"Ray Jardine is a paradigm buster."
—Doug Walsh

"I have read both The Pacific Crest Trail Hiker's Handbook
and Beyond Backpacking and absolutely love them. Besides
lightening my pack immensely !!! Ray has given me a greater
appreciation for nature. I recommend these books to all my
hiking buddies. His philosophies and advice have changed my
life in the best of ways!"
—James Gibling

"We were interested in Ray and Jenny for a number of reasons: their achievements as long distance hikers (PCT 3 times;
Triple Crown etc); their importance as innovators (Ray's
designing of friends for climbing in the 60's; their own design
of kayak for their recent trips in the Arctic etc). But perhaps
most importantly for the philosophy, motivation and commit-
ment that lies behind these achievements - from our point of
view their whole concept of ultra-lightweight backpacking
together with their philosophy of going with nature. From a
U.K. perspective we see them in a long line of U.S. based
wilderness thinkers and philosophers - Muir, Emerson,
Thoreau, Abbey etc. We view them as immensely important
and they were right at the top of our list for this second series
of Wilderness Walks."
—Richard Else
Series Producer/Director, Triple Echo Productions
BBC Wilderness Walks.

Beyond Backpacking

Ray Jardine's
Guide To
Lightweight Hiking

The ALL-trails version of Ray's classic
The Pacific Crest Trail Hiker's Handbook

Practical methods for all who love the out-of-doors,
from walkers and backpackers, to long-distance hikers

— **Ray Jardine** —

Beyond Backpacking - Ray Jardine's Guide To Lightweight Hiking

Second Printing. Published in the United States by

AdventureLore Press
Box 804, LaPine OR 97739
www.AdventureLore.com

For additional copies of this book, call:
1-800-247-6553 or 419-281-1802

Library of Congress Catalog Card Number: 99-72758
Ray Jardine, Beyond Backpacking
AdventureLore Press, LaPine Oregon
ISBN 0-9632359-3-1
Printed on 100% recycled paper

To Jenny:
Companion in nearly two decades of adventuring,
full-time assistant in the preparation of this book,
best friend and "better half."
Beyond Backpacking is as much hers as it is mine.

And to our readers:
"fellow-adventurers on a bright journey to understand
the things that are." —Richard Bach
May you cast your visions far,
load your backpacks lightly and leave your cars at home,
and may you cherish and protect the lands you explore.

For ye shall go out with joy, and be led forth with peace;
the mountains and the hills shall break forth before you into singing,
and all the trees of the field shall clap their hands.

— Isaiah 55:12

Special Acknowledgments

I would like to thank the many readers of my previous books who wrote with questions. These helped broaden the scope of the book, and many of my answers are incorporated here, I hope adequately.

The writing in this book is my own, with a little enlivening from Jenny. At the same time, I would like to offer a heartfelt acknowledgment and thank-you to Brett Tucker, who worked as a free-lance editor through most of the book's processing. Brett went through the original manuscript with a fine toothed comb, analyzing every detail, suggesting clarifying changes, and pointing out omissions of many things I tend to take for granted. His contributions to the project have been invaluable.

I would also like to thank Demetri Coupounas, who proofread the final manuscript and provided a number of thoughtful suggestions. He and I also worked endless hours developing the line of GoLite clothing and equipment.

Thanks also to Kerrie Donaldson from the Land Down Under, for her assistance. And in appreciation to some very special friends: To Karl Diederich, long-distance hiker, sailor and engineer, who has been lending advice to this work since its beginning almost a decade ago. To Richard Else and Margaret Wicks, series producers of the BBC television series "Wilderness Walks," to series host and wilderness advocate Cameron McNeish, and to the rest of the film crew for their good company during our time in the wilds. To martial arts instructor Paul Bonner for his friendship and support. To Carol and Reinhard for sharing their wisdom about things to come. To David and Jen Nimmo for their encouragement. To my brothers and sisters of the Goose Tribe, for their love and sharing. To Stalking Wolf and Tom Brown Jr., and the students walking their Paths. To Errett Callahan who taught me about being a mentor. To Verlen Kruger for showing what can be done. And to my parents and Jenny's for their continual support and prayers.

Contents

Obstacles

Longer Journeys

Back to Basics

Introduction

All too often the term "backpacking" conjures images of plodding along the trail with a crushing load on one's back, and with a pair of large, awkward boots encumbering the feet. For decades this "Standard Backpacking Method" was the norm. The deep fatigue, the pain in the knees, and the blisters on the feet—these were accepted, albeit regrettably, as part of the experience.

I started breaking away from this style in the early 1970's, looking for ways of facilitating the hiking without sacrificing the comfort and safety. For nearly thirty years I have devoted my energies mainly to adventuring, and this has given me plenty of opportunity to apply my aerospace engineering approach to the design and construction of my own lightweight outdoor gear and clothing, and to refine my hiking and camping techniques accordingly. From 1987 to 1994 my wife Jenny and I logged over 15,000 miles of hiking, including five summer-long journeys each in excess of 2,000 miles. All the while I examined and reexamined our hiking equipment and methods with an eye toward refinement. In effect, each journey became something of a multi-month field test, as we put our ideas into practice. These ideas had to work because we depended on them. But sometimes they did not work very well, and we always seemed to return home with new ideas for the next trip. The process has been evolutionary, and it has led to a new approach, a lightweight system of gear and philosophy—tried, tested, modified, and tested again.

My quest has not focused on what works best for Jenny and myself alone. I am also concerned with what works for other hikers—those with varying levels of experience and skill, diverse hiking goals, and who hike and camp in different regions. To that end, in 1992 I chronicled the initial phases of my lightweight gear and associated techniques in my now out-of-print *Pacific Crest Trail Hiker's Handbook*. This was the first time that such ideas had been widely popularized, and since then the concept of lightweight hiking has taken a strong hold. But that original book was not the end of the journey. Over the years I have continued to refine my packweight and develop methods of even greater effectiveness.

At this point in time it seems fitting to organize my ideas into this new book: *Beyond Backpacking*. In these pages you will find much of that original, tried-and-true information detailing my recommended gear and clothing, the associated techniques of using it to best advantage, and my camping methods in general. You will also find stories from my own experiences that led to their development.

In the *Handbook* I described the benefits of this specialized, lightweight clothing and equipment, yet I left no way for readers to obtain it, other than to contrive it for themselves. So in this new book I devote a full chapter to making your own gear, showing how to get started, where to get the materials and patterns, and detailing the many interesting possibilities. Of course, not everyone will want to make their own. To this end I also worked with a manufacturer to make my ultralight gear available commercially. So whether you prefer to make your own or buy it, the gear is now obtainable. And in this book you will learn how to use that gear most effectively.

The Standard Backpacking Method with its profusion of heavy-duty equipment actually prevents us from reaching our full potential as accomplished wilderness enthusiasts. The all-inclusive, "everything-but-the-kitchen-sink" approach only detracts from our outings. I am not promoting minimalism, but simply a reduction in what is not necessary. And I have found that this reduction, when thoughtfully and skillfully done, actually enhances both our safety and comfort.

Underlying the physical skills, techniques and gear is a far more fundamental and philosophical aspect to my lightweight approach. I feel that our wilderness outings should be more than just physical walks along trails, and our camping experiences more than pitching a tent and zipping ourselves inside. More important is our presence in the wilds: how we carry ourselves, how softly we move upon the landscape, how aware we are of the patterns of life around us and how we interact with them. This "earth philosophy" is the motivation behind all my lightweight gear, techniques and methods. And it is the underpinning of this book. I and many others both present and past refer to it as the Connection. It is a bridging of the gap between human and nature, a bringing together for a greater awareness and deeper understanding—of the natural world around us in all its glory, of our relationship with that world, and of our own inner nature.

So whether you are planning a weekend cross-country ramble, a two-week hike in a popular backcountry area, or perhaps a summer-long trek, *Beyond Backpacking* will help you simplify your gear and lighten your packweight. No matter what your level of experience or physical fitness, this book will show you how to increase your safety and enjoyment in the out-of-doors. And I hope that it will motivate you to continue walking your own path to that wilderness Connection.

Nature Enriches

The purpose of a wilderness journey
is not to get from one end of the [trail] to the other,
but to enjoy the landscape,
and adapt to its ever-changing moods.

— Bill Mason

Exploring the wilds,
in search of our selves

How many times have I looked up from my desk to gaze out the window. I see the trees waving in the breeze, clouds drifting past. Sometimes I catch sight of a few ravens gliding by. They represent a sense of freedom that beckons me to leave my writing and go explore the nearby woods, or to enjoy a pleasant ramble down by the river. I see other birds flitting busily past my window, a pair of young squirrels darting playfully around the yard, a rabbit nibbling at the grass. All these creatures stir me to come out of my world and be a part of theirs.

How nature tugs at the soul. Certainly the lure of the wilds is different for each of us, and our reasons for wanting to go hiking and camping vary widely. Many people appreciate the temporary respite from everyday stress and distraction, the snarling traffic, blaring radio and tv commercials, ringing telephones, the schedules and responsibilities. Most revel in the wild sunrise heralding the new day and its adventuresome prospects. What childlike wonder to discover a bird's nest hidden in a grassy hollow, holding a clutch of tiny, mottled eggs. Myself, I long for the freshness—the scent of pine or sage. And I can almost taste the spicy pasta cooking on a small, crackling fire toward the end of a long and rewarding day on the trail.

For some people, the wilderness brings a sense of satisfaction and connection that comes with living more simply, almost primitively—tapping into that genetic link to our prehistoric past. Some find that out in nature they can more easily differentiate their wants from their needs.

And of course, the adventure of it all. The natural world stretching before us, full of challenge, discovery and lessons to be learned.

Henry David Thoreau wrote:

"I went to the woods because I wished to live deliberately, to front only the essential facts of life, and see if I could not learn what it had to teach, and not, when I came to die, discover that I had not lived."

For me there is another dimension to this idea. Perhaps others have felt this as well. That we go into the wilderness to discover more about ourselves, about who we really are. I think the influences of modern society keep many of us from being our real selves. In reacting continually to pressure, we tend to take on personalities not our own. But when we step into the wilderness, we free ourselves of those influences, at least temporarily, and we begin to discover more about ourselves.

That is why I love to hike and camp, and explore the wild places. And when I set off down the trail with just a small bag containing all I need slung over my shoulder, I feel invigorated. My legs are striding, my lungs expanding, and my heart is pumping the life back into me. Marathon runner George Sheehan put it well when he wrote, "I ran to regain control of my life." I tend to view my hiking journeys in much the same way.

Nature has a way of reawakening our senses and speaking to our hearts. The voices of those ravens riding the wind—they call to us to come live more deliberately for a time, and see what we can learn about the world around us, and the world inside us.

The Myth
of Heavy-Duty Gear

Grandma's legacy

The wilderness can seem to hammer us with fatigue, rain and bug bites, or it can enrich us profoundly with the joys of adventure and discovery. The determining factor is our attitude. A negative or fearful mindset will enervate even the strongest-bodied hiker. A positive, more self-confident frame of mind will buoy almost anyone along any trail.

A negative or fearful outlook often calls for a magnum-sized backpack full of heavy-duty gear touted to protect a person from the gamut of nature's vicissitudes. A positive attitude allows us to safely and comfortably adopt lightweight gear, and to dispense with the extraneous. The choice is ours: whether to armor for battle, or to take a lighter, friendlier approach.

Emma "Grandma" Gatewood (1888-1975) did not look like much of a hiker. But sometimes looks can be deceiving. During an illustrious hiking career that spanned eighteen years, she thru-hiked the Appalachian Trail (AT)—not just once, but twice—and she section-hiked it a third time. She also hiked the Chesapeake and Ohio Canal Towpath from Washington, DC to Cumberland, Maryland; the Long Trail in Vermont; the Baker Trail in Pennsylvania; and the Buckeye Trail in Ohio. And on the

100th anniversary of the Oregon Trail she walked its entire 2,000 mile length in fifteen days less than what most of the historic wagon trains had taken.

Grandma Gatewood started hiking at an age when most people retire to their armchairs. And even then her accomplishments were outstanding. During her second AT thru-hike she took no rest days, and completed the rugged journey in only 4½ months, finishing just a few days before her 70th birthday. Her secret? "I had always lived on a farm and was used to hard work," she told one reporter. "I was in good physical condition, so I decided to hike that trail, and I just started out." And in her spunky style she quipped, "Most people are pantywaists. Exercise is good for you."

What set Grandma apart was her disdain of the latest and most robust equipment. Backpackers wore sturdy boots to protect their feet; Grandma wore Keds™ sneakers. They used expensive parkas and "lightweight," bug-proof tents. She used a rain cape and a plastic shower curtain. They carried expensive frame packs that distributed their heavy loads evenly. Grandma didn't carry a heavy load. Her items of extra clothing and gear were few, and she carried them, along with her food, in a home-made bag simply draped over one shoulder.

Grandma's legacy encourages us in our own abilities, and reminds us of today's excess in heavy-duty paraphernalia. She was obviously a strong and gutsy woman, but I doubt whether she would have hiked a fraction of those miles lugging the standard elephantine load. And what is more, I cannot think of a single item of modern clothing or gear that would have added to her success.

The bulk of advertisements and articles in today's outdoor magazines are telling us quite the opposite: that we need a wide selection of the very best in heavy-duty gear in order to survive out there, let alone have a good time. But Grandma Gatewood proved otherwise. Then as now, her example stands as convincing evidence that a simpler, lighter-weight approach is just as workable.

I am not suggesting that we abandon our gear and adopt a minimalist approach. But I do think that the bulk of today's equipment is not essential to hiking and camping enjoyment or to safety.

If we do not need our gear to be heavy-duty, then why is most of today's gear so heavily constructed? Why do the "best" backpacks weigh 7 pounds rather than 1? Why do the latest tents weigh 5 pounds rather than 2? Why does the footwear weigh 6 pounds rather than 1 1/2? I see two reasons. The first has to do with the inconvenience to the manufacturer when gear is returned for repair or replacement. The second has to do with marketing pressure driven by today's fiercely competitive climate.

Product returns = more weight

Let's say that someone buys an expensive backpack, first verifying that it is fully guaranteed. If a seam rips out or a strap tears off, the disgruntled customer returns the product for repair or replacement, probably having to pay the postage, and of course suffering the loss of valuable time. This is bad news also for the manufacturer, who thinks in terms of profit and public image. And it is particularly inconvenient for those who import their products, as most do. So the manufacturer responds by enhancing the design, not by reinforcing the overstressed area, in most cases, but by simply increasing the weight of the affected component, be it the fabric, fastener, or whatever. In time, after dozens of packs have been returned for repairs—each with a different problem—the manufacturer will have made the product massively stronger, and of course that much heavier. This ultra-durability and its associated weight is a convenience to the manufacturer, and to the mainstream consumer who insists on "bomb-proof" products. And while it might be acceptable for expeditionary use, it is decidedly overkill for hiking in relatively accessible areas, particularly for those hikers who know how to take good care of their gear.

The backpacks that Jenny and I used on our most recent thru-hike weigh less than a pound. Actually, mine weighs 13 1/2 ounces, and Jenny's is two ounces less. And even though we made them of lightweight materials, they handled those 2,700 miles perfectly. In every likelihood, most hikers would be happier with such lightweight gear as long as that gear is well designed and constructed, and treated with care. But the marketeers would have us believe otherwise, and in order to convince us of our need for their heavy-duty wares, they sometimes resort to some rather fanciful tactics.

Your life depends on (our product)

Thumb through a few outdoor magazines and you may find advertisements pitting a hostile environment against you and some piece of heavy-duty gear. Here are a few examples:

- Excerpt from an ad for a jacket: Exploring the farthest reaches of our planet means protecting yourself from its fury.

- Fabrics: Out here, Mother won't wipe your nose. She'll rub your nose in it. When it's just you and Mother Nature, you better be prepared. Cause Mother can have a bad attitude.

- Clothing: OK, now technically we can't guarantee that you'll end the day with as many limbs as when you started. But when you consider what we put into our (clothing) you gotta like the chances. (Wear our clothing), thereby improving your odds of making it home in one piece.

- Boots: How can you expect to touch the face of god when your feet are firmly planted in hell?

- Fabric: Sometimes even when the wind is with you, it's against you.

- I hope I don't get mauled by a mountain lion. Good thing I ate a (popular energy bar).

These ads use a common tactic: they attempt to arouse your fears of nature, and then they rescue you with the company's wares as the ultimate weapons against the big, bad, natural world. My intent is not to discredit any particular product or company, but merely to highlight the advertising methods.

Here are a few more examples:

- Clothing: Rocks have eyes and they are mean. They aim for skin. Right for where it stings. Hoping to lift off pieces of you to keep with them on the ground.

- It's nice to know that even when you're not breathing, your jacket is.

- Tent: The wind howls because it can't get to you.

- Shorts: You never know what dangers you'll have to face out there. So we've provided some (shorts) that can take on just about anything.

- Fabric: One million sweat glands are conspiring against you. Retaliate. [Not only is nature out to get us, but our bodies are conspiring against us also.]

But are we really as alien to our natural environment as these advertisements would have us believe? Is nature so hostile and dangerous that we dare not venture forth without the most durable and heaviest gear? Accidents do happen, but they are more related to overconfidence and inattentiveness than to any lack of heavy-duty gear.

Any type of gear, heavy or light, requires competence in its use. But the marketeers are trying to convince you that the heavier gear is safer, more durable, and of higher quality. But even heavy-duty materials can be cheaply put together. And just because a product uses those materials does not mean that it is well designed. The best designs are those that address the hiker's needs. That calls for lighter-weight materials, expertly put together.

Perceived obstacles

The idea of nature-as-adversary has a long history, and we find plenty of examples in today's magazine articles and books. I came across one that described the Appalachian Trail as "one seriously tough mother." The author went on to say that "[The Appalachian Trail's] peak bagging philosophy manifests itself into one grade-A butt-kicking experience. Then there's the heat, humidity, and rain to consider as well as the bugs and snakes."

This kind of attitude reflects the advertising slant that we examined above. And yes, if a person ventures into the wilderness with the assumption that it is out to get him or her, then that person is likely to encounter the envisioned obstacles, one after the next. Not genuine obstacles most of the time, but perceived ones. But I find that our perceptions of nature are cultivated by our attitudes, and that our attitudes hinge upon our own free will, whether we choose to maintain a negative mindset or positive. To illustrate this, here are a few words from Emma Stephens, who at the age of 55 thru-hiked that same AT:

"My trek left me feeling very proud of myself. I hiked through 14 states. That means I walked it like the pioneers did, but instead of a mule carrying my supplies, I carried them. (I am not comparing myself to a mule, but a little stubbornness is sometimes a good thing!) I hiked alone for about two of those months and thoroughly enjoyed it. I liked making my own decisions about when and where to stop and how long to hike each day. Throughout the hike I would wake up in the morning to the birds singing, and very often at night go to sleep with the sound of a creek or waterfall as a lullaby. Can you do that in the city? Each day was a new adventure. What would I find? Hills, rocks, creeks, deer, bird nests, bear, turkey, old foundations, huge old trees that designated a homestead many decades ago, wild berries, moose, a new friend... I would not trade this experience for all the rocking chairs in Texas!

"I guess my final advice would be: Do it! The pride and sense of worth and accomplishment you will come away with will be very hard to beat. Oh yes, it will be hard, you will be wet, cold, hot, tired, and sometimes scraped and scratched, but almost never will you be discouraged. This will be six months of my life that will live on in my memory forever. And I don't think my family will forget it either. They are so proud of me."

Grandma Gatewood disassociated herself from the glossy marketing mainstream, yet she enjoyed a lengthy and successful backpacking career on par with the best of them. How? By exercising her strong will to succeed, and relying on resources within. "It's about as nice a thing as anybody can do—walking," she said. "And it's cheap, too!"

Packweight

On a long journey even a straw weighs heavy.

— *Spanish proverb*

Objectivity
through trial and error

I started hiking as a youngster, following my dad into the remote, alpine backcountry of Colorado in quest of the perfect trout lake. My backpack was reasonably large for a kid my size. It was actually more like an army-surplus rucksack, and my sleeping bag took up all the room. That was in the early 1950's, and I'm not sure that goose down and nylon sleeping bags even existed back then. If they did, we certainly did not have them. Ours were cotton, with cotton batting insulation. They were heavy and not very compressible; about all we could do was roll them up. My dad carried a packboard lashed with what seemed to me like a ton of gear. He hiked in his rubber hip waders because his packboard had no room for them.

Dad gave me a larger pack every few years, while handing down my smaller ones to my two younger brothers. And of course with each new pack he encouraged us to share more of his load. This meant that as we grew up, our packweights were always maxed out. But we loved going on those trips, and considered the heavy burdens a part of the experience.

By the time I left for college I had backpacked many hundreds of miles, with family, friends and on my own. And almost always it was with a large pack. After college I divided my spare time between rock climbing and mountaineering. On the mountaineering trips, my friends and I would drive to the mountains on a Saturday, carry our heavy packs into "base camp," then Sunday we would rise early, climb the peak, and return to camp. There, we would pack up, then hike back out to the trailhead and drive home. After a couple of years of this I decided it would be more adventurous to dispense with the camping gear and simply climb the mountains alpine style—bivouacking high on the peaks if necessary rather than tenting at a base camp. This was the first time I had considered the idea of reducing packweight, and it ultimately cost me all of my mountaineering friends. They were not about to give up their conventional base camping methods, despite the heavy loads associated with them.

So I found new partners and started scaling the mountains alpine style. For a sleeping bag I used a thin, three-quarter length bag of goose down and nylon, augmented with a down jacket. My pack was still very heavy with climbing hardware, but by minimizing our baseline packweight, my partners and I were able to climb the mountains by their more technical routes.

Slashing packweight

In 1970 I began instructing for a wilderness program, and this was when I began cutting my packweight in earnest. Each course ran from 23 to 28 days, and the resupplies came every 5 to 7 days. I needed to be very careful about how much gear I loaded into my pack because the rest of the load had to be food enough to see me to the next resupply. Also, these trips were fairly ambitious. I usually hiked in the company of my students, but in the latter stages of each program I would shadow them, which required that I circumvent their more direct routes. And because I needed to reach our pre-arranged waypoints ahead of them, I had to hike more expediently. This meant that I needed mobility. All this encouraged me to refine my packweight. I carried a tarp rather than a tent. I wore running shoes rather than boots. I carried no stove but cooked on a small fire. In fact, I would invariably get so caught up in the minimalist approach that I would intentionally short myself two or three days' food.

After the summer courses I would return to Denver where I had access to an equipment manufacturing company. The company president was my good friend and climbing partner, Bill Forrest. Bill and I had climbed the Diamond on Longs Peak together several times, and the "Nose" of El Capitan in Yosemite. I had worked in his shop designing and sewing all sorts of climbing and hiking gear. And in fact I had invented and prototyped the climbing protection devices called "Friends" there. Bill was similarly inventive and resourceful. Among numerous other products, he invented and fabricated a climber's backpack haul-bag combo. This pack was so successful that I used it for more than a decade's worth of hiking and climbing. And it provided the basis for the packs that Jenny and I make and use today. Basically it was little more than a large bag fitted with shoulder straps—so simple in its design, yet so functional.

Packweight metamorphosis

As Jenny and I began preparing for our first big thru-hike, back in 1987, we realized the need to minimize our packweights. Yet as much hiking and backpacking as I had done—and Jenny had done a fair amount herself—we still felt intimidated by the prospects of hiking the Pacific Crest Trail's two and a half thousand miles in one go. Especially because neither of us had done much serious hiking for several years. This insecurity about the prospects of hiking such a distance sapped our objectivity. We perused stacks of catalogs, studied equipment reviews galore, and visited backpacking stores to try out all the most "advanced" and durable gear.

For backpacks we chose magnum-sized, internal-frame models of the latest design. Then we proceeded to modify them. We cut off every unneeded strap, tab and buckle. We removed the internal seam binding (the long nylon strips that hide the raw edges and stitching). In fact we disassembled the packs almost completely and re-shaped the nylon pieces for improved function, before sewing them back together. In the process we also applied sealing compound to all the seams, in a futile attempt to waterproof the packs. And we shaved down the aluminum stays with a belt-grinder to minimize their weight. As a result, we reduced the weight of these packs by only half a pound; the remaining 6½ we could do nothing about. Still, we accepted the weight because we felt that the packs had to be large and robust. For after all, we had a lot of gear and clothing to load into them.

We were training on the snowbound flanks of Pikes Peak in the dead of winter, so naturally our selection of clothing was slanted toward the cold. We purchased the latest polypropylene shirts and pants, Gore-Tex® rain jackets, and a load of expensive socks. But we also sewed many items ourselves. These included waterproof stowbags, a home-made gravity-feed water filtration system, and clothing such as shirts, pants, fleece jackets, mittens and hats. We also sewed together a tarp while preparing for the journey, but ultimately decided against it, in favor of a commercial tent. The marketing literature for this tent was so convincing that, save for running a clothesline across the ceiling, and fitting loops for hanging our eyeglasses at night, we made no other modifications to the tent—an oversight that was to cost us later.

In order to save weight and bulk in our sleeping system we bought a single goose-down sleeping bag with a full length zipper. Unzipped and placed over the top of us, it covered us both together. We also bought a couple of full length, closed-cell foam pads, 3/8" thick. Under these pads we sewed a thin groundsheet of nylon, around which we added a zipper—running down one side, across the bottom, and back up the other side. This matched the zipper on our sleeping bag. The result was an integrated two-person sleeping system with a goose down top and a foam bottom.

We began our thru-hike with ungainly loads. With these we hiked for a month through southern California. And when we loaded the packs with mountaineering boots and a three week supply of food for the trip through the snowbound High Sierra, my pack must have weighed 75 pounds and Jenny's around 60. After struggling through the high country we began to realize that much of our clothing and gear was not essential, and in fact that its weight and bulk were working against us. For example, we carried a variety of clothing, and of course we never used all of it at once. One day we wore this, and another day we wore that. Eventually we found that we could reduce the variety in our garments without compromising comfort. So we started sending home extra shirts, pants, shorts, sweaters, things that we liked to wear, but that we could do without. This was more a mental shift, differentiating our wants from our needs. And we found that we didn't mind the lessened variety in shirts and pants, as long as we kept them laundered. And by washing socks every day, we did not need a five day supply of those. As a result of sending the superfluous items home, we reduced our baseline packweights considerably.

Our summer proved richly rewarding, but it sure was a lot of work! In fact, this first mega-hike was our most difficult, simply because we carried such heavy packs. Had it not been for our many months of very serious pre-hike training, I doubt whether we would have completed the hike with those heavy loads.

The four-pound tent we used for most of that trek was the latest and lightest design, but it failed us during one particular rainstorm. The rain fly was cut too high above the ground, and the pounding rain rebounded through the gap and soaked everything inside. We hitchhiked to the nearest town and ordered a new tent. This tent was a pound heavier than our first one, and it leaked during the next rainstorm.

The boots we wore through the snowbound Sierra were, like the tent, the latest and greatest. But they performed poorly, mainly because they were always wet, and the wetness made them heavier still. We sent them home at the first opportunity. From that point on, I wore running shoes and Jenny wore lighter fabric boots.

More thru-hiking

After a couple of years pursuing other interests, we decided to hike the PCT a second time. We chose to carry the same packs, but we did make new clothing all around. And we modified our sleeping system to make it more serviceable. We bought new rain jackets to replace the ones we had worn out, and we equipped ourselves with umbrellas. We sewed a rain awning to the fly of our original four pound tent, and extensions along the sides to rebuff the splashes. Throughout this trip our baseline packweights averaged about 22 pounds which was still fairly heavy, but much better than previously. And for the first time our equipment was beginning to work for us. We experienced a lot of rain, but the umbrellas shielded us beautifully, allowing us to carry on hiking many times when other hikers remained tent-bound. The new rain awning allowed us to keep the tent's doorway open, and this provided more ventilation, keeping us and our clothing drier. Jenny wore lightweight fabric boots about half of the distance; I wore this type of footwear only through the snowbound High Sierra. Otherwise we wore running shoes, with excellent results.

A full summer's trek has a way of wearing out equipment, so the following year we again amassed new clothing and gear before setting off on the Continental Divide Trail, (CDT) Canada to Mexico, through the states of Montana, Wyoming, Colorado and New Mexico. Once more we used our old, weather-beaten packs, which meant that we were still burdened with their 6½ pounds. Nearly all the rest of our gear was evolving, however. For example we abandoned the zipper arrangement on our foam pads—we realized that the open sleeping bag did not need to be attached to the foam pad. At night we simply draped the bag over us.

While preparing for our Appalachian Trail thru-hike (Georgia to Maine) the following summer, we felt that the severe up-and-down nature of the trail would call for a radical reduction in packweight. Simple physics suggested that the more weight on one's back, the more work required to climb each steep hill—of which the AT has many hundreds. And with the experience gained on our previous long distance walks, we were growing weary of carrying unnecessary weight. This next trek would be so much more enjoyable, we reasoned, without having to lug all that along. Just as importantly at that point, we were going through a mental shift that would open the doorway to our current ultralight system. With thousands of trail miles behind us, we were much more confident in our abilities. No longer shackled by our own doubts and fears, the marketeer's hype lost its hold on us. This was when we regained our objectivity. As such, we began to shed our need for heavy-duty gear. We finally realized that we were far better off without it.

We set aside our 6½ pound mega-packs and started shopping for lighter models. Finding nothing even remotely suitable, we made our own. We used the latest commercial four-pound tent, but again sewed on a rain awning. We outfitted ourselves with a selection of running shoes. As an experiment in saving weight, we dispensed with the stove, and planned to buy food along the way and eat it cold. We also reduced our "kitchen ware," to almost nothing. No pot, bowls or cups. For water bottles we used empty soda bottles. Tiring of buying a new a goose-down sleeping bag each season, we made a lightweight quilt of synthetic insulation, and this proved surprisingly easy to do.

June 8, 1993 found us at Georgia's Springer Mountain, and the start of the Appalachian Trail. We had built thin aluminum internal stays into our home-made backpacks, along with webbing hip belts and quick-release buckles. But by the end of our first day we realized that the hip belts were neither beneficial nor necessary, due to the lightness of our "loads." So we cut the hip belts off. At the first way station we dispensed with them—along with the aluminum stays. As we trekked northward, nearly everyone we met expressed disbelief when we told them that our goal was Katahdin, the northern terminus of the trail. In fact, our too-late start and too-small packs essentially ostracized us from the traditional back-packing community, both on the trail and off. People regularly mistook us for day-hikers, and when we told them we were thru-hikers, they some-times informed us that we had no chance of finishing the hike that year. But our lightweight packs and running shoes worked very well, and we reached the summit of Mt. Katahdin in 88 days, or just under three months.

The following summer we planned to hike only 700 miles along the

PCT from the Canadian border south to our home in central Oregon. For this trek we again replaced all our equipment with home-made gear that was even simpler and lighter. We finally dispensed with the tent and hauled out that nylon tarp I had made seven years earlier. This tarp offered far more living space and rain protection, at a fraction of the weight and bulk. We abandoned most of our heavier garments, since we had rarely worn them on previous hikes. Even in the coldest weather we found that the exercise of hiking warmed us very nicely. And when not hiking we were usually settled comfortably beneath our quilt.

The 8-1/2 pound packs at the completion of a 2,700 mile journey, 1994.

During that trip we spent the first couple of weeks hiking mostly in snow. Still, the tarp worked beautifully, as did the quilt, mainly because we sought out snow-free and more sheltered sites. In fact, the trek went so smoothly and easily that when we reached central Oregon we decided to hike the remaining 1,960 trail miles to Mexico. And it was during this phase of the journey that we brought the many aspects of our current system to fruition. The 8½ pound baseline packweight had come of age.

Packweight and daily mileage

During our first thru-hike, with loads that were ponderous to us (but lighter than what most other hikers were carrying) we averaged 17 miles a day. On our fifth journey, with baseline packweights of 8½ pounds (not including food and water), we averaged 29 miles a day. The reduced packweight made that much difference. Without the huge load, the hiking was no longer such a chore. In many ways a thru-hike is a series of day hikes; I think that the advantages of lighter-weight packs are equally beneficial to all hikers, regardless of the duration of their trips.

During each PCT thru-hike we kept track of our daily mileages, as well as our hours on the trail each day. And we could easily remember the locations of each camp. With this information I was able to make some useful comparisons. While hiking southbound and nearing a resupply point with packs empty of food, (meaning less weight) we far outdistanced our northbound daily mileages coming out of those same stations loaded with food (more weight). I extrapolated the data and plotted the

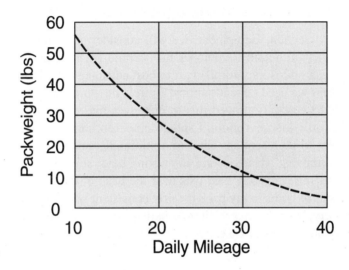

results to give an interesting correlation between packweight and daily mileage. This graph assumes a constant energy expenditure, hiking at a comfortable pace of 2.5 miles per hour. This graph can give you an indication of your expected daily mileage, relative to the weight of your pack. This is total average packweight including food, water, stove fuel and gear. Obviously the graph gives only an indication, due to the variables in terrain, weather, physical conditioning, motivation, type of footwear, and so many other factors. Despite these variables, keep in mind that at any point along the line of the graph, the hiker exerts a constant amount of effort. For example, the hiker carrying a 58 pound pack expends about the same amount of energy in 10 miles as the hiker carrying 10 pounds does in 30 miles.

If you are setting out on a day hike, with no intentions of traveling more than 5 or 10 miles, then a packweight of 8 or 10 pounds will have little effect on the ease and mobility of the hiking. If your plans are more ambitious, and you will be covering more than 10 miles while carrying more than 10 pounds, then you would benefit by conditioning your body for your wilderness outings ahead of time, gradually building up to your target packweight and distance—depending on your existing level of physical conditioning. Loads over 15 pounds are rare among day hikers, unless those hikers are carrying some kind of equipment for a specific purpose such as photography, or unless the conditions necessitate carrying a large load of water.

Advantages of the lighter-weight system

In the next section, Equipment, we will consider each item of recommended gear in detail. Remember that behind each piece of gear and clothing is a philosophy for using it to best advantage. And too, that the type of gear we need depends almost entirely on what we *think* we need. Jenny and I certainly proved this to ourselves during those five multi-thousand mile journeys afoot. I should note, too, that I do not consider my system to represent any kind of a minimalist approach. To me, the word "minimalist" denotes long exhausting days, shivering nights, self-denial and suffering. My gear lists near the back of the book show that the number of items in my pack is fairly consistent with what most other hikers carry. It's just that each item is perhaps more carefully thought out, specially built in many cases, smaller and lighter and with fewer redundancies.

But before we can reduce the loads on our backs, we have to lighten the loads in our minds. In other words, we have to believe that lighter-weight gear (and less of it) will work equally well for us. Lacking this conviction, we will never try any of it, and our beliefs will remain unchanged. Or we may try an item or two, use them incorrectly and unsuccessfully, and revert to our old heavier gear once again. Either way we remain stagnant. In years past about the only way to try this lighter-weight gear was to make it yourself. However, much of this gear is now commercially available under the GoLite brand (more on that shortly). And if you are interested in saving money, see my chapter on Sewing Your Own Gear.

Whether you decide to buy the gear or make it yourself, consider a few examples of my home-made gear, as compared to the more traditional heavy-duty varieties.

- Compare one of my packs—weighing 13½ ounces and costing $10.40 to make—to a store-bought backpack weighing 7 pounds and costing $275.00. My pack is 12% of the weight and 4% of the cost.

- Compare my present two-person quilt—rated at 20°F, weighing 1 pound, 15 ounces, and its $34.00 worth of materials—to a pair of commercial sleeping bags costing $400.00 and weighing 6 pounds together. The quilt is 32% of the weight and 9% of the cost. Compare the equivalent 15½ ounces per person and the 20°F rating to *any* commercial sleeping bag: it's no contest.

- Compare my current silicone tarp—weighing 1 pound and costing $28.20 to make—to a commercial tent weighing 4½ pounds and costing $250. The tarp is 22% of the weight and 11% of the cost.

These three items alone save us **20 pounds** and **$1,117**.

Lightweight gear goes commercial

In the first editions of *The PCT Hiker's Handbook*, I detailed my system of hiking gear and philosophies. Those books inspired thousands of letters, and one thing was clear: Most people do not care to sew their own gear, for whatever reasons. So in effect their lack of sewing skills was preventing them from using or even trying my type of lightweight gear.

Then one day Demetri "Coup" Coupounas contacted me, saying he wanted to form a new backpacking equipment company selling products based on my designs. The idea did not enthuse me initially; the last thing I wanted to do was become involved in the outdoor retail market. But I also reasoned that if Coup were to produce my lightweight hiking gear commercially, it would become available to those who do not sew. So I acquiesced, on condition that I would contribute only my designs; I wanted no part in the company's operation.

The company is called GoLite, and they offer a free catalog. They are at 15785 Arapahoe, Boulder, CO 80303. 888-546-5483, www.golite.com.

Overall, I am pleased with GoLite gear. It is lightweight and functional, and the designs are reasonably close to my specifications, certainly far closer than anything else on the market. Naturally, I have no say in the company's pricing, naming of products, style or placement of logos, choice of colors, and promotional material. Nor is everything they sell of my design. For specifics, see www.transport.com/~ray316 (or search "Ray Jardine's Adventure Page").

All said and done, I still encourage you to make your own. You will feel good about the money saved, and you will be very proud of the items you produce. Something bought commercially is a mere possession, while something you make yourself becomes an extension of your own energies, and a very meaningful part of yourself.

Lightening the load: the six pound object

Imagine pulling a six pound object from your backpack and leaving it home. That would lighten your load considerably. You may not have anything in your pack that weighs that much. But how about the pack itself? Most large packs on the market weigh from five to seven pounds, and more. Yet they add nothing to the journey; they are merely containers for the equipment, clothing and food. To me it makes no sense that the container should be the heaviest article of gear.

The ultralight packs that Jenny and I used on our most recent thruhike each required about 12 hours at the sewing machine, and cost $10.40 in materials. Throw-away models? Hardly. Their condition has not deteriorated in more than 3,500 miles of use. With a lighter load, the pack does not need to be nearly as robust, nor does it need a frame or hip belt. However, this does not mean that these packs are limited in what they can

The GoLite pack

do. During our most recent PCT thru-hike I carried up to 50 pounds in mine (mostly water) while traversing the desert regions of southern California. See the Sewing chapter for guidelines on making such a pack yourself.

The first time you pick up one of these packs you will be amazed at how light it is. And yet it still has quite a lot of carrying capacity, especially taking into account its three external pockets. Use this pack on short hikes initially, and take only what you need. The last thing you want to do is cram it full of heavy, bulky gear. Besides, all those things would not fit. So don't load the pack to the hilt, and especially don't load the extension collar—that is only for occasional use, for example when setting off on a multi-day hike with an extra large load of food. Also, resist the temptation to lash things all over the outside. Note, too, that the heavier the load, the tighter the shoulder straps should be, to prevent the pack from riding too low on your back. As a general guideline, try to keep the weight below twenty pounds. Structurally, the pack will carry much more than that, but the lighter the load, the more comfortable and enjoyable your journey will be. For this reason you might want to try some of the other lightweight equipment as well.

One of the main benefits of these packs is that virtually anyone can pick one up, put it on, and head on down the trail. We do not have to be muscle-bound athletes, which is good news because that would exclude most of us. At any rate, no longer must we struggle beneath the standard elephantine load. And now that we can carry less weight, I think many people will be more inclined to venture into the wilds, and more often—since the hiking is no longer so much work.

The tarp

Most lighter-weight commercial tents weigh four to five pounds. Yes, there are lighter shelters out there, like bivy sacks or flimsy little one-man tents, but they tend to be cramped and extremely restrictive of ventilation. The two-person tarp of my latest design weighs 16 ounces. This is one-fourth to one-fifth the weight of even the lightest two-person tents currently available. Of course I enjoy the tarp's lightness, but I also like

its roominess. Scrunched inside a small tent, I have to keep most of my gear out in the vestibule, where it is much less accessible. Beneath the tarp I remain more a part of the landscape; I can still see and hear everything around me. This facilitates my connection with nature greatly—even while in bed. If using a stove, Jenny and I sometimes cook beneath the tarp, particularly in rainy weather. We tend to sleep much better under a tarp than inside a tent, and awaken more refreshed. The tarp allows for fresh air and wonderful ventilation, and it reduces the condensation in the quilt and clothing come morning. We pitch the tarp sideways to any wind, and if the wind is strong we pitch the tarp lower and secure the windward edge flush to the ground. Either way, this configuration shelters the two of us very nicely. I also believe that a properly pitched tarp is stronger than most tents, particularly lighter-weight tents. I describe the tarp more fully in the equipment section, and give instructions for pitching it properly. To make one yourself, see the Sewing chapter.

I should point out, too, that the majority of nights we hikers spend in the backcountry are mild. We are not automatically going to encounter the ultimate storm the minute we step out the back door with lighter-weight gear. But should it happen, a properly pitched tarp will handle it. Pitching a tarp is not difficult, but the method differs from that of pitching a tent. The best way to make the transition from tent to tarp is to carry both on a few shorter outings. Pitch the tarp and sleep under it, and keep the tent packed in its stowbag and close at hand, just in case.

The tarp complements my 8½ pound system nicely, but it also works well in combination with more traditional gear. Carry it instead of your tent, especially in fine weather. Or, carry it in addition to your tent—it is so lightweight and compact that you can carry both. At camp you can use the tarp as a "garage" for sheltering your pack and supplies. You can also use it as a lightweight but spacious cooking shelter. If rain starts pouring from the skies, you can pitch the tarp over your tent for added protection. This would be particularly useful should your tent start leaking. Or you can pitch the tarp over your tent's doorway to create a wealth of add-on living space. In a pouring rain this would shelter the tent's entryway, and allow you to keep the door wide open for better ventilation, even in a deluge.

The quilt

My latest two-person quilt is rated at 20°F, and weighs one pound, fifteen ounces. In no pair of commercial sleeping bags could two people sleep comfortably in 20°F temperatures for less than a pound per person; that kind of performance is unheard of in the sleeping bag industry. I designed the quilt as part of our 8½ pound system, but Jenny and I have found it so effective that we are convinced it would be perfectly suitable for anyone. The part of the sleeping bag beneath you does almost nothing to keep you warm: as you lie on the insulation you compress it flat. The quilt dispenses with that part of the sleeping bag, and therefore it saves you its unnecessary weight and bulk.

The arrangement of two people sleeping under this type of quilt is very effective at reducing packweight and bulk; the two people share each other's warmth. But the quilt works equally well for one person. Either way, you would normally use the quilt instead of your sleeping bag. But on very cold nights you can use the quilt to extend the range of your sleeping bag, simply by throwing it over your bag and perhaps safety-pinning it in place. Or if your bag has room, you could use the quilt inside it as a luxuriously warm liner. The quilt also makes a great blanket for sitting outside in the mornings before the sun has warmed the day, and again in the evenings. When hiking in cold weather it makes an excellent comforter during rest stops. Use it anytime you want to avoid getting your sleeping bag wet; the ultralight materials of the quilt will dry much faster than those of a sleeping bag.

Crawling into a sleeping bag, especially the mummy type bag, imparts a certain sense of security, as though once we have zipped the bag tight and cinched it around our face, nothing out there in that cold, dark night can get at us. But in reality the nighttime world is not much different from the day. Save for a few insects, there is not much out there that has any interest in us. And while the quilt may not offer mummy type security, it will keep us just as warm as would an equally rated but much heavier sleeping bag. I say this based on experience in extreme conditions. Jenny and I use a quilt, not sleeping bags, on our Arctic sea-kayaking expeditions. Why? Because they are just as warm as sleeping bags, for considerably less weight and bulk.

But what about bugs crawling around at night? If the night is cold, then the bugs are dormant. On warm nights they are active, certainly, but remember that apart from a few mosquitoes, the bugs, snakes, and mice would rather keep away from us, even when we are asleep. The "size ratio" is to their disadvantage. Jenny and I have slept under a quilt hundreds of times, both out in the open and beneath a tarp, and we have not been bitten at night by any creature other than the occasional mosquito. This is not to say that it could not happen, but I think the odds are quite against it.

However, the ants. These little fellows are fond of getting into everything, including our clothing at night—not to bite but merely to have a good wander around in search of dead insects, crumbs or whatever. They can be distracting when crawling on bare flesh. So, on warmer nights we sleep in the bug-proof "shell" garments.

Many people detest ants, but I am fascinated by them. If you have never studied them then you are missing some great entertainment and education. And studying ants is something we hikers normally have plenty of time for, during the rest stops. I wonder how many ant-miles one of these tiny creatures walks per day. Have you ever noticed the huge loads they often carry? Not only are they indefatigable workers, but they are also amazingly organized. And many times I have watched scores of them come out of their hole all at the same time for exercise and fresh air. So too, ants are nature's tireless house cleaners. A hiker slaps at a mosquito and it drops to the ground—the ants quickly haul it off. Without the ants, the earth would be one big pig pen. Here is an interesting experiment: Locate a line of ants marching toward who knows where, and dribble a bead of white flour across their path. This will confuse them greatly, but eventually they will find their way around the flour and resume course. Now pour a bead of freshly-ground whole-wheat flour across their path. Immediately they will start feeding on it. They know real food when they find it. At any rate, all aspects of the natural world are fascinating, were we to take the time to watch, listen and participate. Whenever an ant or two show up at my bed, I let them go about their business. Knowing they mean no harm, I simply turn over and go back to sleep.

When first using your new quilt, you might keep your regular sleeping bag handy. Frankly, I doubt that you will need to revert to the bag. If you find yourself chilling, figure out why. Maybe you oriented your tarp incorrectly and the wind is coming in through the end. Maybe you camped on compact ground, or in a valley filled with katabatic air (see the Stealth Camping chapter). Once you become comfortable with the quilt, you can leave your sleeping bag home.

For details on how to make a quilt, see the Sewing chapter.

The self-inflating mattress—not

The self-inflating mattress is so popular with backpackers that it is almost an icon of the traditional approach. Yet on our hiking journeys and outings, Jenny and I sleep on pads of closed-cell, polyethylene foam, 3/8 inch thick. These are no sacrifice in warmth and comfort because we select soft, naturally insulating terrain. Where the ground is damp, we lay down a waterproof groundsheet. Self-inflating mattresses are said to be necessary when the ground is covered in snow. Yet even when tromping through the snowbound high country in late spring, we have found the ground snow-covered only at the higher elevations, and even there we find occasional patches of exposed terrain for camping on. Below treeline, which is where we normally camp, the ground is most often covered in natural insulation—leaves, pine needles and duff, and these can make for a very comfortable bed. The idea is to avoid camping on compacted ground, such as that found at the popular and overused campsites. In desert-like regions where the ground is bare, we look for non-compacted sites, where, in most cases, the dirt is quite soft.

The natural insulation approach is so effective that it requires only short pads. Ours are 36 inches in length, about the size of our torso-print. To cushion our heads we use makeshift "pillows" of jackets or other spare clothing; these overlap the top of the pads. And to insulate our legs we use spare clothing also.

By camping more in tune with nature and sleeping on natural bedding, you can save yourself a lot of packweight and space. Should you feel a bit of chill working up through your groundsheet or foam pad, simply stuff a few items of clothing under you, or put them on. The spare garments are just lying around, so why not use them? Read more about all this in the Groundsheet and Sleeping Pad chapter.

Shell garments and rainwear

One of the better ways to reduce packweight is to eliminate redundant clothing. At home we like to wear a variety of things, but in the wilds we can dispense with variety and concentrate more on performance, making sure that each garment is functional, and in fact multi-functional. In this respect my shell garments and rainwear excel. You can make or buy these garments. Wear the shell jacket and pants as protection from mosquitoes and blackflies. When not needed, simply stuff them into your backpack. They are so lightweight and compact that you will hardly know they are there. The same is true with my waterproof-breathable rain jacket and pants. They are extremely lightweight and compact, and you can carry them on all your outings, in case you encounter an unexpected storm. Read more about the shell garments and rainwear in the Clothing chapter.

Sharing gear with a partner

Jenny and I share a lot of our gear, mainly to save weight and bulk in our packs. Most hiking partners can share at least some gear, how much will depend on the nature of the partnership. It's a matter of how tolerable each person is to encroachment of personal space, and the extent to which each person is willing to rely on the other. Remember that even the closest alliances can separate, whether intentionally or not. Partners who venture ahead or lag behind are well known for selecting the wrong fork in the trail. With this in mind, each member of a group should maintain a certain amount of autonomy by carrying items for safety and well being. At the very minimum these would include a sealed packet of matches, food, a relevant map, money and identification, and at least some type of shelter.

Sharing the tarp or tent will save packweight and space, but the partnership would use this method only when certain they will remain together for the entire hike. Sharing a quilt saves weight and adds shared body warmth; obviously this is a couples' approach. If sleeping beneath a single shelter, two people could share a double-size groundsheet. Should they decide to separate they could cut it in half. Two people camping together could share a single stove, fuel bottle, and cookpot. Should they split up, the stoveless person could revert to the cook-fire, (as described in the Campfire and Cook-fire chapter) but would have to make do without a pot until reaching a store that sells one. Hikers in close partnerships could also share guidebooks, camera and film, first aid kits, pocket knife, compass and many other small items. With the right mindset and relationship, this would hardly be an inconvenience, especially in light of the potential weight savings.

Synergy in motion

Jenny and I were in Oregon during our southbound PCT thru-hike, when late one afternoon we found ourselves hurrying along in an attempt to reach our next resupply station. Our box of supplies was waiting for us at the little store inside the Timberline Lodge on Mt. Hood, and that store was about to close for the day. The late evening and early morning hours are among our favorite for hiking, and we knew that if we did not hurry, we would have to forfeit them and make an early camp somewhere near the lodge. So at my suggestion Jenny handed me her backpack, pocketed some cash and her ID, tied her shell jacket around her waist, and took off at a trot. We figured she could reach the store in about an hour. This left me carrying two backpacks. Since I normally carried mine on one shoulder only, I simply slung Jenny's pack onto my other shoulder and continued ahead—carrying what I quipped was my 17 pound "pack-pack."

Farther along I overtook a pair of backpackers obviously on journey, so I slowed my pace and walked with them a ways. The woman and her husband said they were hiking the section of PCT from the Columbia Gorge to central Oregon, and that they had left the Gorge five days ago. I mentioned that Jenny and I had started in Canada, and that we had left the Gorge yesterday. After a few minutes of pleasant chat I bid them goodbye, with hopes of meeting them again at the lodge.

Jenny and I were sorting our supplies inside the lodge when our friends arrived. It turned out that they had read the first edition of our *PCT Hiker's Handbook*, describing some of our earlier lightweight methods. But these people admitted that they simply "didn't believe any of it." Now they were brimming with questions.

The reaction of these backpackers was typical of the many we met that summer. On paper, our lighter-weight methods may seem "radical" and idealistic. But when these people saw how easily we were doubling and sometimes even tripling their daily mileages, they tended to become less skeptical. The irony was that we were exerting ourselves no more than the backpackers. We were using our energy mainly for forward progress, rather than for load hauling.

I see mileage as an effect rather than a cause. Not something to be struggled for, but merely a by-product of a more efficient style. My main focus is on the natural world, my place in it, and how that relates to the joys and the lessons learned along the way. I also find that when we reduce our barriers—our detachment—from the natural world, we stand to better our wilderness connection. If you are planning a longer journey and would like to easily increase your daily mileages, read the chapter Supercharging Mileage. A lighter pack *can* make the journey more expedient, if your summer's plans call for it.

Works as a system, or independently

Originally I designed my gear and methods to work as a system—each item and technique complementing the others like pieces of a jigsaw puzzle, and nothing used out of context. For example, I advocate hiking in running shoes or sandals. But before backpackers can safely retire their boots, they need to reduce their packweight. To do that, they must first reduce the quantity, size, and weight of the items that fit into their backpacks. And then they would choose smaller and lighter packs. If striving for the 8½ pound baseline packweight, this is the best approach. I call it synergy in motion.

However, for the person interested in reducing packweight more modestly, nearly every one of my recommended items works well in combination with a selection of more traditional gear. The ultralight backpack can be used on day or weekend hikes, loaded with a modest supply of heavier gear. The quilt can be used in place of the sleeping bag, all other gear remaining the traditional type. The tarp can be carried in place of the tent. Each item saves weight, and of course the more items adopted, the more weight saved. But they do not have to be made or purchased all at once. In fact, you might try only one or two new items at a time, giving yourself a few trail miles to become familiar with them. For the long-distance hiker this will probably mean practicing with the new gear during the conditioning hikes.

Benefits to families with children

Backpackers with children are often eager to share the joys of the outdoors with their kids. However, traditional gear is so heavy that it limits the possibilities enormously, especially for those with younger children. What usually happens is that the entire family remains at home during the formative years, waiting for the youngsters to grow strong enough to carry their own things. Lighter-weight equipment changes all of this. Each member of the family can carry all his or her own gear. Or if the children are very young, then mom and dad can carry their gear as well, with little extra strain. This means that the whole family can enjoy these outings together, and I think this is particularly beneficial for the kids during their early years.

Children especially will appreciate the lighter gear, the smaller packs, comfortable lightweight shoes and clothing. They will have fun in a tarp of their own, and they will enjoy sleeping in their own small quilts. This simple, lightweight equipment combined with mom and dad's contagious joy of the wilds can turn the overnight trips into positive experiences for the children, and they will eagerly look forward to subsequent outings.

Phases of packweight reduction

Whether you are planning a 10-mile loop, an overnight outing, or a months-long trek, every additional ounce of weight on your feet and back will magnify itself. So why drag along items of luxury and comfort designed to resemble what you are leaving at home? They will only subtract from your comfort while on the trail. Make it easy on yourself by carving your packweight.

Traditionally, hikers have cut a few inches from the handles of their half-ounce toothbrushes, trimmed the margins off their maps, combined all their candy bars into a single bag and dispensed with the individual wrappers, and with a sense of accomplishment called the job done. As a result, the 50 pound pack is trimmed to 49.9 pounds.

Phase 1: Concentrate on heavy items first

When reducing packweight, concentrate on the heavier items first. Replacing a 7 pound pack with a 1 pound pack saves a whopping 6 pounds! Replace a 5 pound tent with a 1 pound tarp and save 4 pounds. Wear lightweight and functional clothing rather than heavy and bulky "all-conditions" attire. The weight on your feet makes a difference too. Try hiking in lighter-weight shoes. And consider sharing some gear with a partner.

Phase 2: Leave superfluous gear behind

Every item that goes into your pack will add to your load. Conversely, when you eliminate an item of equipment from your inventory, you reduce its weight by 100%. This leads us to the second phase of packweight savings: avoiding the superfluous.

Consider a typical set of cookware and utensils: the nesting pots and lids, the handle tool, the frying pan, spatula and the cooking oil, the baking device, mixing bowls and mixing spoons, the plates and silverware, the insulated coffee mug and the Sierra cup. It's a nice thought, dining in elegance in the wilds; but all this camp cookery only subtracts from one's wilderness connection. Why? Because it makes the hiking much more difficult, and the camping more of a hassle trying to keep all the cookwear clean, free of flies, and organized. Virtually every type of *nutritious* food can be cooked in a single, lidded pot, (or broiled or baked over an open cook-fire) and eaten with a spoon.

The hiking wardrobe is notorious at expanding the bulk of one's pack. This is mainly because we are so used to variety in our clothing. Jenny and I learned that we could get along just as well—in fact better—with only the basics. I should note, though, that even in continuously fine weather, I consider a back-up set of storm clothing essential. At the minimum this would include an insulated jacket and a rain jacket.

Gadgets are probably the worst offenders: the nifty multi-pliers tool, camp chair, and items of entertainment such as thick paperback books, radio, cassette or CD player, deck of playing cards, backgammon set. I have seen cell phones, machetes, butane curling irons, and lawn chairs; not exactly lightweight, and all of it superfluous. Leave all these things behind, and you will be well on your way to a lighter pack.

Phase 3: Select the lightest and most functional

In this phase we select the lightest and most useful of the usual profusion of small items, such as the knife, flashlight, compass, cookpot, camera, water bottle, eating utensils, first aid kit, personal hygiene kit, and so forth. Each fractional ounce by itself is not much, but in quantity they add up fast.

Reading the map, on the CDT in New Mexico.

I have seen hikers with headlamps that weighed a pound. I have known thru-hikers to use large metal spoons to scoop peanut butter from glass jars. Look at your gear with a critical eye. A small plastic bag containing only the basic first aid items is a fraction of the weight of a comprehensive kit that comes in its own nifty zippered case. How about your water bottle? In place of the standard, heavy duty, wide-mouth bottle, use an empty soda bottle with a screw-on lid.

Phase 4: Cut and whack

Most commercial products come with guarantees or warrantees that become void if you modify the product. This leaves you feeling that the company still owns the products long after you have paid for them and taken them home. But the truth is, your purchases belong to you, and you may modify them any way you like. And by doing so, they are far more likely to serve your specific needs.

Heavy-duty backpacks are notorious for their extraneous straps, loops and hooks, bells, whistles and doo-dads. Cut off anything you will not use. Be assertive, and remember that if you whack too much you can always sew it back together. Do the same with all your gear, cut and whack to your heart's content: the toothbrush handle, the maps (cut away whatever portions you will not need, not just the borders), cut the bandana in half, chop a small wedge from the bar of soap. Instead of carrying an entire guide book for the trail you will be hiking, cut out only the pages you will need. Leave the sewing thread behind, and use dental floss for any sewing repairs.

Phase 5: Tabulate

Use a kitchen scale that shows ounces and fractions of ounces, and record the weight of every piece of your gear, every item of clothing, your pack, shoes, the items in your first aid kit—everything. When you catalog your gear in black and white, you will see it more objectively. Usually you will find ways of ridding your outfit of more weight.

Phase 6: Reason and reject

The final phase takes place after you have selected and tabulated your gear, but before actually loading it into your pack. Scrutinize each item, and ask yourself: Do I absolutely need it? You can do this at home prior to departure, and at the resupply stations. This phase is particularly effective on longer journeys that allow more opportunities to experiment with your selection of gear, and to determine which items are essential and which are not. Remember that even if you think you might need a particular item someday, this is no justification for carrying it (unless for emergency). If you are not using it, and are not likely to be using it fairly soon, then consider ridding your pack of it.

Brett Tucker tells me of one of his pack-clearing experiences: "I remember hanging out in front of the AT Conference office in Boiling Springs, Pennsylvania, where they have a hook-scale for measuring packweight. The summer's thru-hike was long; we had come only about half way, but had already grown tired of our heavy packs. And so a bunch of us were soon engaged in a hilarious free-for-all, as we spent the afternoon culling items from our packs, re-weighing the loads, and culling some more. Items were held up and roundly scrutinized by all present. Tents, stoves and cold weather sleeping bags were boxed up and shipped home. One guy even sent home his entire pack and bought a daypack at a nearby outfitters."

Let's look at a few more important considerations for packweight reduction.

Tuning in

- **Time the hike appropriately**. By timing your outings to the most favorable seasons, you will usually enjoy the best weather. A high country trek during the month of May is bound to be cold and sodden, whereas that same route in August will usually be drier and warmer. This kind of planning will reduce your need for cold-weather clothing and all sorts of other winter-related gear, including climbing ropes, crampons, snowshoes, expedition tents, heavy mountain boots, and extra fuel to melt snow. On a bona fide winter mountaineering trip, these items might be desirable, assuming you have the skills for using them properly and safely. But by delaying the start of your hike until the snow has melted, you can do away with the need for all this winter gear. Springtime snow usually melts amazingly fast, and often just a week or two can make a big difference. You still need to carry a certain amount of gear to handle adverse conditions, but by timing your outing properly you will reduce your chances of encountering those conditions.

- **Tune in to the environment**. This goes hand in hand with timing the hike. The more you bend and flow with nature, rather than stand up to it, the lighter you can travel without sacrificing your margins of safety. For example if a storm threatens, you would descend to lower, more protected terrain and make a secure and comfortable camp.

- **Carry an umbrella**. In good weather the umbrella may seem superfluous, but when the clouds let loose day after day, or when the sun beats down from a clear sky, the umbrella will be worth every ounce.

- **Food weight does not count**. Camping usually stimulates the appetite and hiking always increases the need for calories and nutrition.

Don't scrimp on the quantity or the quality of your food for the sake of saving a few pounds of packweight. A hard-working body needs a good supply of wholesome food.

• **Always carry emergency items**. Like the food, your emergency items are exempt from the quest of packweight savings. Always keep a few emergency items with you. These would include a fire starter kit (stick matches or spark striker, birthday candles, and some dry tinder) in a waterproof plastic bag, a small, sharp knife, and a set of cold weather and storm-proof clothing (an insulating sweater or jacket, a rain jacket, mittens and a warm hat).

Packweight myths

In this chapter we have explored ways of reducing packweight, and have examined the many benefits. Now let's look at some of the standard arguments in favor of traditional, heavy-weight gear.

Myth: The longer the hike, the more gear it requires.

The longer the hike, the *less* gear it requires. This is because the more weeks and months we spend on the trails, the more skill we tend to develop. The more skilled, the less we need to rely solely on equipment, and so the less equipment we need.

Myth: Those who traverse deserts and high snowy ranges need lots of heavy-duty gear and very large, sturdy packs to carry it in.

This argument is a favorite with companies selling these products, with those who are paid to market and "review" them, and with the occasional backpacker trying to impress others with fanciful escapades. For the person who traverses deserts, lightweight gear is essential. And when necessary, a lightweight but well designed and properly constructed pack will carry a heavy load of water. The person traversing snowbound mountains finds similar benefits in lightweight gear, mainly because it greatly facilitates the progress. Cold weather clothing does not have to be massively built.

Myth: The day or weekend hiker can carry a lot of gear and not worry about the weight. These trips are short, and the extra load will not affect the hiker physically or mentally. The hiker can handle the load, and wants an enjoyable, laid-back trip with all the luxuries.

Lightweight methods and gear are well suited to day and weekend hikers, because they reduce the chances of injury caused by lugging a heavy load. Gear-laden short trips tend to discourage a person from making longer trips, because the hiking is so much work.

Myth: Our equipment must be rugged and durable. It *has* to be heavy.

Indeed, we should choose gear that is reliable and durable, but it certainly does not have to be heavy. Well-constructed gear can be made of lighter materials, and such gear can hold up extremely well.

Myth: The backpacker needs a full load of equipment for a safe and comfortable trip.

A bloated selection of hiking and camping gear is very heavy. Lumbering beneath a heavy load is anything but comfortable and enjoyable for most people, even those in excellent physical condition. The heavy load subtracts from the safety by increasing the person's chances of injury, and by reducing his or her ability to descend expediently to lower and more protected terrain in the event of a sudden storm. A load of heavy-duty gear is no substitute for good judgement, mobility and skill.

Myth: The backpack may feel very heavy at home, while preparing for the hike, but once we get started and get into shape, it won't be so bad.

Initially, a 60 pound pack feels merely heavy. After the first few days of actual hiking, though, it will begin to feel more like a crushing burden. A heavy pack will steepen every hill, and lengthen every mile. It will sap enjoyment and increase the chances of injury. Never will the hiker accustom to carrying it, and always will removing it from the back bring immense relief.

Myth: To live the good life, we must ensure our comfort, both at home and in the woods.

The tendency is to simulate the comforts of home. Never mind that at home you do not have to carry those things mile after mile, over hill and dale.

Myth: Strong hikers don't mind carrying heavy packs.

Brawn and brute strength is one approach, but careful thought and planning are almost always more effective.

The Standard Backpacking Reasoning: It is better to have a piece of gear and not need it, than to need it and not have it.

The Jardine Approach: If I need it and don't have it, then I don't need it.

Few of us learned to ride a bicycle by reading a book; we had to go out there and learn by actually doing. And so it is with adopting a lighter-weight approach. Instead of merely reading and discussing, philoso-phizing and debating, go out there and give it a try. Camping and hiking with less gear requires a new attitude and a willingness to experiment until you discover what works best for you.

The joys of a lighter pack

Section 1

Equipment

The Backpack

Most hikers consider the backpack one of their most important items of gear. Yet Grandma Gatewood did not carry one. She used a home-made bag, as we saw, closed at one end with a draw cord. It had no shoulder straps—the entire bag simply draped over one shoulder. With this she hiked many thousands of miles. Contrast her duffel-type bag with the massively built backpacks found in backpacking stores and catalogs today which are complicated, overbuilt, and not very functional. Trends are beginning to change, but still we find the market dominated by internal frame packs weighing five to seven pounds, and more.

We hikers are trying to carve ounces from our gear, and the backpack manufacturers are adding them back in pounds. How do they get away with this? By including all sorts of complex gimmicks, such as devices of ergonomic fit, adjustable and even interchangeable suspension systems, stylized and garish panels, eye-catching loops of contrasting webbing, rugged, outdoorsy-sounding brand and model names, and much more—all of which effectively diverts the customer's attention away from the pack's weight. Of course, the manufacturers assure us that these packs will carry our loads in comfort. Why do we need the comfort? Because our loads are so heavy. And at five to seven pounds, the backpack itself is one of the main culprits. What good is ergonomic fit to someone struggling beneath a heavy load? Is there such a thing as suffering in comfort? The way to make hiking more comfortable, and more energy efficient, is not to design a backpack to carry a heavy load more comfortably, but to reduce the load. And one of the most effective measures in reducing that load is to reduce the weight of the backpack itself.

As mentioned, the pack that I carried on my most recent thru-hike weighs 13½ ounces; Jenny's is 11½ ounces. These packs worked great, and because we constructed them properly, minimizing the stress points and optimizing the reinforcements, and because we treated them with reasonable care during the trip, they returned home in like-new condition. And with about 3,500 trail miles now on them, they are still going strong.

The reduced weight of one of these backpacks will carve *pounds* off your load, not mere ounces. And its somewhat smaller size will limit the amount of gear you can burden yourself with.

Pack size

Hiking with a smaller and lighter pack requires a certain shift in thinking. We would not expect the usual pile of camping gear and clothing to fit into a smaller pack. We need to reduce the size of the pile, and in the chapters to follow we examine ways of doing that.

Actually, my pack is not as small as it might seem. When loaded, it is 11½" wide, 9 1/3" deep, and 20½" tall, not taking into account its extension collar. The pack has a volume of 2,200 cubic inches. The three outside pockets add another 400 cubic inches, and the extension collar another 1,100. The all-up capacity, then, is 2,600 cubic inches, or 3,700 with the collar, which is not bad for a 13½ ounce thru-hiking backpack. The pack I designed for GoLite is 10% larger and only fractionally heavier.

I consider these packs suitable for any length of hike. If you can go on an overnight hike with a smaller assortment of lightweight gear, then you can go for months carrying that same selection. This is because the gear you need for camping one night in the wilds is about what you would need for camping a hundred nights. The same holds true for your clothing, rainwear, and so forth. The only real variation is your food, and if you are setting off with a large supply of that, then you can put some of your load into the pack's adjustable extension collar. More on that to follow.

Measuring pack volume

Published specifications for pack volume are not highly reliable, since the methods of measurement are not standardized among manufacturers. The way I measure pack volume is very straightforward, and you can try it with your current backpack. Visit your local shipping store and ask to borrow a large sack of recycled plastic "peanuts." Take them home and fill your pack with them. Be careful not to jam the peanuts in tightly, since that would give a false reading. Use a very light pressure with the open hand to settle them into the backpack. Pour the peanuts from your pack into a cardboard box, and use the same light pressure of your hand to level them. The volume of your pack is now represented in the cardboard box. Measure the box's length and width. Then slide a yardstick down the inside of the box, without disturbing the peanuts, and measure how many inches high the peanuts are. Multiplying these three numbers together (length x width x height) gives you the backpack's volume in cubic inches.

Extension collar

The extension collar is a length of extra material that pulls out of the pack's main body and extends above it, to create more carrying capacity when needed, for example if you are starting off from a trailhead with an extra large supply of food. With the extension collar loaded, the backpack tends to ride top-heavy. Carrying it this way can be something of a balancing act, and in precarious situations it could be unsafe. In most situations the extra food will be consumed in a day or so, if not hours, and the extension collar will be folded back down out of the way, reducing the pack to its normal cruising size.

Pack features

Backpacks used to be simple affairs, hardly more than bags fitted with shoulder straps. These uncomplicated rucksacks worked quite well—until people started carrying heavier loads in them. Responding to the demand, and in many cases actually creating that demand with various advertising methods, designers and manufacturers have been producing ever more complex backpacks. My feelings are that this complexity has gone way beyond our needs. This is why I have "backwards-engineered" the pack, simplifying and reducing its features to the most basic and functional.

Frames and hip belts

Actually, pack frames and hip belts go back many years. Would you believe at least 5,000? The Iceman, whose frozen corpse dates back to the Stone Age, carried a frame pack. And from evidence that researchers have pieced together, it appears that he used a hip belt attached to that frame. The hip belt even had a front pouch for keeping small items handy. The story of Iceman, how he was found, and the fascinating details of his life that researchers have pieced together are found in *The Man in the Ice*, by Konrad Spindler (Harmony Books: 1994). See also "Building The Ice Man's Pack Frame" by John Mills, in Volume 4, Issue 3 of Wilderness Way magazine.

During our second thru-hike, whenever my pack was nearly empty of food and water, and therefore when it was at its lightest, I would hike with its hip belt unlatched. I found that I walked easier without the restriction. On our fourth thru-hike, Jenny and I set off along the AT with the initial versions of our ultralight packs. Half-way through the first day we realized that the hip belts were doing us no good, because our loads were so modest. So we cut the hip belts off. And without hip belts, the internal frame stays were no longer needed, so we dispensed with those also.

Pack frames, whether they are internal or external, aluminum, plastic, or stiff foam, are designed to take a part of the crushing load off the shoulders, and transfer it down to the hip belt and onto the hips. Does this sound like fun, carrying a load so heavy that your shoulders alone cannot bear it? With a much lighter load, the shoulders can cope very well, and we do not need the frame or the hip belt. And when we remove the hip belt and frame, we cut a fair percentage of the pack's weight.

Another function of the pack frame is to cushion the hiker's back from any pointed objects inside the pack, such as the stove, a pair of crampons thrown in haphazardly, a massively spiny Coulter pine cone, and possibly a large, craggy meteor found in some field. But the stove we can position on the side opposite the back, the crampons we can safely leave at home, the Coulter pine cone we can leave lie, and the chances of finding a meteor are very slim. So rather than rely on a frame for padding, we can use our available soft goods, namely the spare clothing, tarp, groundsheet, foam pad and quilt.

Coulter pine cone

You might experiment with carrying a lightly loaded pack with its hip belt unfastened. If the shoulder straps alone tire your shoulders to extreme discomfort, then you are probably carrying too much weight. If you need to carry more weight, then build up to it gradually, over the course of several outings.

Hikers accustomed to carrying heavy loads, and who switch to lighter gear and hip-belt-less packs, (and possibly to lighter footwear) will often find themselves walking with surprising buoyancy. In fact, they may fairly jounce along the trail, with the small pack banging them in the back with every step. With a lighter load one should smooth the stride, making it less aggressive and jerky.

Hip belt stabilizing straps

Let's take another look at the industry standard, overly-complex back-pack, and examine it in terms of bio-mechanics.

As we walk, our pelvis moves in three ways. It swivels as though we are dancing the "twist," opposite the arms as they swing forward and back. It see-saws, one side up, the other down, then vice versa. And it shuttles side to side as our body weight shifts from one leg to the other. The motions of our shoulder girdle mirror those of our pelvis, but in opposite phase. Our spine connects the shoulder girdle and hips, and it accommodates these opposing motions by bending and twisting. An internal or external frame pack with its hip belt cinched acts as a brace, limiting the natural movement of the spine, and restraining these motions. Over the long haul this saps energy. Furthermore, by constraining the spine, designed for suppleness in absorbing shocks, both the hip belt and the frame increase one's chances of injury—for example should one step off a root or rock without thinking, and land too hard. Crunch!

All this harness restraint works great for jet fighter pilots, securing them in their seats as they make radical G maneuvers. But the restraint is detrimental to hikers ambling along the trail. At the very least you could cut off any hip belt stabilizing straps (read: pelvis immobilizing straps), since these only cinch the load tighter about the hips, and render the hip belt even more inflexible. You will walk more efficiently without this kind of restraint. Of course, for even better results, carry a lighter pack with no frame and hip belt at all.

Shoulder strap adjustments

In order for the frame to properly transfer the load down to the hip belt, the whole assembly must fit the hiker's body like a glove. Five thousand years ago, Iceman's hazel and larch pack frame and leather hip belt probably fit him perfectly. Today we can no longer custom fit a complex back-pack by making adjustments to it with a knife and bit of lashing, such is the price of progress. Instead, the pack manufacturers must devise ways of accommodating the broad range of hiker sizes. They do this by making the packs in a few select sizes, and by contriving various adjustments in the height of the upper shoulder straps' attachments. One such adjust-ment is with "lifter straps." These attach to the pack straps several inches down from the upper attachments, and allow the user to raise or lower the shoulder straps according to torso shape and size. Another method is with complicated assemblies for adjusting the upper shoulder strap attachment points themselves. However, once the hiker makes all the adjustments to achieve a proper fit, these adjusting mechanisms are of no further advan-tage, even though the hiker must carry the extra weight of these contriv-ances from then on.

A pack that lacks a frame and hip belt does not require the added complexity of adjustments. Not only is such a pack lighter, but it is more reliable.

My ultralight pack has one small adjusting buckle on each shoulder strap, where the strap attaches to the bottom of the pack. These buckles enable one to adjust the length of the straps, depending on how many layers of clothing are being worn. I find, also, that the more weight in the pack, the more I tend to cinch the shoulder straps, keeping the pack riding higher on my back, at the correct level. Loose straps allow the pack to ride too low and to tip back away from one's body, both of which can feel sloppy and cumbersome.

Compartments

Some types of commercial packs have horizontal partitions between the main loading area and a lower, sleeping bag compartment. The sleeping bag compartment is then accessed externally with a heavy zipper. This arrangement supposedly allows for better weight distribution, accommo-dating the lighter sleeping bag below, and the heavier food items above. The old, monster packs that Jenny and I struggled under for so many miles started life with such compartments. The zippers were heavy and difficult to open, especially with cold hands. Worse, the weight of food bearing down on the sleeping bag compromised its loft very seriously, despite the divider. After the first season we cut the partitions out, and stowed the heavier food items in the bottom.

The need to balance a pack properly, placing the heavy items in such and such a place, and the less heavy ones just so—is a requirement of the elephantine backpack. A lighter assortment of gear does not need to be carefully balanced. And with a little extra forethought in stowing things into the pack, you will spare yourself of the frustration of forever having to dig down into the pack looking for something. The idea is to stow each item according to its priority. Place the things you will need during the day near the top. (See Loading Sequence, below.)

External pockets

My latest pack has three external mesh pockets. One pocket, located on the right side of the pack, is for my water bottle—kept there for accessibility. This pocket is made of mesh to allow the bottle's condensation to evaporate. On the other side is a pocket for the fuel bottle, also mesh to permit the fumes to evaporate. And on the rear is a large pocket for stowing the tent fly or tarp when it is wet with the morning's dew. Each of these pockets is fitted with elastic in the top hem, to help secure the contents.

Back in the days when I carried a backpack heavy enough to warrant a hip belt, I stitched a home-made camera bag to the belt for easy access. This kept my little camera out of the way when not needed, but handy when it was needed. I now carry the camera in one of the mesh pockets on my small pack. Because the pack is compact and mobile, and because I carry it on one shoulder only, I can easily swing the entire pack around and reach into the pocket when I need the camera. Of course, in very hot weather I bury the camera in the pack to insulate it.

Hikers have asked me about the advisability of using a separate "frontpack" for added carrying capacity—like a small pack worn backwards, with the pack riding against the chest, or some kind of specially designed frontpack that attaches to the backpack's shoulder straps. Supposedly these help balance the load of the backpack. But in the process they also increase the klutz factor, hampering one's mobility and restricting the visibility down at one's feet. The more paraphernalia hanging all over your body, the more cumbersome, and the more you will trudge along instead of enjoying a pleasant ramble. So rather than looking for ways of adding carrying capacity, a better plan is to rethink the gear selection, and find ways of reducing it.

Hikers do not need frontpacks to balance their loads. They balance them simply by leaning forward. In fact you can gauge the weight of someone's load by looking at his or her degree of forward lean. With a heavy pack this lean is pronounced; with a lightweight one it is hardly noticeable.

Thumb loops

As you hike along the trail your arms swing like pendulums, in cadence with your gait. But because you are not using your arm and hand muscles, their vessels enlarge and the blood tends to "pool" in the fingers and hands. Several hours of this can swell and stiffen these extremities. To alleviate this you can raise your hands occasionally and hook the thumbs behind the backpack's shoulder straps, at chest height. Or you can insert your thumbs into makeshift thumb or wrist loops secured to the shoulder straps at chest height. Not only will this help reduce the swelling in the fingers and hands, but it will relieve the shoulders and encourage the chest cavity to expand more fully with each breath.

Sternum strap

If there is one technical innovation that we might call breathtaking, it is the sternum strap. This "chest corset" is a common feature on today's backpacks; it even appears on most of the smaller day-hiking models. Never mind that it constricts hikers where they need it the least—directly across their lungs, which in the normal course of hiking are laboring to expand with each breath. Technically, the sternum strap's only function is to pull the shoulder straps together, keeping them from sliding off the shoulders. And indeed, the straps can slide off the shoulders of someone wearing a pack that is sized for someone much larger. In effect, then, the sternum strap allows a wider range of fit. And while this may benefit the manufacturer's sales, it does little for the hiker's breathing. The sternum strap also makes the pack more difficult to remove in an emergency.

Try hiking with the sternum strap unfastened. If you find that the shoulder straps slide off your shoulders, then maybe your pack is too large for your body size. Or maybe the straps are not designed properly. Either of these would be all the more reason to make your next backpack yourself, tailoring it to your needs. Or to buy a pack that fits properly. If you must wear a chest corset, position it as high as possible on the shoulder straps.

Compression straps

Most commercial packs come with compression straps. Cinched tight, these act like a boa constrictor, reducing the size of the pack. Theoretically this makes the pack ride with better stability as you jog along the trail. But how often do you find yourself jogging along a trail? If you need that kind of speed, on rare occasion, then you could try the cruising mode, which is free of jouncing (as described in the Hiking Pace chapter). Compression straps bring the pack's center of gravity closer to the body. This is important with heavy packs, but not with lighter ones.

Compression straps also reduce the size of the pack, when the extra volume is not needed. With a smaller selection of lightweight gear, we do not need the extra volume to begin with, so why not simply carry a smaller and lighter pack? And when you need more carrying capacity for that fresh load of provisions, use the extension collar.

Fear of pruning

Most companies specify that if you buy one of their products, and if you modify it in any way, then you void the warranty. I remember a pair of shoes that burst a heel-cushioning bubble after only a few hundred miles on the trail. I sent the shoes back for replacement, but was denied it on the basis that I had cut the tongues out. I seriously doubt whether the tongues had anything to do with the bubble failure, and suspect that the company was using that as a boilerplate excuse for not backing up their product. This was in the earlier days of that particular model, and no doubt the company has corrected the problem. But the fact remains that many times a manufacturer will use such an excuse to its own convenience. The non-modification clause in the guarantee tends to leave you feeling that the company still controls the product after you have purchased it. It makes you reluctant to cut the tongues out of a pair of shoes, to cut off compression straps, to remove company logos, and to make the scores of other modifications that would be very beneficial to your gear inventory, and to your wilderness experiences.

My feeling is that we pay our money and take our chances. First we inspect the product, looking for any defects or weaknesses. Then once we make the decision to purchase, we buy the product and take it home, confident that it belongs to us, and that we may modify it in any way we like. If we modify it in such a way that weakens it, then that is our fault, not the company's, and we should not expect a replacement. Instead, we break out a needle and thread, and make the repairs ourselves. Or if the product does later prove defective through no fault of our own, then maybe the company will accept that fact and make the replacement. If it does not, then that would not be the end of the world.

For many people, the idea of taking a pair of scissors to a commercial backpack is unthinkable. But remember that a pack is nothing more than a collection of simple pieces of material all sewn together. There is nothing magic about it. And just because you *might* need the extraneous features someday, that does not mean you have to carry them needlessly for 20 miles or 2,000. Prune them, and in the unlikely event that you later find that you need them, sew them back on. And just because you trim something off, that does not mean that the pack will suddenly fall apart, or become useless. Rather, the pack will likely become more serviceable, as its weight and complexity decrease.

Loading sequence

Generally, our hiking belongings fall into three categories: food, clothing and equipment. And each of these we can further separate into what we will need while hiking and resting—placed higher in the pack for accessibility—and what we will need at camp—placed lower in the pack, out of the way.

When filling my pack, for overnight trips or longer, I begin by loading the bulk of the food into the bottom. Next goes the quilt in its waterproof stuff sack, then the tarp if it is dry, again in its stuff sack. On top of this goes the cookpot and stove. To keep these from digging into my back, I place spare clothing behind them, stowed inside their waterproof stuff sack. Depending on the conditions, I keep my shell jacket and pants, sweater, mittens and warm hat near the top, along with the day's supply of snacks, lunch, water filter if any, and perhaps a ditty bag containing the compass, foot care kit, and so forth. The fuel and water bottles go into the outside mesh pockets. And if the tarp is wet with rain or dew, then it goes into the central, large mesh pocket.

My packs have no foam padding to cushion the back, since I find it unnecessary. If you think about what is going into the pack—quilt or sleeping bag, clothing and so forth—most of it is soft. As described, these are my padding. Actually, my recommended 36" sleeping pad fits very nicely inside one of these packs when empty. Roll the pad loosely, place it into the pack, then allow it to unroll and fill the pack's interior. In effect it acts as an internal foam liner, adding stiffness and cushioning.

Donning the backpack

When Jenny and I hiked the Appalachian Trail, we noticed that almost every chair-size rock or log near the track had a beaten path in front of it. Backpackers carrying massive loads were apparently using these objects to rest on, thereby reducing the distance they had to stoop when sitting down. These benches also made it easier for them to stand up again and get going.

I have carried many a large load, mainly while climbing and portaging. So I know how it feels. But in most hiking scenarios I see no need to carry a load so gruesome that it requires the trailside object-cum-chair approach. Of course, a big load of food and water can increase the packweight dramatically, so when shouldering a heavy pack, one must be careful not to injure the back. This is especially true when dehydrated, because at such times the spinal disks are far more susceptible to injury.

If you are traveling with a partner and you both have heavy packs, you can reduce the chances of injury by helping each other lift the packs to your backs. But when hiking solo, you might try the following method: Grasp the pack by its haul loop and one shoulder strap, and hoist it to bended knee. Support it there momentarily, then heft the pack to shoulder height and quickly turn your back into it, inserting one arm into its shoulder strap. The pack is now hanging from that shoulder. Take a few steps, turn around to check for anything left behind, then insert the other elbow into the remaining strap loop. Shouldering that strap, you then bring the arm through at your convenience.

The single-shoulder carry

For decades I carried my pack on both shoulders, but when finally I reduced the size and weight sufficiently, I found it far more comfortable and less restrictive to carry the pack on one shoulder only. And while this may seem like an unusual method, it has some very practical advantages.

First and foremost it improves the ventilation and reduces the sweat-

On the PCT in 94

ing. Carried on both shoulders, the backpack acts like an ultra-thick layer of insulation, causing the hard working back muscles to sweat-soak both shirt and pack. This is far less a problem with the one-shoulder carry.

Also, my shoulders do not become nearly as tired as might be expected, since I can switch shoulders every ten or fifteen minutes and allow the opposite shoulder to relax completely.

In the unfortunate event of someone sliding pell-mell down a snow slope or being swept downriver, a backpack attached securely to that person's back would essentially immobilize them, in most cases compromising their safety enormously. The single-shoulder carry is much safer in such an event, since the pack in most cases will simply drop away. However, before you try this method during snowfield traverses or while fording rivers, make sure you are well accustomed to it during your normal hiking.

I do not design my packs differently to accommodate the single-shoulder carry; the positioning of the straps does not change. And actually I do use both straps, although not at the same time—except in rare instances, such as when I need to lug a heavy load of water, or when I want the pack to stay put as I clamber hand and foot over rugged terrain. The Appalachian Trail's Mahoosuc Notch, .9 mile of boulders, comes to mind here.

You may have used the single-shoulder method at one time or another without giving it much thought, perhaps during school days when toting a "book bag." It is the same idea. In any case, the single-shoulder carry is a viable option with a lighter-weight pack.

Pack cover

In years past I spent a lot of time trying to waterproof my packs. First I tried waterproofing all the seams—without success due to the complexity of construction in the commercial packs. Next, I bought commercial pack covers, and found them heavy, and so baggy that they flogged in strong wind. Nor did they prevent the rain from soaking my pack and its contents. Worse, they acted as catch-basins, pooling the rain in the sagging bottom. Tired of dumping so much water out of my store-bought pack covers, I started making my own. I custom fit them and went through several design improvements. Jenny and I hiked with these for thousands of miles, but still we found them less than ideal.

Finally we reverted to something that has been around for decades and works quite well: plastic trash bags. We place one inside each of our packs, as a liner, and simply twist the top closed and fold it over before closing the pack. A more durable alternative would be an internal waterproof liner.

———————

Backpacks come in many different makes and models, and choosing the right one can be perplexing. We see internal frames and external frames, hip belts and lifter straps, lumbar pads, stabilizing straps, compression straps, daisy chains, loops and buckles galore. But do we really need all this gadgetry? More importantly, do we need to carry huge loads? I think that most of us could get by quite nicely with a simple rucksack fitted with a couple of straps. Grandma Gatewood would probably have suggested that we don't even need the straps.

Tarp and Tent

A night spent sleeping under the stars can be one of wonder and beauty. My first experience with this was as a youngster, "camping" in the backyard of my parent's home. My brothers and I would throw our sleeping bags down on the grass, and sometimes a few of our neighbor friends would join us. This was independence and freedom; camping at its best. We even built a little brick fireplace and fried eggs over an open fire in one of mom's old skillets. We poured ketchup over the eggs, and to us it was the best breakfast in the world.

That was nearly fifty years ago, and since then I've done a lot of camping. I still remember those trips into the Colorado high country with my dad and brothers; those crisp evenings before the campfire, the craggy, snow-clad peaks towering all around. The tents we used were two-person, army surplus pup tents, made from two pieces of canvas joined along the ridgeline with buttons.

My grandfather owned a ranch, and as Boy Scouts we camped there on a regular basis, using the same type of pup tents. During the summer months my family sometimes lived on the ranch. By day I drove the tractor, working the crops. At night I slept in my own private camp in the forest. When I awoke one morning and startled a gray jay off my sleeping bag, I realized that I was starting to develop a special kinship with nature.

During my early twenties I worked as an aerospace engineer, spending my weekends climbing mountains and technical rock. Many nights I slept in my tent. But my fondness for tents came to an end when I started climbing the mountains alpine style, bivouacking at day's end rather than hauling along a tent and setting up camp.

After retiring the necktie and leaving the office cubicle, I worked for seven years as a wilderness instructor, mostly in the Colorado Rockies. During this time neither I nor my students used tents. Instead, we used tarps. In later years our tarps were made of nylon, but the first several

seasons they were nothing but sheets of clear plastic. At the start of each summer we would reel off what we needed from a store-bought roll, and that was that—cheap, easy to use and durable. We draped these plastic sheets over cords strung between trees or poles, and secured the corner lines to the tarps with sheet bend knots (see the Knots chapter). These knots are remarkably strong; I never saw one tear out.

Simple though these tarps were, they had many advantages and very few disadvantages. They cost a fraction of what a tent sold for. They had no zippers or poles to break and render them immediately unserviceable. They weighed less than half of what tents weigh, yet they provided far more sheltered living space. But most importantly to us, they permitted the best possible ventilation. We, our clothing, and our equipment stayed much drier. These tarps proved themselves eminently suitable for weeks of continued use, even during inclement weather. And in those high Colorado Rockies there was plenty of that.

Another advantage to the tarps was that in mild weather we were not so inclined to use them. They were not like tents where the tendency is to pitch them rain or shine, and the perceived security draws a person in and compels him or her to shut out the world. Where possible we slept in the open, and this was a marvelous experience for everyone. With the starry canopy overhead and the earth's gentle embrace beneath, we found that our simple, low-tech style allowed us a more profound interaction with the natural world.

All in all, we had no need of expensive shelters, clothing or gear designed to protect us from so-called "nature's wrath."

Modern tents

A decade and a half later, when Jenny and I were planning our first thru-hike, I made a tarp, based on how well this type of shelter had worked for me in the past. Yet after studying the more prevalent backpacking books and being swayed by marketeers' hype, we decided to go with a commercial tent instead. Neither of us had ever hiked anything nearly as long as the Pacific Crest Trail, and we felt that the very best gear would improve our chances of success. So we settled on a 4 pound, 3-season tent of the latest design. We carried fairly heavy loads that summer—typically 30 or 35 pounds, including food and fuel—and when it came time to make camp we were too tired to enjoy day's end; all we wanted was to crawl into the tent and collapse.

In the mornings we would usually find our sleeping bag and clothing very damp with condensation. This meant that we had to spend a lot of time drying things out, and it was not uncommon to see other hikers doing the same. I remember one fellow stopping to chat, and during our conversation he matter-of-factly pitched his free-standing tent inside-out, to dry.

During the night the hiker's body gives off several pounds of moisture. Some comes from the breath, which is always saturated. And some comes from the skin, in the form of insensible perspiration. This moisture is warmer than the ambient air, so it rises to the tent's ceiling. And there it is trapped, in much the same way that warm air is trapped inside a hot-air balloon. Most tents have a so-called ventilating gap all around the perimeter of their rain flies; and hot air balloons have gaping holes in their bottoms. Neither ventilates the interior, since the buoyancy of the warmer air keeps it from dispersing.

To this day I know of no tent that ventilates adequately. Large, open ports would help, a few at the top to expel warmer, moist air, and a few close to the ground to take in fresh, drier air. But these ports would need to be nearly as large as the doorway itself. I've seen marketing claims about how well certain tents ventilate, but in my experience the only time they do is during gale-force winds. Otherwise, their doorways (of both fly and tent body) need to be kept wide open.

The problem with keeping the doorway open is that with most tents, it allows rain to enter. So when selecting a tent, look carefully at the design. With its door wide open, would rain fall directly into the tent? Or would rain drip or run into the open doorway? Many tents cannot pass this simple test, as though their designers were unfamiliar with the realities of camping in extended rainy weather.

The reality is this: After the first day or two of rain, the interior moisture will build to the point where you will need to keep the doorway open. If you cannot do this without admitting rain, then of course you will have to keep the door closed, in which case the interior dampness will pervade your clothing and sleeping gear. This extra moisture will add pounds to your packweight. More seriously, it will reduce the value of your insulation. In cold weather this could send you into a survival-type situation. This is not a weather attack, but an equipment failure.

Tent failure

The build-up of moisture is one way a tent can fail its user. There are others. Jenny and I were on the trail in central Oregon during that first PCT hike, when an uncommonly severe storm moved into the area. It began with several inches of snow—and this was mid-July—then it turned to rain which cascaded from the sky. We hiked through it for half a day, then made camp. This was before we had learned to carry umbrellas, so we were ill-equipped to hike in such heavy and prolonged rain. Or to camp in it either, we soon found out.

During this storm we spent forty-two hours in the tent. Whenever we opened the door for ventilation, the rain ricocheted in. When we closed the door to shut out the rain, we soon found ourselves inundated with condensation. Moisture given off by our bodies condensed on the tent walls, dripped down and absorbed into the sleeping bag. Outside, rain rebounded under the fly, soaking the tent's interior walls even further. Groundwater also worked its way between the tent floor and the underlying groundsheet, and oozed up through the floor.

No matter how we tried, we could not stop the pervading, warmth-sapping moisture. Every hour our sleeping bag and clothing grew more wet, and lost more of their ability to keep us warm. Waiting out the relentless storm, we began to realize that time was working against us, that our equipment was slowly but inexorably failing us. Eventually we packed up and made our soggy way out of the mountains and down to the nearest town.

On the theory that we needed a more substantial tent offering better coverage, we mail-ordered a new one, and of course spent the next several days waiting for it to arrive. Setting off again with the heavier load, we felt more confident—until the next rainstorm a few nights later when the new tent exhibited the same problems.

The Jardine Tent Awning

These difficulties with the tent inspired us to make some changes. So while preparing for our second PCT hike we sewed a simple awning to the tent fly, extending over its doorway. This awning allowed us to keep the door fully open in any kind of weather, even during the heaviest of rain. It also sheltered our backpacks. I describe how to make such an awning in the Sewing chapter.

The awning worked very well during that second trip, so while preparing for our third trip, the Continental Divide Trail, I cut away the entire vestibule from the tent fly. This modification created a huge open doorway, greatly enhancing ventilation. And the subtracted weight of the vestibule compensated for the added weight of the awning. In lieu of a door we always tried to pitch the tent with its foot pointing into the wind, and its doorway facing away from the wind. Where this was not possible, due to the ground's slope, we simply lowered the awning so that its front edge was close to, or against, the ground.

This tent and awning combination was reminiscent of the old time canvas tents, which had open, sheltered doorways. In rainy weather the campers built a small fire out front, allowing the heat to radiate into the tent's interior and dry their damp belongings. For an excellent example of this see Bill Mason's "Campfire Tent," featured in his book *Song of the Paddle* (Bibliography). In a dire situation my awning design could provide much the same benefits, when used with extreme care. Actually Jenny and I have used it this way only once. If you build a drying fire in front of your tent awning, (or in front of your tarp) keep it at a safe distance, and keep it small. A tent catching fire could be a disaster.

The tarp proves its worth

While preparing for our fifth thru-hike I finally let go of the tent idea. Those thousands of miles of trial and error finally convinced me that tents do not work as well as tarps, at least in summertime conditions here in the "Lower 48." During our fifth journey we used a tarp, and with excellent results. It measured 8 feet 8 inches square, weighed 28 ounces, and we made it out of urethane-coated nylon. This material is very durable and makes an excellent tarp, but for the truly weight conscious I now recommend silicone-impregnated nylon, which has only recently become available.

My current silicone-nylon tarp is 8 feet 10 inches in length—not including the beaks (see below). This two-person unit is also 8 feet 10 inches wide, when flat on the ground. Pitched fairly low-lying in moderately blustery conditions, this tarp is 7 feet 9 inches wide, which is wider than most two-person backpacking tents are long. Pitched in this configuration, it provides 69.75 square feet of living area. In a pinch, four people could sleep under it quite comfortably. Jenny and I find it luxuriously roomy. The tarp weighs 16 ounces, including all its cordage but minus any stakes. A one-person tarp would be the same length, but would of course be narrower (7 feet 2 inches) and would weigh about 13.5 ounces.

Strength—tarp and tent compared

The tarp is an integration of straight lines and triangles, and these are in tension. The tarp has no weakness of curved members in compression, which accounts for its superior strength over tents. And thanks to its all-tension geometry, it can be constructed of thinner and lighter materials.

And speaking of strength, should a tent pole break in strong wind, the tent can become uninhabitable. In other words, in conditions so severe that your life depends on your tent, this is when the tent is most likely to fail you. Not so with a tarp. If a tarp support breaks, you simply replace it with a stronger stick from the forest. And if one cannot be found, then the tarp will still work without it. Many times I have pitched a tarp with just one end elevated.

Using a tarp in strong wind

The tarp's adjustability makes it eminently adaptable to varying conditions. The stronger the wind, the lower you pitch the tarp, and the stronger the tarp becomes.

When I was teaching those wilderness classes in the San Juan mountains of Colorado, the students and I once spent two weeks hiking and camping directly atop the exposed Continental Divide. I would not recommend trying this; we were doing it more as a challenge, and during that period the weather was free of thunderstorms. We did experience powerful winds, however. In fact the winds were so strong that they might have flattened most backpacking tents. Yet our plastic tarps worked very well, and we found that pitching them low to the ground was quick and easy. To do this, we simply spread our plastic groundsheets, set our back-packs in the center to act as supports, covered everything with a tarp, then placed smooth rocks all around the tarp's perimeter. In so doing, we cre-ated the ultimate in low-lying aerodynamic structures. To enter, we crawled through a gap on the downwind side. And of course no matter how tightly we secured the tarp's perimeter, the gale-force winds provided ample ven-tilation.

During our fifth thru-hike, when Jenny and I used a tarp, we tried to pitch the tarp with its ridgeline broadside to the wind, and with its wind-ward edge lowered right to the ground. Where this was not possible, due to the local topography, we pitched the tarp very low lying. Sometimes if the wind started angling into one end, we deployed an umbrella at that end. Even without an umbrella, one can keep the effects of wind at a minimum by orienting the tarp properly and by pitching it very low.

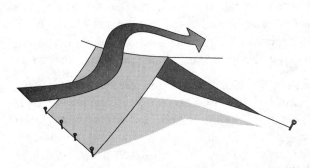

To pin the wind-ward edge of a tarp to the ground, insert the stakes directly into the tarp's guyline webbing loops, without using the guylines them-selves. If not using stakes, secure the guylines several inches away from the edge of the tarp, using rocks, logs, etc., then cover each guyline with a heavy rock. Never set a rock on the tarp itself, since it could abrade the thin fabric and make holes in it.

When selecting a site, look for natural protection from the wind, such as trees, rocks, logs or tall bushes. At the same time, avoid pitching the tarp directly against any of these objects, because they could abrade the tarp fabric as it vibrates in the wind.

Variable geometry aerodynamics

In my most recent tarp design I added a very useful feature. Both ends of the tarp are drooped. I call these drooped ends "beaks." The lower you pitch the tarp, the wider you spread the two halves apart at their base, and the more the beaks point downward. In so doing they partially close off the ends of the tarp, and help block both wind and rain. Once the tarp is pitched, the position of the beaks is fixed. But while pitching the tarp, you can point the beaks nearly horizontally (by pitching the tarp high, and angling the walls steeply), or you can point the beaks straight down vertically (by pitching the tarp very low, and spreading the edges wide). Or you can pitch the tarp so that the beaks are anywhere in between those two positions.

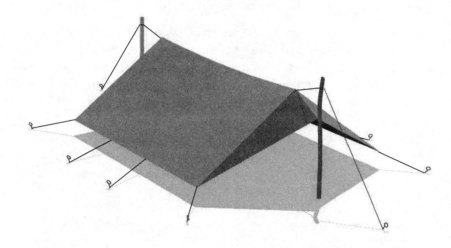

The tip of each beak is fitted with a short guyline. This is tied to the nearby support pole or tree, but only tight enough to support the beak, since this line does not support the main tarp body.

Warmth—tarp and tent compared

Our bodies give off moisture during the night in the form of vapor— invisible molecules of H_2O in the gaseous state. This mixes with the air, and the heat of our skin warming the air tends to buoy it upwards. It rises into our clothing, not wicking because it is still vapor. Emerging from our clothing, it continues rising into our quilt or sleeping bag, passes through that, and into the ambient air. All along the way it cools, from skin temperature (warm) to ambient air temperature (cooler). As it cools, it may reach the temperature of condensation, called the "dew point," at which time the molecules of vapor condense into molecules of water. If this condensation happens outside our sleeping gear, then all is well, particularly if we are sleeping beneath a tarp. The ambient ventilation (out-side breeze) carries this excess moisture away, although some of it con-denses harmlessly on the tarp's underside, as dew—in the same way that dew collects on the surrounding vegetation. If we are sleeping inside a tent, which by its nature restricts ambient ventilation, then the moisture accumulates. And the vapor of our breath, which is always saturated, only adds to the accumulation. Some of this vapor condenses on the tent walls, and the rest of it works its way back into our bedding and clothing. Suffice it to say that the humidity level inside a tent is much greater than that beneath a tarp. And high humidity inside a tent works against us.

On very cold nights, as the vapor of insensible perspiration passes through our clothing and quilt or sleeping bag, it reaches the dew point somewhere inside that sleeping gear. The vapor then condenses into mois-ture and becomes trapped in the insulation, wetting it. If the ambient humidity is low, and if we are sleeping beneath a tarp, then much of this moisture will wick to the surface of the quilt or sleeping bag, evaporate, and be wafted away. Air at a certain temperature can contain only so much water vapor, and this amount decreases as the temperature falls. So if we are inside a tent on a cold night, then the tent's air soon reaches 100% humidity (saturation) and the moisture trapped in the quilt or sleep-ing bag will stay trapped. Or more technically speaking, the rate of evapo-ration is counteracted by an equal rate of re-absorption.

The net effect is that on cold nights a tarp is warmer than a tent. The tent traps moisture, and this moisture saps our body heat. The moisture also adds considerably to the weight of our clothing and sleeping gear, increasing our packweight the following morning. In regions of higher humidity and low nighttime temperatures, all the above problems are amplified, and the tarp becomes even more favorable.

Effectiveness in rain—tarp and tent compared

Supposedly the tent's most salient feature is the protection it offers from rain. But if you have ever pitched a tent *in* the rain, then you know how discouraging the job can be. First you preen the site of sticks, pine cones, and small rocks, while fully exposed to the rain. Then you lay out the groundsheet, which starts acting as a rain catcher. Quickly you pull your tent from its stowbag and spread it on the groundsheet, at which time the tent begins soaking water from the groundsheet, and from the sky, like a sponge. Hurriedly you fumble with the poles; they get wet and slippery, and by the time you get the tent erected the whole thing is soaked. You throw the fly over the tent, attach its corners to the tent poles, and peg out the vestibule—provided your tent has a vestibule. And if so, then you stuff your wet pack beneath it. You yourself are soaked; you remove your rain jacket, place it in the vestibule atop your pack where it cannot possibly dry, and you slide into the tent. Welcome to a wet, decidedly uncomfortable home. But not to worry, you begin mopping the interior with a hand towel, wringing it out the front door when necessary. And soon your abode has become at least tolerable.

In the afternoon's heavy rain you probably did not stop to cook dinner. Now that you are in your tent, you may feel like cooking. But alas, for safety's sake you cannot cook inside the tent, tempting though that might be. Fumes could accumulate and asphyxiate you. The stove could ignite the sleeping bag or tent, or it could tip over and scald you with boiling liquid and soak everything. You could reach out and cook in the vestibule and hope that the carbon monoxide does not waft into the tent and accumulate to dangerous levels. Except that your backpack is probably occupying the vestibule. Maybe you could shove the pack out into the rain, and light the stove in the vestibule, and take your chances with the fumes. Ok, for safety's sake you venture back outside in the pouring rain, and crouch beneath the partial shelter of a tree. And there you sit, hunkering over your sputtering stove for what scant warmth it provides, soaking wet and becoming more miserably chilled all the time. This is high technology? Frankly, I doubt whether our primitive ancestors lived as miserably.

You can pitch a tarp in the rain without all the worry and rush of keeping things dry. Once pitched, you crawl beneath it and bring in your backpack, setting it to one side. After gently preening the ground of any sticks, pine cones, and small rocks—while fully protected from the rain— you lay out your groundsheet, dry side up. Next, you remove your damp clothing, wring it out if necessary, and hang it from a clothesline strung lengthwise along the underside of the tarp's ridgeline. Right away you put on dry clothing and crawl into the quilt or bag. Welcome to a warm and dry home.

The luxury of being able to cook under a tarp while reclining in dry comfort is another of the tarp's many benefits. Simply reach beyond the groundsheet, ignite the stove, and cook a hearty meal. Keep the stove away from the sides of the tarp where it is lower, and keep your clothing, bedding, and all other flammable gear well away from the stove. And locate your stove in such a place that should it tip over, it will not spill hot liquids onto you or your groundsheet.

Heavy rain rebounds into the tarp's interior just as it does into the gap around a tent fly. But because the tarp is so much larger than a tent, this rebounding does not come close to you or your gear. And unlike a tent where this splatter inevitably wets the fabric, beneath a tarp it either soaks into the ground or it evaporates. The same happens with the water running off the tarp's perimeter. Any ground water will flow away from you, as long as you have selected a site that is slightly elevated or at least naturally absorbent.

While camping on sloped ground, if the rain starts pouring so hard that it courses downhill, you might have to use a stick to scrape a V-shaped trench in the ground uphill of your tarp. This will channel the groundwater away from your living quarters. Only in extreme need would you have to dig such a trench, however; I have done it only twice. If you resort to this method, be sure to fill the trench and eradicate all signs afterwards.

If you cannot find a slight rise or a slope, you may have to camp on level ground. Should the rainwater start running into your living quarters, simply dig a few small holes for it to drain into.

Striking camp in the rain

On those mornings pouring with rain, breaking camp is far easier when using a tarp rather than a tent. Still beneath the tarp, you load your pack. Then you deploy your umbrella, step outside and set the pack beneath a sheltering tree if one is available. You then take down the tarp, give it a few vigorous shakes, and stuff it into the external mesh pocket of your backpack, or stuff the tarp into its waterproof stow bag. You can do all this beneath your umbrella. Persistent rain will prevent you from airing the tarp during the day, but this means only that the tarp will be a little heavier. The wetness will not affect its performance the following evening.

Using a tarp in the snow

The tarp is not meant as a four-season shelter, but I have camped beneath tarps during fairly heavy snowfall, without incident. Should you be caught in an unexpected snowstorm, pitch the tarp tighter and with the roof more steeply inclined, encouraging the snow to slide off. When the snow begins to stick to the roof, simply tap it with your open hand from underneath. This will dislodge the snow and force it to slide off the tarp. If the snow is accumulating rapidly, you will find it piling up along the sides, and this will help seal off the sides and add to the overall protection. But at some point the snow may begin pressing in on the tarp, at which time you may need to dig away some of it.

Using a tarp in bug season

The tarp does not offer substantial protection from biting insects. Back in the 1970's I experimented with sewing a width of netting around the tarp's perimeter, but I found that this idea had a host of disadvantages. First, it did not rid the enclosure of mosquitoes, blackflies, ticks and other insects. Many of these insects were on the ground, in the grass or forest litter, prior to my pitching the tarp over them. All the netting did was cage them, and make me available to them at night while I slept. The netting added a certain amount of weight to the tarp, and this increase was not justified when the bugs were largely absent—which was most of the time. And the netting greatly restricted the needed cross-ventilation on hot days. The netting sewn all around the tarp also prevented me from pitching the tarp higher in fine weather, and it got in my way when I pitched the tarp very low in stormy conditions. And when I pitched the tarp low in rainy weather, the netting got soaked and muddy, creating more of a mess.

Abandoning the idea of sewing the netting to the tarp, I designed a separate "NetTent" that hooks to the underside of the tarp. This adds about a pound to the system, and provides around 24 square feet of enclosed living space. And because it has a floor, it is very effective at keeping the bugs at bay. The floor serves also as the groundsheet on all but the wettest terrain, saving the weight of a separate groundsheet. But the best feature of the NetTent is that I can leave it behind in reasonably bug-free conditions. Carrying only the tarp saves me the NetTent's one pound of packweight.

When Jenny and I hiked the PCT for the third time, we used a simple piece of netting sewn to the quilt, and found it very effective, even when the mosquitoes were swarming in great numbers. This netting was 54 inches long, and 72 inches wide—extending about 10 inches to either side of the quilt. The netting was not flat, but tucked on both sides to form an enclosure, which we could support with an open umbrella beneath it, or suspend from the tarp overhead. But most often we simply pulled it over our faces at night. It was very effective against the bugs, and on chillier, bug-free nights we found that it kept our heads warmer. When not needed we rolled it down and tied with special tabs, holding it out of the way.

On nights too warm for the quilt we slept only in the mosquito-proof clothing, and head-nets if the insects were bothersome. In the wee hours when more warmth was needed, we simply dragged the quilt over us.

Bug-proof netting is a fairly recent innovation, yet it is hard to imagine camping in the summertime without it. How did people manage in times past? I think the answer lies mostly in our physical make-up, compared to that of our distant, and even our fairly recent ancestors. Our consumption of refined foods has changed us, I think making us more attractive to flying and biting insects, and more reactive to their bites. I say this based on my own experience, and that of other outdoor enthusiasts.

Using a tarp in snake country

How does one avoid nighttime encounters with snakes while sleeping under a tarp? Aren't these warmth-seeking reptiles drawn to us? While we do generate a great deal of infrared heat, we are much too large to constitute a prospective meal. And while asleep we certainly do not constitute a threat. Snakes use their warmth-seeking abilities only on creatures more their meal size, such as mice. Never mind the "true life" stories of some unsuspecting camper waking up with a rattlesnake in his sleeping bag. Our imaginations run wild so easily, but I think these stories are fictitious. I am not saying it could not happen, but if snakes were attracted to the heat of sleeping people, then tent campers would often find snakes outside their tents and even underneath them, which is unheard of. And what about the countless numbers of people who slept out in the open, in times past? I think that the chances of a nighttime encounter with a snake under a tarp are extremely slim.

Tall tales aside, we would still use a bit of caution when selecting a place to pitch a tarp—or a tent—when in snake country. For example we would not pitch our shelter near a pile of rocks. And if the surrounding brush is thick, then we might probe it with a long stick before setting our pack down near it and establishing camp.

Methods of pitching a tarp

Pitching a tarp is an elementary skill, and basically there are only two things to remember. The first is to avoid established campsites with their compacted and dished ground. Instead, find a less-trampled site, preferably somewhere remote and pristine, at a place where the ground is slightly raised above its surroundings. In most cases finding such a site is a fairly simple matter. The second point to remember is to secure the tarp's guylines only to objects that are strong and stable.

The A-frame mode

The illustration at the beginning of the chapter shows the tarp pitched in its usual configuration: the A-frame mode. The ridge line could be stretched between two ridge poles or sticks, or two trees, or one stick and one tree. Often, the ground at the base of a tree is slightly raised, thus providing excellent drainage. However, trees are known for dropping branches during storms. Jenny and I generally use two sticks because they allow greater freedom in the choice of a site. Normally we start looking for ridge sticks well in advance of making the evening's camp. Where trees are sparse we start looking for the sticks an hour before making camp. Where trees are entirely lacking we carry a couple of sticks with us. In the desert we have used dead stalks of agave plants as ridge sticks. And as a last resort we have even used our umbrellas. Trekking poles would work, and if too slippery for the ridge line clove hitch friction knots (see Knots chapter), then you could wrap the poles with a bit of adhesive tape for a better grip. Metal trekking poles might not make the best tarp supports in a lightning storm. At any rate, the thing to avoid is laying the tarp directly on the quilt or sleeping bag, as this greatly restricts the beneficial ventilation, and will usually make the sleeping gear very wet with condensation.

If using stakes, secure the guylines to them with clove hitches. The clove hitch can be tied anywhere along the length of the guyline, it is adjustable, and it automatically unties itself when you pull the stake out of the ground and slide the stake out of the knot. With very thin line, the clove hitch around a stake can be difficult to remove, in which case you can use a clove hitch with a quick release.

Attaching the ridge lines to their support sticks

With the plastic tarp, the ridge line is one continuous piece of cord, running tree-to-tree under the tarp's ridge. The nylon tarp works differently. It has two shorter cords, each connected to the tarp, one at each end.

I normally attach the ridge lines to their support sticks, again using clove hitches. These knots slide up and down the support sticks when not tensioned, so they allow us to set the height of the tarp to suit the conditions. In lieu of clove hitches, one could simply wrap the ridge line around the support stick a number of times, then run it down to the stake. Either way, position the sticks close to the tarp but not quite touching it.

Normally you would choose ridge sticks of about the same height, but if necessary you could use a shorter stick at the foot end, such that the tarp's ridge slopes down from head to the foot.

When securing a ridge line to a stake, tree or bush, wrap it once or twice as necessary to prevent vertical slippage. Bring it back and secure it to itself using a taut line hitch. (See the Knots chapter.)

Raising the tarp

Spread the tarp on the ground, and attach its ridge lines to the support sticks as described above. The temptation is now to stand the ridge sticks upright, except that they would fall over as soon as you let go of them. You might be able to jam the sticks into the ground a ways, making them stand upright on their own. This is not the best idea, since later in the process you may need to adjust their location. If you and a partner are pitching the shelter together, then one of you could hold one stick upright while the other person secures the corner guys, then you could repeat the process at the tarp's other end. Fortunately for the solo hiker there is an even easier method. Simply secure all four corner guys to their anchor points (stakes, rocks, tree trunk, etc.) positioned at the approximate locations. Raise the ridge sticks one at a time and secure their ridge lines out to their own ground anchors.

Then adjust the positions of the corner guys to create a taut, even pitch.

In strong wind, be sure to use stout ridge sticks. Secure the ridge line clove hitches to these sticks lower, so that the tarp is pitched closer to the ground. And be sure to tension the ridge lines quite tightly.

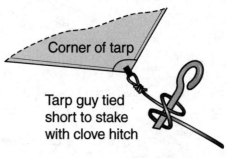

Corner of tarp

Tarp guy tied
short to stake
with clove hitch

Slide stake out
of knot to untie

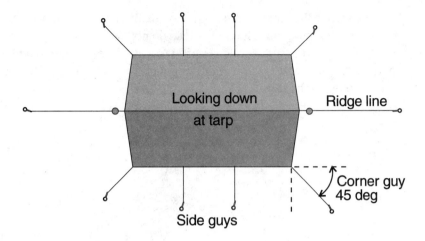

Side guys

Corner guys

Always angle the corner guylines 45° out to the side, as viewed from above. Tension them medium-tightly. Look at the tarp for wrinkles. If you see any, then you know that the corner guys are not angled or tensioned properly.

Side guys

In addition to the four corner guys, you can further secure the tarp against strong wind with the side guys, two on each side. Tension these only lightly, otherwise they will lower the tarp's mid-section.

Lifters

The lifter lines lead from the central area of the tarp to lifter sticks, and then down to their anchors. Their purpose is to raise the ceiling and provide more interior living room. My tarp has lifters on each side. These

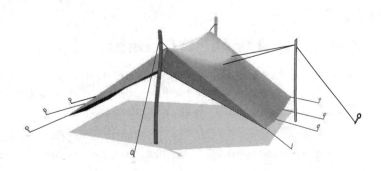

also help stabilize the tarp in gusts, and they maintain headroom beneath a light snow accumulation. The lifter sticks do not need to be very stout, since there is very little pressure on them. Wrap the lifter line around the support stick twice and tension it only enough to create a bit of extra headroom beneath the tarp.

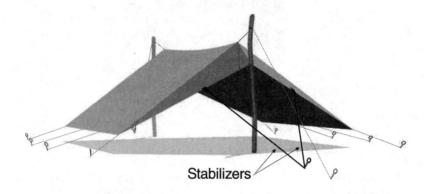

Stabilizers

Stabilizers

The stabilizers are tabs and lines attached to the beak ends of the tarp. They are used to stabilize those end panels in strong wind. Ordinarily we do not use them because they get in the way and add to the guyline tangle. But when the wind is blowing strongly they add considerable stability. Each end of the tarp has two stabilizer tabs. To use them, attach their lines, and bring these lines together at their far ends and secure them to a single stake.

My tarps have extremely fine lifter lines, side guys, and stabilizer lines. This is because these points of attachment are not heavily stressed, compared to the others. But with very thin lines, one must avoid tying knots that will later need to be untied. Here again if using stakes, tie a clove hitch along the length of a line, and consider adding a quick release.

Guyline anchor points for tarps and tents

As the wind speed doubles, the pressure it exerts on a tarp or tent quadruples. This is why we must attach the guylines to objects that are very secure. Tent stakes are suitable only in firm ground.

Where the ground is not firm, tie the guylines to large, flat-bottomed rocks, to logs placed endwise to prevent them from rolling, or to the base of bushes. Even small bushes can be very strongly rooted, and guylines tied to them properly can be quite secure. To do this, wrap the guyline twice around the bush at its base (twice prevents the line from sliding up the stem) then secure the end of the guyline back to itself with a taut-line hitch. If concerned about the line cutting into the bush's bark and doing harm, you can wrap the base of the bush with natural materials—dry grasses, pine needles, or leaves—to make a protective pad.

Clotheslines

Every tarp and tent should have a clothesline overhead, running the length of its interior. With a tarp, the clothesline runs from one end to the other, under the ridgeline. You can also string a clothesline under a tent awning. Clothes hung to dry overnight inside a tent will rarely dry, but this is still a good way of separating wet clothing from the sleeping gear. If the clothing is soaking wet, wring it out before hanging it on the line.

Holders for eyeglasses and wristwatch

If you wear eyeglasses and use a tent, you could attach a small loop of cord to the tent fabric somewhere overhead—not to the waterproof fly, but to the breathable tent wall or ceiling. From this loop you could hang your eyeglasses at night, out of harm's way yet handy when needed. You could attach the cord by sewing it to the fabric, or more simply, you could use a hot ice pick, or a hot nail held with pliers, to melt through the fabric in two places, half an inch apart. Run the cord through both holes, and tie it on the outside of the tent where the knot will be out of your way. If you use a wristwatch alarm to awaken you in the early morning, you could make a similar loop to hold the wristwatch. With the watch hanging near your head, you will be much more likely to hear it when its morning alarm sounds. If using a tarp, you can sew small loops of narrow webbing inside, and seam-seal the stitching on the outside. You can also hang your eyeglasses and your wristwatch from the overhead clothesline.

In the chill of early morning, the eyeglasses will normally fog when first putting them on. One solution is to pre-warm them. To do this, while still lying under the bedding, place your glasses on your chest for a couple of minutes. Speaking of eyeglasses, be sure to tighten the tiny connecting screws before leaving home. You can also apply Loctite® Threadlocker 242 or the equivalent to prevent the screws from working loose.

Tarp and tent color

In terms of performance, black is the least desirable color for a tarp or tent fly. Black would gain more heat by day and lose more by night. Other very dark colors share these disadvantages. Light colors, such as white and bright yellow or gold, can be too glaring under them, at least when the sun is still in the sky. The best color in terms of technical performance is silver-colored aluminized material. The best color in terms of low-profile camping is something that blends in with the surroundings, helping the shelter remain unobtrusive.

Bivy sacks

Most bivy sacks are lighter and more compact than tents, making them seem like an attractive option. I do not favor them because of their lack of ventilation. A bivy sack is also heavier than a tarp for a fraction of the living space, and it tends to be more expensive. It provides little or no shelter for the backpack and other belongings, no place to set the wet clothing, no convenient place to cook out of the rain. Its singular advantage is its small footprint, useful in areas with little open ground, such as on high and rocky mountainsides. This type of adventuring is beyond the scope of this book; for the safest and warmest trip we would camp in the lower regions.

An easy transition

One of the best ways to familiarize yourself with a tarp is to practice pitching it in your backyard, at a nearby park, or some other convenient location. Then during your first few overnight outings with the new tarp, you might consider carrying a back-up tent as well. If the weather is favorable, keep the tent handy. If the weather is threatening, pitch both the tarp and the tent, but sleep under the tarp. If for some reason your tarp setup fails, and you are forced to move into the tent, figure out what went wrong, and make the necessary corrections the next time.

Generally there are only three things that can go wrong with a tarp. One is that rainwater runs under it and invades your living quarters. Once again, this is caused by camping on dished ground. The solution is to camp on slightly raised ground. The second thing that could go wrong is that a chilling wind blows through the interior. Again, pitch the tarp sideways to the wind, and with the upwind edge of the tarp lowered to the ground. This offers even better protection than most tents with their non-closeable gaps beneath their rain flies. The third problem is human error—a knot coming untied, a poor choice of support sticks, not enough tension on the guylines, or the wind pulling a stake out of the ground.

A sense of connection

The tarp is about a fourth the weight of even the lighter tents, and it offers up to twice the living space. It keeps us drier, and in many cases warmer. But of all its very fine features, perhaps its best one is that it allows us to stay more in tune with our surroundings. A tent can offer a false sense of security. Its walls might encourage its occupants to relax and shut down their senses, but these walls are no barrier to any kind of real threat, should one develop. Security comes not from thin nylon walls, but from staying alert to unusual sounds, watching and reacting when necessary. Without a tent enveloping us, we can also become more connected to the wilderness around us. The night is as full of wonders as the day, so why barricade ourselves off from them and spend the quiet, starry hours in oblivion? We can do that at home, inside our houses.

Comfortably reclined beneath a tarp, we can watch the sunset if we are retiring early, and well into the night we can listen for animals roving about, and any changes in weather. Awakening at dawn we can watch the sky as it begins to lighten, signaling the new day. In my experience a tarp provides the best of both worlds: an effective and efficient shelter, yet providing a wonderful sense of openness.

Groundsheet and Pad

As the name implies, the groundsheet is a thin, protective sheet (plastic or coated nylon) placed on the ground. Onto this goes your tent if you are using one. Or, if you are using a tarp instead, you would pitch the tarp first, then spread the groundsheet under it, to serve as your "floor."

One might imagine that sleeping beneath a tarp on wet ground would be pretty miserable. On very wet ground, even a tent has its limitations. But if the ground is absorptive, and if it slopes away from you in all directions such that more rain will not intrude, then a groundsheet spread over it will begin to dry that ground. And after sleeping there all night you will often find, when breaking camp the following morning, that the ground is no longer wet.

When used with a tent, the groundsheet helps protect the tent floor from abrasion, from soiling, and from picking up sap. The groundsheet gets soiled, but when breaking camp you simply fold it dirty-sides together. The groundsheet will not protect the tent's floor from punctures, since the groundsheet itself is thin and punctures fairly readily. This is why we must preen the site beforehand of anything sharp or pointed, such as sticks, stones, and needle-tipped pinecone scales. This gentle preening makes the area more comfortable to sleep on as well, reducing the need for a thick foam pad.

Most tent floors are made of nylon coated with polyurethane, or rarely, silicone polymer. Although touted as waterproof, these coatings are not completely impervious to water when pressed tightly against something wet. In this case, moisture can migrate through them, although minutely. You may wake up some mornings and find a bit of condensation beneath your sleeping pad. This intrusion of moisture is usually so slight that it is of no concern. And this is why I do not use a separate groundsheet beneath my NetTent, except in extremely wet conditions.

Groundsheet materials

Ordinary polyethylene makes an inexpensive and very serviceable groundsheet. This is sold in hardware stores as "poly" or plastic sheeting. A thickness of 3 mil (3 thousandths of an inch) is about right. Moisture from wet ground will not migrate through it, at least when new and puncture free. It is surprisingly durable, but also somewhat heavy. The person more concerned about packweight could use a polyethylene sheet of less than 3 mil thickness, and carry a few extra inches of duct tape for repairs.

For the lightest possible groundsheet, use a piece of mylar, sold in most sporting goods stores under such names as "Emergency Space Blanket." It looks somewhat like aluminum foil, but is an aluminized polyethylene—a very thin, lightweight plastic with a reflective, silver-colored coating.

Another heavier but more durable option is the All Weather Blanket, made by Metallized Products and again available in sporting goods stores. I've also seen this product advertised as the Space Blanket. The All Weather Blanket is a four-layer laminate: one side is a reflective silver color, and the other side is a ripstop-like plastic in various colors. This product is not puncture-proof, neither are polyethylene and mylar; but I have not found this to be a problem. One caution about colors: If you choose the bright orange or red, be careful about airing the blanket colored-side up, since an aviator could misconstrue your "signal" as a call for help.

Trimming to size

Cutting the groundsheet to the appropriate size will reduce excess weight and bulk. If you are trimming the groundsheet for use with a tarp, spread the groundsheet on the ground, lie down on it, and draw a line around yourself, leaving about twelve extra inches all the way around. If you will be tarping with a partner, then both of you would lie down, a "sleeping distance" apart, and each would delineate your own side of the groundsheet. Leave even more groundsheet if you want extra "floor space" for some of your things. Use a pair of scissors to trim the sheet along your line. The two-person groundsheets that Jenny and I have used on numerous outings are 48" wide at the head, 34" at the foot, and about 7' long.

If you are cutting a groundsheet for use beneath a tent, pitch the tent on it, then draw a line on the groundsheet around the tent's perimeter. Cut about an inch inside the line, making the groundsheet that much smaller than the tent's footprint. The trimming not only eliminates excess weight and bulk, it also eliminates channeling. Any margins of groundsheet left exposed will collect rainwater running off the tent fly, and direct it unfavorably beneath the tent.

Once you have used a groundsheet for a few days or weeks, you may begin to find various small holes in it, normally the result of inadequate site preening. These holes do not need to be repaired. My groundsheets are usually riddled in such holes, and I have not noticed any decrease in performance. Before I realized this, I patched the holes with small bits of adhesive tape. Of course, any larger holes, as well as tears in the material, are genuine candidates for taping. Duct tape works about the best, and it is also effective on mosquito netting, the tarp or tent fly, waterproof bags, and even water bottles. Duct tape is fairly heavy, though, so I usually carry just a few feet of it, rolled and flattened. A more lasting way to repair tears in a urethane-coated tarp or tent fly is to apply a thin coating of AquaSeal. For fabrics that are silicone-coated, use a thin layer of silicone sealant.

The sleeping pad

As discussed in the Packweight chapter, the problem with items of luxury and creature comfort is that lugging them along the trail is very *un*comfortable, due to their weight and bulk. So when selecting your equipment, be careful to choose only the essentials. And of these, try to select the lightest in weight, without sacrificing function.

In this regard, the self-inflating mattress falls short. It is heavy, bulky, expensive, and susceptible to damage. And it is practically impossible to customize to your specific needs. Yet the self-inflating mattress is one of the last items that most campers would leave at home. Why? Because it offers comfort when camping on hard ground, and warmth on cold ground. The inference with this reasoning is that all ground is hard and cold. But is this true? In the established campsites it usually is, especially where decades of campers have scraped away the cushioning layers of forest litter and duff—right down to the dirt. And where this dirt has usually been heavily compacted by innumerable boots and steel-shod hooves.

Such is not the case with undisturbed areas far off the beaten track, where soft, cushioning leaves or needles, or deep and pliant layers of duff or leaf detritus, offer very comfortable camping. Even bare dirt in pristine, untrammeled areas is reasonably soft. Places like these do not require self-inflating mattresses. Neither do they call for scraping together the natural insulation for the best possible cushioning and insulation. We simply use it as we find it—nature's perfect bedding.

But how can we be assured of finding such places every night? Simply by spending a little extra time each evening exploring the surroundings, looking for them. Granted, if the search is cursory, and if the mind is still caught up in the cold-and-compacted-ground way of thinking, then all ground will probably look raw and uninviting. But if we let go of that old mindset and allow nature to provide for our needs, then almost invariably we will find comfortable places to sleep.

To me, the shortcomings of a thick mattress go far beyond its weight and bulk. Due to its thickness it lessens one's connection with the earth. Heavy boots do the same. They reduce the communication from the earth into our feet and on up through our body and into our mind and heart. The connection works in the other direction too: from the heart to the mind, to the body, the feet, and down into the earth. I believe that we are meant to walk on the ground by day and lie on it by night. The earth communicates with us in ways that science is only beginning to discover, and the less we insulate our feet and bodies from the earth's vibrations, resonance and energies, the more we benefit.

The thin foam pad

In most cases a thin foam pad will suffice as a sleeping pad, and a good option is a closed-cell polyethylene pad with a thickness of about 3/8 inch. Often, even this pad is unnecessary. Still, many people have serious doubts about the effectiveness of a thin pad, let alone using no pad at all. Perhaps the main reservation is the lack of a bedroom-like ambience. I find that the concept of comfort has many levels of interpretation, from the hedonistic to the plain and simple. The more time we spend in the wilds, the more we are able to differentiate between our actual needs and our wants—and the less it usually takes to make us comfortable. The end result is still comfort—we are not sacrificing that—we are merely making a few mental adjustments.

What about camping on snow? Early season hikers often encounter plenty of that. Yes, but that does not mean that they have to sleep on it. Jenny and I have hiked well over a thousand miles on snow, and we have always managed to find bare earth to camp on. We do this by ending our days at the lower elevations where the snow is not as pervasive. And when we choose to remain in the higher country, we look for isolated pockets of snow-free ground. These often exist right up to treeline.

On our thru-hikes we slept on 3/8 inch foam pads, and with excellent results. But this is not to infer that we had toughened ourselves to the cold. To the contrary, extended wilderness trekking tends to deplete a person's metabolic reserves. The longer the outing, the more carefully the hiker has to guard his or her body heat. And the best way to do that is to select sites that do not sap that body heat.

These thin foam pads are available typically in sporting goods and variety stores. Before each journey I buy a new pad (they are generally 72" long and 20" wide), and cut it in half, making two shorter pieces. Jenny gets one, and I the other. Then we trim each piece to shoulder and hip width, eliminating unnecessary weight and bulk. The pads need only match our "torso prints." Specifically, my pad is 36" long by 20" wide at the shoulder. It starts tapering at 24" and tapers to 17" wide at the bottom.

The pads do not need to be under our heads, since we use pillows (rolled-up jackets, or stuff sacks filled with spare clothing). And the foam pads do not need to be under our feet, either, because they are tucked comfortably in the quilt's foot pocket. Nor do the pads need to be beneath our legs, because we insulate them with our empty packs, empty stowbags, and whatever spare clothing remains. This leaves no parts of our bodies un-cushioned and un-insulated. It sounds a bit austere, I know, thanks perhaps to the old hard-and-compact-ground way of thinking. But it works very well, especially because we first choose our sites with care. In fact, in warm weather and areas of good ground cover, Jenny and I do not use the foam pads; we find that we are more comfortable without them.

What about camping inside a shelter, like the type found along the Appalachian Trail? If you intend to sleep on those hard wooden bunks, then yes, you will probably need the extra cushioning. Or you could sleep in the woods, instead, on softer, more compliant ground.

Changeover

If you are serious about cutting packweight, but are not yet ready to let go of the self-inflating mattress, you might try carrying both the mattress and a full-length thin foam pad. Use the pad to sleep on, and keep the mattress in reserve. When it is time to make camp, continue beyond the established campsites, and locate a more suitable place in the woods—

one that features natural cushioning and ground insulation. Before erecting your shelter, spread out your groundsheet and foam pad, and lie down on them. Then, shift a few feet one way or the other, feeling for just the right spot—one that better matches your body contours. I call this the "sweet spot," and find that it can make all the difference in comfort. Then pitch your tarp or tent right there. And should you find the need for a little extra padding or ground insulation, place a few items of clothing under you.

The inflating mattress kept in reserve will allow you the freedom to experiment with these lighter methods. Then once you have become adept at them, you will feel more confident about leaving the mattress at home.

The next stage is to cut the foam pad in half, making two shorter pieces. Carry both initially, but with the intent of using only one piece— beneath your torso. Keep the other in reserve. This encourages you to look even more carefully for just the right camping place. Then when you are confident with that, leave one piece at home.

These transitions may sound daunting, but with a carefully selected location and the right attitude, you may be surprised at how little you need to camp comfortably, and to enjoy a very pleasant night's rest.

Quilt and Sleeping Bag

For years I slept in mummy-style sleeping bags—decades actually—but never quite got used to them. They always seemed a bit claustrophobic and were usually too warm. Eventually I solved these problems by opening the bag and using it as a blanket. This method worked so well that by the time Jenny came into my life, I had not slept in a zipped-closed sleeping bag for ten years, even though I had used sleeping bags most of that time. So it was only natural for us, during our outings, to share a single sleeping bag, draped over us like a blanket. This saved us half the weight of two individual sleeping bags, half the bulk and half the cost.

Trial and error

During our first thru-hike we used this open sleeping bag method, but with an added development. As mentioned earlier, we positioned it over a two-person foam pad fitted with a full length zipper. Zipping the two together kept the cold air from wafting in around the sides, and prevented the bag from shifting position during the night. In effect we created a two-person sleeping bag with a goose-down upper and a foam pad lower.

This system was reasonably successful, but by the time we had finished our third thru-hike we had long since quit using the zipper. We found that we slept warmer without the bag attached to the foam pad. This was because the zipper, attaching the edge of the bag to the edge of the foam pad, held the edge of the bag away from our bodies, creating an undesirable air space. Without the zipper, the edges of the bag rested comfortably against us, and this was much warmer.

So we slept with the sleeping bag simply draped over us. Gravity held it in place nicely, and we now had more control over the temperature under the bag. In cold weather we could pull the sides of the bag close to us for warmth, and in mild conditions we could drape it more loosely.

Our method of sleeping under, rather than inside, a single sleeping bag was working well, but still we faced the problem of loft degradation. In the course of carrying, stowing and unstowing the goose down bag month after month on those summer-long journeys, we found that the bag lost about half its original loft by trail's end. Having to buy a new bag every year was expensive, so while preparing for our fourth thru-hike we abandoned the commercial bags and started making our own. I had made a goose down sleeping bag previously and found it somewhat complicated due to the internal baffles. But this time we used modern synthetic insulation which required no baffles. The final product was little more than a layer of insulation sandwiched between two layers of nylon fabric, the whole thing being sewn together around its edges. And because we quilted it to keep the insulation from shifting, we adopted the term "quilt." (See illustration in the Sewing chapter.)

The quilt

The quilt worked so well that we used it on our fourth and fifth thru-hikes, and on virtually all our outings since. One might imagine that the idea of the quilt would not be applicable in very cold weather, but we have used quilts on all of our Arctic expeditions, and have found them eminently suitable—particularly since a second expedition-weight sleeping bag would take up valuable space in the kayak. Whatever kind of trip we are planning, we adjust the thickness of insulation to meet the expected conditions.

Quilt for one person

I designed the quilt with couples in mind, but have found that it works equally well for individual use. While at home Jenny and I sleep beneath quilts left over from various trips; and we each get our own. For one person sleeping alone in the wilds, a two-person quilt would be lavishly large, yet still lighter and more compact than the equivalent commercial sleeping bag, due to its use of ultralight materials. A one-person quilt would be cut narrower (see Sewing chapter), and would of course be that much lighter.

Like an insulated blanket

At home, most people sleep on beds with blankets draped over them. The blankets trap the rising warm air. And because the blankets lie flush against the mattress all around the person, the blankets seal off any gaps. The quilt works the same way, and in fact the quilt is nothing more than an insulated blanket.

One might be reluctant to try a quilt due to the possibility of dislodging it while tossing and turning in the night. In reality, sleeping beneath a quilt is no different than sleeping under blankets at home, and with only a minimum of practice a person learns not to dislodge the quilt while turning over. This is true even for someone accustomed to tucking the blankets between the mattress and box spring. Keeping the quilt in position becomes automatic, even while asleep.

Together, the quilt and a torso-shaped foam pad make an extremely effective sleeping system. I say this after having used these items on many a comfortable night in all sorts of conditions, including weeks of winter-like weather in the High Sierra and the North Cascades, as well as many months in the frozen Far North. Simple though it is, the quilt is the answer.

The foot pocket

Imagine a sleeping bag with a full-length zipper along one side. Unzip the bag all the way down to the foot, then zip it back up a foot or so. Lie down, place the bag over you like a blanket, and insert your feet in the "foot pocket" formed by the partial zipping. This is how Jenny and I use our quilts. Except that our zippers are not full-length like those of sleeping bags, because we find no need to zip our quilts more than the short ways. This foot pocket positions the quilt over the feet, preventing the quilt from sliding off the feet during the night. And the pocket prevents the quilt from shifting toward the head area when inadvertently tugged on.

Securing the quilt to the foam pad

If you are concerned about the quilt sliding off, you can secure it to your foam pad with a few patches of hook-and-loop such as Velcro™. To do this, sew a 2-inch square of "hook" patch to the quilt's outer surface at shoulder level, one on each side, near the edges. Glue a pair of corresponding "loop" patches of Velcro to the upper surface of your foam pad, a few inches in from the edge. With your feet comfortably nestled in the zippered foot pocket, the quilt is effectively pinned down at the far end. And with the two Velcro patches securing the sides, the quilt will be well anchored in a stable triangular pattern.

The reason for gluing the Velcro a few inches in from the foam pad's edges is to eliminate the chilling air space between the sides of the quilt and your body. Basically, the Velcro holds the quilt in a tucked-under fashion.

I rarely use the Velcro tabs, myself. On very cold nights I may tuck the edges of the quilt beneath my shoulder for a bit of added warmth when I first crawl in, but after half an hour or so I will have warmed sufficiently and can then simply drape the quilt loosely about me.

Drying a quilt or sleeping bag

Regardless of whether you carry a quilt or sleeping bag, be sure to air it daily to rid it of the moisture accumulated during the previous night. Down bags benefit the most from airing because they need to be kept dry in order to preserve loft. But even synthetic-fill bags and quilts will shed a pound or two as the entrapped moisture evaporates.

The reason that Jenny and I use zippers for creating the quilt's foot pocket—rather than simply sewing the edges together—is so that we can unzip the pocket and open the quilt fully for maximum exposure to the drying air.

And remember that the sun does not have to be gleaming down from a clear blue sky in order to dry a quilt or bag. The clearer the sky the better, but even beneath a fully clouded sky you can spread your gear to dry—any time between mid morning and mid afternoon—in the absence of rain, of course. Much of the sun's energy penetrates the clouds and will dry your sleeping gear surprisingly well. The cooler the day, the more important it is to avoid spreading your gear on vegetation, which tends to collect moisture. On dank days, look for a patch of rock or gravel that angles toward the sun's position. This type of surface holds rela-

tively little moisture and tends to be warmer than the surrounding terrain.

If the ground is completely saturated from a recent rain, you can simply drape your quilt or bag over you and carry on down the trail like an emperor in a luxurious robe. This procedure will not dry the sleeping gear completely, because of the moisture pumped into it from your body, but it can help considerably.

Further uses

When not hiking, use the quilt at home, on your bed in winter or on the couch as a comforter while reading. Consider making or buying a spare quilt to keep in your car for emergencies.

Shredded newspapers

Imagine for a moment an expensive, premium quality sleeping bag made with prime northern goose down. Let's say that this bag has a thickness—measuring only that part of the bag that would cover the person—of two inches. As we will calculate below, this bag has an Effective Temperature Rating (ETR) of 20° Fahrenheit. Now imagine this: A sleeping bag filled with two inches of very fine steel wool would be just as warm. Another one filled with two inches of finely shredded newspaper would be equally warm. And let us not forget modern technology: a sleeping bag filled with two inches of the latest synthetic fill: 20° Fahrenheit once again.

How can all these fill materials provide comparable insulation? The answer is that the individual fibers themselves are so thin that they are not able to conduct heat—or to insulate against the cold. The fibers are not what provide the sleeping bag with its insulating ability; all they do is trap tiny pockets of air. It is the air, warmed by our own body heat, that provides the insulation.

Goose down or synthetic fill?

Warmth is an important quality in a sleeping quilt or bag, but we hikers have additional requirements. We need our sleeping gear to be reasonably light in weight. And we like it to fit into small stuff sacks, and come out looking about like new. So we use insulating materials that are low in density and high in loft-retention.

Among these, prime northern goose down offers the greatest warmth and compressibility for the least weight. Put another way: for a given loft, (thickness of covering) goose down weighs the least and compresses the best. Technology is gradually closing the gap, and the performance differences between goose down and the best synthetics are no longer very great. This is good news because goose down has a few shortcomings that for most of us might outweigh its advantages.

Wet and cold

Down loses most of its loft when wet. If allowed to become soaked, it becomes fairly useless. My most vivid experience with this was during a sea-kayaking trip in what is usually sunny and warm Baja, Mexico. That particular October was rainy and frigid. I carried no tent; I slept beneath the kayak's sail, hardly large enough to cover me. And as the days and weeks progressed, the goose down sleeping bag became wetter, flatter and colder.

If you try to wring the water out of a soaking wet goose down bag, you make it even flatter. This is not to suggest that when goose down becomes saturated all is lost. Left with no alternative, you can restore its ability to insulate by drying the bag in front of a campfire. This can be effective, but it is slow, and often risky because the heat can melt or even ignite the material, and sparks can burn holes in it. And what if the skies are pouring with rain? This is where a tarp comes in handy. You can light a small campfire maybe ten feet from the tarp, then sit beneath the tarp and hold the wet sleeping bag toward the fire, allowing it to absorb the radiating warmth. I have done this only once, during a period of heavy and prolonged rain. And that was my last journey with a down-filled sleeping bag.

Synthetic fill materials also lose their ability to insulate when wet. For after all, water absorbed into the insulation, whether that insulation is down or synthetic, replaces the tiny pockets of insulating air. This water conducts away body heat. But at least when synthetic insulation becomes wet, even soaking wet, you can wring it out and restore much of its loft. There is no need to dry it before a campfire to ensure your survival in cold and stormy weather. In the event of such a predicament, this wring-and-restore feature can make a big difference.

Speaking of survival, one must never underestimate the benefits of a hearty campfire. This is why one should always carry an emergency fire starter kit containing strike-anywhere stick matches (or zirconium type flint-strikers), a few birthday candles, and a small bundle of dry tinder. In a storm situation already fraught with predicaments you might be tempted to try warming yourself and drying your clothing—inside your tent per-haps—with a camp stove. This is rarely a good idea. All fossil fuel stoves generate large amounts of moisture as a byproduct of the combustion. The more they burn, the more water they pump into the surrounding air. And of course the more asphyxiating carbon monoxide they produce.

Preserving loft

Earlier I mentioned that a sleeping quilt or bag tends to lose loft over time. This is true with both goose down and synthetic materials. Let's look at ways of minimizing the problem.

Most importantly, never use a compression stuff sack to contain any item made with low density insulation. This includes quilts, sleeping bags, and insulated parkas, hats and mittens. Compression devices are very effective at reducing bulk, but they are equally effective at destroying loft. The first time you cinch down those compression straps, you snuff out, permanently, approximately 10% of a sleeping quilt or bag's loft. And you can subtract an additional 2% for each subsequent compression. And of course the quilt or bag loses that percentage of its ability to keep you warm. Even more damaging than using a compression stuff sack is to sit on a quilt or sleeping bag when it is contained in any kind of a stuff sack. Low density insulation cannot stand up to such crushing loads. The more carefully you treat your insulating gear, the better it will serve you. This is especially important during a long journey that runs into the late fall season, during which time you may need the most from your gear's warmth. For best results, use the largest stuff sack practicable, refrain from stowing heavy gear or provisions on top of it, and resist the temptation to sit on it.

Certain manufacturers claim that their proprietary insulation materials do not lose loft. But even if a sleeping bag does not lose its loft, it may not be your best choice if it weighs five to seven pounds. So if you read such claims, be sure to check the product's weight. The discussions in this chapter deal with the more efficient, lighter-weight types.

Even after a synthetic bag has lost much of its original loft, it still remains serviceable. But when a down bag loses its loft, the down tends to shift uselessly to the sides, leaving patches of almost zero insulation covering you. And no matter how well you fluff it up before retiring, the down will slide off you during the night. So if you decide to purchase a down bag for a summer-long trip, consider one that has baffles that restrict the movement of the down in the sideways direction. Also consider one having a moderate "overfill" so that the compartments will still be fully inflated after some loft degradation.

Effective Temperature Rating formula

So far we have discussed the two basic types of sleeping bag insulation: down and synthetic. And we have seen how a given thickness of insulation would offer a certain amount of warmth, regardless of composition. Now let's determine how much insulation we might need.

Obviously, the colder the night, the more insulation we will need to stay warm. But when we try to quantify the matter, we run into difficulties due to the many variables. Everyone reacts differently to nighttime temperatures. Some people do not mind being a little chilled, while others prefer incubation. Another variable is the type of fabrics used on both sides of the insulation, and their permeability. If those fabrics are overly breathable, then the warm and moist air will escape too voluminously, and much warmth will be lost. The color of the outer layer affects the amount of heat it will radiate away. Another variable is the ambient humidity. Yet another is the local wind chill factor. Aside from all these, the variable with the greatest influence is the amount of clothing we wear while sleeping; more on that in a moment.

In practical terms, we can speak of the quilt or bag's "Effective Temperature Rating." This is the hypothetical lowest outside air temperature at which a sleeping quilt or bag would preserve one's body warmth. I have quantified the matter into an easy-to-use formula that gives a very useful approximation.

In this formula, the letter "T" represents the thickness of that part of the quilt or bag covering the person. Since warm air rises, the part of a sleeping bag beneath the person contributes almost nothing to warmth.

My formula:

$$ETR = 100 - (40 * T)$$

Again, "T" is the quilt or bag's thickness, in inches, covering the person. When we multiply this by 40, then subtract the result from 100, we arrive at the ETR, the quilt or bag's Effective Temperature Rating, in degrees Fahrenheit.

Let's say that on a summer journey taking us to the cool mountain heights, we are carrying a sleeping bag having 2 inches of insulation in the part that covers us. Plugging the 2 inches into the formula: 100 – (40 * 2") gives this bag an ETR of 20°F. In other words, when sleeping in this bag we can expect to remain comfortable down to 20°F.

The ETR is only a guideline, but a very useful one. It gives us an easy means of comparing commercial and home-made bags and quilts, independent of manufacturer's claims. And until an independent lab starts testing these items in some definitive and standard way, then I think the ETR can be applied universally.

Measuring thickness

Here is an easy and reasonably accurate way of measuring thickness of insulation: Lay the quilt or bag on a flat surface. If measuring a sleeping bag, unzip it, and open it so that it is not doubled— measure only the part that would cover you. Lay a yardstick gently on the quilt or bag. Stand a ruler on the quilt or bag, alongside the yardstick, and press it down onto the underlying flat surface. Read the thickness measurement on the ruler at the yardstick.

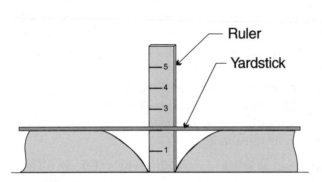

Beware of design oversights

I have heard certain manufacturers claiming that their products have higher effective ratings, based on certain unspecified properties. But I have yet to see any justifiable evidence supporting these claims. At the same time, we need to be aware of possible design oversights that can reduce a quilt or sleeping bag's ability to retain body heat, independent of its thickness and ETR.

Foremost among these is the use of an outer fabric having excessive air-permeability. As the warm air rises from our body during the night, it flows up through the quilt or bag covering us. If the materials are too breathable, then they allow that warm air to escape unimpeded.

On the other hand, if the quilt or bag's shell fabrics are completely impermeable, then this would be another design oversight. A certain amount of breathability is necessary in order to dissipate the accumulation of body moisture. But not so much breathability that it sets up an undesirable convection. The best compromise is an outer fabric that is only slightly breathable. This you can test by simply sucking air through it and feeling for its resistance.

In the same way that a chain is only as strong as its weakest link, a quilt or sleeping bag is only as warm as its thinnest part, and this leads us to another possible design oversight. If its thickness is two inches in one place but only one inch somewhere else, then the bag's temperature rating would be—not 20°F as in the forgoing example—but closer to 100 − (40 * 1") = 60°F. Beware of this type of design problem in commercial bags, and avoid it when making your own.

Wearing a hat at night

When sleeping in cold weather, the tendency is to hunker down into the quilt or bag, covering your head and face with it. This is rarely a good idea, because the moisture from your breath will condense into the quilt or bag, and reduce its warming ability while adding to its weight. Leaving the head exposed to the cold, ambient air is not a good idea either. This will degrade the warming ability of any sleeping system. The best idea is to wear a warm cap pulled down over the face. You can sew one of these in only a few minutes; see the Sewing chapter.

Wearing clothing while sleeping

Earlier I mentioned the tendency of some people to prefer more insulation than others. Partly the differences are physical. Their at-rest metabolisms drop lower than most, resulting in less heat production. But also they may be less tolerant, emotionally, of cooler, nighttime temperatures. Either way, they need more insulation in their sleeping gear. However, this does not necessarily mean they need thicker quilts or sleeping bags. In most cases they can easily make up the difference by wearing more clothing at night. Actually, this is a general rule applying to everyone. To increase the performance of your sleeping gear, wear more clothing.

The idea of wearing clothes at night is certainly nothing new. When Robert Peary and his small band of hardy adventurers trekked to the North Pole, they did not carry sleeping bags. There, in an environment far more demanding than what most of us will ever encounter, they slept in their clothing. They wore thick, fur parkas, and simply pulled their arms inside them at night to create ready-made sleeping bags.

In most cases our hiking clothing is not warm enough to sleep in by itself. But we certainly can wear our clothing at night to augment the quilt or bag's thermal insulation. This lessens its needed thickness, and is a very effective way of reducing packweight and bulk.

Certain manufacturers claim that a sleeping bag needs raw body heat in order to keep the occupant warm in very cold weather. That is, that the bag requires the heat generated by an unclothed, or nearly unclothed hiker to provide the best warmth. This is nonsense. By telling us that we need to sleep in the buff, they can sell us a heavier and therefore more expensive sleeping bag. An unnecessarily thick sleeping bag is more expensive, heavier to carry, and it robs valuable space in the backpack. In actual fact, the clothing we wear inside a sleeping bag, or under a quilt, does not diminish warmth, it adds to it.

To me it makes no sense to carry an excessively large, bulky and heavy bag throughout the day, and then to sleep alongside a pile of perfectly adequate, insulating clothing at night. In my quest for a lighter packweight, I have come to believe that the opposite approach makes far more sense: that is, to carry a thinner, lighter-weight quilt or bag, and to wear those clothes when the nights are chilly. This approach saves money, packweight and bulk, without compromising nighttime comfort in the least. And as a bonus, I find it quite pleasant to rise on the coldest of mornings already dressed in warm clothes.

If planning to wear your hiking clothing during the night, while sleeping, you will need to keep this clothing reasonably dry during the day. This means that you must be careful not to sweat soak it while hiking. To accomplish this, dress in layers and remove a layer or two whenever you start to sweat. The layering and dynamic-wearing approach (see Clothing chapter) will not eliminate sweating—a hard-working body naturally perspires, whatever the temperature—but it certainly will minimize sweating, while allowing the sweat to evaporate. Also as you hike in the cooler hours of late afternoon or evening, your perspiration will be much reduced, so that you are likely to arrive at camp in hiking clothing quite suitable for wearing at night.

Clean clothes are the most comfortable for both hiking and sleeping. They are not as warm when dirty because our body oils and accumulated "trail patina" reduce the fiber's loft while conducting away more heat. For this reason it is important to launder the clothing dundo-style (as described in the Hygiene chapter) every few days and more often in hot, muggy weather. Clean garments last longer, too.

What if your clothes are muddy and you would rather not soil the inside of the quilt or bag with them? In muddy hiking conditions I normally wear shell pants, while being careful not to wear too many underlayers that would lead to sweat soaking. If my shell pants are wet or muddy when I make camp, I hang them under the tarp and retire in the other garments. The shell pants will perform equally well the following day, wet or dry, clean or muddy. And because they are easily laundered and quick to dry, I do not leave them muddy for long.

In fact, the shell pants are so fast drying that unless the rain is continuous, the pants are usually dry once I reach camp. When dry they offer surprising additional warmth when worn at night, in the quilt or bag, because of the extra insulating air they entrap.

Those who wear socks inside their quilt or bag would do well to change into clean ones before retiring. You might think of wearing wet socks on cold nights in hopes of drying them, but in my experience this rarely works. What it does, instead, is chill the feet. Wet socks are better dried on a clothesline, or in dire conditions against one's stomach inside a shirt, after vigorously ringing them out, of course.

Regulating body heat

Should you decide to try wearing your hiking clothing inside your usual sleeping bag, you may soon find yourself overheating—your clothing adds to the bag's insulation, as we've seen. But rather than remove the clothing and crawl back into the bag, you might try this: unzip the bag and position it over the top of you like a quilt, as you lie directly on your foam pad. Then experiment with moving the bag laterally so that one edge is fractionally off your body. In this way you can very effectively regulate the temperature. The next step is to wear your hiking clothing beneath a thinner quilt.

Breathability in the quilt or bag

Waterproof-breathable and vapor-permeable fabrics have some very useful applications, but I feel that they actually reduce the performance of any sleeping system made of them. They restrict the transportation of water vapor exuded from our skin during the night. Not entirely, but enough to increase the accumulation of moisture in the insulation. This entrapment of moisture reduces the thermal value and it adds weight. And during the day, these materials greatly hamper one's air-drying efforts.

Around-the-world-walker Larry Amkraut had this to say about a waterproof-breathable sleeping bag: "I once had a [popular brand name of fabric] sleeping bag that cost $520.00 nicknamed Lazarus, because it came out of the stuff sack in a lump and I had to stretch it out lengthwise and width-wise and then fluff it up, bringing it back from the dead. Eventually I sent it home, in exchange for a different type."

The best plan is to place our protective, waterproof layer overhead, in the form of a tarp or tent. Between that and ourselves should be a flow of ventilating, moisture-purging air. Against our bodies we want only breathable materials, allowing the transportation of our body moisture into that air. Simply put, the tarp is our shelter, the quilt or bag is our insulation.

Vapor barrier liners

Sleeping bag liners made of waterproof, vapor barrier (VB) materials might seem compatible with minimum weight camping. After all, they prevent our body's insensible perspiration from reaching the sleeping bag's insulation and permeating it, and therefore they keep the insulation at its lightest and warmest. For use in polar regions, VB can be suitable, since the constant sub-freezing temperatures make air-drying impractical. But I am not an advocate of VB in temperate climes, even at altitudes where the nighttime temperatures fall below freezing. VB would actually increase our load, not because it is heavy, but because it prevents us from wearing our clothing at night. Any clothes we wear inside the VB liner will get soaked in perspiration, and when we step outside in them the next morning, they will turn positively frigid as the moisture in them begins to evaporate. This means we should not wear them inside a VB bag. And because of this, we lose the benefits of using the clothing to reduce the thickness of the bag's insulation. The VB would reduce the needed thickness of our quilt or sleeping bag, but not nearly as much as our clothing does.

Also, the human body was not designed to live in a plastic bag. Our skin needs to "breathe." Not only does it constantly exude moisture in the form of insensible perspiration, and sometimes in the form of sweat, but our skin also emits small amounts of gas such as carbon dioxide, as well as certain soluble and in-suspension by-products. This is why doctors sometimes call the skin our second liver, because it helps detoxify the body. Our clothing, sleeping system, and shelter must be able to pass these byproducts. When it comes to our health and comfort, breathability in our garments is very beneficial.

The stuff sack

To keep the sleeping bag or quilt dry while stowed inside the backpack, use a waterproof stuff sack. The waterproof stuff sacks of my design are less than one-third the weight and a fraction of the cost of the usual commercial varieties. I describe how to sew these in the Sewing chapter. You can make them any size, to hold clothing or whatever. After stuffing the items into them, squeeze out some of the air before twisting the top collar closed and folding it into the draw string casing.

For the quilt I prefer a stuff sack that is about 2 inches taller than the width of my backpack. After loading the heavier food items into the bottom of my pack, I load the quilt vertically, then turn it horizontally, side to side. This provides for a lightly compressed fit.

If you are not inclined to make or buy a waterproof stuff sack, you could use a non-waterproof one and simply line it with a plastic trash bag. Place the plastic bag inside the stuff sack, rather than outside, to protect the plastic from abrasion. This approach adds a bit of weight and fuss, but it works well.

Airing the quilt or bag

When stopping at day's end to make camp, make a habit of pitching your shelter soon thereafter, and spreading the quilt or sleeping bag open to the air. Not on the ground where it would absorb moisture, but atop the tarp or tent, weather permitting; or otherwise within it. This allows the insulation materials to "loft up." Shaking the quilt or bag to encourage the lofting process is unnecessary, and can stress the insulation and its attachments.

When removing a quilt or bag from its stuff sack, pull gently. Yanking is extremely hard on the synthetic fill, because it can pull the filaments from each other and from their stitching. For this reason, stuff sacks are best made of silicone-impregnated nylon, which is quite slippery and therefore offers less resistance to the item being withdrawn.

Colors

Technically, the quilt's upper surface should be light in color. This reduces the quilt's radiant heat loss. If the under surface is also light in color then it will reflect body heat back to the sleeping person a little better. But I make the under surface of my quilts dark in color for an even more important reason. When I stop hiking in mid-morning to air my gear, I air the quilt mainly dark-side up to speed the drying process. Also, when sleeping in the open in an area where I prefer not to be noticed, I sleep with the quilt dark-side up.

Umbrella

I first saw the idea of hiking with an umbrella in Peter Jenkins' book *The Walk West: A Walk Across America II* (Morrow: 1981). Peter and his wife had attached umbrellas to their pack frames as shade in the hot and arid Southwest. Jenny and I adopted the idea for our second PCT thru-hike, and found the umbrellas so functional for both sun and rain that we have carried them on all our treks since.

The umbrella is not the lightest way to go, especially because the hiker must also carry a rain jacket as a back-up, in case a storm brings lightning, or rain-laced winds of gale force. But it does allow a person to hike far more comfortably and efficiently in anything less, from drizzle to downpour to snowfall, and in intense sunshine. While protecting us from these elements the umbrella also provides superb ventilation. We need this ventilation when hiking with any degree of vigor—in any climate, hot or cold. It helps keep us comfortable and free of the sweat-soaked clothing syndrome. In my experience, the umbrella is well worth its weight.

Rainy-day comfort under the umbrella

Most of us know the pleasant feeling that comes with crawling into a shelter after a day of tramping in the rain. The umbrella offers much the same protection and comfort, without having to wait for day's end, or even having to stop. As you hike under the patter of raindrops, the umbrella keeps most of the wet off of you. And it covers the top portion of your backpack. When you need to stop and withdraw something from the pack, the umbrella held overhead shields the pack's contents. Have you ever seen hikers in rain jackets lounging around at rest stops—out in the open—during a heavy rain? It doesn't happen. But the umbrella makes those rest stops quite plausible, and therefore it makes the hiking itself far more appealing, since you need to rest every so often. If the rain is slanting with wind, look for a rest stop beneath a sheltering tree, and if you cannot sit on the downwind side of the tree, simply place your umbrella close in front of you to block the wind. So, too, on a rainy late afternoon you can sit cooking dinner, using the umbrella to shield both you and the stove.

When hiking in exceptionally rainy weather, at day's end you will still be wet, at least from the thighs down. The umbrella does not keep you perfectly dry all of the time, but most likely it will keep you free of the associated hassles of rainy weather. With it, you can walk along in comfort, free of the rain jacket's restraining hood, able to see ahead and all around, while still protected from the dollops.

While hiking beneath an umbrella, my preferred attire is the usual spandex shorts and short sleeve polyester shirt (described in the upcoming Clothing chapter). If the day is chilly, then I add the shell jacket and pants. These retain quite a lot of warmth, even when wet, and they breathe very nicely. Then if the day is chillier still, I wear insulating garments under the shells, and a warm hat when necessary.

Holding the umbrella overhead

The umbrella can be tiring to hold overhead for any length of time, which is why I do not hold it this way, except in very hot weather when I need the best possible ventilation. Most of the time I let the umbrella ride with the lower edge of its canopy resting on my backpack. In calm weather the "brolly" will stay there on its own. Even so, I hold on to the handle in case a gust of wind tries to send the umbrella flying. I learned the necessity of this after a few spirited chases. I usually hike with a thumb tucked under my pack strap anyway, so holding onto the umbrella's handle at the same time is no extra effort. And that way I can reach up with the other hand if I need to douse the brolly quickly.

In areas of dense vegetation, overhanging rocks or low tree limbs, it is a simple matter to draw the umbrella partially closed until the obstacle is astern.

The umbrella in wind

Point the umbrella into the wind to block both wind and rain. When hit by a gust, partially close the umbrella and aim it into the gust. This keeps the wind from getting under the umbrella and possibly damaging it. In brisk headwinds you can hold the umbrella in front of your face, and hike along while peering over the top. This arrangement provides full-torso protection, while allowing you to see where you are going.

Jenny using an umbrella on the PCT in 1994.

Jenny and I have carried umbrellas on four mega-hikes, as well as on the hundreds of training hikes preceding them. And we have carried them on a great many shorter hikes as well. Only once has one come apart, and that was during a storm experienced while hiking in the Three Sisters Wilderness in Oregon, near where we live. The incident actually turned out to be very instructive: I was using the same umbrella I had carried all summer on a thru-hike, so it was pretty well worn. My hiking partner that day was using a new umbrella, and, interestingly, his came apart also. These two umbrellas were made by the same company, and were the same size and model. And both, I soon learned, had the same structural defect: a weak wire securing the tines to the shaft.

The fact remains that any umbrella will blow apart in a vicious gust, structural defects or no. So in the event of more powerful winds, it's a good idea to stow the umbrella and don the waterproof-breathable rain jacket.

For sun protection

An umbrella will shield you from much of the sun's harmful ultraviolet radiation. It also blocks a great deal of the sun's heat. And it will block a great deal more heat if covered with a film of reflective mylar.

It took me a while to discover all this. While tramping through the

Mojave Desert regions of the PCT our first year, in 115-120° F tempera-tures, Jenny and I concluded that there must be a more tolerable way to deal with the extreme heat. At the time we were trying to adhere to the traditional methods of desert travel: rising at first light, hiking until the day grows intolerably hot, resting in the shade during the afternoon, then setting off again as the heat begins to subside. The strong sunshine is what made us uncomfortable, far more so than the high temperatures. In fact, life in the shade was almost pleasant. Unfortunately, mid-day shade in the desert seemed to be a figment of someone's imagination. When the sun was directly overhead, the shade beneath the scrawny desert flora was far too small to squeeze into. What we needed was portable shade.

On our second PCT hike we carried our own shade, in the form of umbrellas. These blocked the sun's ultraviolet radiation, allowing us to hike throughout the day, even in the hottest weather, as long as we carried and drank plenty of water. But the sun's heat still penetrated the umbrella's canopy, and this led me to the idea of covering them with reflective mylar.

The mylar covering

As mentioned in the Groundsheet section, the type of mylar most suitable for hiking applications is a thin plastic sheet with a reflective, silver-colored coating. This is sold in most sporting goods stores (usually 7 feet by 4½ feet) under such names as "Emergency Space Blanket." A piece of this fitted to an umbrella blocks nearly 100% of the sun's ultraviolet ra-diation and about 80% of its infrared heat. Jenny and I now use the mylar covering on our umbrellas whenever the sun beats down fiercely.

To fit a piece of mylar to your umbrella, lay the umbrella head down onto a sheet of mylar. Draw a line on the mylar around the umbrella, but about an inch away from it. Using scissors, cut along this line to create an octagonal piece of mylar about an inch larger than the umbrella all around. This piece will lie on top of your existing umbrella canopy, and the edges of the mylar will wrap around each umbrella tine tip. The tines are the metal rib-like pieces. Where the mylar wraps around a tine tip, secure it in place by wrapping it several times with a very small rubber band. The most suitable bands are about ¼" in diameter, of the type often available from your local dentist or orthodontist. But of course any small rubber bands will do. Between the tine tips, fold the mylar under the canopy and secure it to the canopy's underside with a few small pieces of duct tape.

With heavy use, the aluminized reflective coating will eventually scuff away, leaving the mylar ever more transparent. This reduces its reflectivity, and therefore its ability to block the sun's heat. Take care, then, to protect the mylar from abrasion. For best results, do not attach the mylar to the umbrella until you need it. Let's say, for example, that you are planning on a hike that will take you, in part, through a desert region. Normally you would carry the mylar neatly folded in a small plastic bag. Before putting it into that bag you would cut it to the appropriate size and include the rubber bands and a very small, flattened roll of tape. When you reach that desert section, you attach the mylar to the umbrella, and carry on. Then when you have crossed the stretch of desert and are back into the shaded forest, you would remove the mylar by unwrapping the rubber bands and carefully peeling away the tape.

When the umbrella is fitted with mylar, avoid shoving it down inside the pack, where the other gear inside the pack would chafe against it, and over time would rub off the reflective coating. Instead, strap it to the outside of your pack—head up, handle down. If using a pack of my design, the handle of the umbrella goes into the pack's side pocket, and the body of the umbrella fits behind the side strap.

The reflective coating on a piece of mylar should last for several weeks of continuous use. On longer journeys you might include a spare piece of pre-cut mylar, rubber bands and tape in a resupply box. For repairs of small rips or punctures, use a bit of duct tape.

Modifying a commercial umbrella

The type of umbrella I use has a 21-inch radius, and weighs 14½ ounces new. I select the type with the fewest complexities. The collapsible, or multi-folding type is not suitable because the extra joints mid-way along the tines are weak points. I then modify the umbrella extensively—taking its weight down to 9 ounces, and its length to 25 inches. I describe the modification process in the Sewing chapter.

Umbrella colors

Darker colors absorb more of the sun's thermal radiation. In the case of the umbrella, darker colors also re-radiate more of the sun's heat down to the hiker. Therefore, darker colors provide very little relief from the heat. In hot, sunny weather, lighter colors are much cooler. The ultimate umbrella color, in terms of its ability to reduce direct solar heating, is of course the reflective mylar covering.

In cool, rainy weather the umbrella's color is of little technical concern. In these situations, hikers might like subdued, earth tones, or they might prefer something more colorful and cheery to brighten an otherwise wet and cloudy day.

========

Rain or shine, with or without the mylar, the umbrella is an extremely functional piece of gear. I would not think of setting out on a hike without one.

Remaining Equipment

Stove

There is nothing quite like the cheery hum of a gasoline-type stove. At dawn it quickens the heart with prospects of the new day. And in the evenings it soothes the spirit with its promise of a hot drink and a well-deserved meal. The problem is, the cheery hum is more like an industrial roar. It drowns out the more interesting and enlivening sounds of nature all around. Like an auditory fence surrounding a person, it severs the connection with the wilds. So in this section on stoves we will look, also, at a few alternatives.

Cooking on an open fire

The flickering glow of a campfire has always attracted people in mystic, spiritual ways, and inspired them to contemplation. Strictly in terms of the wilderness connection, the open fire is also the best way to cook. But today's dwindling natural resources and increasing numbers of campers suggests we limit our campfire cooking to the cook-fire method, as described later, in the Campfire and Cook-fire chapter. Unlike the larger campfire that acts as an incinerator, the cook-fire has very little impact on the local supply of firewood, since it uses only pencil-size kindling. And because of the small size of its fuel, the cook-fire burns that fuel to powdery ash. This ash is easily buried a few inches below the surface. Properly cared for and eradicated, the cook-fire has very little impact on its surroundings. The cook-fire is my choice for cooking meals, where open fires are permitted.

The can stove

Where open fires are prohibited you might be able to use the type of stove that burns natural materials—twigs, bark, pine cones, etc. These stoves tend to be more permissible because they contain the flame in some type of metal enclosure. When in doubt, check with the local authorities. I refer to these stoves as "can stoves" because I have made a number of them from cans. If constructed properly they work surprisingly well, although not on par with the cook-fire or the gas stove.

To make one of these rustic stoves, remove the top of a large (46 fluid ounce) juice can, then cut a few sizeable air-intake holes in the can, along the bottom edge. These holes should extend about a third of the way around the can's circumference. The fresh air enters the can through these holes, is heated by the fire, then is expelled out the top of the can. Therefore, when using the stove, it helps to position the intake holes into the wind. If you make the holes too small they will plug with ashes, but you can clear them from the outside by poking a stick into the holes. The best way to cut the holes is with a sheet metal nibber, after drilling a starting hole, or punching it with a large nail. You can also use only the nail. Simply punch the outline with numerous holes until the tab breaks free. Use a block of wood under the metal to keep the can from collapsing. Whichever method you use, be careful not to cut your fingers on the sharp edges. In addition, cut a few holes along the top edge to act as pot supports. Without these, the pot smothers the flame.

Certain manufacturers are making much more complex can-type stoves with battery-powered fans. The fan supplies the burning materials with plenty of oxygen, so the flame is spectacular. I have experimented with these stoves, but much prefer the simple can type, mainly because it does not need a battery, and because it is lighter.

If you are using a can-stove or its battery-operated counterpart, you will need twigs and other natural materials to fuel it. These you can collect along the way, prior to cook time. If the woods are wet, then you will need to carry, well ahead of time, at least enough kindling to get the stove going. Once going, it will dry what kindling you add that is moist, as long as you add it slowly. As with preparing to build any fire, search for dry twigs at the base of trees and beneath overhanging rocks and logs. On a very wet day you can also carve slivers from the inside of larger dead branches, where the wood will be dry in any kind of weather. Before packing up, make sure to extinguish the last of the embers.

Alcohol stove

Alcohol is made from hydrocarbons, (usually plant cellulose) as opposed to petrochemicals. Thus, stoves that burn alcohol are more akin to stoves that burn wood. Although their heat output is somewhat lower, these stoves burn quietly. They also tend to be fairly simple in construction, and relatively light in weight. The Mini-Trangia alcohol stove, for example, weighs 3.1 ounces, including its burner cap but not including its pot support and wind screen, both of which can be improvised of lighter materials. A number of web sites and magazine articles describe ways of making even lighter alcohol stoves from various types of cans, and pot supports from bent coat hangers and so forth. I have made a few of these, and find they work fairly well. But they do need to be stowed inside a sealed can when not in use, to contain the fumes. The Mini-Trangia comes with its own fume-containing burner cap, with a very effective sealing gasket.

These alcohol stoves burn denatured ethyl alcohol, which is rarely available at the trailside stores. But it is almost universally available at hardware stores. In a pinch these stoves will also burn the drugstore variety ethyl and isopropyl alcohols, but with more soot and less heat, due mainly to the additives and the higher water content.

For those planning long distance treks involving resupply packages, the question arises as to whether or not you can legally ship alcohol stove fuel with the supplies. The answer seems to depend on who you talk to. What I learned is that ethyl and isopropyl alcohol are not legal to ship by air, but are ok to ship by ground, with the following stipulations: maximum amount of fuel per parcel—1 quart, if in metal container, or 1 pint if in a plastic container. Also, the sender must note on the outside of the parcel the type of fuel contained, how much, and in what type of container.

Butane-Propane stoves

Butane and propane are flammable gaseous hydrocarbons, with small differences in their molecular constituents. Specifically, butane is C_4H_{10} and propane is C_3H_8. Propane puts out more heat for its weight, and it pressurizes better at low temperatures. But it is more dangerous in small containers, which is why most backpacking stoves, lanterns and lighters use butane, or at least a mixture comprising mainly butane.

Camping stoves that operate on canisters of compressed butane or propane are legal in most wilderness areas, and they have certain advantages in terms of convenience. They burn more quietly than the gasoline-type stoves. They are easier to ignite; and once lit, their valves regulate the flame better. They burn essentially soot-free, and properly cared for they rarely clog. The cartridges are not legal to ship by air, and they are rarely available in the trailside stores.

Still, we cannot escape the fact that the empty cartridges are an ecological disaster, considering the huge quantities of them going into the landfills. Some types are recyclable, which is nice in theory but rarely practiced.

Kerosene

Kerosene (known as paraffin in England and Europe) has the reputation of producing soot, and stoves that burn it are known for consuming both time and patience. I have not noticed kerosene for sale in many trailside towns.

Gasoline, white gas and Coleman™ fuel

The longer the outing, the more one must consider fuel availability when choosing a stove. This is one of the many reasons I prefer the cook-fire over any kind of stove. And although the can-stove is no panacea, it, too, offers the option of gathering natural fuel along the way. Even so, most hikers prefer the greater utility of stoves that burn petroleum-based fuels. And in many ways these preferences are justified, the industrial roar notwithstanding.

But what about the ethics of burning stove fuels in the wilderness? Doesn't this deplete the earth's fossil fuels and add to air pollution? In an absolute sense, yes. But consider the mind-boggling quantities of liquid hydrocarbons burned by cars, trucks and jetliners every day. Even compared to the gas you burn in your car en route to the wilderness—usually without thinking about the environmental consequences—the small amount you burn in your stove is insignificant.

There are very few differences between gasoline, white gas, Coleman fuel, MSR fuel, Blazo, Naptha, and the likes. White gas is a liquid hydrocarbon mixture, blended from petroleum. Gasoline is white gas with over 200 additives to help improve automobile performance. Unleaded gasoline is gasoline without the addition of lead, to help ease emission toxicity. Coleman and the other cooking fuels are little more than white gas with coloring dyes added.

The stove's jet is the tiny hole that sprays the fuel vapor, under pressure, into the open combustion chamber. The size of the jet (hole) is mainly what determines the type of fuel (kerosene, white gas, or unleaded gasoline) the stove will burn most efficiently. The two most common petro fuels used by hikers are the white gas types and unleaded gasoline. The white gas types are widely available near popular camping areas, and of course unleaded gasoline is available at virtually any gas station. Either type of stove will burn the other type of fuel, but not as well, meaning that its jet will require more frequent cleaning. When burning unleaded gasoline in a stove designed to burn white gas, try placing a small piece of aluminum foil over the air intake, closing off about 25% of its area. This reduces the air-gas mixture ratio. More on cleaning the jet to follow.

A common error is to overestimate one's fuel needs, and carry too much. In most cases an 11 ounce fuel bottle is sufficient for one or two hikers.

Distance hiker Jason Ontjes reminds us that "despite claims to the contrary, fuel bottles do leak." He wisely suggests wrapping the fuel bottle in a plastic bag and carrying it below the food. My own style of backpack has an external mesh pocket meant for the fuel bottle, where any leakage can evaporate. If your pack does not have such a pocket you can easily sew one onto it. See the Sewing chapter. And be sure to depressurize your fuel bottle after each use, to minimize leakage.

Most stove comparisons give the weights of the stoves, but this is only a part of the picture. When debating the pros and cons of various types, keep in mind the weights and bulk of the fuel and fuel bottle, windscreen, primer and cleaning kit.

Jet cleaning

The impurities of combustion are well known for clogging a stove's jet and weakening its flame. Some stoves come with a "shaker jet," which is a weighted cleaning needle fitted loosely inside the jet's lower passage. Supposedly, all one has to do is invert the stove and shake it, thus running the needle in and out of the jet, thereby cleaning it. Actually, this idea is not new. Decades ago, many of the white-gas stoves had internal cleaning needles controlled by the regulating valve itself. All you had to do was turn the flow to maximum, and this shoved the cleaning needle out through the jet. It worked perfectly, and in ten years of cooking on such a stove I never had to disassemble it for cleaning its jet or anything else. My experiences with the shaker jet stoves have not been as trouble free.

The job of cleaning a jet manually is an inglorious one, but I can at least offer a suggestion that will help ensure the job is done correctly. I arrived at this after many hours of fiddling with gas stoves in the Arctic. It has to do with a small piece of fine steel wool.

Regardless of whether your white gas or unleaded gasoline stove has a shaker jet or not, carry a jet-cleaning kit. This kit should contain a jet removal wrench, as supplied with the stove, and a jet-cleaning needle, which typically does not come with the stove but is usually available at backpacking shops. These jet needles are far thinner than any sewing needle or pin. Brett Tucker says that he uses a piece of high E guitar string (.009 gauge unwound steel). I also recommend the jet cleaning kit include that small piece of steel wool.

Start by unscrewing the stove's jet with the wrench. Tear off a pinch of steel wool and twist it to a size that you can just force into the back cavity of the jet nipple. Use this to scour out the cavity. Tear off another small pinch and repeat the scouring until the steel wool comes out clean, and the inside of the jet is shiny. Then comes the important part. With the steel wool inserted loosely into the cavity, prod the other side of the jet with the cleaning needle. This forces the jet's debris into the steel wool. Without the steel wool, the needle would poke the debris into the cavity and leave it there. Then the next time you use the stove, the debris would re-clog the jet.

The cleaning needle is delicate and must be protected. The best way I have found is to duct-tape a portion of it (not the part that goes into the jet) to something flat and hard, such as the side of a small plastic bottle in your first aid kit, or whatever you happen to have. Along with the jet-cleaning needle you could also tape down your sewing needle.

Prohibited baggage

If traveling by air to your intended trail, be aware that camp stoves, fuel bottles and fuel are not permitted in either checked baggage or carry-on bags. Sometimes—but not always—you can bring with you a partially disassembled and air-dried stove, and possibly an empty and air-dried fuel bottle with its lid removed. If in doubt, call your airline representative. However, you should still plan to buy your fuel at your destination. You may also have to buy your stove and bottle there, or your could mail them, using UPS Ground or Parcel Post, (checking with your UPS or postal authorities) to a destination near your trailhead where you would then pick them up.

The dangers of carbon monoxide

Cooking inside a tent may be convenient in foul weather, but it is decidedly unsafe. The stove could explode, and while such incidents are uncommon, they are not unheard of. The stove could ignite a too-close article of clothing, the sleeping bag, or the tent itself. One careless swing of the elbow could knock the stove over, spilling scalding liquid, soaking everything, and melting a hole in the tent's floor and groundsheet.

Another very real danger is that of the stove filling the tent with deadly carbon monoxide. As the hot gases of combustion rise to the ceiling, they accumulate—despite an open doorway and the ground-level ventilation around the fly's perimeter. These gases are odorless, and what makes the poisoning so dangerous is that it produces no appreciable symptoms. One minute all is apparently well, and the next minute the person is sprawled on the floor, unconscious—never to recover unless someone drags him or her outside to fresh air. In his book *Arctic Manual* (Macmillan: 1944), Vilhjalmur Stefansson wrote, "If you watch carefully, a feeling as of pressure on the temples can be detected for some little while, perhaps only a few moments, before you keel over."

Stoveless hiking

Jenny and I have experimented extensively with non-cook foods. And we have hiked for weeks without a stove, eating pre-cooked and dehydrated foods. So it can be done, but we have never found it satisfying. Nor have we found it particularly energizing. In our minds, the energy and vitality provided by freshly cooked meals is well worth the trouble.

Two reasons for not cooking come to mind. One would be the danger of attracting grizzly bears, such as in Glacier and Yellowstone National Parks. This is a valid reason. The other is the reluctance to carry a stove and its fuel due to its weight and bulk, to say nothing of the difficulties of obtaining more fuel along the way. In such a case the cook-fire might be a suitable alternative, depending on local conditions and regulations. Read more about the cook-fire in the Campfire and Cook-fire chapter.

Cookpot

Traditionally, backpacking cookware was made of steel. Then aluminum became common, then stainless steel, and now we have titanium. Cookpots made of titanium are more expensive than their aluminum and stainless steel counterparts, but they are lighter than stainless steel, and stronger (although a little heavier) than aluminum.

I have used aluminum pots for many years, but after researching the matter I now suspect that aluminum in contact with food and water may pose certain health risks. Some cookpots come with plastic, non-stick coatings. These coatings facilitate cleaning, and they prevent the food and water from contacting the aluminum. Yet I wonder whether even these coatings are safe. I have seen reports that indicate that most types of plastic are themselves health hazards, when used with food and water. However I am not quite ready to start carrying glass water bottles.

Some types of cookwear come with the company's name and logo printed on the lids. One way to remove these is to dab on some paint remover, followed by a light brushing with fine-grit sandpaper. And while you are at it, you might use a coarser grit sandpaper to roughen the bottom of the pot so that it will not slip so easily when perched atop the stove. Most everything here is based on experience, and the sandpaper treatment is no exception. The first evening of a long sea-kayaking trip, Jenny and I watched our brand new cookpot slide off the stove and send our meal crashing into the sand. I roughened the bottom of the pot with a rock, and we cooked a second dinner.

A pot with a 1½ quart capacity is usually adequate for one person cooking solo. Two people cooking together could share a 2 quart pot. In either case the cookpot should have a lid of some sort, as this will help keep the contents clean during the cooking process, while retaining much of the heat. If your pot comes with a lid, you could use that; or to save a bit of weight you could use a sheet of aluminum foil instead.

A handle extending from the side of the pot is a convenience, but unless it folds flush against the sides it creates unnecessary bulk and difficulties when stowing the pot inside the backpack. The separate handle, the type that clamps onto the side of the pot, is a good idea in concept, but it is another item to carry and to keep track of, and possibly to lose. If you use one of these, make sure that it is in serviceable condition. You would not want it to slip off a heavy pot of boiling water.

I prefer a simple wire bail. This supports the pot from above, and when not needed it swings down out of the way. If your cookpot does not have a bail you can easily drill a pair of holes in the pot, one on each side near the top, and run a wire through them. For specifics see the Campfire and Cook-fire chapter.

If you use a cook-fire, or a stove that burns natural materials, then the outside of your pot will blacken with soot. This is actually beneficial because a blackened pot transfers heat to its contents better. To prevent the pot, in turn, from blackening the contents of your pack, stow it in its own stowbag. If you use a gas stove and want to reduce its fuel consumption without adding another gadget to your inventory, simply blacken your cookpot. Suspend it over a wood fire for a few minutes, and let it blacken with carbon.

Cup, bowl and spoon

To reduce packweight, bulk, and the inglorious task of post-meal cleanup, carry only the bare minimum of cookware.

A small, plastic bowl can be eaten from during the meal, and afterwards it can serve as a drinking cup. And if that bowl has a tight-fitting lid, then you can shake and mix drinks in it, carry cooked food in it stowed inside your backpack, and fill it with prepared food from home or a trailside store or restaurant. During our first three thru-hikes Jenny and I used three-cup capacity, cylindrical-shaped lidded bowls made by Rubbermaid.™ On the AT we improvised, using small cottage cheese or deli tubs, or at times the bottom section cut from a soda bottle. Continuing with the weight saving measures, on our fifth journey we dispensed with bowls and cups altogether, eating our hot meals directly from the cookpot, and drinking the infrequent hot beverage from the pot as well.

On all our journeys we carry one plastic spoon each. Our preference is the tablespoon size made of polycarbonate, and sold under the brand name Permaware.™ See the Hygiene chapter for ways of sterilizing your utensils.

Water bottles

Having tried all sorts of commercial water bottles, I much prefer ordinary soda bottles. These are designed to contain liquids in the most efficient manner, being strong, lightweight—and inexpensive. Some types have fairly wide openings, up to 1½", and these are a bonus. The narrow-mouthed soda bottles also serve well, as long as they come with screw-on caps. After discarding the sugar-chemical slurry, strip away the label and you have a very serviceable water container. If the bottle does become damaged you can usually repair it with duct tape, and then you could plan to buy a new soda bottle at the next outpost along your way. Most importantly, by changing bottles every few weeks you avoid the accumulation of mold.

Water bottles, bags and bladders are well known for cultivating stubborn splotches of fungi known as "water mold." This mold can impart an unpleasant, musty taste to the water.

The type of water bags worn against the hiker's back tend to accelerate the formation of water mold, since the heat of the body warms the water and encourages microbial growth. And while these "hydration systems" may be convenient for someone humping a load so massive that they cannot stop and drink from their bottles often, these "wearable" bottles are largely superfluous to someone with a smaller, lightweight pack that is easily handled.

At any rate, the foul taste of the water mold can be difficult to remove from any type of container. One way to remove the mold is to fill the container half full of treated water, and add a scoop of clean, dry sand. Take care, of course, to keep the sand off of the threads, because it can score the seal. After screwing the lid back on, shake the container vigorously to abrade away the mold. Dump out the mixture, then rinse the bottle and lid with more treated water. Use a small, sharp twig to clean the threads inside the lid.

I typically carry a single, quart size soda bottle on the trail. And when traversing long, dry stretches I also carry a 2½ gallon water bag.

Knife

Everyone has their preference as to what type of knife they like to carry while hiking. I have seen everything from magnum-sized hunting knives with 8-inch blades, to the "everything-but-the-kitchen-sink" type Swiss Army knives. However, I think that in most cases a small folding knife with a single blade serves just as well.

My preferred knife is the diminutive Victorinox Classic. With its 1¼" folding blade I open food packages, sever cord, slice vegetables, carve into wet branches while making dry tinder, and cut packaging tape to length. The scissors I use to cut adhesive tape and 2nd Skin, to cut fingernails and toenails, and to trim hangnails. With the knife's file I round my trimmed nails. And I use the tweezers to remove any splinters or ticks. All this utility costs me a mere 0.8 ounces.

Such a small but useful knife is easily lost among the leaves and pine needles at camp. To make it more conspicuous, both on the ground and while contained within the ditty bag, I affix a short length of bright orange parachute cord.

Any kind of blade can dull with use, especially when cutting cardboard. If you are planning a long distance hike, one that will require resupply boxes, you will probably find yourself sitting outside various post offices cutting cardboard boxes down to size for sending things home or ahead. Cardboard is very abrasive, and for this job you could use a small, disposable-blade utility knife. Rather than carry this with you, you could place it in your drift box (see the Resupply chapter).

The Tub

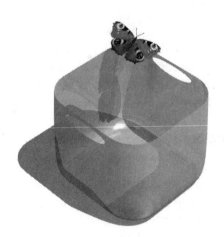

The tub is a versatile addition for the hiker out for more than a few days. Jenny made the one we used on our first two thru-hikes. She simply cut the top off a 2½ gallon collapsible water jug (Reliance™). We found all manner of uses for this tub, including collecting wa-

ter, carrying water to camp and storing it there, settling sediment, containing water for filtering, pouring water into the Hiker's Friend water filter bag (see the Sewing chapter), laundering clothes, and pouring water onto ourselves when bathing. At 2.8 ounces the tub is reasonably light-weight, and because it folds nearly flat it occupies little space in the back-pack.

In our quest to shed packweight we have since realized that the cookpot works nearly as well for many of those jobs.

Wristwatch

The hiker's wristwatch, if he or she chooses to carry one, should be small and lightweight. It should be waterproof to at least six feet so that one does not have to be careful not to get it wet. The watch should also have an alarm and a night light. And it should show the date and the day of the week, since on the longer trips you can easily lose track of them. In most cases the day of the week is not important, except when you are heading for a resupply station. Post offices normally close on weekends, and in some small towns nearly everything shuts down. Knowing the day of the week will help you plan to arrive at your resupply towns on weekdays.

Stopwatch

During your training forays you can use the stopwatch feature of your watch to time the duration of your outings. This data you can enter into your training log. Also during the training hikes (not on the actual jour-ney) you could use the watch's countdown timer at the rest stops. Set at ten minutes, it would remind you to be moving along. This is a good way to condition yourself against the tendency to linger at those rest stops.

Dead reckoning

One of the more important uses of the wristwatch is for dead reckoning. This term comes to us from those who sailed the square-rigged sailing vessels, and the method was, and still is, an important component in any navigational plan. It works on the idea that speed multiplied by duration equals the distance traveled. For example, if we hike at 3 mph for 2 hours, then we know we have covered 6 miles. I try to look at my watch at each known point, such as a signed trail junction, a high pass, a lake, or a road crossing. If later I become confused as to my whereabouts on the map, I look at my watch again and "DR" my distance hiked from the last known waypoint. On moderately graded trails I find that an assumed hiking speed of 2¾ mph in my calculations yields the most accurate results. Of course, on steeply graded trails this figure will be much reduced.

Wristwatch holder

I like to rise at the first hint of dawn, and while on journey I use an alarm to wake me at that time. If I wear the watch on my wrist during the night, the chances are good that I will not hear the alarm. So each evening when retiring I remove the wristwatch and place it near my head. In the days when I used tents, I sewed a hook-and-loop tab to the tent wall, onto which I hung the watch. Or, as described earlier, one could sew such a loop to the underside of a tarp, and waterproof the seams on the outside with sealing compound, which is what I have done on my current tarp.

The watch band

Particularly on longer hikes in warm climates, the wrist can swell considerably during the day's walking. The watch band will have to be long enough to accommodate that. The difference in the size of my wrist, from when I rise in the mornings at home, to when I retire at night during a thru-hike, is four holes on the watch band.

A plastic watch band can restrict ventilation and irritate the wrist. You can replace the standard band with one perforated in holes, or you can punch the holes yourself, using an ordinary paper punch. Or you could replace the plastic band with one made of a breathable, quick-drying webbing.

Compass

I prefer a basic, uncomplicated compass with only the features I need. These are: a rotating housing, and a minimal-friction bearing.

If you do not know whether your existing compass has a quality bearing, here is a simple test. Lay the compass on a table. After the needle has settled, rotate the compass base with imperceptible slowness. Note the angle at which the bearing releases and allows the needle to swing back to magnetic north. Repeat the test in the other direction. If the discrepancy is more than one or two degrees in each direction, the bearing is not a low friction type. The Silva 7NL, (also known as Type 1-2-3) weighs 0.7 ounce including its lanyard, and is my long-time favorite.

Those proficient at taking field bearings by hand can achieve an accuracy of $\pm 1^{1}/_{2}°$. Those who are not might prefer a type of compass having a sighting mirror. Sloppy navigation can cause unnecessary confusion, which could lead to a perilous situation. But it depends on the trail.

On the CDT I used my compass so often that I frequently carried it in my shirt pocket. On the PCT I used the compass only rarely, but a few times it saved the day. On the AT I did not carry a compass.

Some types of compasses feature built-in adjustments for the local magnetic declination. This feature is of little benefit to the person who cannot remember whether the adjustment is supposed to be set to the left or right. The problem is that most hikers are never quite sure whether to add or subtract the declination. My mnemonics might be of assistance.

- Along the PCT and CDT, the compass needle points a little east of true north, as though honoring the AT.

- Along the AT the needle points a little west of true north, as though honoring the others.

Depending on whether you are hiking in the east or west, you will therefore know whether the needle points left or right of true north. If you are hiking in the Midwest you could examine a map showing magnetic lines of flux, and locate the line of zero declination relative to your own location.

Now that you know which way the needle points, you need to know whether to add or subtract the declination:

Field-to-Map—Add.

F—M—A

First Man Adam.

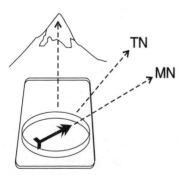

The compass needle points to magnetic north

When taking a bearing to a distant mountain, then setting the compass down onto a map, you are going from field to map. Field to Map, Add. F-M-A (First Man Adam). You *add* the declination before setting the compass onto the map.

When reading a bearing on the map, then raising the compass and pointing it in the direction you want to go, you are going from map to field. You are reversing the procedure, and therefore you would subtract the declination.

This method is for use in the western states, but it works also in the eastern states by adding the negative declination. For example, along the Appalachian Trail in Maine the declination is about 20 degrees west of true north, or minus 20. So you would add the minus 20 to the field bearing before plotting it on the map.

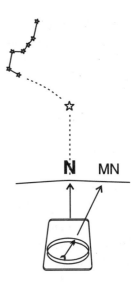

Most maps give the local magnetic declination of the area they depict. You can measure declination directly by taking a bearing to the north star (Polaris).

Innate sense of direction?

Years ago, a climbing partner and I were descending one of Colorado's 14,000-foot mountains, when a cloud moved in and reduced visibility to a scant hundred feet. Coming to a drop-off, we rigged a rappel sling and used our rope to rappel down. Continuing for another three hours, we eventually came to something that stunned us momentarily senseless. Our rappel sling! There was nothing for us to do but use it a second time. In another hour the sky cleared and eventually we found our way down to camp. Somehow we must have walked all the way around the mountain, but this was incomprehensible since we felt that we were descending in a diagonal fashion the whole way. I mention this experience to suggest how easily one can stray off track.

Aside from simple disorientation, experiments have shown that a blindfolded person trying to walk level ground from point A to point B will wander far off track, while believing that he or she is traveling in a straight line. The tendency to deviate is caused mainly by a difference in leg strength, left and right. I have witnessed the same effect (with the differences corresponding to different arm strengths) when paddling with a group of sea-kayakers, crossing a large bay. Some will veer far to the left, and some to the right. And after regrouping at the distant headland, everyone claims to have been the only one paddling in a straight line. In fact, I have seen people veer so far away that they nearly disappeared from sight.

The standard reasoning as to why we cannot detect the deviation is that we are not blessed with an innate sense of direction. Or are we? We know that birds and many types of animals can sense which direction is which. Apparently they have some kind of a gland in the beak or head that contains magnetic iron, and this acts like a compass. Scientists say that humans have the same type of gland. Obviously modern mankind has lost touch with this little device, but many of the more primitive, earth-connected peoples apparently used it very effectively. It might be possible for modern-day people to get back in touch with this long-lost skill. One way to practice is to hike along a trail, or cross-country, and try to remain aware of your direction of travel. Check your external compass every so often and see how well your internal compass is doing.

Of course, if the day is clear or only partly cloudy, then you can simply remain aware of the sun's position. You do not have to actually look at the sun to do this. Instead, watch the direction of the shadows as the day waxes and wanes.

Flashlight

Despite my interest in packweight reduction and my quest for connection in the natural world, I find a small flashlight very useful on extended hiking journeys. Not because I cannot see my surroundings without one—in all but the thickest forests I usually can, using only the subdued light of the stars. But because a flashlight allows me to night-hike at my daytime pace. In rattlesnake country, it also helps me avoid unfavorable encounters. When searching out a good campsite, the flashlight illuminates any poison ivy or oak. And after settling into camp, I like to spend usually half an hour writing by flashlight in my journal.

The best way to use a flashlight at night is to hold it as close to the ground as you can comfortably reach. Doing so produces the best shadows and therefore the best definition. Holding it at eye level washes out most detail. This is why everything looks so flat in a cave when using a headlamp.

When your flashlight begins to fade, you can extend its life by using it only intermittently. Switch it on, then switch it right back off. This will give you a quick glimpse of the way ahead, enough for you to "memorize" the scene. Then when you have hiked to the end of your memory, repeat the switching on-off process. You can use a disposable butane lighter in the same way, even one that has run out of fuel. Simply flick the Bic and memorize the terrain ahead in the flash. I once found my way out of a mile-long cave this way, when my lamp ran out of carbide.

For the brightest and lightest-weight flashlight, choose one with a krypton or halogen bulb powered by one AA or AAA battery. In my experience the krypton bulb is good for about 5 alkaline battery changes; fewer if using lithium batteries. Keep a spare bulb inside the flashlight, and familiarize yourself with the bulb changing procedure ahead of time, when you can see what you are doing.

At the time of this writing, AA lithium batteries cost two or three times as much as alkaline ones. They last about three times longer, and they far less. One should never dispose of batteries in the wilds, they are harmful to the environment and should be recycled. If you cannot find AA lithium flashlight batteries locally, try phoning the company "1-800-Batteries" at 1-800-228-8374. As of this writing I know of no source of lithium AAA batteries.

Brightness aside, by far the most efficient flashlights are those incorporating the high-intensity LED bulbs, again powered by lithium batteries. The C. Crane Company (1-800-522-8863) says that their "LWL" lasts 50 hours at full brightness on one AA-size lithium battery. This flashlight is 3½ inches in length, completely waterproof, and from the factory weighs 1 ounce minus the battery. I grind the excess plastic away, reducing its weight to 0.85 ounce. I also wrap the clear plastic head (not the lens face) with a layer of duct tape to reduce lateral glare.

The Photon Micro-Light® II weighs a mere quarter of an ounce, and comes in a variety of light-colors. The two-battery models are brighter, and said to last 7 hours between battery changes. The one-battery models are less bright but longer lasting. The green will shine supposedly for 7 days, and works great for nighttime journal writing. I have night-hiked with all currently available colors; red is my personal favorite because it doesn't hamper peripheral vision. These units are not waterproof, and must be cared for accordingly. Purchase them at http://www.photonlight.com.

When not on journey I rarely carry a flashlight. Unless in known rattlesnake country, I much prefer to hike at night by ambient light alone. A flashlight blinds one to the surroundings, with the exception of the red Photon Micro-Light. Hiking at night without a flashlight necessitates a slower pace, but allows for a deeper wilderness connection. The eyes will adapt to the ambient light, and rather than rely almost entirely on eyesight, you can shift into a more whole-body awareness. Using this method, you can find your way even in complete darkness. Just make sure to lift your feet a bit higher than normal, to avoid any roots and rocks.

Journal

When you journey into the backcountry your senses will expand, and you will start to notice more detail. You will make observations, perhaps learn lessons, philosophize, and possibly find some answers. Being in the wilderness also lends itself well to contemplation, and this is why I find that keeping a trail journal is extremely worthwhile. Recording those bits of wisdom, the observations, and the many interesting details of your hike may not seem important beforehand, or even at the moment, especially when you are tired. But months and years later you will probably enjoy reminiscing, and reliving your experiences through your trail journals. In your trail journal you can write whatever you like. You can keep only the most basic log, noting where you camped and how many miles you hiked. Or you can record some of the details of what you saw, who you met, and how you were feeling. Journal writing has no limits.

As long-distance hiker Mike Anderson points out: "The more you put into your journal, the more you will get out of it." And as Oscar Wilde quipped: "I never travel without my diary. One should always have something sensational to read on the train."

Each evening Jenny and I write an average of three pages, on both sides. As a weight savings measure we make our own writing pads ahead of time, containing only as many pages as we will need, since an excess of paper can be surprisingly heavy. Figuring the number of days hiking between any given pair of resupply points, and multiplying this number by the three pages per day, I know how many pages we will need on that stretch of trail. I remove that many pages from a narrow-ruled pad that measures 6" by 9", and either staple them together along their top edge, or tack them together with a couple of stitches, using a hand awl.

I carry our trail journal in a resealable plastic bag, along with maps and any other paperwork, which again I try to keep to a minimum. And I make an effort to send each section of journal home from the resupply stations.

Ditty bag

The ditty bag is small, and usually made of lightweight nylon fabric. It holds the hiker's assorted knick-knacks. For details on size and construction, see the Sewing chapter.

As anyone who has done much camping can attest, to leave small items lying about camp is to possibly lose them. After using an item, make it a practice to return it into its bag. Also, if the smaller items are brightly colored, then you will locate them easier in the ditty bag, and you will be less prone to leaving one behind at a rest stop or a camp. Also at camp, if you keep all your belongings centrally located, you will be far less prone to losing something. Those socks hanging to dry in that tree— over there. They are much more likely to be left behind. Also, when setting off from camp, or from a rest stop, walk a few paces then turn around and inspect the area for anything you might have forgotten.

Zippers

To extend the life of a zipper, and to make it slide easier, rub some wax on the teeth. Any kind of wax will do: beeswax, paraffin, even an old candle. You can buy spray lubricants for zippers, but these are anything but beneficial to the ecology, and wax works just as well.

The sawing action of the zipper teeth—even nylon coil or plastic molded teeth—will eventually wear out the slider. A worn slider will slide, but it will not zip the two halves together. To improvise a temporary repair, reduce the size of the slider's aft end by crimping it slightly. In lieu of pliers, try using one small rock as an anvil, and another as a hammer.

Fire starter kit

The fire starter kit is one of those items best kept tucked away in one's pack for the proverbial rainy day. It is not for igniting the stove or cookfire on a daily basis; for that you should keep a separate container of matches or a small butane lighter, preferably along with the stove or cookpot where it will be handy. The fire starter kit is strictly for emergencies. Whether the journey is 5 miles or 2,000, adverse weather always has the potential to thrust a person into hypothermia, regardless of the time of year. It is always a good idea to carry a fire starting kit. Keep it small and lightweight, and keep it absolutely dry. The kit should contain:

- Kitchen "strike-anywhere" stick matches in a plastic bottle. The bottle should have a screw-on lid with a serviceable gasket, for example a vitamin or spice bottle.

- A few birthday candles, in the same bottle.

- A small handful of dry tinder in a waterproof plastic bag.

The kitchen "strike-anywhere" stick match burns hotter and longer than a cardboard book-match, and the stick of the match adds more to the kindling. It is also more wind-resistant, much more so than the common butane lighter. While packing for the trip, strike one match to make sure that your supply is dry and functional. Also, check the gasket of the bottle's lid for leakage. To do this, empty the bottle, screw on the lid, submerge it in water, and squeeze. Any bubbles indicate a defective seal.

An excellent alternative to matches is the zirconium rod. When scraped with a piece of steel, for example a knife blade, the rod emits an abundance of extremely hot sparks, capable of igniting all but the most reluctant tinder. These rods are commonly termed "flint strikers," but this is a misnomer since they are not made of flint. Zirconium is a lustrous gray, metallic element resembling titanium. Unlike matches, the rod is not put out of action by water, but it will deteriorate in time if left soaking wet. The lightest and smallest "flint" striker I know of is sold by the C. Crane Company, mentioned earlier. It goes by the name of the "W.S.I. Hot Spark Key Chain." By removing the key ring you have a tiny fire starter that weighs .39 of an ounce.

If you have tried starting a campfire when the woods are drenched, then you understand the importance of carrying dry tinder. For best results, collect the tinder when the woods are dry, and keep it that way inside your pack. The possibilities for tinder include dry grasses, seed heads, pine needles, and inner bark from downed trees. A small resealable bag of tinder weighs only a fraction of an ounce, but it can make a ton of difference when needed.

Pepper spray

Jenny and I have always carried a large pepper spray canister in the Arctic, as protection from grizzly and polar bears. One day here in our community I decided to try the spray on a particular dog fond of disrupting our daily walks. I sprayed the aggressive creature in the face, at a distance of about eight feet. The dog's only reaction was a small sneeze. This prompted me to look for a different type of canister for the Arctic, one with better range.

A small canister of pepper spray or mace can be clipped to the hiker's clothing or backpack strap, or placed less obtrusively in a pocket. At night it should be kept within easy reach. The risk of attack by an aggressive bear, dog, or person is quite remote, but that does not mean that the hiker has to remain defenseless. I know two people who are alive today, thanks to one small canister of mace.

Pepper spray contains oleoresin capsicum, a natural derivative of hot peppers. Some states restrict its purchase. Canadian law forbids it altogether, meaning that PCT, CDT, and other crossing-the-border hikers cannot carry it into that country.

Trekking poles

Many hikers feel that trekking poles or hiking sticks help them across uneven terrain. That is perfectly fine, as long as they are not influenced by advertisements attempting to impart magic-like qualities to trekking poles, inferring that the poles almost spring the hiker along. One ad reads, "Designed to take the stress out of walking." What stress? That of carrying too heavy a load, perhaps.

How much stress do trekking poles relieve? One advertiser claims that their poles can eliminate an average of six tons of stress per mile on a hiker's legs, feet and back. Let's look at how this might work. Dividing 5,280 feet (one mile) by the length of an average stride—roughly 2-2/3 feet—we get 2,000 steps per mile. The advertiser's six tons (at 2000 pounds per short ton) divided by the 2,000 steps = 6 pounds per step. In other words, what they are saying is that you push down on each of the two poles with an average of three pounds of force, with every step. We could compare the whole scenario to walking on crutches. When you push down on them you relieve your legs and feet of that much weight. The advertiser wants you to believe that by pressing down on the poles with six pounds of force (three pounds per pole) this reduced stress accumulates in some magical way throughout the course of a mile of hiking.

When we compare that six pounds to the weight of the hiker's body, clothing, footwear, and backpack, we realize that the poles are not saving much. Especially because the trekking poles lend assistance only when pressed down on, usually for only a part of each step. But while the trekking poles are "relieving six tons of stress" from your lower extremities, they are adding it back to your upper extremities. That six pounds of force has to go somewhere; it travels through the hands, wrists, arms, elbows, shoulders and torso.

In actual fact the poles add to the *total* stress, because of their weight. Let's say that each pole weighs 16 ounces. Two pounds lifted from the ground between each of 2,000 steps equals two tons of unfavorable stress that the poles add—per mile—to your entire body. So all in fun, let's turn the advertiser's claims around: Getting rid of the trekking poles can eliminate an average of two tons of stress per mile on your arms, legs, feet and back.

Poles or sticks can serve as third and fourth legs, helping the adventurous arthropod maintain balance on rocky terrain. This extra balance is necessitated mainly by a heavy, cumbersome pack. Those who carry reasonably lightweight packs would rarely need the extra balance, particularly if they have practiced my balance-enhancing exercise, detailed in the Physical Conditioning chapter. While negotiating blocky terrain, climbing or descending sometimes hand and foot, you must stow the poles, or toss them ahead of you. And of course on steep snow with an ice axe in your hands, you certainly cannot use the poles.

On level ground, trekking poles and walking sticks interfere with the natural swing and gait of the arms, making the walking less efficient. They prevent you from carrying an umbrella, one of the most useful items of rain protection imaginable. The clackety-clack can be wearisome to the ears, and the scrapes and scars on the rocks left by carbide-tipped trekking poles are particularly unsightly. Many of our popular hiking trails now bear these scars. The poles might seem to make good brush pokers while checking for rattlesnakes, but they are not nearly long enough for that. And they would seem to provide an extra set of legs for fording creeks, but they are not reliably strong enough for any substantial depth and swiftness of current. For river crossings, your best option is to find a very stout stick lying around.

Swashbuckling up the trail with a trekking pole in each hand is supposed to give "a total body workout." No doubt we hikers could use a little more exercise of the upper body. But in terms of maximizing distance covered and minimizing the total load, trekking poles are superfluous. By far the best way to reduce stress is to reduce the packweight.

Ski poles

Ski poles are sometimes used while hiking, like trekking poles. But they must never be used as a substitute for the ice axe on a steep snow slope.

Should the hiker fall and accelerate wildly down a steep slope, the attempted self-arrest could snap a pair of ski poles like matchsticks.

Ice axe

For your own safety, carry an ice axe wherever you might encounter steep slopes with snow covering the trail. You can expect to find such conditions just about anywhere in the high country, from October through June. This means that even the casual day hiker visiting these regions during any season except mid-to-late summer may require an ice axe.

The AT thru-hiker can generally get by without an ice axe. But along the PCT and CDT, an ice axe, and self-arrest skills, are essential to safety. For instructions on the use of the axe, see the Snow chapter.

My ice axe measures 20 inches along the shaft, and 9 inches along the head. I normally stow it outside my pack, in such a way that it will not snag overhead branches, and so that it will not cause injury in the event of an accidental slip—for example while rock-hopping across a creek. My pack features a pair of loops that hold the axe in such a way that I can remove the axe without first having to stop and remove the pack.

The ice axe should be fitted with a lanyard (a loop of nylon cord or thin webbing) about three feet in length. One end is tied to the head of the axe, the other is secured to the hiker's wrist during use. The lanyard prevents the loss of the axe in the event of an unexpected slip, when one's reflexes could fling the axe into space.

Snowshoes

Snowshoes can be quite useful when negotiating soft and moderately sloped snow. But while most trails seem gently graded, they are often cut across steep slopes. When these slopes are covered in snow, the "trail" becomes steeply sloped in the lateral direction. In such conditions snowshoes are decidedly unsafe, since they cannot be edged into the slope like skis, for security. They tend to slide off the trail sideways.

Most hikers who have carried snowshoes have not found them sufficiently useful to justify their weight and bulk. Proper timing can eliminate their need altogether. Snow that is soft enough to require the use of snowshoes has not yet consolidated. This condition indicates merely that the hiker is there too early in the spring season—or far too late after summer has passed into autumn.

In early season you may find yourself slogging in mush, or postholing. This is especially true in the late afternoons when the sun has been softening the crud all day. At night, if the sky is clear (allowing radiant cooling) the surface will probably re-freeze. In the very early mornings, then, this frozen crust will probably support your weight, and this is the best time to make tracks—miles of barely indented ones.

Skis

Skiing across the alpine heights in early season requires a very high level of proficiency. This is especially true in light of the consequences of a skiing-related injury in the remote backcountry. If a person is sufficiently skilled, and if the snowpack is deep and pervasive, then skis might be well worth considering. However, in late spring when the snow has coalesced, one can walk on the snow's surface most of the time. So in terms of making miles, I think waiting and walking is easier and more expedient.

Gaiters

Gaiters are a type of ankle covering, designed to keep the snow from entering the boot tops. Many hikers use knee-high gaiters while ambling along a bare trail. The intent is to keep the gravel and dirt out of the shoes, and to protect the legs from poison ivy and oak, and insects such as blackflies, ticks and chiggers.

I find gaiters necessary only on endless miles of snow tromping. On snow-free terrain, anything covering the clothing and footwear restricts ventilation and causes overheating and sweating. Rather than try to keep the dirt and gravel out of my shoes, I tie the laces loosely so that I can stop when necessary and remove and empty the shoes without having to untie and re-tie the laces. But in a long day of hiking I usually stop to do this only once or twice. At each rest stop I remove the shoes and bang the small amount of dirt and grit from them. Back in the days when Jenny wore lighter fabric boots, she improvised a pair of gaiters by cutting the toes off a pair of old socks. These she slipped over her lower calves before putting on the boots, then she pulled the bottom part of the makeshift gaiters down over the top of the boots. These kept the grit out of her boots. The shell pants (Clothing chapter) worn in conjunction with the usual lightweight nylon socks will protect the legs from poison plants and biting insects. If the blackflies are particularly bothersome, you could apply repellent to your calves just under the pant legs, or you could simply tuck the pant legs into your socks.

Crampons

Strapping on a pair of crampons and venturing across a steep and frozen snow slope might seem like a safe way to go, but without the skill to use these implements they can be very dangerous. First, they allow a person to more easily climb out into a very exposed position, and second, they can then fail that person. They can do this in a number of ways, mostly through mistake or misuse. In order for crampons to function properly, obviously the person wearing them must remain upright. But while negotiating a steep slope, one could easily lose balance and fall. Among the possible scenarios, the person could catch a crampon prong on the other crampon, on its strap, or on a pant leg or gaiter. A crampon strap could work loose, or a tooth or other metal component of the crampons could fracture. The person could stumble on an unseen dip or rise. Or he or she could experience a moment of vertigo, due to an unfamiliarity with the exposure, and lose balance. Moreover, if the snow is wet it can stick to the bottom of the crampons and accumulate with every step until the hiker is walking not on perforating spikes, but on slippery snowballs.

As discussed in the Snow chapter, the proper stopping technique for someone sliding down a slope requires a three-point contact with the snow. The three points are the pick of the ice axe, and the toe of each boot. But the person wearing crampons cannot so much as touch the crampons to the snow's surface. Otherwise they will grab the snow and possibly cartwheel the person wildly out of control.

If you need crampons to climb a frozen slope, then in most cases you are there too early in the day. The morning's warmth will probably soften that snow within a few hours, and allow you to kick perfectly adequate steps.

Climbing rope

First and foremost, a rope must never be used to assist a river crossing. For a discussion of the dangers, see the Creek Fording chapter. In skilled hands, a rope can sometimes increase the safety on a snow slope. If one person slips, the other can stop that person from sliding off the mountain by holding the rope in a special way known as belaying. As with any piece of equipment, this requires know-how.

One person hiking solo would have no use for a rope when negotiating a steep snowfield, or for any other aspect of a hiking journey. Two people hiking together, both of them well experienced at snow travel, would not need a rope, either. They would both be adept at the ice-axe self-arrest, and at judging and avoiding the dangers of a snow slope to begin with. Where the rope can be handy is when one person is experienced and the other is not. The experienced person can use the rope to safeguard the inexperienced partner. With two inexperienced people the rope can be doubly dangerous, for if one person slips, the rope could wrench the other off balance too. So if you are thinking of carrying a rope for snow safety, be sure that at least one person in your party has plenty of experience with its use.

For the weight-conscious, a 20 foot length of 7-millimeter Spectra rope might be best. Spectra is very strong and lightweight, but it is also slippery and does not hold some of the more basic knots very well.

Early one morning Jenny and I climbed up to snowbound Glenn Pass, in the Sierra. The ascent went well, but as we began heading down the other side we found the snow frozen hard. Stomp as we did, our boots barely indented the surface. This was not a problem for me because I was accustomed to edging aggressively with my boots. I was also used to the exposure of the mountainside dropping away far below. But not so, Jenny. She slipped and quickly self-arrested, but not before her weight came partially to bear on our safety rope. We were using a 20 foot length of polypropylene, which I learned that day is so slippery that it does not hold a bowline knot very well. In an instant my knot untied itself from around my waist, and I found myself hanging onto the rope with my hands. This meant that I could not drop down into a self-arrest—I would need both hands on my axe for that. Fortunately, this was not an immediate concern because I was quite secure on my feet. Jenny was in no danger either, she was pinning herself securely to the slope with her ice axe. But the slope was frozen so hard that she could not kick footholds, and that meant that she had no way of standing back up. And because I no longer trusted the knots in the rope around her waist, I could not use the rope to assist her to her feet, lest it suddenly come lose and throw her off balance. So I stomped my way down and moved into position beneath her, and used my axe to quickly chop her a set of footholds. With these she easily stood up. I tied a figure eight knot around her, secured with a couple of half-hitches—leaving plenty of free end. I did the same with my end of the rope around me, and together we proceeded down the slope without further incident.

Re-Centering

Choosing all the right gear can be a challenge in itself, but regardless of the length and nature of your outings, if you compile your gear carefully, taking only what is necessary, and leaving behind the superfluous, then you are likely to travel more easily, and with your mind focused more on your natural surroundings. Also, the more time you spend in the wilds, gaining experience and developing skills, the less you may be attracted to gear that is heavy-duty and overly complex, which tends to isolate and alienate its user from the wilderness environment.

So as you peruse the many tempting racks of clothing and display cases, stop occasionally and re-center yourself. Think about how that gear is affecting you emotionally. Judge whether or not it will lead you to a more meaningful outing, with a better understanding of the natural world and a closer connection to it. And do not let any of that gear become your main focus. Otherwise, the chances are that the real beauties of the hike—the priceless gifts of nature—will be lost.

I like to think that life is more than money and merchandise. So I try to encourage the making of one's own outdoor clothing and gear. And no doubt a person could strike a compromise and do a little home sewing and a little shopping, and come out very well. But the experience is more important than the gear. If an item of equipment helps you achieve a closer connection with the natural world, then that equipment is worthwhile. If it fails to serve this purpose, then maybe you could modify it, or discard it and try something else. But the important thing is simply to go, and to enjoy your outings for all they are worth, which will surely be a great deal.

Clothing

I have yet to see any problem, however complicated,
which, when you looked at it in the right way,
did not become still more complicated.

— *Poul Anderson*

Sometimes we are not quite sure which is the greater obstacle: the elements, or the heavy-duty clothing designed to protect us from them.

Hot weather, cold weather, intense sunshine, snow, insects, humidity, wind, rain and brush. Welcome to life on the trail. These are some of the livelier conditions you may find yourself hiking in, and that can test your clothing. And naturally, you want your hikes to be enjoyable. But if, for instance, you are cold and miserable due to a lack of warm clothing, the fun will quickly disappear. At the same time, a heavy load of inappropriate clothing can make your outings just as unpleasant. So in this chapter we learn how to put together an efficient clothing system, one that will serve you well in your journeys.

Whether our chosen trails are long or short, the conditions we encounter along them will determine our needed range of clothing. Basically the conditions depend on such factors as the time of year, the elevations, and weather. The elements could be harsh and quite variable, or they could be fairly benign. Either way, we benefit by equipping ourselves with an efficient system of clothing.

The reason we would strive for efficiency in our clothing, and think of it as a system, is that we must carry it all. And by now, the advantages of a lighter weight pack should be evident.

But to achieve a lighter load, must we go so meagerly equipped that we sacrifice comfort and possibly even our safety?

Actually, going into the high country with a minimalist attitude, with the idea that we do not need sufficient clothing to handle cold weather, can be very risky. When we venture into the wilds, we must protect ourselves against a loss of vital body heat. This applies to every one of us, from the least experienced to the most. And because of our differences in hiking style, mental attitude and body metabolism, each of us will need to experiment, to determine what clothing works best for us, individually.

So our goal is not to dispense with warm clothing in an effort to minimize packweight. Rather, it is to put together an efficient and lightweight system of garments that work together synergistically, in the widest possible range of conditions. Think functionalism, not minimalism.

The search for what works best

In my pursuit of the most functional wilderness wardrobe, I have headed into the wilds with what seems like every imaginable type of outdoor wear. With these garments I have gone day hiking, overnight tripping, weeks-long wandering, and full-summer thru-hiking and its preliminary months of conditioning forays. And in the process I have put this clothing to the test in climates ranging from the freezing Arctic and Arctic-like alpine regions, to the moisture-sapping desert heat of the southwest and the sweltering kind of muggy heat often typical of the eastern states.

For quite a few years I relied on commercially manufactured outdoor clothing. Very little of it worked well for me. I often had the feeling that the designers were more intent on creating outdoor fashion statements. And while I appreciated appearances, experience had taught me that a garment's performance was more important.

So I began making my own outdoor clothing. Free of commercial restraint, I spent many years creating, testing and returning to the proverbial drawing board for further refinement. Eventually I evolved a system of garments that proved to be the most serviceable.

At first glance these garments might seem overly simplistic. Yet they are the lightest in weight and the least in bulk. They are warm on cold days and cool on hot ones. They are breathable in order to minimize sweating, and easily laundered by hand and fast to dry. They are comfortable, durable, highly versatile, and very packable. And taken as a whole, their efficiency is unmatched.

Garment descriptions

What follows is a list of these garments comprising my clothing system. This list reflects my own personal inventory. In the Sewing Your Own Gear chapter I describe how you can make most of these items for yourself. Or you can buy many of them from GoLite.

Jenny and I have found these articles eminently suitable during normal hiking season. Depending on your hiking style, you may wish to experiment with these or other options. My intent here is simply to offer the benefit of our experience and to serve as a catalyst in your own thinking.

• **Shell jacket and pants**: Designed to protect the skin from thick brush, to block the wind, and to rebuff ticks, which seem to find these garments too slippery to cling to. Also designed to thwart mosquitoes, blackflies and other biting and crawling insects. The shells also provide a moderate amount of chilly weather comfort, especially when worn over the other garments.

I call them "shells" because I often wear them as a protective outer layer over one or several inner layers. But in warmer weather I might wear them alone, for example on a hot day as protection from bugs or brush. These garments are so versatile that I carry them on all my trips, regardless of whether I am day hiking or thru-hiking. I often sleep in my shells when out in the wilds. And I even wear them in the Arctic while distance-canoeing and sea kayaking, and when relaxing around the tundra camps.

My shell jacket and pants are performance oriented, no-frills items. Made of nylon or polyester, they are single-layer, lightweight and loose fitting. I use uncoated fabrics for optimum breathability, allowing sufficient ventilation for the hard working body, even in warm weather. Yet the shell garments still block the wind very nicely. And the fabrics are woven with sufficient tightness to block stings and bites from mosquitoes and blackflies. Unlike mosquito netting, the shell jacket and pants can lie directly against the skin, for example at the shoulders and elbows, and the bugs cannot penetrate the fabric. As mentioned, these garments are ideal wherever the trail is overgrown in brush. And throughout the journeys they are easily washed by hand and quick to dry.

I have added no extraneous zippers, flaps or designer features, since these only add weight and bulk. The jacket has a full-length, front-opening zipper for greatest ventilation when needed. It has zippered cargo pockets for stowing mittens and so forth. And it has a small breast pocket with a zipper for keeping small items handy, such as compass or keys. The sleeve cuffs and waist band are elasticized and fit snugly to block mosquitoes.

The pants have an elasticized waist band and leg cuffs, and a small chafe patch inside each ankle where the shoes may brush against the pant legs.

• **Polyester shirt**: My hiking shirt is short sleeve, loose fitting, and made of lightweight polyester. In the right weave this fabric is highly breathable, amazingly fast drying and therefore easily laundered. Other 100% synthetic fabrics such as nylon (Supplex® and taffeta) would work reasonably well. As with all my recommended garments, the shirt is very simple. It opens fully in the front for ventilation, and it closes with buttons. It features a standup collar to help shade the back of the neck. In other words, it looks like a casual dress shirt, except that it has no cotton in it. It can be worn alone in warm weather or as an inner layer in cold weather. It is also my garment of choice when hiking in very hot temperatures where going shirtless would be socially inappropriate. And when freshly laundered, dundo style (see Hygiene chapter), it is very suitable for wearing in the trail towns.

• **Hiking shorts**: These are less restrictive than long pants and of course cooler. This is important on warm days since the muscles of the legs will work more efficiently if kept cool.

One option is loose fitting shorts made of nylon taffeta or Supplex®. These are breathable and quick-drying. Side pockets add utility but reduce breathability and ease of drying.

Leg chafe can be a serious problem with many hikers, and ordinary loose fitting shorts will rarely prevent this. Leg chafe results when the moist skin of the upper thighs rubs together while walking. The resulting irritation may prompt the hiker to apply a lubricating ointment, but this only clogs the pores and collects dirt. Or the person might stuff a bandana between the legs; this can help in an emergency but only marginally.

My solution is to wear shorts made of spandex, like bicycle shorts but without the padding. Spandex is a nylon-blend stretch knit commonly known under the Lycra® trade name. Spandex shorts fit somewhat snugly around the upper legs, especially on the inside of the thighs where we may need the chafe protection. Because they are sheer, and since they stay put, the material can rub against itself all day long with no discomfort to us. I like them snug enough to prevent chafing, yet loose enough for long term comfort.

I have hiked over 15,000 miles in spandex shorts, and find that one pair will easily last me an entire summer. I choose black because this color is by far the least revealing; still, I avoid wearing them in the trail towns, although most townspeople are becoming more accustomed to seeing bicyclists and joggers wearing them.

Spandex shorts could serve as underwear. But underwear, as we normally think of it, is just another complication. In warm weather, the extra layer promotes and retains more sweat. Some hikers prefer to wear the spandex underneath to eliminate chafe, and a pair of looser fitting shorts over them for appearances.

Another option to shorts is the skirt. Jenny has hiked many thousands of miles in skirts. Made of polyester, they are comfortable, she says, and fast drying. I have heard of guys hiking in "kilts," but have not tried such an arrangement myself.

• **Thermal shirt**: This is a long sleeve, pullover shirt made of a thermal (wicking) fabric such as polypropylene or Thermax. It can be worn alone, in combination with the short sleeve polyester shirt, or as "long underwear" beneath other layers, such as the shell jacket. This shirt is reasonably fast-drying, yet because the fabric is thicker than the ultralight polyester shirt, it is more insulating. Worn for its added warmth, for example on cold days while hiking, at rest stops, around camp, and while sleeping during extra-chilly nights. In unseasonably cold weather one could wear two or more of these shirts in combination (same with the pants, below).

• **Thermal pants**: Made of the same material as the thermal shirt, these pants keep the legs warm while hiking or resting in chilly to moderately cold conditions. They are rather loose fitting for ease of knee articulation, and can be worn alone or under the shell pants when the cold is accompanied by wind, and of course at night.

• **Insulated jacket**: The typical fleece jacket may be comfortable to wear around camp, but it tends to be fairly heavy for its rather limited warmth.

With this in mind I designed an ultralight insulated jacket for GoLite. This jacket is lighter than most fleece jackets, even with its insulated hood attached, yet it is much warmer. The jacket features a full-length, front-opening zipper for utmost ventilation when needed, and a pair of zippered hand-warming pockets. Wear it while resting alongside the trail, and while lounging around camp. Normally one would not hike in it, as this would cause overheating in all but the coldest climes. One can also sleep in this jacket, or use it as a pillow or as a cushion under the legs for added ground insulation.

• **Umbrella:** This is my primary protection from rain, used instead of the rain jacket in all but the most blustery weather. The umbrella provides superior ventilation as it shields us from the rain. In so doing it can make the difference between a soggy, dreary day on the trail, and a pleasant one.

The umbrella also offers welcome relief from intense sunshine, such as in open, treeless regions. In extreme heat and sun, I cover my umbrella with solar-reflective mylar. While not essential, this affords even greater protection from the sun's intense heat and ultraviolet radiation. See the Umbrella chapter for more details.

• **Rain Jacket:** Used in rain accompanied by wind too strong for the umbrella. Like my other garments, the rain jacket is a no-frills item. Made of a two-layer waterproof-breathable fabric, it is light in weight, loose fitting, breathable and packable. It features a hood and a full-length, front-opening zipper for improved ventilation when needed. In fact, my rain jacket is virtually identical in design to my shell jacket; the only differences are that the rain jacket is made from waterproof-breathable material, it lacks the pockets (to save weight), and it is fractionally larger. When fully unzipped it can be worn backwards, the advantages of which I describe in the Cold chapter. For more information on the rain jacket's features, uses and limitations, see the Rain chapter.

• **Rain Pants:** While hiking in the rain I do not normally wear rain pants since they tend to restrict the needed ventilation. The problem is one of condensation inside the rain jacket and pants, and I describe this fully in the Rain chapter.

To me, the rain pants are a complement to the rain jacket, but mainly they are an emergency item kept in the pack for an unexpected rain or snow storm. Rain pants can also be useful while ambling in rain and wet brush at a leisurely pace, and while sitting around camp on a drizzly afternoon.

The rain pants are made of the same material as the rain jacket and are very basic in design. They have an elastic waist with a drawcord, and leg cuffs that are left open (no elastic) for better ventilation.

• **Socks, thin nylon**: For hiking in warmer weather I prefer thin nylon socks, sold inexpensively in clothing and department stores. These socks are highly breathable, meaning that they contribute only marginally to foot sweating. They are easily washed by hand and quick to dry. In fact, I sometimes rinse them in cold water, dundo style, wring them out, and put them right back on! In my opinion the thin nylon socks perform better than expensive sports socks, and in cool to moderately cold weather I wear two or three pair for added warmth. The right kind of thin nylon socks are extremely durable, typically lasting me thousands of trail miles. The wrong kind, namely the ultra-thin varieties, can wear out in a single day. I test my newly purchased socks for durability during my training hikes.

• **Socks, medium weight, wool-synthetic-blend**: For cold weather hiking I sometimes wear medium weight (thickness), wool-blend socks. I say "sometimes" because where possible I much prefer wearing multiple layers of thin nylon socks, even in very chilly weather—and especially in wet weather. Why? Because the thin nylon socks dry a lot faster, meaning that in intermittently wet weather my feet do not stay wet. That said, medium weight wool-blend socks are faster drying than heavy weight wool-blend socks, so in very cold conditions you might keep in mind the layering principle, and double or triple up on the medium weight socks.

For snow travel in lightweight, breathable boots, I suggest taking along a few pair of medium weight wool-blend socks. But consider giving the layered thin nylon socks a try also, to determine whether their warmth and quick-drying properties work well for you.

Wool provides reasonable warmth when wet, but wool by itself is poorly resistant to abrasion. So select socks that have a blend of synthetics, preferably with more wool than synthetic – for example 70 percent wool and 30 percent nylon.

Even with the synthetic blend, these socks are not long lasting. Three hundred miles is about my limit with wool-blend socks, which on a longer hike is around ten to fourteen days. Even with everyday washing the wool-blends slowly glaze and lose loft. And once softness is lost, the socks begin "fossilizing" into what feels to the feet more like sandpaper. If you anticipate long periods of cold and wet conditions that would call for wool-blend socks, consider carrying a few extra pair or place extras in your resupply parcels.

• **Mittens, fleece**: These are nice to have, even in only moderately cold weather. As the hands swing to and fro in the normal course of walking, circulation is impaired. So once the hands become chilled, they tend to stay that way. Mittens prevent the hands from chilling in the first place. I prefer fleece mittens because they are lightweight, warm and reasonably fast drying. Mittens made of wool are, here again, heavier, bulkier and much slower drying. But caught short, you could improvise with spare socks.

My hands tend to sweat in thick mittens, particularly while hiking, so I often carry a second pair made of a thinner, thermal material.

Mittens are much warmer than gloves. Gloves have more surface area and most of this lies between the fingers where it robs them of heat. In mittens, the fingers share their heat.

• **Bomber hat**: Made of fleece or other synthetic fabric, and preferably covered with a waterproof-breathable shell. Wear the bomber hat during cold days along the trail, at rest stops and at night while sleeping. Wear it also in wind too strong for the umbrella. In cold, wet and blustery conditions, the bomber hat with its waterproof shell protects the head and neck without restricting one's field of vision like the hood of a parka does.

• **Skullcap**: In addition to the bomber hat, I usually carry a simple "skull-cap" made of a lightweight thermal fabric for use when the bomber hat would be too warm. I make the skullcap long enough to pull down over my face at night while sleeping. The material is easy to breathe through, yet it keeps the face nicely warm. On very cold nights, one can wear the bomber hat over the skullcap, and on extremely cold nights the detachable hood of the insulated jacket. These hats enable you to keep your head out of the quilt or sleeping bag, preventing your breath from soaking the bag's insulation and reducing its warmth while adding to its weight.

The bomber hat and skullcap are essential components of my cold weather clothing system. This is because one's head tends to radiate away a comparatively large amount of body heat. I often use one of these hats as my primary means of regulating body temperature while hiking. Which hat depends on the temperature. The minute I begin to overheat, I remove the hat. Should I later begin to chill, I put the hat back on – before putting on more clothing because often the hat alone provides the needed warmth.

• **Wide-brimmed sun hat**: Used in moderately sunny conditions, when the mylar-covered umbrella is not needed. Used also **in** strong sunshine when the wind is too gusty for the umbrella. My sun hat is made of nylon taffeta and has an encircling brim. The brim is stabilized by an internal wire running around its perimeter, keeping the brim from flopping down in front of my face in gusts of wind. I have not come across a wide-brimmed hat with the wire stiffener already in it, so I install my own. When the hat is not needed I stow it inside my pack carefully to prevent bending the wire, or I tie the hat to the outside of the pack. The hat also has a chin strap made of thin cord, for use in strong wind.

• **Head-net**: Made of no-see-um netting, for use when the mosquitoes are swarming. Used on the trail, at the rest and meal stops, and at camp. In swarms of bugs the head-net can be worn under the hood of the shell jacket, reducing the sometimes irritating hum and whine. Otherwise the head-net can be worn over the wide-brimmed hat, which keeps the netting away from the face and off the top of the head.

• **Shell mitts and booties**: Made of shell jacket material (breathable nylon) and worn in buggy conditions, along with the shell jacket and pants and head-net. The shell mitts protect the hands by virtue of the fact that insects cannot penetrate them, even where these mitts contact the skin. In this regard, mitts and booties constructed of no-see-um netting are wholly inadequate. The shell mitts and booties spare you from the effects of chemical repellants. The shell mitts can be worn anytime; while the booties are very useful at buggy trail stops where you may want to remove your shoes and moist socks in order to relax in comfort. Both the shell mitts and the booties are suitable for use on bug-ridden nights when you are sleeping beneath an open tarp or under the stars.

• **Shower booties**: Made of coated nylon, these protect the bare feet from athlete's foot fungus and other parasites usually endemic to the floors of public shower stalls and on motel room floors, showers and bathtubs. The booties have elastic around the tops, much like a pair of upside-down shower caps.

The layering approach

When the temperature drops, hikers may tend to overprotect themselves by wearing clothing that is too thick and heavy. This can cause overheating and sweating, even while hiking in the coldest of temperatures. And when the garments become sweat-soaked, they are far less serviceable.

Enter the layering approach to keeping warm (and cool). Here, we select garments that are thin and lightweight, and in harsher weather we wear these garments one on top of another.

As an example, say we start out on a beautiful, sunny morning, hiking in a lightweight polyester shirt and a pair of shorts. A frontal system moves into the area and the shirt and shorts are suitable for a while, but we begin to feel the temperature dropping as the morning progresses. So over the shirt and shorts we don the shell jacket and pants, and for the next few hours this becomes the most comfortable arrangement. Any more clothing would make us sweat. But as the ambient temperature continues its decline, soon we need a bit more warmth. So we remove the shell jacket, don a thermal shirt over the polyester one, and put the shell jacket back on. Now wearing three layers on the torso we continue ahead, once again in comfort. Then in a few hours, as the temperature drops further, we remove the shell pants, put on the thermal pants over the shorts, and put the shell pants back on. And we pull on our warm hat and mittens.

This layering approach is important in several ways. It affords a greater comfort range by enabling small adjustments, as we don and doff relatively thin layers. It keeps us comfortably warm without sweat-soaking everything. And it makes for faster drying of all our garments, since each is less thick than the heavy-duty types. The faster our clothes can dry, the less the storms will affect us.

The key here is comfort. Never should we allow ourselves to become chilled (or overheated). If we feel the need for more layers, we put them on. And don't forget about the insulated jacket, and the quilt, which at the rest stops and evening camps can serve as a wonderfully warming robe.

Cotton and hypothermia

The ubiquitous cotton T-shirt. Comfortable when clean, rather less so when dirty, and very slow to dry even in warm weather. In fact, the cotton T-shirt is so slow to dry that the hiker usually does not bother washing it. And with the passing of days and weeks, as the shirt grows ever more soiled and odiferous, it begins acting as a people repellant and a bear attractant.

On a cold day, when cotton becomes wet—from sweat for example—it can sap vital body heat. Cotton fibers are hydrophilic, meaning that they absorb moisture. This is why the hiker who wears cotton, and who sweat-soaks those garments in cold weather, will be socializing with hypothermia at every rest stop. Even as little as one percent cotton in a garment is unfavorable.

Certain synthetics (like polyester and polypropylene) are hydrophobic, meaning that the individual fibers do not absorb moisture appreciably. (Nylon is fractionally absorptive, making it somewhat slower drying than the true hydrophobics. This is why my hiking shirts are polyester and polypropylene or Thermax, rather than nylon.) Any synthetic garment is as cold as a cotton one when wet. However, the synthetics are faster drying; so in essence they are much more forgiving, which helps explain their popularity in today's outdoor apparel.

Wool is an exception; it can preserve at least a measure of warmth when wet. However, because of its weight and bulk, most hikers find it of limited use. The only wool applicable to lightweight hiking, in my opinion, is the wool-blend socks.

People sometimes experience reactions to synthetic fabrics. Generally, the fibers themselves are inert, but some of the chemicals added to them can cause sensitivities. Which is not to infer that cotton garments are chemical-free either, by any means. But for most people, synthetic hiking garments offer the best performance, comfort and safety.

Clothing for hot weather

The hotter the day, the more ventilation our skin needs. And even thin clothing restricts ventilation, especially when sweat dampened. Meaning that the less clothing we wear in hot weather the better—not just for comfort but for our well being. In very hot weather I prefer spandex shorts, thin nylon socks and running shoes. When I need to wear a shirt, as social conditions necessitate, I wear the polyester one. In warm to hot weather Jenny normally wears nylon shorts or a polyester skirt, and a polyester shirt or perhaps a Supplex® tank top. If hiking in forest shade, additional protection from the sun is rarely necessary. But out in the open where the sun beats down with fiery intensity, the umbrella (especially one covered with mylar) proves its worth.

Optimum color

Often the tendency is to choose the color of our garments based on personal preference. But when we are hiking in various weather conditions, color plays a significant role in a garment's performance.

Light colored clothing blocks solar radiation better, meaning that it absorbs less heat. This is extremely important when hiking under a hot sun, especially during the height of summer. Light colors also radiate less heat away, helping us stay warmer on cold, cloudy days and at night. And light colored clothing is less attractive to flying and biting insects. Ticks, which are generally brown, are more conspicuous on lighter colored clothing.

Dark colored clothing absorbs more solar heat, and this works against us on a hot, sunny day. On a cold, sunny day, the dark color may generate needed warmth, but only for the parts of our body facing the sun. That same dark clothing will radiate valuable body heat on the shaded side of us. However, because dark clothing is again a good radiator of heat, we can use it in hot, shaded regions, at least when we need to cover ourselves fully because of mosquitoes or biting flies.

If I had to choose only one color, it would be a light one, since most of the hiking I do is in sunshine. Even in the Appalachian Trail's "green tunnel" a lighter color will not attract as many flying insects and will make the presence of any ticks more obvious.

Laundering

Washing clothes by hand is rarely convenient. But clean clothes are far more comfortable to wear and they are warmer and longer lasting than soiled ones. Also, they are less prone to attracting unwanted wildlife into your camps. So if you will be hiking for more than a few days you will greatly benefit by washing your clothing regularly. And if your garments are light in weight, the washing will be easily done.

I try to rinse my polyester shirt and spandex shorts near the end of every day, along with my socks, usually at my dinner stop if water is handy. If I have soap, then I rub a small amount on the garments. Soap is not critical; rinsing alone will suffice. Whether or not you use soap, be careful to wash and rinse your clothes well away from the natural water sources to keep from polluting the water. Normally the best way is to use the dundo method, which I describe more fully in the Hygiene chapter.

This involves collecting water in a water bottle or cookpot, then moving well away from the water source and pouring that water over the garments. Hold the shirt or a sock in your hands and scrub it against itself vigorously. Mix in a very small amount of soap if available, scrub again, and rinse well. The rinse is the most important step, since any remaining soap residue can irritate the skin.

On our first two thru-hikes Jenny and I carried a "tub." Filled with water and carried away from the water source, it served as a basin for hand laundering clothes. See the Remaining Equipment chapter for details about this 2.8 ounce option.

If you are planning an extended trek, remember that your garments will probably wear out. Regular laundering will help forestall such problems, but still you may need a replacement shirt or two, along with a supply of extra socks. Plan ahead and include these in your resupply parcels.

Clothing stow bags

Dry clothing inside your pack is precious cargo. But since backpacks tend to leak in rainy weather, and pack covers often fail, your spare clothing may become wet unless you take precautions. To protect your garments, keep them in a waterproof stow bag of some type. It could be a coated nylon stow bag, such as those described in the Sewing Your Own Gear chapter, or something as simple as a plastic garbage sack. In very wet weather use a second, larger bag as a liner inside your pack. These will thwart the soaking rain and the sweat soaking in from your back. After a day of hiking in cold or wet weather, make camp and slip into your dry, stow bag-protected clothes. Hang the wet items where they can dry: inside your tent, under the tarp or under the protection of a tree.

In an emergency or unexpected situation you can usually turn to nature for added warmth. Look for a natural windblock, and build a fire. Stuff your clothing with natural insulating materials such as grasses, leaves, pine needles and moss. These provide the same dead-air spaces that the insulating jacket and sleeping bags do, and depending on how much of these natural materials you use, their potential for warmth is practically unlimited. They even work reasonably well when wet. If you become cold at night, cover your quilt or sleeping bag with the same kind of natural materials.

Footwear

It is better to wear out one's shoes
than one's sheets.

— Genoese proverb

Our footwear is the link between our feet and the ground; between our envisioned goal and the path that leads us there. Many forces of nature will test this link every step of the way. So whether we aspire to an occasional ramble through the woods near home, or a multi-month thru-hike, we would do well to give this vital link—our footwear—some careful thought.

Hiking barefoot

Our feet are naturally light in weight, flexible and full of sensory receptors and transmitters. As we walk barefoot, the nerves in our feet provide our brains with a wealth of tactile information. This sensory data helps augment our sense of orientation and balance, and it brings us more in tune with our environment. In fact, there is something Neolithic and sensual about hiking barefoot through a quiet forest, or on a trail of soft dirt. Even sun-warmed and glacier-polished granite can feel wonderful. In terms of the best connection with nature, barefoot is the ultimate in "footwear."

Brief stints of barefooted hiking have much to recommend them. Done with care, and for short distances—say, half an hour a day—they can also be very therapeutic. This is especially true for the blister-footed hiker in the early stages of a longer journey. Walking a short distance barefoot is a great way to toughen ailing feet, both internally and externally. And it usually works wonders for leg pains, a fact that points to the footwear as the most likely cause of the pain. To avoid a stubbing or puncturing injury, slow down and watch where you are placing your feet.

At the same time, not many of us could get away with hiking great distances barefoot. Depending on the climate and the individual, this would create overly-thick calluses. Thick calluses are the result of the abrasion of walking combined with the excessive ventilation. Because of the dryness, thick callus is subject to cracking. The cracks are unable to heal, because callus is dead tissue. Yet the cracks can cause considerable pain, since they work down into the underlying live tissue.

Moccasins

Jenny and I have hiked many miles in moccasins, and find them the next best thing to going barefoot. We have even worn them on cross-country trips of a hundred and more miles. We make our own moccasins based on a hard-sole design of the Ute Indians. For more information on making moccasins, see the *Craft Manual of North American Indian Footwear* by George M. White, and the moccasin making section of *Blue Mountain Buckskin*, by Jim Riggs.

The technique for walking in moccasins is different than that for walking in shoes. Mainly, one does not strike the ground with the heel. Heel stomping is unnatural, and it requires extra cushioning. Rather, we land on the outside of the forefoot, then roll to the middle of the forefoot, then lower the heel. In this way we walk gently upon the earth in a more graceful and connected manner.

Sturdier footwear

The human foot contains 126 ligaments that interconnect 26 bones. These interconnections form working, flexing joints that allow the foot to better accommodate irregularities of terrain. Stiff footwear restrains much of this beneficial flexing. The stiffer the footwear, the more it restricts, and therefore the more clumsy and difficult the person's walk.

If barefoot or moccasin-shod, the hiker must place the feet carefully, and with much less force than if wearing sturdier footwear. In shoes or boots, hikers can tromp along with considerable vigor. This allows them to hike at a faster pace, but it also increases their chances of incurring a stress-related injury, and of course it alarms the wildlife. Still, sturdier footwear has its advantages. Shoes or boots protect the toes when accidentally kicking rocks, roots and pointed sticks. The carbon-rubber soles allow the wearer to walk with very little thought to the sharp rocks, cactus spines and needle-tipped pine cone scales underfoot. The soles insulate the feet from temperature extremes. And they act as barriers to parasites that could auger into the feet when stepping on manure in various stages of decay, something that is unavoidable on many trails.

Experimentation and experience

Growing up in the foothills of the Colorado Rockies, I hiked a great many trail miles and climbed scores of peaks in stout, leather boots. In the early 1970's when I began instructing outdoor programs, I started hiking hundreds of miles each summer. For the first few years I hiked in leather boots, but I also carried a spare pair of running shoes in my pack for use around camp. The shoes, I realized, were much more comfortable. So in my third year I began hiking in them. This worked surprisingly well, except that I had to carry the boots in my pack, and they were much heavier and bulkier than were the shoes. I quickly grew tired of carrying that extra weight, so I simply left the boots at home.

Hiking in running shoes was practically unheard of at the time. Most people believed that without the support of boots, the ankles would buckle under the load of a backpack. Yet my ankles did not buckle, or even complain. This was true even though I have steel pins in one lower leg from a spiral fracture during a skiing accident, and a flattened arch from a karate sparring mishap. In spite of these old injuries, or perhaps because of them, I found that with less weight on my feet I could cover the miles with much less difficulty. Most importantly, the soles of the running shoes provided better traction. What I discovered back then was that the aggressiveness of sole tread is entirely secondary to the frictional properties of its rubber. The day I started wearing running shoes was the day I stopped slipping on wet rocks and crashing into creeks. Another benefit was that the shoes were more economical. This was important because the summer's earnings had to last me the entire year.

Years later when Jenny and I first hiked the PCT, the snowpack in the High Sierra was 120% above normal. We spent the entire month of May wallowing through snow, en route from Kennedy Meadows to Tuolumne Meadows. We had planned on a wintry adventure, and most of our gear handled it reasonably well, except for the sturdy leather boots. Once they became soaked, they stayed that way. And each time we applied waterproofing compound we only made them heavier. Reaching Tuolumne

Meadows we sent the boots home. I switched back into running shoes, and Jenny her lighter-weight fabric boots, and we continued on to Canada.

During our second PCT journey we again traversed the High Sierra early in the season, but this time late enough so that the snow had con-solidated—meaning that we could generally walk on top of it without sinking in. Even though snow covered the ground most of the way, we hiked from Kennedy Meadows to Tuolumne in twelve days. This was less than half our previous time. We both wore lighter-weight fabric boots on the steeper sections, and running shoes on less steep snow and the occasional stretches of bare ground.

On the Continental Divide Trail we wore running shoes the entire way, and with excellent results. Even on the steeper snow slopes in Gla-cier National Park we found the shoes perfectly adequate, but of course we carried ice axes and a short length of climbing rope as a safety backup. Because running shoes dry so much faster than boots, we did not worry when they became wet during the drenching spring rains and the scores of river crossings in Montana. Yet we did experience one problem among the prickly weeds of New Mexico, near the end of the trip. The stickers dropped into the spaces between our ankles and the shoes, and made walking painful. Lacking gaiters that would fit over our running shoes, we used a bit of duct tape, and that solved the problem.

Running shoes proved ideal for our thru-hike of the Appalachian Trail; more on this to follow. On our third PCT hike, which took us south-bound, we wore ultra-lightweight fabric boots during the initial few weeks through the snowbound North Cascades. In weight, these "boots" were only marginally heavier than a pair of lightweight running shoes. The specific make and model is no longer in production, but I mention them only to illustrate the possibilities. Once out of the snow we retired the "boots" and wore running shoes the rest of the way, along with sandals for a bit of variety.

Boot fallacies

During all these experiments in boots and running shoes, I have tried to look at the pros and cons more objectively, rather than simply accept the standard practices. What follows is my reasoning, based on my own dis-coveries and those of others.

The ankle-support myth

Most hikers who wear stout boots believe they need them for ankle support. But if hikers need boots for ankle support, then logically they would also need crutches for hip support and braces for lower back support. Which of course is nonsense. What hikers need is not ankle support, but ankle strength. Weak ankles are a result of walking mostly on flat floors, sidewalks and stairs. By design, these level surfaces do not stress the ankles in the sideways direction. Civilized, yes, but they leave the ankles unprepared to handle the irregularities of natural terrain. Boots attempt to rectify this, but a far better solution is to strengthen the lateral muscles and ligaments of the ankles and feet. Our ankles were meant to sustain the weight of our bodies and packs, without external support, and to transport us over rugged ground for hundreds and even thousands of miles. And in every probability they will do so, safely and without problems, if we first strengthen them by conditioning for our hikes ahead of time. See the Physical Conditioning chapter for details.

Hiking rugged terrain safely

One of backpacking's greatest fallacies is that sturdy boots allow a person to negotiate rugged terrain safely. The truth is, boot-clad hikers suffer leg and foot injuries practically every day of the summer, in all kinds of terrain and weather. I know several people who have broken legs or sprained ankles while wearing sturdy boots. The summer that Jenny and I hiked the Appalachian Trail, four people suffered serious mishaps on the slopes of just one mountain (Mt. Moosilauke), all in sturdy boots. Boots actually contribute to these accidents in a number of ways.

Boots and heavier hiking shoes reduce one's tactual awareness of the terrain underfoot. In lightweight footwear you can feel the earth beneath you, and this is a big advantage. If you happen to step on something that might twist your ankle or throw you off balance, you immediately sense this. Your feet rush the message to your brain, and the brain directs you to quickly lift that foot, and put it down somewhere else. This is known as autonomic reaction, and it is something innate in everyone. Yet heavy footwear prevents the feet from foreknowing of these missteps. And once you place your weight down fully, it could be too late.

Heavier footwear reduces the accuracy of foot placements, while restricting your mobility and dexterity. The person wearing boots or heavy shoes might aim to step between two basketball-sized rocks on the trail, and miss. Down for the count of ten. Why? Because of the difficulty of aiming a heavily-weighted foot in motion, and of regaining balance after a poor placement.

Can you imagine driving a cement truck on a twisting, winding race course? No, a sports car would be better. And to me, that is the difference between heavy footwear and lighter running shoes. The more rugged the terrain—with rocks and roots, steep slopes, difficult tread and boulder hopping—the more maneuverability we need. The lighter the shoe, the more maneuverability it provides.

Protecting the bottom of the feet

But don't we need stiff-soled boots to protect our feet from bruising—for example when stepping on sharp-edged rocks, or when accidentally kicking trail-embedded rocks and roots? Yes, massive boots protect the feet from these things, but they also cause the hiker to kick and stumble on them in the first place. By virtue of their size and weight, they make the hiking more clumsy.

During one of our journeys Jenny and I walked a ways behind a fellow who hiked with a unique style. Several times a minute he kicked roots or rocks, slipped on mud, or skidded a ways recklessly down intervening snowbanks. But each time he immediately corrected, and threw himself adroitly back into balance, as a matter of course and apparently without giving it any thought. Jenny and I were wearing running shoes, and just as subconsciously we were avoiding those rocks and roots, and treading the mud and snow more deliberately so as not to stumble and slip. For this fellow the terrain was full of obstacles that required sturdy boots. To us, the trail seemed mostly obstacle free, and our soft shoes performed very well.

One might argue that hikers in running shoes spend all their time "watching their step," and that they therefore miss most of the scenery passing by. The fact is that boots do not exempt anyone from the need to watch where they are stepping. Inattentiveness could lead to injury due to a slip or stumble. This is not to suggest that we should constantly watch our feet. Instead, we move our eyes in a continuous sweeping motion, from the immediate foreground to the scenery, back and forth. With practice this sweeping pattern becomes routine. It helps us avoid kicking rocks and tripping on roots, while at the same time it allows us to enjoy the scenery. And in the presence of rattlesnakes or copperheads this same awareness could spare us an unfavorable encounter.

The Appalachian Trail has a reputation for terrain so rugged that it requires stout boots. Following Grandma Gatewood's example, and our own usual practice, Jenny and I hiked its full length in running shoes. We found the trail remarkably rugged in many places. In particular, veteran hikers told us that we would never make it through the notoriously rocky sections of Pennsylvania in our running shoes. But we had no problems with the rocks there or anywhere else. One might imagine that our running shoes slowed us down as we watched every step. Actually, they shortened our trip duration dramatically. Not because they allowed us to hike faster—we always try to maintain a very moderate pace—but because they made the walking easier, and therefore they allowed us to spend more of each day hiking comfortably.

Kicking steps in steep, hard snow

But don't we need stiff soles in order to kick steps in steep, hard snow-pack? Yes, and this is why the hiker should travel through the alpine regions in spring and early summer equipped with two types of footwear: One, a lightweight boot of moderate stiffness for trouncing steps in steep snowpack; and two, a softer shoe for making easier miles across open ground. The boots do not need to be board-stiff to provide adequate purchase. They could be lighter-weight fabric boots that feature good "toe-bumpers" (the welt around the toe area) for kicking steps, and sturdy edges for biting into hard, steep snowpack. The skier on steep, hard snow digs in with the edges of the skis for purchase and security. The hiker does the same with the boots. On steep snow it is the edges that provide security, much more than the lug soles. When the snow is frozen too hard to kick steps with your lighter-weight boots, you have two options. You could chop the steps with your ice axe. Or more preferably, since the spring snow typically freezes at night then re-thaws in the morning, you could simply wait a few hours for the morning sunshine to soften the snow.

Snake protection

Aren't stout boots good protection from venomous snakes? For the feet, yes. For the legs, no. And remember that pit vipers use their infrared (heat) sensors to decide where best to strike. The hiker's legs would constitute equally suitable targets unless covered by exceptionally thick pants or snake chaps. In snake country, boots do not exempt the hiker from the need for vigilance.

Advantages of running shoes

Let's take a look at the advantages of running shoes.

Kinetics of the footstep

Imagine you are resting beside the trail, watching a hiker striding past. The hiker is moving ahead at a steady pace—say three miles an hour. But each foot is starting and stopping with every step. (You might better visualize this by "walking" two fingers across a tabletop.) When a foot is on the ground and the hiker's weight is on it, that foot does not move. Its forward speed is zero for that moment. Taking the weight off the foot, the hiker's leg muscles accelerate it quickly forward, taking the next step. This quick acceleration requires muscular effort. How much effort depends on the mass of the leg, foot and the footwear. We cannot reduce the mass of our legs or feet, but we certainly can select less massive footwear. As an extreme example, imagine walking with your feet encased in concrete blocks. The heavier the footwear, the more difficult the walking; the lighter the footwear, the easier the walking.

More miles, no extra effort

I estimate that each 1¾ ounces removed from a shoe or boot (3½ ounces for the pair) can add about a mile to a hiker's daily progress. One-and-three-quarter ounces is not much. It is about the same weight as a pair of expensive cushioning insoles. But it is enough to degrade progress by one mile each and every day.

Let's put this into better perspective. Replace a pair of medium-weight leather boots weighing 3 pounds, with a pair of medium-weight running shoes weighing 1 pound, 5 ounces, and with *no extra effort* find yourself hiking 7½ more miles each day.

Imagine that two people begin a thru-hike of the PCT together. They are equally well conditioned, they carry packs of equal weight, and they eat the same kinds of foods. The only difference is that one wears stout boots while the other hikes in lightweight running shoes. On the first day the boot-clad backpacker covers, say, 11 miles. With no more effort the hiker in running shoes walks 18½ miles. The running shoe hiker reaches the first resupply station, 50 miles into the journey, 1½ days ahead of the other. And he reaches trail's end a whopping 1¾ months ahead.

All other factors being equal, the thru-hiker in running shoes is capable of covering the trail in seven weeks less time. But what usually happens is that this hiker simply takes it easier, hiking the trail in 4½ or 5 months while spending less time on the trail each day. The lighter footwear simply makes the journey less of a chore. And on shorter hikes we can reap these same benefits, hiking further each day if desired, or at least covering our intended miles with less effort.

The handicap of stiff soles

Stiff soles place great demands on the hiker's calf muscles and Achilles tendons. Technically, we could discuss this in terms of the shoe or boot's longitudinal center of effort. This is the theoretical point about which the sole pivots with each step. The stiffer the sole, the further forward is its center of effort, and therefore the greater the effort of walking in that shoe or boot. As an extreme example, imagine walking with boards strapped to the undersides of your feet and extending in front of your toes. The farther the boards extend forward, the harder your calf muscles must pull in order to lift your heels. The stiff shank of a boot or a stiff-soled hiking shoe acts in the same detrimental way.

Therefore, when trying on a shoe or boot prior to purchase, test the stiffness by grasping the toe in one hand and the heel in the other, and bending the sole as it would bend when taking a step. Compare this stiffness to your everyday street shoe or trainer. If the hiking shoe or boot in question is quite stiff, it will add considerably to the stress in your legs.

Mid-foot cushioning

Another reason I prefer to hike in running shoes is the heel and mid-foot cushioning they provide. Foot ailments are common among runners, so the makers of running shoes have gone to great lengths to design their products for maximum comfort and cushioning. The makers of hiking boots think differently. In general, they are more concerned with heavy-duty construction and durability.

Running shoes easier to break in

New boots are often quite difficult to break in. In the process they tend to "break in" the hiker's feet, instead. For after all, the boots are tough and durable, like the advertisements state. If the boots fit properly, then all may be well. But if they do not fit properly, then they will continue to conform the hiker's feet to their shape. This can weaken the feet, and while such an arrangement may be tolerable for a mile or two, it can eventually lead to pain and even injury. Running shoes are more soft and supple, and require very little break-in time, if any at all.

Tread softly for minimum impact

A stiff-soled boot providing maximum security on steep snow can be very damaging to the exposed alpine soil and its sensitive plant ecology. Hiking and backpacking are gaining in popularity, and the detrimental impact of lug-soled footwear is becoming ever more pronounced. This is particularly apparent in places where the ground is soft or moist, such as in delicate springtime meadows and along high alpine trails. For this reason, when you descend out of the snow you should change into your softer-soled running shoes at the very first opportunity.

Renowned climber Steve Roper originated the Sierra High Route, one of the more rugged and challenging treks in America. In his guide book to this route, *The Sierra High Route, Traversing Timberline Country*, (Sierra Club Books: 1997) Steve recommends wearing running shoes to reduce the impact on the fragile alpine ecology. This is a strong statement in favor of both wilderness preservation and the suitability of running shoes for handling difficult terrain.

Footwear for cold and rainy conditions

The prospects of extended wet weather used to intimidate me. I knew that my socks and boots would become soaked, and that they would stay that way for days. When I freed myself of the boots, and started wearing running shoes instead, I left behind the anxieties the boots were causing.

Boots in rain

We have all seen magazine ads showing boot-clad hikers stomping melodramatically through puddles. These ultra-wet conditions are supposed to necessitate heavy boots. But are boots capable of keeping the feet dry? In my experience, leather boots might deter the pervading wetness for a day or two, depending on their quality and the amount of sealing compound recently applied, and as long as water does not simply run down into their tops. But eventually they will probably become waterlogged. And when they do, they are that much heavier. This is not a big problem on a weekend hike, when we can take the boots home, and set them aside to dry. Nor is it a serious bother for when we are hiking hut-to-hut, where we might be able to dry the wet boots, at least partially, overnight. But during longer hikes, wet boots can be a genuine concern. Not only are they heavier than dry boots, which are heavy enough to begin with, but they take a long time to dry—even in good weather. In rainy weather they may never dry. Even in dry weather, waterproofing compound applied to leather boots reduces their breathability. Waterproofing compound only adds to the problem of dank, uncomfortable feet. And lack of comfort aside, sweaty, boot-bound feet are much more likely to blister.

But what about boots laminated with an inner ply of waterproof-breathable material? Don't they permit the inside moisture to escape while holding the outside water at bay? In theory, yes. But when used in boots, these materials tend to break down rather quickly. Even if the materials could hold up, their breathability is minute, compared with that of more permeable fabrics usually—but not always—used in running shoes. Also, the high-tech membrane only *seems* to obviate the need to apply sealant. The outer boot material, left untreated, will soak water like a sponge. The membrane then inhibits drying by restricting cross ventilation. One could apply a sealing compound in order to reduce external absorption, but this would further restrict breathability, and it would cause the intervening sandwich of leather to retain the entrapped moisture from sweat indefinitely. One could apply a breathable sealing liquid, but these tend to be short lived in harsh conditions.

Running shoes in rain

When I hike in running shoes, I know they will not become massively heavy when soaked, and that they will dry fairly quickly at the first opportunity. This leaves me squishing along, feeling almost impervious to the rain, sloppy snow and wet brush. Our feet are waterproof and they do not mind being wet, as long as they do not become too cold—which they do not if we are hiking and generating metabolic heat. And as long as we spend our nights comfortably warm and dry under our quilt or inside the sleeping bag, which of course we do. What we need, then, are not boots to keep our feet dry, but lightweight shoes and socks that will dry faster once the rain stops. With these, we will spend far less time with wet feet.

During our CDT thru-hike, Jenny and I encountered several weeks of frigid rain in Montana. We figured this was a good test of our running shoes, particularly since we often forded dozens of creeks a day, usually without stopping to remove shoes and socks. The creek water was only momentarily numbing; our feet re-warmed after walking only a short ways.

Dealing with wet shoes and socks in camp

After you have spent a long, wet day on the trail, you would remove wet shoes and socks as soon as you have pitched your shelter and finished your camp chores. Snug and dry under the shelter, you reach outside and wring out your socks, then hang them from the tarp's clothesline, or from a line rigged inside the tent or underneath its awning. If the nighttime air temperatures are likely to drop below freezing, you could place your wet socks under the edge of your foam pad instead. They will not dry there, but neither will they freeze into stiff boards. In sub-zero weather you might also place your shoes under your groundsheet. Otherwise leave the shoes out, but protected beneath the tarp, or your tent awning or vestibule. By morning you will find them probably much less wet. And if the morning's weather proves fine, and if the dew is not on the trailside vegetation, then your shoes will likely dry within a few short hours of tramping.

Creek fording footwear

When it comes to creek fording, I normally prefer to remove my shoes and socks, and wear two pairs of spare socks. The socks provide some cushioning against sharp stones, they insulate my feet somewhat from the cold, and they receive a hasty laundering in the process.

If the water is flowing strongly, and if no deeper than what I can handle safely—which is well below the knees in swift water—then I wear my shoes for better traction and maneuverability, minus the socks.

Shoe requirements

The variety of running, hiking and cross-training shoes on the market is almost overwhelming. And in response to competition the manufacturers are continually shelling the market with new models. I cannot recommend specific ones that have worked well for me because without a single exception they have gone out of production. But I can list the guidelines I use when selecting new shoes.

- Reasonable cost—midway between the cheapest and most expensive.

- Lightweight—$10\frac{1}{2}$ oz. each, or less. (This is the average weight of men's size $10\frac{1}{2}$—the industry standard. The weight will be proportionally heavier for larger sizes and lighter for smaller ones.)

- Ample tread for traction, but not massive tread that would cause excessive damage to the land.

- Adequate heel support, (not ankle support) keeping the shoe centered under the heel (see below).

- Excellent cushioning beneath both the heel and ball of the foot.

- Highly breathable uppers, allowing perspiration to evaporate.

And a few qualities to steer away from:

» Visible gas or liquid filled cushioning devices molded into the sole's *bottom* surface—that which contacts the ground. These can burst on contact with sharp rocks.

» Gaping indentations in the sole that reduce the footprint area. These are less stable, and since they create more pressure in contact with the ground, they are harder on the ecology. As an extreme example, picture a woman's high-heeled shoe. The "sole" of the heel spike has very little surface area. It would sink deeply into softer ground, and is very unstable.

» Stiff soles, and extra wide or flaring soles.

» Foam linings. These over-insulate and restrict ventilation.

» Built-in elastic sock. These also restrict ventilation.

Shoe construction: lasting

Before buying any type of hiking footwear, remove the insole and inspect the lasting (the inside bed of the actual shoe itself). This will not be possible with a cheaply made shoe that has the sock liner glued into place. Nevertheless:

- Inside a *board-lasted* shoe or boot is a sole-shaped piece of cardboard or other stiff material, glued in place.

- In a *combination-lasted* shoe, a piece of cardboard covers only the rear half of the foot area.

- Inside a *slip-lasted* shoe you will see fabric joined by a hand-sewn seam running the length of the shoe.

Board-lasted shoes and boots are less costly to manufacture. The board (cardboard) last adds stiffness, and naturally it comes in various qualities. Some merely abrade and roughen when wet, while others actually begin to disintegrate. And the glue securing the boards in place some-times—but of course not always—dissolves. Bereft of its last, a board-lasted or combination-lasted shoe can be unwearable. Given the choice, I usually choose slip-lasted footwear.

Insoles

The insole is the removable, foot-shaped pad that comes in most running shoes and boots. The heel and toe areas of the insole are normally molded in an upward curve. I pull out the insoles in my new shoes, and using a pair of scissors I trim away those curved portions at the toe and heel. This provides more space and reduces the chances of blistering.

In my earlier days of long-distance hiking I fitted expensive insoles beneath the factory-equipped ones for added cushioning. Eventually I realized that the extra cushioning was beneficial only because I was wearing the shoes too many miles and breaking them down internally—even though the shoes still looked fine on the outsides. The problem with trying to extend the life of a shoe or boot is that sooner or later it can begin harm-ing one's feet. Pains can surface suddenly and without warning, for ex-ample, in the middle of a long section between trailheads. A better plan is to replace broken-down footwear with a new pair.

Orthotics

That karate sparring mishap that flattened my arch also left me with an over-pronating ankle. So before embarking on my first long hike I con-sulted a sports podiatrist. He cast a plaster mold of the bottom of each foot, and supplied me with a pair of custom plastic orthotics. Invented by the late Dr. George Sheehan, the well-known running advocate, these are removable inserts worn inside the footwear. My orthotics provided sup-port not beneath the arch, but behind the arch on the forward part of the heel. I wore them during the pre-hike training, and eventually determined that the non-injured foot was gaining no benefit. I wore the orthotic in the other shoe the full distances of our first two journeys. As the injured foot became stronger, it outgrew its need for the orthotic.

Pronating ankles are not necessarily incapable. But they can cause pain in the ankles or knees. Here is an easy way to test your feet as to whether they might benefit from orthotics. Place a sheet of paper on the floor. Wet your foot then step naturally onto the paper. The moisture should leave a well-defined footprint. If most of the foot area is visible, but a small area is scooped out at the side, then your arch is probably normal. If the entire outline of your foot is revealed, your ankle might be over-pronating. Also, ask someone to stand behind you and watch as you walk away from them bare-footed and bare-legged from the knees down. They should be able to tell whether your ankles are flexing inward as you place your weight on them.

If your ankles over-pronate, the calf-stretching exercises (see the Stretching chapter) will help reduce any associated problems. During the stretch, do not allow the ankles to flex inward.

If you experience a knee pain that you think might be related to an over-pronating ankle, try this simple test: walk on terrain sloped down and away from the painful knee. For example if the left knee hurts, walk on ground sloped down and to your left. If this seems to help, it might indicate a weakness in that ankle.

Supination is the opposite of pronation: the ankles turn outward with each step. Supination is rare, and seems to cause few problems among hikers. However, turning the ankle forcefully outward, when stepping clumsily on a rock or root with the inside of the foot, can result in a sprained ankle. This is best avoided by watching where you place your feet, and far more importantly by strengthening your ankles during a pre-hike training program.

Heel support

Most hikers have "normal" feet and do not require orthotics. And hikers with properly strengthened ankles, the result of pre-hike training, do not require ankle support either. But almost everyone needs good heel support in their shoes. Heel support means simply that the shoe's heel-cup is fairly stiff. This keeps the heel of the shoe centered beneath the heel of the foot. This is important if the shoe is to work well on uneven terrain. When you walk on laterally sloped ground, your heel tends to slide off the shoe's footbed, but good heel support prevents this.

However, most shoes made for good heel support are also fairly heavy. Eleven ounces (average for a men's size 10½) is getting up there, and many such shoes climb into the twelve ounce category. When studying running shoe catalogs, pay attention to both the weights and the advertised extent of support provided by the various shoes. Better yet, visit a shoe store and examine the models personally. To test a shoe for heel support, simply squeeze the heel cup laterally. The stiffer the heel-cup, the more heel support it provides. It is that simple. What is not so simple is finding shoes that have good heel support, yet which are light in weight and easy on the wallet. They do exist, but sometimes finding them takes a bit of searching.

Wide and thick soles

The sole of the optimum running shoe should be about the same width as the bottom of your foot, or slightly wider. And the sole should be reasonably thin.

An overly thick sole raises the vertical center of effort, reducing stability. A too-narrow sole also reduces stability. With either problem your foot can sometimes "fall off" the shoe. This happens when you step inadvertently on the side of a rock or root. The sole twists to match the slope of the rock, and your foot slides off the sole. And because the fabric is flexible, the sensation is that of falling off, or out of, the shoe.

A far greater problem is that of the sole being too wide. In addition to a shoe's longitudinal (front to back) center of effort, a shoe has a lateral (side to side) center of effort. Wider soles might seem to provide more lateral stability, but this is true only on flat ground. More often, we hike on irregular ground. When you step on a protuberance with the very edge of a too-wide sole, it can torque your ankle tremendously. And the wider the sole, the more apt you are to step on something with its edge.

We can look at the wide-sole problem another way. Suppose you are traversing a steep slope. Narrow soles will allow you to walk on their edges, keeping your ankles more vertical. Wide soles stress the ankles so much that you cannot walk on the soles' edges. Instead, you have to walk with the soles flat against the steeply sloped ground. This torques the ankles sideways, and can stretch and weaken those outer tendons and ligaments.

Reflective material affects photographs

The reflective material used on most running shoes is intended to alert night-time motorists. But it can wreak havoc with your photographs. In any situation where you use a fill-in flash, in day or night, the burst of light from the flash can rebound from the reflective material of the subject's shoes, and over-expose that part of the photo. The same can happen with the sun's reflection when the subject is walking away from a sunset or sunrise. The solution is to slice away the reflective material from the shoes, or to cover it with paint, or simply to remember to point your camera a little higher, keeping the reflections from the shoes out of the picture.

Proper fit

If you are planning a long trek, it is usually best to purchase your footwear larger than normal, to accommodate the swelling of your feet. You may not notice your feet swelling while hiking only every other day during your training exercises. But once you start hiking many miles on a daily basis, your feet will most likely begin to increase in size. This is especially true if you are hiking in hot and arid climes. Some of this enlargement is due simply to the feet strengthening to the task. The muscles are growing in size, and the blood vessels are expanding. And some of the enlargement is due to blood pooling and fluid accumulation. This is perfectly normal; healthy in fact. But to accommodate this swelling, buy your shoes 1 to 1½ sizes larger than usual for hiking in cool to moderately warm climates, and 1½ to 2½ sizes larger in hot climates. Otherwise, as the swelling progresses, your feet are likely to become very cramped inside the shoes. Hiking in tight shoes or boots is a sure way to painfully blistered feet—and maybe to bruised toes and blackened toe nails as well. You might be very reluctant to buy footwear sized that much larger, especially in the presence of a "helpful" salesperson. But as my own experience has shown, and scores of hikers have affirmed, buying shoes or boots that fit properly in the city is a big mistake. They can become unwearable within the first couple of days on the trail.

However, unless your feet are exceptionally wide, I would not recommend buying extra wide shoes, usually denoted as EE, EEE or EEEE. No matter how enlarged your feet become, these extra wide sizes will be far too roomy in the rear-foot areas. Even when swollen, your feet are likely to wallow in them. Conversely, some brands of shoes are very narrow in the forefoot. These are best avoided also, even if your feet are quite narrow. Once on the trail you may find the extra space to your advantage. Many women hikers wear men's shoes on the trail because these tend to be wider in the forefoot where the extra space is beneficial.

Modifying your shoes

After many miles of hiking in hot weather, you might find that the sensitive areas on your feet are multiplying out of control. This is the time for surgery. Not on your feet, but on the shoes.

First, cut out the tongues: cram the tongue deep into the shoe's toe box, then carefully slice the tongue-to-uppers stitching. With the tongue done away with, slit the shoe's upper forefoot, down its centerline an inch toward the toe of the shoe. This slit allows the shoe's forefoot to expand laterally, creating more space for your foot. After hiking in the shoes awhile, you can elongate the forefoot slit if necessary, but only in small increments. Avoid slitting all the way to the vicinity of your toenails, as they might then begin snagging the slit with each step. If you slice too far, you can always break out the sewing needle and thread, and stitch a cross-hatch pattern back along the slice, leaving it plenty wide. No matter how far forward the slit extends, the cross-hatch stitching will prevent interference with the toes.

After you have removed the tongues and slit the upper forefoot areas, you will have increased the shoe's ventilation tremendously. This helps your feet stay cool and dry. It also admits more dirt, yet even this can be an advantage. I call it "dura-dirt" because it can be difficult to scrub off, but actually it helps toughen the feet, as long as you do scrub it off at day's end. The gap left by the missing tongue also admits the occasional bit of gravel. I handle this by lacing my shoelaces so loosely that I can slip out of the shoes without having to untie the laces, and slip back into them in the same way. But of course I tighten the laces before crossing steep terrain and making the more serious creek crossings.

If a shoe is chafing your foot day after day, consider slicing the shoe to make it larger, or cutting out a hole where the material is causing a persistent blister. Another common problem with some shoes is that they rub or exert pressure on the Achilles tendon, creating tenderness in the back of the heel. Trying to walk far in such shoes or boots is a sure invitation to injury. You can relieve the pressure by slitting the shoe an inch or so down the back. If you are wearing fabric boots that irritate the Achilles tendon, make a 2-inch slit along the back of the boot, only in the area of pressure.

Protecting the stitching

All exposed stitching on a pair of shoes or boots is vulnerable to abrasion. For longer life you can coat that stitching with fast-setting, 3 to 5 minute epoxy. Fast-setting epoxy is more flexible than the slower setting types. While mixing the epoxy, add an equal amount of rubbing alcohol. This acts as a thinner, and encourages the mixture to soak into the fabric and the stitching. Use a toothpick to dab the epoxy on, and smear some also wherever the uppers might need extra protection from abrasion. Mix the epoxy in small batches, on tin can lids for example.

Reducing footwear-related injuries

Most types of running shoes offer excellent cushioning, and this cushioning is very beneficial to the hiker. But it comes at a cost. With the passing of many miles the cushioning materials slowly break down—even though the shoes might still look fine on the outsides. These materials do not break down evenly, and the result is a shoe that transmits unbalanced forces with every step. These imbalances can ultimately lead to a stress injury.

A budding stress injury is signaled by a sharp or burning pain with each step that manifests itself for no apparent cause. The pain can be anywhere from the foot up into the lower back. Hiking pains can stem from other problems, such as a lack of pre-hike training, too heavy a load, severe and prolonged dehydration, inadequate nutrition, lack of calf-limbering exercises, and of course, from stepping down crooked when hopping across a brook or slipping off a wet log. Most often though, the pains are caused by the footwear. So whenever you begin experiencing a pain that stabs with every step, suspect the footwear first.

The solution is obvious: change into a different pair of shoes. More on this in a minute.

If the cushioning in running shoes is prone to breaking down and causing stress injuries, then why not wear boots instead? Because boots, too, are well known for causing stress injuries. This is not because their cushioning breaks down, since they usually have very little, but because they do not fit the hiker's foot perfectly. And this imperfect fit creates imbalances that can gradually grind away at the hiker's foot.

For every person who manages to hike a couple thousand miles in a single pair of boots with "no problems," several others are not so fortunate. The boot advertisements claim comfort and impunity for untold miles across all sorts of rugged terrain, but such is often not the case. Hiking-related stress injuries occur with both running shoes and boots, and I discuss the matter in the Stress Injuries chapter. However the matter bears looking at from a different angle here.

Suppose you buy a pair of shoes or boots that, due to a quality control problem, has a sizeable lump under the ball of one foot. It could be a glob of hardened glue, or a fold in several layers of material. It is an internal problem, not visible. You do notice something a little odd, but decide to break in the shoes or boots gradually over a few weeks' time. Later, you embark on a hiking journey in these shoes and for the first few weeks all seems well. What is happening is that your foot is trying to adapt to the lump as best it can. But as this irregularity hammers incessantly at your foot, eventually you may start feeling a nagging pain at that spot—or just as likely, somewhere else. It could just as easily be in the leg, knee, hip or back.

Every shoe, boot, and sandal has its irregularities. These are not normally as pronounced as in my example, and they might not be lumps—they could be areas that twist or cramp the foot in some unnatural way. You may not feel them, and if they are minor and your feet manage to accommodate them, then you may experience no problems. But if your feet cannot accommodate them, then in all likelihood they will eventually, over many miles of hiking, begin to cause a stress injury. Moreover, as the footwear starts breaking down and wearing out internally, other irregularities can manifest and grow pronounced.

This does not mean that shoes or boots are worthless, only that they have their limitations. And when we know about these limitations and take the appropriate measures, we can easily side-step the limitations. We do this by removing the offending shoes, boots, or sandals at the first sign of pain, and never wearing them again, at least while hiking; and by changing into a different pair.

Carrying spare shoes

From my own experience, a pair of quality running shoes lasts me anywhere from three hundred to a thousand miles. And when the shoes finally "hit the wall," they suddenly start causing pain. One minute all is well, and the next minute I am hobbling. At times like these, ten miles to the nearest trailhead can be a vast distance. Many thousands of hiking miles have taught me to carry spare footwear, and to include spares in various resupply parcels. I know the life of a shoe (or boot) is limited, so I plan accordingly.

Hikers preparing to cover any distance would be well advised to carry spare footwear. This could be a pair of very lightweight running shoes, or lightweight sandals. If nothing else, these would allow you to change back and forth several times a day, for variation. Think ahead and know that your feet will be closer to the center of your personal universe than they are now. Give them plenty of choice in footwear all along the way. Wear one pair to the next resupply station, then send them ahead in your drift box. Think variety!

Here is a common argument in favor of boots: "If the running shoe idea requires that we carry spare shoes to make it work, consequently increasing our overall load, why don't we just wear one, good-fitting pair of boots, and forget about the spares?" Let me give a few reasons. First, the weight on your feet is critical. Second, two pairs of lightweight shoes are lighter than one pair of durable boots. Or, one pair of lightweight shoes and one pair of ultralight sandals are lighter than one pair of lighter-weight boots. And third, weight is not the only problem. Boots sap the hiker's energy and decrease forward progress. They are clumsier to walk in. And they are more damaging to the soil and vegetation.

Along these lines, I received a letter from a thru-hiker-in-planning who wrote: "The main issue I'm looking at is economics. I would believe that shoes not designed for a lengthy trek would break down more rapidly, causing you to have to purchase more and more pairs. Why not buy just one pair of boots that will last the whole way?"

One pair of sturdy boots costs more than several pair of moderately priced running shoes. But let's overlook the expense of the footwear for a moment and consider the costs of the journey as a whole. To start with, we must consider the worth of one's time spent planning, preparing and training, and the cost of lost wages during the actual journey. Then there is the cost of equipment, provisions, postage on the resupply parcels, transportation to the start and from the finish, and groceries, meals and perhaps a few motel rooms along the way. The price of the footwear, be it one pair of boots or half a dozen pairs of running shoes, is a fraction of these costs. Now let's look at cost effectiveness. The success of the journey will depend—entirely—on the footwear. Many are the hikers who set off on their journeys trusting in a single pair of boots, and who return home prematurely with major foot problems. Trusting in a single pair of

A selection of footwear for a long-distance hike,
and the reason why.

boots is neither wise nor cost effective. So if you decide to wear boots on a multi-month hike, make sure you have access to backup footwear.

Sandals

I first saw people hiking in sandals on the Appalachian Trail in '93, but it wasn't until my friend Chris Townsend recommended I try a pair that I actually wore them for hiking myself. Chris was using them on all sorts of trips and raving about them.

The following summer Jenny and I wore sandals for about five hundred miles on the PCT, sometimes with socks and sometimes without. The extra ventilation and foot room were very nice. The cushioning was quite good, at least in the types we wore—in some other types it is lacking. But with almost any type of sandal the heel support is practically non-existent, and as with running shoes this requires strong ankles—especially for the person carrying a full pack. With the straps well secured, sandals work great for creek crossings. Some sandals have a raised lip around the sole, and this helps protect the toes when stumbling, or kicking rocks or roots. Sandals also expose the feet to more dura-dirt.

Slipping into a pair of sandals can be a welcome and therapeutic change for one's painfully blistered feet. However, the straps of the sandals can sometimes create new blisters, as they rub against the skin in areas that the hiker's regular shoes do not. A thin pair of socks or a bit of tape applied to the feet beneath the straps can be effective remedies. And as time goes on, your feet will become more resistant to chafe, since the extra ventilation encourages the skin to toughen. In fact, the ventilation is so good that the fungus responsible for the infection of athlete's feet does not stand a chance—although the mosquitoes certainly do.

Hiking in sandals requires a few novel techniques. Pebbles tend to work themselves under the sole of the foot, and usually you can remove them with a few shakes of the foot. The more obstinate stones require a few well-placed kicks of the sandal against a rock or log. Bits of gravel can also work through any small holes in a sock, and about the only way to remove them is to sit down and remove both sandal and sock. When hiking in sandals you must be particularly careful of sticks lying on the trail. Not noticing, you step on the far end, which raises the near end, and when your other foot swings forward it is speared by the near end. Ouch! I remember one that put me down for fifteen minutes of first aid. That was a good lesson in treading more carefully.

After about five hundred miles in those sandals I started feeling what I thought was a wood sliver in the ball of my foot. Closer inspection showed it to be a crack in the callus. I applied triple antibiotic ointment and carried on, but every day the crack grew larger, even though I continued to apply the ointment. In a few weeks the crack became positively gaping, and others began forming as well. Realizing that the callus was becoming too thick and rigid, I tried grinding it down with rough stones, but to no avail. I would have applied a callus-dissolving solution, had I been carrying one. Clearly, the sandals' ventilation was too much. So I started wearing more layers of socks, in an effort to reduce the ventilation. And sure enough, three pairs of thin nylon socks solved the problem. The cracks did not heal shut, but at least they quit worsening and hurting. In the end I reverted back to wearing running shoes, and wearing the sandals only occasionally.

Future technology in trail footwear

In the coming years we will undoubtedly see new types of footwear designed for hiking and active outdoor wear. Regardless of their design, they will still need to conform to the basic needs of our feet, as discussed throughout this chapter. Weight is very important. If that new model that has attracted your interest weighs much over 11 ounces (men's size 10½), think twice before buying it. Another important feature is heel and midfoot cushioning. Another is adequate (but not excessive) breathability. And until someone figures out a way to make the shoe mold to your foot and stay that way, don't forget to buy several pair, of different makes and models.

Why different makes? Because companies tend to use the same basic molds and "lasts" to make all their models. For the best variety, choose from a wide selection of brand names. Runners are well known for their strong preferences for specific brands and models of footwear, and I think this is one reason they experience so many stress injuries.

Ordering footwear by mail

While hiking a longer trail, you might find yourself in need of a new pair of shoes, sandals or boots. At your next waypoint you could telephone a friend or home-base person and request a pair be express mailed to you there, or to your next stopover. Or with a credit card you could order new shoes direct from such companies as Eastbay (800-826-2205) and Road Runner Sports (800-551-5558). Before placing the call, arrange with someone locally to receive your package, since these companies might not ship to General Delivery. If all else fails you might have to hitchhike to the nearest town and buy a pair. The problem of needing fresh footwear is very common, and is so much more easily solved ahead of time by including spare shoes in your resupply parcels. Those shoes you decide you don't need, you can mail home and use later—possibly on your next hike.

―――――――――――

The technology represented in today's running shoes is considerably improved over that of Grandma Gatewood's era. Today's running shoes offer better cushioning, stability and motion control. I am not suggesting they are the ultimate in long distance hiking footwear. But I do think that by following the guidelines in this chapter, lighter-weight footwear will help you enjoy a successful and trouble-free journey.

Section 2

Hiking Considerations

Food

Part of the secret of success in life
is to eat what you like,
and let the food fight it out inside.

— *Mark Twain*

Meeting our needs
or merely suiting our preferences?

Most of us who enjoy hiking and camping consider the meals and snacks an important part of those outdoor activities. But not all types of today's processed foods are nutritious; far from it. So in any worthwhile discussion on food, we need to consider not simply the whims of our taste buds, but more importantly the physiological needs of our bodies and brains.

What constitutes a good hiking diet? To help answer this, I have structured the first part of this chapter as a general guide to recognizing overly processed junk food in its various disguises. The second part of the chapter gives suggestions for more wholesome trail foods.

Not all "food" is food

The subject of food is complex, and each of us has our own food preferences. Basing food choices solely on preferences must have worked reasonably well in centuries past, when foods were not so heavily processed. But today we have to be more careful. The types of foods we enjoy eating might not be the most beneficial. In fact, some might not even be food.

Also, some of our food preferences may not be our own. Many of the larger food companies bombard us with advertising. This advertising pervades our lives, and is continually suggesting preferences to us. The inference is that the products most heavily advertised *must* be the best. And our emotional responses being what they are, we often agree.

Many, if not most food companies lace their products with taste-enhancing chemicals designed to trick our brains into interpreting the foods as tasting good. High-tech processing ensures that these "foods" are quick and easy to prepare. And modern packaging is aimed at making the packaging attractive. These food companies are large and prosperous, and they use every resource in their arsenal to sell their wares. We, the consumers, are their prey.

Manifestations of poor nutrition

The nutritional value of a food relates to its capacity to provide a person with strength and endurance, to aid cellular growth and repair, and to facilitate mental acuity and stability. We store this nutrition in the cells of our body, to be used as needed. The exercise of hiking depletes these nutritional reserves more quickly, and this is particularly the case on longer journeys. So unless we replenish these nutrients regularly, we will usually start to suffer various effects.

Poorly-nourished hikers often find themselves low on energy and endurance. They usually assume that hiking is inherently tiring, and that the steepness and length of the trail is to blame for their weariness.

Malnutrition can also manifest itself in the hiker's mental outlook. The poorly-nourished brain is largely incapable of producing positive emotions. The sun, rain, snow, the hiking companions and even the trail itself might become intolerable. Endless miles of beautiful surroundings glide past, and most of it is disregarded. In more severe cases this can lead to a sour attitude. Apathy, disharmony, intolerance, the list goes on— and any of these can sap the life, and the enjoyment, from the wilderness journey. Such is the price of poor nutrition, and over the long term we can also expect an inexorable decline in health and well being.

But if these symptoms of poor nutrition are discouraging, they are also avoidable.

Processed flour (white flour)

Processed flour is the nation's most popular food staple. Americans eat more of it than anything else. Yet it is so lacking in nutrition that it hardly qualifies as food. Yes, it fills the stomach and satisfies the palate, but it provides very little nutrition.

The backpacker's larder usually contains plenty of items made of white flour: bread, bagels, crackers, spaghetti, macaroni, flavored pasta mixes, couscous, and certain types of Chinese noodles. These items are acceptable in moderation, but certainly not as one's primary source of sustenance. Let's look at the reasons why.

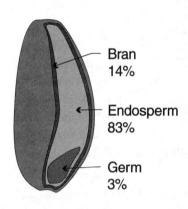

Bran
14%

Endosperm
83%

Germ
3%

In its natural form, the kernel of wheat is protected by an inedible hull. Even after winnowing to remove the hull, the kernel remains alive, waiting to germinate. In fact, in favorable conditions it can lie dormant for decades, thanks to its surrounding layer called the bran. The bran serves to protect the inside from invasive microorganisms, and the bran is a very nutritious part of the kernel. At the heart of the kernel is the germ, the part that would grow if the kernel were planted. The germ is also very high in nutrition. And lastly, the endosperm lies within the bran, surrounding the germ. The endosperm is mostly starches, and contains very little nutrition.

The process of milling breaks down the grain's protective bran, and exposes its germ to air-borne microorganisms. These start feeding on the germ, and begin turning it rancid. To prevent rancidity, the milling machinery removes the germ. And for better texture and color, it also removes the bran. What remains is the endosperm. This lifeless part of the grain is then further processed, refined, bleached and treated to become the nutritionally desolate version of wheat known as white flour. It has a long shelf life because microbes cannot subsist on it very well, and neither can we.

To compensate for robbing the products of their nature-given nutrients, the food industry "enriches" them with all manner of chemicals. The word "enrich" incorrectly leads us to believe that these chemicals are good for us—even though they restore none of the nutrition and only a fraction of the vitamins and minerals. Most of the chemical additives are artificially synthesized vitamins. Under an electron microscope these appear very different from the associated vitamins found naturally in food. Some of the "fortifying" chemicals are added to make the product taste better. Others are texture and color additives to make the product *seem* more like real food.

One of the best references on this subject is *Beating the Food Giants*, by Paul A. Stitt (Bibliography). In fact, this book is so informative that I consider it essential reading for anyone concerned about the quality of their food. The author details his work as a foods research scientist, citing a number of shocking studies and experiments involving, among many other things, the nutritional value of white flour. He says that the food giants do their best to stifle these types of studies because "too often these tests show their 'foods' are incapable of sustaining life."

Nutritional bankruptcy

How do we know whether a certain bread, for example, contains the nutrient-rich germ and bran? The product description certainly does not tell us. Nor does the label "100% whole wheat bread." This means only that the bread is made from 100% whole wheat, before removal of the germ and bran, and the introduction of the usual barrage of additives. And lest we put too much faith in the list of ingredients, Paul Stitt informs us that "Bread can contain oxides of nitrogen, chlorine, notrosyl chloride, chlorine dioxide, benzoyl peroxide (acne medication), acetone peroxide, azodicarbonamide, even plaster of Paris and sawdust, and the manufacturer is not obligated by the Code of Federal Regulations to warn you of these. Nor is bread the only product that can have hidden additives..."

About the only way we can know whether the germ and bran are present is to grind the grains ourselves, and bake our own bread. If you are doing that, then you know that genuine whole-grain bread is coarse and crumbly (and packed with nutrition). Modern commercial breads of all types do not match this description. This is because they are mostly white flour disguised in all manner of ways. White flour contains a high gluten content, and this gives the bread its fine consistency.

So why do people eat these types of bread? Actually it all started back in the Middle Ages when white bread was first invented. Back then it was called manchet, and later wastel bread. These were made of the "finest and most delicate flours obtainable," and were so expensive that only the aristocracy could afford them. Laborers, servants, and others of few means had to make do with darker, coarser, whole-grain breads. When the industrial revolution introduced machines that could produce white flour cheaply and in quantity, white bread became available to the common class, who wanted to eat the same foods as the wealthy.

Other popular hiking foods

Wheat pasta is made of durum semolina—a fancy term for a variety of wheat, again stripped of its bran and germ. In other words, white flour. While it might make a tasty meal on occasion, don't mistake white-flour-based pasta for highly nutritious food and plan to eat it for every dinner during a long-distance hike. Consumed in such high quantities it will sap your energy, and it can turn your summer's journey from one of enjoyment to one of drudgery. Many long-distance hikers, myself included, have eaten corn pasta for nearly every meal while on journey, and with excellent results. Not so with white-flour-based pasta.

Then there is macaroni and cheese. This, too, is durum semolina (white flour), and the "cheese" is usually artificial. Flavored pasta mixes are made from white flour with various flavorings, as are Ramen noodles. Couscous is a finely cracked durum wheat or millet that has been steamed, dried, and refined (stripped of its bran and germ).

Instant oatmeal is in the same category. To make oats "instant," the bran and germ are removed, and the endosperm is pre-cooked and rolled thin. Another so-called "instant" product is instant rice—the most heavily processed and least nourishing form of rice, even when "enriched." It, too, lacks the bran and germ.

Paul Stitt asserts that "Whole wheat and whole rice is produced in ample abundance in most places of the world. But when rice and wheat are processed, i.e., when the bran and germ are removed, the grains are stripped of all major nutrient value. The [malnourished] people don't get too little to eat. The tragic truth is that the food they do get has been ruined before it gets to their mouths."

Excitotoxins

Many types of foods popular with backpackers contain chemicals designed to make our brains interpret the foods as tasting good. In fact, most commercial foods contain such chemicals. Neuroscientists call them "excitotoxins" because they excite the neurons in our brains to the point of killing many of them, causing brain damage in varying degrees. Evidence suggests that MSG (monosodium glutamate), aspartate and a whole class of similar chemicals play a major role in degenerative brain disease, including Parkinson's, Alzheimer's and Huntington's. When these chemicals appear on a packaged food's list of ingredients, which they rarely do, their names are almost always disguised. Yet despite their damaging effects, the food industry finds them enormously helpful in bolstering profits.

In his excellent book *Excitotoxins, The Taste that Kills*, (Bibliography) Dr. Russell L. Blaylock lists a few hidden sources of MSG:

"Monosodium glutamate, Glutamate, Monopotassium glutamate, Glutamic acid, Hydrolyzed protein (from 12 to 40% MSG), Autolyzed yeast (from 10 to 20% MSG), Yeast extract, Calcium caseinate (8-12% MSG), Sodium caseinate (8-12% MSG).

"In addition, some ingredients always contain MSG: Textured protein, gelatin, yeast food, plant protein extract, yeast nutrient, hydrolyzed oat flour.

"And the following are ingredients that often contain MSG: malt extract, malt flavoring, barley malt, bouillon, stock, broth, carrageenan, maltodextrin (corn), whey protein, whey protein isolate, whey protein concentrate, anything enzyme-modified, xanthum gum (corn), pectin, flavor(s) & flavoring(s), natural flavor(s) & flavoring(s), natural pork flavoring, natural beef flavoring, natural chicken flavoring, 'seasonings,' soy sauce, soy sauce extract, soy protein, soy protein isolate, soy protein concentrate, anything protein-fortified, 'spices'."

Dr. Blaylock also points out that "glutamate, aspartate and cysteine are found in nature," which is how the industry gets away with labeling them as "natural" ingredients. He goes on to say that "the label designating 'natural flavoring' may contain anywhere from 20 to 60 percent MSG. The powerful excitotoxins asparate and L-cysteine are frequently added to foods and according to FDA rules require no labeling at all."

"More and more diseases of the nervous system are being linked to excitotoxin build-up in the brain. For example disorders such as strokes, brain injury, hypoglycemic brain damage, seizures, migraine headaches, hypoxic brain damage, and even AIDS dementia have been linked to excitotoxin damage."

With this list of excitotoxins in mind, you might peruse the ingredients labels of the foods you typically carry with you on your outings.

"Energy" bars

We want our snacks to provide the best energy, keeping us well fueled throughout the day. This often brings to mind the so-called energy bars so prevalent today. Why do we normally associate health and energy with these bars? Mainly as a response to the advertising. But do these products actually provide us with a significant boost in energy? I think of them this way: If energy bars supplied significant energy, then at the Olympic Games, all the athletes would gorge on them prior to competition. These people need energy more than just about anyone, and what do they eat? Wholesome, natural foods, not on the morning of competition but during their months of training. So what are we to make of these supposed "energy" bars? I tend to agree with one description I heard: "high-priced candy bars."

In a survey done by a popular magazine, the bar that won top place received such accolades as "loved the real food texture and awesome energy." Looking at the wrapper on one of these bars, we find that the first ingredient is malted corn and barley. Malted corn and malted barley are sugars. And as if these do not make that particular bar sweet enough, the fourth ingredient is honey. The fact is, simple sugars are ineffective at replenishing glycogen stores, essential for working muscles. The most effective replenishment is complex carbohydrates, such as freshly cooked whole grains, legumes, squash and potatoes.

The second most popular "energy bar" in the magazine comparison is practically the de facto standard in today's sports "energy" market. This bar lists its first ingredient as "high fructose corn syrup with grape and pear juice concentrate." In other words: sugars. The third ingredient is maltodextrin, which is an excitotoxin. A few ingredients later we come to: "natural flavors (no MSG)." The protein content in this bar is derived mainly from powdered milk, which hikers often carry anyway. And according to my calculations, the bar's vitamin and mineral content is the equivalent of a two cent vitamin pill.

We need to be wary of the type of advertising that attributes magic-like qualities to products made of ordinary ingredients. Full page, monthly advertisements are phenomenally expensive, and they are paid for by unsuspecting customers. And because we see these ads in so many magazines, we get the impression that the products are very popular. Why are they popular? Because they work so well, we are led to believe. The market is flooded with tens of thousands of similar products promoted as sports foods, snacks and drinks. These products bring to my mind the cartoons of Popeye eating the proverbial can of spinach and suddenly turning into a whirlwind of energy. The sports foods industry is exactly as the name implies, an industry. And like most industries, its motives are profit.

The calorie myth and candy craving

Some hikers believe that their foods must be high in calories for sufficient energy. If calories gave us energy, then we could eat a dozen candy bars a day and practically fly along the trail. Sugars are high in calories, but they do not provide us with usable energy. Nor do they encourage recuperation from strenuous exercise, cleanse our muscles of their byproducts, help repair micro-damaged muscle fibers, or help strengthen our muscles and increase their stamina. Sugars are also quite useless at promoting mental acuity and encouraging what is perhaps the journey's most vital ingredient—a positive mental attitude.

Jenny and I ate a fair amount of candy during our first thru-hike, in an attempt to bolster energy. But rather than energize us, the candy sapped our energy. Most people are familiar with the "sugar-high, sugar-low" syndrome caused by the pancreas over-reacting and secreting an over-abundance of insulin. During our last few mega-hikes we avoided candy bars altogether, and with very positive results.

If our journeys degenerate into battles, in terms of lost energy and mental buoyancy, then I think those battles are usually won or lost in the grocery stores, rather than on the trails. And the good news is that the more we avoid these products, the easier they become to resist.

Coffee

During our first PCT hike, my wristwatch alarm sounded at 5:30 am. Jenny would reach out and ignite the stove, and set on the coffee pot. We would rise, pack our gear, then hastily chug two cups of café-campo (camp coffee) before shouldering our packs and setting off, usually by 6:15.

I had been drinking coffee all my adult life—ostensibly to stimulate alertness. In reality, I was addicted to the caffeine, as indicated by the low-level headaches I experienced for several months after I stopped drinking coffee. Jenny stopped also, and before long we both began to notice an increase in mental acuity. Free of the daily drug infusions, we found that we ate better, slept better, and were generally in better physical shape. Aside from these physical benefits, we quit drinking coffee for a deeper reason. The more we connected with the natural world, the less we liked the idea of being controlled by a substance.

During our second PCT hike, the alarm sounded at 4:40 am. We would rise, pack our gear, and set off typically by 5:00. Whereas breaking camp used to take us 45 minutes, now released of the coffee rites we were afoot in 20 minutes.

But by drinking the morning's coffee, weren't we helping to rehydrate ourselves? Absolutely not. Coffee is a diuretic. By definition, a diuretic is a substance that increases the flow of urine. We drink the coffee brown, our kidneys filter out the particulates and solvents, and it comes out clear. Then our bodies begin the work of flushing the excretory organs, with water stolen from the cells. The result is a net loss in fluid, and a net loss in energy. By refraining from the morning coffee, not only were we able to maintain an improved fluid balance, but we also gained an extra 25 minutes every day. We used that time for hiking, but we could have used it for sleeping, journal writing, or simply relaxing and enjoying our surroundings. The fact is, boiling the water, brewing the (expensive) coffee grounds, letting the concoction steep and cool, and then drinking the brew like addicts was wasteful of both time and stove fuel. For us, it was a pointless morning ritual that had little to do with enjoyment. Rather, we drank the coffee for the effects of its caffeine. And this artificial high added nothing to our wilderness experience.

Favorable substitutes

We still enjoy coffee-like beverages at some of our evening camps, and at home. My personal favorite is Cafix, which is a caffeine-free grain and fig beverage. Other coffee substitutes include Inka, Pero, Roma, etc. In moderation these are not diuretic.

Alcohol

The last thing hikers need are beverages that dehydrate them. Alcohol, like coffee, is a powerful diuretic. This is why responding to thirst by opening a can of beer is a poor idea. Just a few beers will severely dehydrate the body and greatly reduce energy levels in the process. In fact, a hangover is mainly the result of plunging so rapidly and acutely into dehydration. Hikers who do enjoy drinking alcohol socially from time to time would therefore be wise to drink large quantities of water along with the alcohol. The same holds true for coffee and the "energy" sports drinks. To help stay hydrated, drink lots of water with these beverages. But for the best possible results, drink only the water.

Unwrapping the freeze-dried fallacy

Freeze-dried foods are generally light in weight, convenient, appealing, tasty, and readily available in backpacking stores and catalogs. So of course they are popular with many backpackers, despite the counter-ecological packaging. Freeze-dried food is also very expensive because it requires large-scale equipment in its manufacture. This equipment freezes the food to minus 50° F., applies a vacuum, quickly heats the food to 120° to promote sublimation, and then removes the vapor with low-temperature condenser plates.

During my first summer as a professional wilderness instructor I subsisted on a diet of mainly freeze-dried meals, as supplied by the company. During my second year I began to suspect that these were not providing the needed nutrition, so I experimented with more nutritious foods from the supermarket. My job as an instructor entailed backpacking almost continuously throughout the summer, and I found that despite the heavier load of fresh food, my energy levels and hiking enjoyment skyrocketed.

I suspect that those who eat freeze-dried foods are feeding, instead, on the reserves stored in the cells of their own bodies. And of course the excitotoxins these foods contain trick our brains into interpreting the products as tasty and satisfying. On a label from a popular brand of freeze-dried Chicken a la King, for example, I counted eight different excitotoxins.

Packweight and food weight

The "foods" we have looked at thus far are all relatively light in weight, and this partly accounts for their popularity. And granted, thus far in the book we have gone to great lengths to reduce packweight. So it would seem logical to concentrate on lightweight food when planning our trail menus. But in fact this would be a serious mistake.

I think of packweight in terms of the total load, *minus* the food and water. This may seem incongruous, considering that we have to carry it all. But I make this distinction for two important reasons. First, the food and water are consumable. Heading out from a trailhead or resupply, we might carry about 2½ pounds of food for each day. Along the way we eat most of the food. But as the food weight drops from, say, a dozen pounds to nearly zero, our baseline packweight—the equipment and clothing— remains more or less constant. Our supply of water varies considerably throughout the day; so like the food, its weight is outside the baseline. This is one reason for discounting the weight of food and water, but the second reason is the more important one. Even though reducing our packweight is extremely beneficial, reducing our food weight is entirely counterproductive. We must never scrimp on quality food. Ultralight (and nutritionally empty) meals are about as useless to a hiker as a pogo stick would be to an astronaut. Neither provides enough usable energy to get them where they want to go.

Continuing with the analogy, rocket fuel is incredibly heavy, but it is also packed with enough energy to propel both it and the spacecraft sky- ward. Take it from me: rocket engineers work only with those fuels ca- pable of delivering the payload the highest and farthest, in the most prac- tical manner. And we hikers should do the same.

When we consider our hiking inventory, we must remember that the weight of each item, while a major concern, is less important than the item's function. In my experience, most lightweight "foods" are not func- tional.

I remember my first week-long climbing trip into an area of sand- stone towers in the deserts of Utah. This was in the days of heavy steel pitons, and my pack was loaded with about 70 pounds of these and other types of hardware. My partner and I could not lighten our gear, so we decided to lighten our food. For one continuous week we ate packaged instant oatmeal. During the first few days all went well, but soon the rigors of climbing sapped what little energy the oatmeal could impart. Nearing the trip's end, we were reduced to lying listlessly in our tents. We failed to climb our chosen tower for want of strength; in fact we probably could have done better by fasting. And that was my last experi- ence with lightweight instant oatmeal.

Traditional backpackers face a similar dilemma. Their packs are so heavy that they can hardly afford the additional weight of heavier food. But with lighter-weight gear and therefore with a lighter baseline packweight, we *can* afford to load up with heavier, more nutritious foods— like fresh vegetables and fruits, and whole grain meals to name just a few. These will deliver us to our distant objective in much better condition—

physically and mentally. They will reduce our need for layover time. And because they can empower us to the next resupply point in fewer days, if we are distance-hiking, then we will not need to carry as many days' supply.

Burning the reserves

During a weekend of strenuous activity, backpackers can gormandize on nutritionally "empty" foods without noticing too many ill effects. Essentially they are feeding instead on the reserves stored in the cells of their own bodies. But there comes a point on the longer journey when the exertion begins to deplete these reserves. The most noticeable result is a profound sense of fatigue. And the person may try to compensate with junk food binges at the stores en route.

During the longer hike, as the person's reserves start bottoming out, the brain senses that survival is starting to become at risk. Subconsciously it knows what it needs—better food. And it knows where to get it—back home where it has always gotten it. The subconscious mind starts prompting us to return home. It does this by suggesting various excuses, ironically that usually have nothing to do with the real problem, which is the nutritional deficit. Instead, some external aspect becomes a scapegoat, and grows more intolerable. The trail seems horribly full of rocks and roots, and the hills impossibly steep. Blisters might seem to be destroying the feet. The trail's propensity to wander might become more outrageous with the passing of every mile. The sun might be too hot, or the rain too drenching. Or perhaps we develop a rekindled passion for a former hobby, such as collecting license plate numbers. These are mental ploys, contrived by a brain trying to direct the body to a supply of nutrients. The problem might seem enigmatic at the time, but the solution is very straightforward: eating quality foods in quantity.

Nutritious foods suitable for hiking

Fresh, wholesome foods are the most capable of sustaining life at the highest levels. Among these are fresh vegetables, fruits, whole grains, legumes, seeds, nuts, meat, fish, eggs, cheese, and much more. Fresh and perishable food will spoil if kept too long in our packs, although in many cases not as quickly as one might think. But since we all have different diet preferences, what follows are my offerings. And they are only that— suggestions to help you make your own informed and intelligent choices in regards to wholesome foods.

Fresh fruits and vegetables

In terms of nutrition, fresh fruits and vegetables are worth every ounce in the backpack. At various times Jenny and I have carried potatoes, carrots, onions, celery, corn on the cob, tomatoes, lettuce, cucumbers, cabbage, apples, oranges, limes, lemons, grapefruit, nectarines, bananas and plums. On shorter hikes we bring these fresh foods from home, and on longer hikes, in places where stores are available, we buy whatever fresh fruits and vegetables they offer. Even slightly wilted, these are well worth their weight in terms of the restorative effects and sense of well being they provide. We can boil the vegetables alone or in a stew, but they are even more nutritious when eaten raw. Corn on the cob is particularly so. If we load these foods carefully in our pack, cushioned and well insulated from the elements, they will keep for several days. Citrus fruit, apples, carrots, potatoes and cabbage are particularly long lasting.

Fresh potatoes

Potatoes are an important option for the hiker out for more than a day. Fresh potatoes are sometimes available in stores along the way. Prior to departing on a long hike, Jenny and I place a couple of potatoes in each resupply parcel going to a place where there is no grocery store. Previously, at the supermarket we select the potatoes individually for robustness, making sure they are blemish free. Usually they arrive at the resupply stations, months later, in fine condition. Some will have budded, and these buds we cut off because they are said to be toxic. Inside the resupply box we store the potatoes loose, rather than in plastic bags which restrict ventilation and can accelerate spoiling. Once, as an experiment we vacuum-sealed a few potatoes in an attempt to preserve their freshness. When we collected the resupply box months later, we found that the potatoes had burst their bags, and that a foul liquid had ruined everything. And while this experience was less than pleasant, it does illustrate that real foods—unlike nutritionally plundered substances—are alive. They grow, mature, and yes—eventually die.

To cook potatoes while on the trail, simply dice and boil them. Otherwise, eat them raw. "New potatoes" taste the best this way. These are not a separate variety, but are simply harvested early. They are small, usually reddish in color, and have thin skins.

Fresh meat and dairy products

The meat eaters among us can sometimes buy fresh or frozen meats in the trail town stores. A few chunks of stew meat, or a small boneless steak, is easily cut into bite-sized pieces and boiled. Keep the boiling very brief to avoid destroying the vitamins. Cook only until the pieces are brown on the outside. Consider drinking the broth as well, as it is full of vitamins and makes a satisfying hot beverage. Of course if you are a bona-fide meat eater and a cook-fire enthusiast, (see the Campfire and Cook-fire chapter) the cooking possibilities become more varied and interesting. Save the BBQs for outside of bear country though. Another meat option is to make jerky on a food dehydrator at home. Beware of commercially processed meats and their nitrates and nitrites, and don't eat spoiled meat, due to the danger of botulism.

One issue for consideration by those of us who eat meat and dairy products is the questionable, and often atrocious methods used in the meat and dairy industry, using growth hormones, assorted chemicals, and types of feed too revolting to mention. Rather than spell out the sorry details, let me recommend a very readable and extremely informative book: *Mad Cowboy, Plain Truth From the Cattle Rancher Who Won't Eat Meat* by Howard F. Lyman (Bibliography).

Way-of-Life grains

Granola has long been a standard breakfast with backpackers. And while it makes a great stomach filler, it is decidedly lacking in nutrition because here again the grains are minus their germ and bran. The commercial varieties are also highly processed, and they contain heavy doses of sugars, stabilizers, preservatives and excitotoxins.

Fortunately for the human race, and especially for hikers, there is still some real food out there. Organic, whole-kernel grain is one of the best. In the future, new technologies may degrade even these with "improvements" such as bio-genetic engineering (Frankenstein food) and Terminator technology. But for now, whole-kernel grains are still real food.

While preparing for our first thru-hike, Jenny and I experimented with different grain mixes and eventually came up with a grain porridge that we call "Way-of-Life." This grain breakfast proved so successful that we continue to eat it today, both in the wilds and at home. It has indeed become our way of life.

Our basic Way-of-Life mixture contains equal portions of barley, oats, millet and corn. We are careful to buy organically grown grains, available in most health foods stores. We also buy whole grains that are in their sproutable condition—meaning that they are "alive" and waiting for the right conditions to germinate. You can check whether a certain batch of grains is sproutable by simply sprouting a small handful of them. Soak them in water overnight, drain them, and place on a dampened paper or cotton towel. Roll the towel up and set it aside. Re-moisten the towel once or twice a day. In two or three days you should see the initial stages of growth, indicating that the grains are indeed sproutable. This method will work with any type of grain, pea or bean. And by the way, after they have germinated they are even more nutritious. If the grains fail to sprout, they may still be alright to eat, but not as nutritious.

Most types of processing kill the grains and reduce their long-term nutritional value. But to speed cooking time and reduce fuel consumption, Jenny and I crack the grains using a hand-operated grain mill. This reduces long term food value, granted, but we are still way ahead of the packaged mixes whose ingredients were processed many months, even years ago, and which contain additives of unknown description. With hand-milling, the idea is to split each kernel into only a few pieces. A blender or poor quality hand mill will grind some of the grains to powder, while leaving the others nearly intact. Most motor-driven grinders impart too much heat, which affects the product's nutrition and shelf life.

To our basic Way-of-Life mixture we often add smaller amounts of other cracked grains, such as triticale (trit-i-KAY-lee), rye, or brown rice. Then we add various enlivening ingredients, which might include sunflower seeds, sesame seeds, chopped almonds, pecans, cinnamon, or nutmeg. To cook two large, hungry-hiker servings, we mix two to three cups of water with one cup of the grain mixture. After bringing to a boil, we reduce the heat and simmer for fifteen minutes—or ten minutes if we had pre-soaked the grains. To pre-soak, we simply let the grains sit in cold water overnight. In terms of cooking times, we find that under-cooked is better than overcooked, that slightly chewy is preferable to glutinous.

Our usual sweeteners of choice are powdered milk and a handful of raisins, or home-dried fruits such as apple, pear, peach, apricot, pineapple or papaya. And when on the trail we add wild berries where available, or sometimes honey or jam. We wait until the grains have cooked before adding these sweeteners, to prevent scorching the bottom of the cookpot.

Pre-soaking the breakfast grains is one way to shorten the morning's routine. But instead of this, Jenny and I often cook them the evening prior, immediately after eating dinner. Leaving the cooked grains in the pot, we place them carefully in one of our packs, then carry them for the remaining hours until making camp. The next morning we may hike with them for a few hours, then stop and eat a cold grain breakfast. These grain meals also make good lunches and dinners. They are very nutritious, and they are long-lasting and inexpensive.

Well-stocked natural food stores offer many other grains, including kamut, spelt, amaranth (which grows as a weed in many back yards), sorghum, buckwheat and quinoa. These are usually more expensive than the basic oats, barley, and millet, but they add variety. Which grains are best is entirely a matter of preference. If they will sprout, then they are nutritious. The fastest cooking whole grains are millet and quinoa: three minutes after the water reaches a boil will suffice, with an additional five minutes off the stove while covered with a lid.

Instant oatmeal is said to be about as nutritious as the box it comes in. Based on my experiences in the desert I think that is a bit of an exaggeration, but why mess with it when home-milled corn meal mush cooks just as quickly. Most store-bought corn meal is de-germed. Home-grinding with whole corn is about the only way to know that your grains are complete. To cook, simply add to cold water and stir occasionally as the water comes to a boil. When it starts to boil, remove from the heat, place the lid on the pot to retain the heat, and allow to cool a little. Add powdered milk to help round out the amino acids, and possibly other sweetener as you prefer. Corn gruel makes an extremely nutritious and very satisfying meal.

Nuts and seeds

Raw nuts and seeds are excellent foods. One must be a bit careful with them, since their natural oils can turn rancid after many months, often becoming bitter and in some cases possibly carcinogenic. Make sure to buy them fresh, and use them before they begin to expire. The most common are sunflower, sesame, pumpkin, flax, almond, cashew, filbert or hazelnut, pine nut, walnut, pecan and peanut (which is actually a legume). Buy nuts and seeds raw, rather than roasted, salted, sweetened or otherwise processed. And beware of the commercially packaged nuts containing the usual plethora of chemicals.

Grain and legume dinners

Cracked grains also make excellent dinners, either by themselves or in combination with cracked peas, beans or lentils. The amino acids found in legumes will largely make up for those lacking in the grains.

Some of the more common dry legumes are black beans, black-eyed peas, chickpeas (garbanzos), great northern beans, kidney beans, lentils, lima beans, mung beans, navy beans, pinto beans, soybeans, split peas and whole peas. The legumes suitable for backpacking are those that cook the quickest and that the hiker likes best. Like grains, they can also be prepared whole, they simply require more cooking time.

Grain mills

Jenny and I grind our grains and legumes by hand, and have for many years. This provides us with a bit of exercise, and it ensures that our grain meals and baked goods are fresh and wholesome. For the first several years we used an inexpensive grinder. It was not very well built, but it did allow us to experiment with grinding our own grains. It also confirmed the benefits of freshly cracked or milled grains, as opposed to the nutritionally bankrupt flours found on the supermarket shelves. Looking to the future we invested in a quality hand mill, and this has served us extremely well. We mounted it on a kitchen counter for ready access, and use it every few days. This particular grinder is the Country Living Grain Mill, made by Country Living Products (360-652-0671). This mill cracks whole grains easily and consistently, and it makes beautiful flour. Other sources for grain mills include: Lehman's Hardware (330-857-5757), www.lehmans.com and New Pioneer Hardware (513-471-9674), www.new-pioneer.com.

Corn pasta

While training for our first long trek, we sampled a variety of processed foods and evaluated the resulting energy boost, if any. Every second day we slogged up the snowbound flanks of Pikes Peak in Colorado, testing our energy levels and stamina in relation to the types of food we were eating. One day we found ourselves covering the miles far more easily and buoyantly, and we thought back to our previous dinner—corn spaghetti. This was the first time we had tried this type of food, and we thought the energy boost was coincidental. However, the more we experimented with pasta made from corn on subsequent hikes, the more we began to realize that its energy boost was real.

During our first thru-hike we ate corn spaghetti twice a week. This proved so successful that on our second journey we ate it two out of three dinners. Not once did it fail to provide the energy we needed, and never did we tire of eating it. Had we included more in our resupply parcels we would have eaten that. In fact, during the latter stages of that hike we were actually rationing our supply, eating the corn spaghetti only in the late afternoons when we needed major energy boosts for the remaining hours of hiking.

During our third long trek we again ate corn spaghetti two out of three dinners. On our fourth thru-hike (the AT) we went without it. As an experiment in saving weight, we carried no stove, opting to buy no-cook foods at stores along the way. But many of these stores were small and sold only snack items, so this plan did not work well. Then on our fifth summer-long trek we went back to corn spaghetti and ate it for almost every dinner.

The reason corn pasta provided such excellent energy and nutrition was that it contained the entire grain. The manufacturers were fairly small-time operations back then, and they were apparently concerned with the nutritional quality of their products. Over the years they have been bought out by large conglomerates who operate more on economics. Now, all the commercial corn pasta that I know of is produced using refined corn flour, which of course lacks the germ. It is essentially the corn version of processed wheat flour. Alas, there go most of the nutrients. Such is the price of so-called "progress."

Today, when Jenny and I journey afoot we prepare a daily portion of Way-of-Life type grain breakfasts, and a daily evening meal based on whole corn, supplemented with legumes to complete the protein. We grind these ourselves from sproutable, organically grown kernels.

Other grain pastas are available commercially, including whole wheat and rice, as well as pastas with vegetable additives. But one should be on the alert for the deceptive practice of disguising plain old durum semolina (white flour) with vegetable colorings and flavorings.

Something I have not tried but think might work as well as today's corn pasta is a product by Ancient Harvest called Quinoa Pasta. This is actually corn pasta with quinoa added. It comes in spaghetti and elbows, and like corn pasta it is available at most health-foods stores.

"Whole wheat" pasta

The food industry is so prone to deception that it leaves me very skeptical of any company claiming to include the bran and germ of every grain in its products. I say "every grain" because of the common and misleading practice of adding a fractional amount of germ and calling the entire product "whole grain," on the basis that it contains some whole grain. One alternative to commercial products is of course to make your own pasta from sproutable grains that you grind yourself. If you find a company that claims to produce whole-wheat pasta, you might telephone them and ask whether they mill their own grains, and if not, then how do they know the flour they purchase and use contains the germ of every grain. If their answers bolster your confidence in their products, then venture cautiously ahead. Keep in mind, too, that manufacturing procedures are subject to change without notice, as economics become more of a controlling factor.

Powdered milk

Powdered *skim* milk is best in warm climes, and powdered *whole* milk in colder ones, where the extra fat content will help keep a person warm. Either way, this staple contains protein and other nutrients, it has a long shelf life, it is light in weight, and it tastes pretty good. Use it to enrich your grain meals and to fortify hot and cold drinks. Don't bother with the directions for reconstituting as printed on the package; just pour the powder into the meal or drink to suit. See *Mad Cowboy* (Bibliography) for various nutritional caveats regarding today's dairy products.

Powdered potatoes

Powdered potatoes are not nearly as nutritious as fresh ones, but they are one of the better dehydrated foods commercially available. They are inexpensive, lightweight, and easy to prepare. Before buying a particular brand, examine its list of ingredients for chemical content. This is especially important when buying in larger quantities for a long journey. Also note that some brands of powdered potatoes are hopelessly bland and unappetizing, while others are quite good. So buy a single package first and sample it at home.

Whichever brand of instant potatoes you choose, ignore the directions on the box. You can eat them cold by simply mixing the product in cold water, and stirring in some powdered milk if you like. Mix them very watery and let them stand a few minutes to thicken, otherwise they will thicken in your throat and stomach, sapping the moisture from you and possibly causing discomfort. As with all dehydrated foods, be sure to drink plenty of water along with them. If you prefer to eat the mashed potatoes warm, simply heat the water first—the potatoes do not need to be cooked. Add cheese or other seasoning. Or add the dry potato flakes to soups and stews.

Instant refried beans

These are quite good, on par with instant potatoes. For a complete protein meal, eat them in combination with potatoes, rice, or other grains, or at least with powdered milk. Instant refried beans are available commercially, although we need to be wary of any taste enhancers. I prefer making my own, by dehydrating cooked pinto beans.

Home-made snack bars

Most commercial granola bars and "energy bars" are packed with sugars and excitotoxins. But you can make your own snack bars, and ensure that they contain a minimum of chemicals and sugars. Look in various cookbooks for recipes of "cookie bars." Also you could examine the list of ingredients on the wrappers of some commercial snack bars, purchase those ingredients at health food stores, mix them imaginatively, and bake. The results are nothing like the commercial products because you can experiment with different ingredients and proportions. I think Jenny's home-made productions are far superior to the store-bought types, mainly because we know what is in them. I encourage you to experiment with your own ideas. If you want to bolster the protein content, add powdered milk. And if you want to equal the synthesized vitamin and mineral content of the commercial techno-wonder-bars, take a multi-vitamin pill every few days.

Snack bars do not have to be sweet; you can make them more like a heavy bread, using freshly milled whole grain flours. Some cookbooks have recipes for hard tack, trail bread, and pemmican. These are excellent alternatives to the sugary cookie bars.

GORP

I suspect that gorp (Good Ol' Raisins and Peanuts, also known as "trail mix") and all its variations will be around as long as hikers themselves. I have certainly eaten my share of it, and during our first few long distance hikes Jenny and I always carried a bag in our packs. In the preparatory stages of those hikes we mixed various ingredients into bags—two cups of gorp per person, per day—and loaded these into our resupply boxes. Besides the raisins and peanuts we included dried fruit, chopped dates, shredded coconut, sunflower seeds, almonds, cashews, walnuts, and sometimes small candies. For even more variety we added chips, snack-type crackers, and dry breakfast cereals made from corn.

The reason we paid such attention to variety was to make it more appealing. We tried making it an art form. We tried making it colorful to look at and fun to eat. We avoided items laden with chemicals. But no matter how varied with ingredients, half way through the hikes we found ourselves picking through the bags, ("high-grading") and eating only the most interesting items. Today we prefer small bags of dried fruit with seeds and nuts. We seem to have come full circle, back to the basics.

In addition to the most basic gorp mixture we snack on fresh or dried fruits and vegetables, home-made snack bars, cheese, Ak-Mak® crackers, etc. Before setting out for the day we load the snacks near the top of our backpacks where they are more accessible.

Hot drinks

We should always drink plenty of pure water for keeping ourselves well hydrated—as opposed to sodas or flavored drink mixes, coffee and beer. Still, a hot beverage can be a satisfying addition, especially on a blustery day. A hot "cuppa" at day's end can provide a welcome ambiance for the journal writing. Possibilities include powdered milk, Cafix (the caffeine-free coffee substitute), hot cocoa and herbal tea.

Home-dehydrated foods

The process of dehydrating foods reduces their weight and bulk, and it gives them a much longer storage life. Unfortunately, it also destroys a high percentage of their vitamins and minerals. Jenny and I ate a considerable quantity of dehydrated foods during our earlier hikes, and found that they provided very little energy, certainly far less than their fresh counterparts. But we still think that home-dehydrated foods are an acceptable way of *augmenting* one's supply of hiking victuals.

Food dehydrating is a simple matter of extracting most of the moisture. This requires a source of low heat to accelerate evaporation, and plenty of ventilation to carry the moisture away. The optimum temperature is around 100°F, but this can vary considerably. As the food loses moisture, it also decreases in weight and bulk. For example, a one pound bag of frozen corn (3 cups) dehydrates to 4½ ounces (1 cup).

For meat eaters, beef jerky is another possibility. Pre-soaked jerky makes an interesting addition to the grain and legume meals. Store-bought jerky is expensive and usually loaded with nitrates, nitrites and MSG, but making your own is easy. Buy lean steak, not necessarily an expensive cut, and slice it in ¼-inch wide strips, across the grain. Marinate the slices in seasonings of your preference. When the strips of meat are well coated, spread them on the food dryer rack.

Fruit leathers are also easy to make. Place the fruit in a blender and pulverize them to a thick paste. Pour the resulting mash onto a drying rack lined with plastic wrap, and place the rack in the food dryer. Use the same technique for savory sauces like spaghetti sauce. Jenny takes the process a step further by letting the sauce dry into hard "chips" and then grinding the chips into a powder in a spice mill. This powder is compact and quick to rehydrate.

You can also dehydrate cooked meats such as ground beef or turkey. And you can dehydrate fruits and vegetables that are fresh, canned, or frozen. In fact you can dehydrate entire meals. Chili works particularly well. Simply prepare it as you normally would, then spread it out on the plastic-coated drying rack. On the trail, rehydrate it by adding water and allowing it to stand for three or four hours. Leave plenty of space for expansion; the re-hydrating food approximately doubles in volume. While the food is re-hydrating, you could place it in your pack, inside a resealable plastic bag or lidded plastic bowl, and safe within your cookpot. At dinnertime, cook the meal for ten or fifteen minutes, or simply eat it cold.

The food dryer

While sailing the world's oceans, Jenny and I often trolled a fishing lure. We lacked refrigeration, so whenever we caught a fish larger than what we could eat right away, we sliced the remaining meat and placed it on the decks, under the tropical sun to dry. After a day or two we had delicious fish chips. These were our first experiments in drying food.

Here at home we use a simple rack that Jenny built of wooden 1x2s. The rack stands about five feet tall, and supports three trays. The trays are window screens, the frames of which are sold in hardware stores as packaged kits with directions for assembly. The fiberglass screen is usually sold separately and is easily cut to size using scissors. Jenny assembled the window screen trays first, then built the 1x2 structure to fit them.

During the warm months we set the rack outside, covered with mosquito netting. The hot sun dehydrates the food very nicely. In the winter we use the drying rack indoors, near our wood stove.

An excellent book on food dehydrating, *Dry It—You'll Like It!* (Bibliography) also gives plans for building your own dehydrator. Or check at your local library for other books on the subject. If you don't care to build your own, you can buy food dryers commercially. The Lehman's catalog, mentioned earlier, offers several models.

Home packaging

For our first thru-hike, Jenny and I packaged our fresh-milled grain and legume meals using a vacuum sealing machine. This extracted most of the air from the plastic bags, and sealed them closed. The resulting packages were hard like blocks of wood, such was the pressure of the vacuum. Our intent was to preserve the food's freshness. During shipment, however, about 80% of the packages lost their vacuum. This happened as the packages jostled against one another, and the rough contents punctured the plastic bags like needles.

Preparing for our second thru-hike, we again used the vacuum sealer— but with much less vacuum pressure. In addition we used a simple non-vacuum sealing machine, and this also worked well. What packaged foods we did not eat on the trail we sent home for consumption during the winter months.

However, while out on the trails we experienced a different kind of problem with the packaging. The weight and bulk of the plastic bags were not so noticeable when the bags were full, but as we emptied them we found it hard to ignore the size and weight of our accumulating trash. This we had to carry to the next resupply point, from where we sent the reusable plastic bags home for later use. Clearly, we needed to minimize our food packaging materials. So we started packing the individual meals in paper, since this we could burn when empty. Specifically, we placed the contents of a grain, legume, or corn pasta meal on a sheet of brown paper, such as that cut from a grocery sack. We rolled and folded the paper to envelop the contents, and taped it closed. Then we identified the contents in writing on the package. This system is still our preferred method today.

Plastic bags with zip tops are neither waterproof nor moisture-proof. Heat-sealed bags are far better, and you can make them quite small to contain seasonings, etc. When cutting one open the first time, cut only a corner off, diagonally. To reseal, fold the corner down and secure it with a small bit of adhesive tape.

————————

The task of preparing quality, wholesome food for a long hiking trip is a major one, yet like the trek itself, the easiest approach is to take things one step at a time. Having considered this chapter, you might begin experimenting with some of these ideas at home, well in advance of your outing. Read other books on nutrition, peruse cookbooks for ideas, cook a number of trial meals at home and test various ingredients. Remember too, that your tastes may change once you have been on the trail a few weeks, as your needs for metabolic fuel begin to spiral.

In addition to the books mentioned in this chapter, there are many others that might be of help in your meal planning. One of my favorites is *Traditional Foods are your Best Medicine*, by Ronald F. Schmid (Bibliography). Keep in mind that no one has all the answers. Each of us must draw our own conclusions about what foods to eat, and what to avoid. However, for best results, keep the nutritional value of your foods paramount.

Water

Walking Waterbags

Seen from space, our blue planet reveals its surface to be mostly water, rather than the land we live on. Water is the sustainer of life, and although we cannot live in it, this precious fluid most certainly lives in us. Our blood is 90% water, and is about the same salinity as seawater. Our brains are 75% water. Our bodies are 70% water. Basically, we are walking waterbags.

These levels of hydration are vital to our health and well being. Yet we lose a great deal of water as we hike along the trail. Every time we exhale we lose moisture, since our expelled breath is always 100% saturated. We lose water through urination, of course. Moisture evaporates from our skin continually, in the form of insensible perspiration. And we can exude tremendous amounts through sweat.

The effects of dehydration

Water lubricates the joints in our hips, knees and ankles—in much the same way that oil lubricates machinery. Dehydration reduces this lubricating effect, stiffening our joints and making them more susceptible to injury. Dehydration actually plays a key role in most hiking-related stress injuries. Moreover, as the body loses water, the blood thickens and decreases in volume, becoming more sluggish. This raises blood pressure and slows circulation. As such, it lowers the delivery rate of fuel and oxygen to the muscles. And it retards the extraction of the by-products of metabolism from the muscles. This makes us feel sluggish ourselves, sapped of energy. The dehydrating blood and restricted circulation also slows the brain's functions, impeding our mental processes and destabilizing our emotions. This can work to take the fun right out of the wilderness experience.

We can avoid these negative repercussions simply by drinking plenty of water.

Water is the best re-hydrator

Most people drink a variety of beverages, but very little pure water. As such, they are dehydrated—often chronically and without realizing it. Sodas, sports drinks, flavoring crystals and so forth add little or nothing to the body's fluid balance. In fact, these drinks can actually be dehydrating, due to the processed sugars and chemical solutes they contain. The body cannot use these and attempts to remove them by flushing them out, using water—"borrowed" from the body's own cells. For all practical purposes, H_2O is the only fluid capable of keeping us adequately hydrated.

But what about sports drinks that supposedly replace lost electrolytes—aren't they sometimes beneficial? In reality those drinks are little more than glorified soda pop. They are loaded with sugar in various forms, and they contain all sorts of added chemicals. If you are exerting in very hot weather and sweating a great deal, your healthiest option is to drink large quantities of water. The minerals and electrolytes you can get in abundance from uncooked fruit and vegetables.

Our sweat is salty, so doesn't that mean we need to replace the salt? Actually, the idea that we need salt is a myth. Salt is sodium chloride, and it is a toxin. What our bodies need is organic sodium, again as found abundantly in uncooked fruits and vegetables. The salt in a person's sweat is a detox, meaning that it is being flushed as a toxin from the lymph surrounding the cells.

So skip the beverages and drink lots of water. And don't be a "sipper." Sipping water may wet the throat and satisfy the mental need to take a drink of water, but normally this is not enough. The best hydrating procedure, unless the water is near freezing, is to gulp it down in quantity.

The psychology of thirst

The sensation of thirst is a poor indicator of when to drink water. By the time we feel thirsty we are already dehydrated. And while a few sips of cold water will usually satisfy thirst, such a small amount is not nearly enough to rehydrate the body. So not only does thirst come too late, but it shuts off too soon. Also, when our water bottles are empty, thirst can be a great tormentor, and the agony only worsens when we allow our minds to dwell on incessant thoughts of the cold drinks we do not have. All this is to suggest that thirst is mainly a psychological effect. It is a tool for helping us stay properly hydrated, but like any tool it has its limitations. So rather than rely on thirst to tell us when to drink water, we are better off tuning in to our body's physical signals.

Signs of deepening dehydration

The surest way to know how well hydrated we are is by remaining aware of our water consumption. For example, suppose that we have been hiking for five hours and have taken only a few small sips of water. Based on this information alone, we know that our body is dehydrated.

Let's look at some of the effects of dehydration, in their general order of occurrence.

- After that half a day's hiking with only a minimum of water, we will notice (if we are paying attention) a marked decrease in urinary output. This is a signal that something is amiss, but unfortunately—as far as the body is concerned—it is a signal that is easily ignored. Nevertheless, this stage of dehydration is common among hikers.

- The more hours spent hiking—without drinking enough water—the deeper the dehydration. Higher altitudes and higher ambient temperatures accelerate the effect. As the day wears on, and as the urinary output continues to decrease in volume, it also begins to darken in color. Although dark yellow urine is pretty obvious, it is still easily disregarded. From here on, though, the body will start signaling in ways that are not so easily ignored.

- Namely, the headache, which is often referred to—incorrectly—as "altitude headache." Show me someone in the backcountry with a headache, and I will show you someone who is severely dehydrated. The dehydration may not be the only problem, but often it is. Unfortunately, most people fail to associate this signal with the dehydration. So rather than correct the problem by drinking lots of water, they take a few pain killing tablets. At least with these they drink *some* water.

- Next comes the queasiness, most often the result of introducing pain killing medication into a severely dehydrated body.

- And of course the constipation. Meaning that the digestive tract has slowed nearly to a stop. When this happens, the person begins feeling seriously ill.

- As the dehydrated hiker continues disregarding these problems, his or her body becomes much more prone to stress injury. Initially this might be indicated by a budding pain, for example in the Achilles tendon, or in the back, or joints. All too often, though, the hiker shrugs it off as "part of the hike," and takes more pain relief tablets, which dulls the aches and pains but only masks the real problem. If the person carries on, and allows the dehydration to continue its spiraling descent, he or she may soon be courting a bona fide injury, perhaps in the knee or spinal disks—of course, calling it "accidental." The fact is, the severely dehydrated body is an "accident waiting to happen."

Any of these maladies make the trip less fun, and thoughts of returning home more tempting. And any subsequent outings, with equally negative results, only reinforce the notion that hiking and camping are not very enjoyable. All for lack of sufficient water intake.

Chronic dehydration plays a key part in many more ailments. An excellent book discussing all this is *Your Body's Many Cries For Water*, by F. Batmanghelidj, M.D. The book's subtitle is "You are not sick, you are thirsty!; Don't treat thirst with medications." In particular, if you know anyone who suffers back pain, neck pain, headache, migraine, anginal pain, high blood pressure, hypertension, high blood cholesterol, asthma, allergies, some types of diabetes, dyspeptic pain, colitis pain, false appendicitis pain, rheumatoid arthritis pain, stress and depression—hand them a copy of the "Batman" book.

One quart per hour

Once deep dehydration sets in, it takes two or three days—not just minutes or hours—of drinking water voluminously to recover. So the best tactic is to consume generous amounts of water throughout the day. As a general rule, drink a quart of water during each hour's hiking, and much more in hot weather.

When hiking longer distances between water sources, do not let the extra weight of the water discourage you from carrying a decent supply. At the same time, it makes little sense to be a water hoarder—carrying it for purposes of security—or to simply ignore the need to stop and drink on a regular basis. Why arrive at a water source with a quart or more still in the bottles? At two pounds per quart, this is wasted effort. The best idea is to carry only enough to meet your needs, such that you arrive at the next source well hydrated, but with bottles empty. With a proper map or guide book in hand, this is generally not difficult to plan.

Shortcomings of "purification"

According to conventional backpacking wisdom, giardia contaminates all wilderness water, and we hikers and campers need to purify every drop that we drink, as well as what we use for cooking and brushing teeth. You can read this in hundreds of magazine articles and books. Jenny and I followed this rule faithfully during our first four mega-hikes. And I was sick with giardia-type symptoms many times.

Obviously, something was wrong. If we were being meticulous about filtering our water, then why was I not staying healthy? Jenny remained healthy, and she was drinking the same treated water as I. Apparently my immunities were lower than hers. But the fact remains that somehow I seemed to be contracting parasites despite the assiduous use of the water filter. The filter cartridges we were using were common, brand-name varieties, and we had no reason to suspect they were not working properly.

Clearly, the conventional wisdom was not working. So we abandoned it and tried a different approach. While training for our fifth thru-hike we drank directly from clean, natural sources, a few sips at first, then gradually increasing in quantity over the weeks and months. In this way we helped condition our bodies to the water's natural flora. Then during the actual journey we drank all our water straight from the springs, creeks, and sometimes the lakes—after carefully appraising each source. And for the first time in years I remained symptom-free; and Jenny stayed healthy also.

I am not suggesting that hikers abandon their water filters. But I do think that our experiments yielded information that can be useful to anyone venturing into the wilds.

I doubt whether my illness had anything to do with the filtration or lack thereof. Rather, it had to do with the nature of the water sources we were using. During the initial journeys we were collecting water from all but the worst sources, and treating it. In several cases that I can think of, I feel that this treatment—or any other available treatment—was incapable of making that water safe to drink. This is why, on that fifth trek, we collected water only from clean sources.

Based on these experiments and their successful outcome, the following are my recommendations: Learn to recognize pristine water, and treat it if you prefer. Learn to recognize water that could be microbially contaminated, if only mildly, and treat it thoroughly. And most importantly, learn to recognize water that is beyond treatment, despite any reasonable degree of clarity. Such water can be extremely virulent, and no water treatment system available to hikers is capable of making that water safe to drink. Do not filter, boil or add purification chemicals to this polluted water. Do not use it for cooking or bathing. In the next section we will learn how to recognize such highly contaminated water.

I also learned that our main sources of protozoa—such as giardia and cryptosporidia—are often our own bodies. Our intestines are breeding grounds for these protozoa, and when we fail to sterilize our hands after elimination, we then proceed to re-introduce the microscopic pathogens in vast numbers, for example when we eat a handful of gorp.

While I am not recommending that anyone forgo the water filter, Jenny and I did find that without it, we drank probably three times as much water as we would have, had we been filtering. Such was the greater ease and convenience of drinking directly from good water sources. And we feel that this extra fluid intake was of tremendous benefit. With no filter to carry, we saved some packweight. And being able to drink freely of the earth's life-force provided a refreshing connection with the natural world. But again this is not to suggest that we drank from any and all water sources. Each one we scrutinized carefully as to its safety. Those we considered unsafe, of which there were many, we bypassed.

Recognizing safe water

Judging the purity of water is a wilderness skill. The more knowledge you gain, and the more experience you build, the better your judgement will be. Later in the chapter we will look at specific types of contaminants and how to handle them, but let's start off with learning how to judge a water source. Remember that the goal here is not to enable you to drink "bush water" straight from the source. Rather, it is to show you how to recognize water that is beyond treatment; water that might look alright, but that can make you terribly sick regardless of how thoroughly you treat it.

The first step is to inspect the water visually.

Stagnation

If the water is stagnant, then processing it by normal means will probably do little to make it potable. This is because stagnant water collects anything and everything flowing into it, while allowing nothing to escape other than what can evaporate. So the concentrations build, year after year. Normally, a stagnant pool of water contains harmful chemicals, depending on what is leaching into it, and from where. It can also be laden with decaying plant matter and teeming with infective microorganisms. In times of need you might be tempted to filter and boil it, and consume in moderation. This is rarely a good idea.

Foam

The presence of mats and balls of foam on the water's surface almost always indicates heavy pollution, usually in the form of agricultural or industrial runoff. Ag runoff can consist of fertilizers, pesticides, herbicides, and livestock and feedlot wastes, none of which can be treated effectively by normal means. Tannic acid alone (discussed below) does not create foam.

Algae

In addition to foam, agricultural and community wastes like sewage, detergents, and decomposing rubbish often encourage heavy algae growth, although sometimes the pollutants are so toxic that even the algae cannot subsist on it. Pure spring water also harbors algae, but of a completely different type that feed on the organic minerals coming from deep within the earth. Normally spring water is safe to drink. And in many cases the algae growing in it is safe to eat.

If polluted water contains algae, and pure spring water does also, then what does the algae tell us about the water's quality? With experience you will learn to recognize the types that grow in polluted water, and the types found only in pure sources. They are quite different in appearance. However, it is more important to consider where the water is coming from. Is it flowing directly out of a high mountain spring? Or does it stem from an area of industry, agriculture or human population? Look at the overall picture, and avoid making assumptions about the water in front of you based on your immediate surroundings. For example, that nice-looking water flowing through a forest—might it possibly have passed through a region of pollution somewhere upstream? Consult your map for clues as to what may lie above or around your location.

Root beer coloration

In some backcountry areas the water often looks like diluted root beer. The coloring agent here is tannic acid, leached from organic growth, most often cedar. The tannic acid is not harmful in such weak concentrations, even when consumed in large amounts. But neither does it purify the water. The coloration tells you nothing about whether the water is potable or not.

Poison

In certain places, most notably in the arid Southwest, seeping springs can have a poisonous, high alkali content, caused by the water dissolving certain mineral salts, namely those of carbonate or hydroxide of alkali metals. The first clue is the presence of brown or dark orange algae, microscopic in size and visible only as a bottom coloring. Sometimes a calcium-like encrustation forms around the water's margins. Alkali water has an immediate and long-lasting bitter taste. It is quite obviously unsafe to drink. Even in low concentrations it leaves a disturbing aftertaste.

In a very few areas of the Southwest, certain small springs contain arsenic. This water will usually be crystal clear, and there will be no algae or plant life growing in it whatsoever. And unlike the cartoons showing bones lying about, the animals and birds know not to drink of it. Remember that good spring water almost always supports algae growth, normally green in color.

Mining operations are well known for polluting water sources in otherwise pristine areas. Gold mining is notorious for contaminating the ground water with strychnine. Strychnine pollution is often indicated by a telltale orange cast to the creekbeds.

Stock pollution

This is the one that causes the most sickness in hikers. Cattle and sheep, horses and mules are egregious polluters, and will very quickly contaminate springs, creeks of all sizes, and all but the larger lakes. After you have long been in the woods your sense of smell will probably become very acute, and you will be able to detect stock manure and urine in the water even in minute amounts. In creeks with cattle grazing upstream, even far upstream, you may find clumps of long, stringy algae, dark green in color. But here again your map is your best ally. The combination of a road and a meadow upstream suggests very strongly that there are cattle grazing in that meadow. Cattle-polluted water is extremely virulent, even in low concentrations.

Beaver Fever

The term "beaver fever" refers to the infection caused by giardia, and I suspect that the term was designed and widely publicized mainly with the intent of turning our attention from the main sources of pollution, which are human-related. How easy to make the beaver the scapegoat when cattle and sheep are grazing in the backcountry by the hundreds of thousands. We know that many other creatures of nature live and/or forage in the water. These include muskrat, mink, otter, birds, fish and amphibians, to name just a few. Most hikers can safely treat this water. Some of my most serious bouts with intestinal infection occurred in the alpine regions of Colorado, far above any beaver. Many times I would climb to the very crest of some rugged range and find the ground littered profusely in sheep manure. When the livestock go that high, there is no way to avoid their pollution.

Examining the water source

The preceding visual clues will help you identify contaminated water. Now let's examine various types of water sources.

Creeks

Mountain creeks, far removed from human activity, are usually suitable for treating. How do you know? You do not, for sure. But you can make an educated guess by examining where the creek is coming from. Looking at your map, do you find mines or human settlements nearby? Are there possibly cattle grazing upstream? If the water is flowing from remote, alpine regions, then the water is probably safe to treat by filtering or boiling.

The lower in elevation, the more contaminated the water, generally. So, before descending into a valley, fill your bottles. But if you are in low country to begin with, and if you come to a creek wending along a valley bottom, beware. Low drainages are well known for collecting all manner of pollutants from farm and industrial runoff, and from human effluent.

Lakes and ponds

When considering the potability of a lake or pond, check its inlet or outlet for the rate of flow. Also look at the lake bottom along the shoreline.

Clean rocks and sand normally indicate a good flow, while a thick, mucky bottom indicates stagnation. The less the flow, the greater the buildup of toxins and pathogens. And as with creeks, the quality of lake or pond water depends also on where that water is coming from.

Floating leaves, twigs and pollen are inevitable on lakes and ponds, and do not usually affect the water quality. When collecting water from such water, you might try wrapping a bandana over your bottle or cookpot to filter out the floaties.

Sacred springs

Not all spring water is pure. The terrain above the spring could be boggy, and that bog water could be percolating into the earth and resurfacing as the spring. This type of water could be contaminated. Or there could be a mine uphill of the spring. Another possible source of spring contamination often found in lower terrain is the polluted aquifer, from which the water is upwelling, artesian-style. This is becoming a more serious problem in the vicinity of toxic waste dumps and old landfills, which leach all sorts of dreadful pollutants.

However, most springs in the higher regions are pristine, and these are the hiker's finest sources of water. In fact, since discovering how beneficial they are to good health, I have come to think of them as sacred—as did many Native American peoples. I did not perceive them as such when relying on water filters. But now when I drink from a pure, flowing spring, I feel like I am making a closer connection with the earth and its life-force. And I think anyone could feel the same, whether they filter that water or not. I see pure spring water not merely as another commodity, but as a priceless gift from the Creator for the continuance of life. And I always give thanks for that, in appreciation of the water's true worth.

Seeps

A seep is a tiny spring that barely flows. And as with their more heartily flowing kin, we would use the same criteria for judging whether their water might be contaminated or not.

We would always tread carefully around the seeps, since they are easily damaged and rendered unusable by the next person or animal. Collecting water from a seep can be a delicate process. The idea is to channel the water while leaving the dirt or debris behind. For a collection gutter, use a non-toxic leaf, or a piece of paper, plastic bag, or aluminum

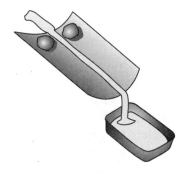

foil. Assuming the seep is flowing slightly, place the gutter in the trickle, then weight it down with a pair of stones at its uphill end. Dig a small hole downstream, at the place where water is dribbling off the gutter. Place a small container in the hole as a catchment. I once bought a single-serving of corn flakes in a café along the Appalachian Trail. The cereal came in a little plastic tub, which I have used ever since as a miniature basin for collecting water from shallow sources.

Where the ground is only moist, you could try scraping a depression. Use a stout stick, and scrape deeply enough so that the hole fills with a reasonable quantity of water, but not so deep that it would impact the landscape. Scoop the precious liquid very gently so as not to stir the sediment. Consider leaving the hole for the wildlife.

Water contaminants

The following is a list of possible contaminants to backcountry water.

- Chemical herbicides, pesticides, fertilizers, etc. These can enter the water through agricultural or industrial run-off. Many of these chemicals are in solution, and cannot be removed by boiling, adding purification chemicals, or filtration by ordinary devices.

- Coliform bacteria such as E. Coli. These bacteria are found naturally in the intestines, and are a necessary part of life. However, an outbreak of them can cause sickness. They stem from human and livestock waste, and can easily contaminate a water source.

- Viruses (ultra-microscopic infectious agents) and amoebas (parasitic protozoa). Very rare in the U.S. wilderness; they are easily disabled by boiling the water they inhabit.

- Cysts, including microscopic worms, parasites and protozoa. The biggest offenders are giardia and cryptosporidia, which can cause diarrhea and intestinal disorders (see below). Both are common in the wilds. When their environment becomes inhospitable, (such as in the presence of iodine, or the absence of water) these parasites can go into cystic form, like hard, round microscopic eggs. Once the cysts are ingested by a "host," the shells are discarded and the organisms infect the intestines.

Giardia

Giardia (pronounced gee-ARE-dee-uh), was named after the nineteenth century French zoologist, Alfred Mathieu Giard. Giardia is a protozoan, which is an animal-like, single cell organism. When ingested by animals, including humans, the organism metamorphoses into a trophozoite (tro-pho-ZO-ite) and attaches itself to the small intestine. The trophozoite is the protozoan in the active stage of its life cycle. Once attached in the intestines, it may begin interfering with the host's digestion. If the interference is pronounced, the result is the intestinal infection known as giardiasis (gee-are-DIE-uh-sis).

Later, the trophozoite multiplies, and the resulting cysts travel down the colon and are excreted in the millions. Thus, the host acts as a breeding reservoir. And if infected stools contaminate a water source, the disease can spread to those mammals later drinking of it.

Giardia parasites have probably always been a natural part of the intestinal flora in mammals. However, giardiasis, the infection, is a different matter. Previously, when people and animals ingested the protozoa or cysts they were not nearly as prone to illness. This is because they produced antibodies that fought off the microbes or at least staved their effects. But within the past several decades, two factors have contributed to the increased risks of our contracting giardiasis.

- As a result of living in civil sterility, our bodies have essentially quit producing the antibodies necessary to maintain our natural immunities. This civil sterility comes from drinking municipally treated tap water or bottled water that is free of giardia (in most cases), and by taking medicinal antibiotics, eradicating any pre-existing giardia parasites in our bodies.

- Humans and livestock including cattle, horses, mules and llamas are polluting the backcountry water in increasing numbers. This has almost certainly raised the giardia count.

Regardless of the cause, when drinking from the natural water sources we risk becoming infected—irrespective of our methods of purification. This does not mean, however, that we will automatically become sick. Most of the time our bodies will be able to hold their own against the effects of the giardia, and we will remain healthy. Staying healthy is mainly a matter of ingesting a minimum of pathogens, while developing immunities to the unavoidable. But when the giardia overwhelms the body's defenses, sickness results.

The typical symptoms are diarrhea and intestinal disorder. The infected person usually experiences a number of loose stools throughout the day. Those who choose to ride the symptoms out, as I have always done, would do well to increase their intake of treated water in order to reduce the malady's dehydrating effects. And they would be extremely fastidious about washing their hands after eliminating. Those who find themselves with increasing symptoms should visit a doctor, since the malady might not be what they think. Dr. William Forgey (Bibliography) recommends carrying Diasorb in tablet form. This is one of the more powerful non-prescription anti-diarrheal medications. Otherwise, you might plan ahead and carry a prescribed medication such as metronidazole (the generic name for Flagyl). But use it only as a last resort, since it will reduce your natural immunities even further.

Cryptosporidia

Cryptosporidia (KRIP-toe-spo-RID-e-uh) is a one-celled protozoan that, like giardia, occurs widely in nature. The infection is called cryptosporidiosis, (KRIP-toe-spo-RID-e-O-sis) or simply "crypto," and is a common cause of diarrhea worldwide. The symptoms are similar to those of giardia: watery diarrhea and intestinal disorders. Drugs are ineffective, but healthy individuals will normally recover on their own, although the symptoms may last a few weeks. Again, persons affected should drink plenty of treated water, and they may also wish to take anti-diarrheal medication.

Cryptosporidia is highly infectious, and can be transmitted in much the same way as giardia. Neither iodine nor chlorine will kill it, at least in the usual concentrations used in "purification." Boiling is the best method of treatment. Filtration is also effective, at least with units that remove particles smaller than two microns.

When we go hiking in other countries we are just as apt to encounter these same types of water contaminants, so of course we would exercise the same precautions. A malady similar in its symptoms to giardia and crypto but much more dangerous is protozoal amoeba diarrhea (as opposed to protozoal giardia diarrhea), more commonly known as amoebic dysentery. This disease kills millions of people globally. The initial symptoms are giardia-like except for one important difference. Giardiasis produces diarrhea day after day. Amoebic dysentery causes alternating diarrhea and constipation.

Many people, myself included, believe that Robert Beck technology (Bibliography) can successfully treat these maladies.

Water treatment options

Filtration is the hiker's most popular method of treating water. Other options include adding iodine or chlorine, and boiling. These methods do nothing to remove or neutralize chemical contamination, and they are ineffective at treating sewage or effluent. As outlined above, be sure you know where your water is coming from.

Boiling

Boiling will destroy water-borne bacteria and other live organic pollutants, and it will deactivate viruses. Once the water reaches a roiling boil the sterilization is complete, and you may remove the water from the heat and allow it to cool. Remember, too, that boiling can be used in addition to filtration, where you want the extra assurance. If you are short on stove fuel, boil the water on a cook-fire (see the Campfire and Cook-fire chapter).

Iodine

As a water purification agent, iodine tablets are lightweight, compact and easy to use. The objectionable taste can be neutralized with ascorbic acid, 50 mg to a liter. The recommended two tablets of iodine for each quart of water, used in perhaps six quarts a day, would seem to be a considerable chemical accumulation. For occasional use I suppose it is acceptable, but surely not throughout an entire summer. To an extent, iodine is cumulative in the body, which is why municipal water treatment facilities do not use it.

If the water you collect from a certain source is cold, and most water in the natural environment is, then after dropping the iodine tablets into it, you must wait twenty minutes for the chemical to take full effect. Imagine hiking for hours between distant water sources, arriving at the next source and having to wait twenty minutes before taking a drink! What usually happens is that the hiker adds the tablets, then waits only a few minutes before drinking. Perhaps the idea is that the iodine will continue working in the stomach. Unfortunately, this does not happen. The stomach lining quickly absorbs the water, along with the iodine in solution, and it leaves the microbes behind, where they then proceed into the digestive tract.

Filtration

Small, portable water filters are popular with hikers. These come in a wide variety of makes and models, take your pick. Filtration units with maximum porosity of about two microns will effectively screen out most protozoa. The finer the filtration, the greater the resistance to the water passing through it, meaning that the harder it is to pump, the slower it operates, and the less water it can treat before clogging.

"Hiker's Friend" water filtration system

Most water filters designed for hikers are operated by hand-pump. I find this method tedious, and would rather spend my time with more connected activities. Which is why I greatly prefer the gravity-feed method. I originated the idea, at least in this modern application, with the invention of the Hiker's Friend water filter system back in 1987, while preparing for our first thru-hike. Jenny and I have since used this system on hiking trips galore, and sea-kayaking trips in Mexico and the Arctic. I recommend it highly. Although the system is not infallible, neither is any other type of filtration system. For a description of how it works, and how you can make one for yourself, see the Sewing chapter.

Other means of contracting pathogens

As I learned during my earlier thru-hikes, no water filter system or other treatment method can keep pathogens from entering our bodies. Assuming we do not misuse the filter, and that the particular filter or its cartridge is not defective in some way, a few protozoa could still pass through the cartridge. However, a more likely scenario involves the microbes entering the body via other channels. One possibility is by washing the face in untreated water. Another is by washing the hands in untreated water, and then munching on a hand-held snack bar, for example. And while giardia is ordinarily a water-borne parasite, it does not need water to survive. Assuming you wash your cookpot, cup and spoon in untreated water, and towel them dry, many cysts could be left clinging to these items.

But there is a far more serious problem to consider here. We, ourselves, can be our own worst sources of protozoa. When we experience even a minor outbreak of giardia or cryptosporidia within the intestines, we become generators of these pathogens. As the protozoa reproduce inside the intestines, they do so by the millions, and the stools become extremely infective. So when returning from the privy or "bushes," be sure to sterilize your hands, preferably with ethyl alcohol gel. If you use an antibacterial soap instead, rather than rinse your hands directly in a natural source, use the dundo method, described in the Hygiene chapter.

Hiking between distant water sources

Nature does not always place water at intervals convenient to us. But she does give us the legs to walk from one source to the next, and the brains to figure out how to overcome any inconvenience.

The 20 mile waterless stretch

Suppose that water sources "A" and "B" are twenty miles apart. Ideally you would plan to arrive at source A in the mid-afternoon. There you would cook dinner. But rather than eat it then and there, you would stow it carefully into your backpack. After filling a quart-size water bottle with treated water, pour two or three quarts of untreated water into a water bag. In very hot weather you would of course collect much more. After enjoying a dundo shower, you would "super-saturate" by drinking as much as your stomach can hold.

Set off, and hike a few hours, then sit down and eat dinner. Refreshed once again, continue with a will another several miles into evening. Then leave the trail and make a pleasant stealth camp, (see the following chapter Stealth Camping). The next morning, rise at dawn and proceed to hike the remaining distance to water source B, arriving there mid-day, and not long after consuming the last of your water.

With this kind of timing, the twenty mile distance between water sources is only a minor inconvenience, except for having to carry the extra water. At no time do you go thirsty or become dehydrated. Twenty mile waterless stretches are fairly common along the Continental Divide Trail and Pacific Crest Trail, but are rare in the east. But in any locale this kind of distance between *pure* sources, or at least easily treatable sources, is common. Hikers using the above techniques should be able to traverse these long stretches without difficulty.

The 30 mile waterless stretch

Now suppose that water sources A and B are thirty miles apart. Reaching source A mid-morning, fill your quart bottle and load your water bag with one gallon. After bathing and super-saturating, press on. Hike until late afternoon, then stop to cook and eat dinner. Clean the cookpot by wiping it rather than washing it with your precious supply of drinking water. Then carry on determinedly into the evening, and make a stealth camp away from the trail. Early the next morning, set off once again, and hike to water source B, arriving there in the afternoon.

By splitting long waterless stretches into two days, you can manage the distance with less difficulty, thanks to the overnight rest provided midway. Of course, you cannot always time your departures from source A according to the above scenarios. In any event, the idea is to hike long into the evening, taking advantage of the cooler hours, and to start off again early the following morning.

Carry your treated water in a bottle, and your untreated water in a larger water bag. Drink the treated water from the bottle, then as it becomes depleted, stop and filter more water into it from the bag. Never carry all your water in a water bag; should it develop a leak you could lose your entire supply.

While hiking long distances between water sources, and carrying a smaller, ultralight pack, I carry the extra water in a soft water bag, or "bladder." This fits in the pack better than, say, gallon-size, rigid-plastic bottles. And when not in use it takes far less space.

The 60 mile waterless stretch

If the present trends of water pollution continue, we may find ourselves hiking ever farther between viable water sources. By reducing our baseline packweight, we can carry more water when needed. And by using the above methods we can stretch our capabilities considerably.

During our third PCT trip, Jenny and I hiked through southern California in late summer. For about 800 miles we hiked in temperatures approaching 100° F. During this time we used our reflective mylar-covered umbrellas, which we found made a world of difference in terms of heat tolerability. Along the way we found most of the creeks dry, meaning that often we had to carry water for 40 and 50 miles between sources. At two gallons per person each day in those temperatures, including what we used for cooking, this meant that we carried 25 to 30 pounds of water. This extra weight slowed progress, but otherwise it did not bother us, mainly as the water also kept us well hydrated and energetic. Our longest stretch of this section was about 60 miles, from Barrel Springs, over the scorching San Felipe Hills, bypassing trickling and probably polluted San Felipe Creek, and up the flanks of Mt. Laguna to the settlement at its summit. We arrived there—dying of thirst? No, actually with two quarts of water. A miscalculation, but at least we knew that we could have hiked much farther had we needed to.

Survival time

How long can a person survive without water? According to contemporary medical knowledge, a person can walk without water in 90°F temperatures for five days. At 60°, survival is said to extend to eight days if the person is active, or ten if inactive.

So should you find yourself without water for a few hours or even a day or longer, as I have many times, this does not mean your life is at stake. Do everything within your power to remain well hydrated; and when that doesn't work, due to unforeseen circumstances, strengthen you will, quiet your mind, and simply carry on—as usual—to the next water source.

Oftentimes the ways of our society are more take than give, especially when it comes to the earth's natural resources. When Native Americans took something from the earth for purposes of sustenance or medicine, they usually left a small offering of thanksgiving in return. It might have been a pinch of medicinal or spiritual herbs, a small feather or special pebble, or a carved twig. These objects were symbolic, representing something in the memory of the giver: a memory of a special place, an event, a lesson learned, or perhaps a meaningful vision or dream. The hiker who considers a natural water source, especially a spring, as sacred can do much the same, accepting the gift of water and leaving some small token of nature in return. And when others pass by, whether they choose to treat the water or drink it straight, these small tokens, set unobtrusively off to one side, may serve to remind them of the water's value, and of their need to protect and honor it too.

Stealth Camping

> I made my bed in a nook of the pine thicket—
> snug as a squirrel's nest, full of spicy odors
> with plenty of wind-played needles to sing me asleep.
>
> — *John Muir*

Forever new
and fresh

Picture a popular region of backcountry in the height of summer. It could be the Sierra Nevada, Yellowstone, or just about anywhere. Now imagine that one night, every camper shines a flashlight into the sky, and that a passing satellite photographs the scene with a powerful lens. The photo would show not isolated pinpricks of light evenly distributed throughout the area, but concentrated clusters arranged in circles, delineating the lakes, and in lines depicting the trail-side creeks. Otherwise, the picture would show vast areas of blackness. This blackness suggests that despite the crowded water-side campsites, the overwhelming majority of the wilderness is vacant.

Hikers who learn to camp away from water sources are at a wonderful advantage. For them, that expanse of blackness on the hypothetical satellite photo becomes the potential for almost unlimited camping.

I coined the term "stealth camping" to denote camping in these vacant areas, away from the established campsites. The word stealth is a derivative of "steal," in the sense of moving or behaving inconspicuously. Most wild animals live by stealth. They move and act with quiet caution, in order to avoid being noticed. And they sleep in secret places hidden from predators. No doubt early native peoples moved covertly in order to locate and approach their intended prey. And they probably camped in stealth to avoid attracting the attention of intruders, both human and animal. My concept of stealth camping is aligned with these ways. We hikers need to exercise at least some caution when near roads or populated areas. And we try to approach animals, not with spear and atlatl, but with camera and appreciative eye. Stealth camping, like the ways of animals and early peoples, keeps us safer and more in tune with the natural world. And it offers a wealth of other advantages. Before we get into the descriptions, let me first outline my objections to the traditional, but opposite, approach: the established campsites.

The drawbacks of established campsites

Outdoor enthusiasts have long been attracted to the natural beauty of lakes, creeks and ponds. This attraction is so strong, in fact, that most people prefer to camp, almost exclusively, along the lake shores and riverbanks. And justifiably so, for these natural water sources are very pleasing, and they often provide a type of contemplative ambience found nowhere else. And of course they make the camping more convenient in terms of water availability. Unfortunately, in the past few decades these campsites have received a great deal of human impact, mostly through overuse. But we are so accustomed to seeing this damage that we hardly notice it.

• Compacted ground

Every summer, campers arrive at their lake and creekside campsites and proceed to scrape away the freshly fallen leaves and pine needles, unaware that these materials are highly beneficial to the ecology, or perhaps simply ignoring the fact. Often they do not stop there, but continue to remove much of the beneficial duff and leaf decomposition. The intent is usually to remove the lumps and bumps, making the tent platform resemble the bed back home. In reality, they are making these campsites less comfortable, and ever more sterile.

All of this cleaning and scraping, along with decades of boot and hoof trampling, have compacted these established campsites into what can seem almost like pavement. Little wonder that these sites require inflatable mattresses or thick foam pads. And not only do humans find such compacted ground uncomfortable and cold, but the vegetation finds it nearly impossible as habitat. The loss of topsoil and the compaction represses regeneration enormously. The result is a long-lasting scarring of the landscape in the name of recreation.

• Dished ground

As these overwhelmed and barren campsites continue to be scraped and trampled year after year, they become dished, meaning that they are depressed, or lower than their surrounding terrain. During a hearty rain, where does the groundwater flow? Into the lowest regions, namely the dished campsites. This calls for tents with "bathtub" floors.

• Dust, soot and desiccated stock manure

If the days are warm and dry, the established campsites are often quite dusty. And this dust is often black with campfire ash. It lingers in the air and penetrates everything, including the tent, clothing, gear, food, and a person's lungs.

If the ground were only dirt and ash, then the dust and soot would be fairly benign. But quite often, especially in the western states, this pulverized mess contains desiccated stock manure. Even though most of the manure is dried, the pathogens and coliforms it contains can remain virulent for years.

• Polluted surroundings

Adding to the filth are bits of rubbish, particularly in the deeply scarred campfire rings with their scraps of aluminum foil and their blackened rocks. One often finds wads of toilet paper stuffed in the crannies of nearby rocks and beneath fallen trees. The creeks and lakes next to these camps often harbor ugly food scraps from someone's dishwashing. Contrary to what many campers expect, the fish do not normally eat this garbage. Equestrians lead their stock to drink at these water sources— downstream of *their* camps of course. And it is not unusual for the horses and mules to urinate and defecate while standing by the water, or even while standing directly in it.

• Marauding animals in the night

One of the greatest worries of many backcountry campers is bears. And where do campers most often encounter bears? In the established campsites, at night.

Bears are not the only animals to frequent these campsites. Camp rodents are also human habituated, and during the night they will chew on gear, gnaw into food bags, and nibble on any food they can get their paws on. In so doing, the rodents may contaminate the food with urine, feces, mites, fleas, and possibly infective microorganisms, possibly including hantavirus.

• Insects

As if pilfering animals were not enough, mosquitoes, no-see-ums, black-flies, horse flies, yellow jackets, and wasps prefer wet areas, especially near standing water. But the water is not the only thing attracting these insects; the rubbish and waste that campers leave behind, and the piles of stock manure attract them also.

• Katabatic (cold) air

Established campsites are typically situated in regions of katabatic air. This air is much colder than that of the surrounding regions. Here is why:

Warm air is lighter than cold air, so it rises. This is what lifts hot air balloons into the sky. During the day, the sun heats the ground, which in turn heats the air immediately above it. The warming air rises, and this we call "adiabatic." This warm air does not rise uniformly, but in columns known as "thermals," and these are what keep sailplanes, hang gliders, and paragliders aloft.

As the sun begins to set, the process reverses. The mountain slopes begin to cool, chilling the air next to them. This cooler air is heavier, so it sinks into the valleys. Sinking, colder air is called "katabatic," and in a way it behaves like water because it flows down the drainages like invisible rivers.

In the evenings, then, the mountain drainages have two rivers; one of water (the river itself), and the other an invisible "river" of cold, katabatic air flowing over the water. Where the slopes above the rivers are steeply inclined, frigid katabatic air can flow down these drainages in veritable torrents.

When the river of katabatic air reaches the valleys it tends to settle over the lakes and valley floors. And there we also find the established campsites—along the rivers and lakes, and in the valleys. All night long this colder, katabatic air hangs over these regions, and those who choose to camp there must endure its effects.

High mountains, deep valleys, calm nights and clear skies tend to accentuate the effect. In the western mountains the layer of katabatic air over a valley at night tends to be, on average, about 20 or 30 feet deep. On rare occasions I have found it to be up to a hundred feet thick. What this means is that during the night and early mornings, established campsites—indeed all campsites in the vicinity of drainages—can be as much as 15 or 20 degrees F colder than their surroundings. How do I know how thick the layer of katabatic air is? Very simply by hiking out of the valley, topping out of the frigid katabatic air, and suddenly feeling a remarkable warming in the ambient air. The temperature difference is that dramatic.

• For want of solitude

When ambling through the backcountry, be it a popular National Park or Wilderness Area, or simply the woods somewhere, the last thing you may be looking for is noisy campers. If solitude is what you are looking for, it will be hard to find at those campsites.

Stealth camping

If you can manage to camp away from the water sources, and from the established campsites, then the many wonderful advantages of stealth camping will be yours. Stealth camping is a cleaner, warmer and quieter way to camp, and it offers a much better connection with nature. In all likelihood no one has camped at your impromptu stealth-site before, and the ground will be pristine. Its thick, natural cushioning of the forest materials will still be in place, making for comfortable bedding without the use of a heavy inflatable mattress. There will be no desiccated stock manure to rise as dust and infiltrate your lungs, nor any scatter of unsightly litter and stench of human waste. The stealth-site will not be trampled and dished; any rainwater will soak into the ground or run off it, rather than collect and flood your shelter. Bears scrounging for human food will be busy at the water-side campsites, and will almost invariably ignore the far-removed and unproductive woods. Far from the water sources you will encounter fewer flying insects, particularly upon the more breezy slopes and ridges. Above the katabatic zones the night air will be markedly warmer. And you can rest assured that your chances of being bothered by other people will be slim.

Hikers and campers normally cause the most environmental damage at the established campsites. We stealth campers have no impact on these campsites because we do not use them. Nor do the wilderness managers have to worry about us impacting our far-removed stealth-sites. We cherish the natural environment, and are very conscious to care for and protect it. As such, we practice no-trace methods exclusively. For after all, our love and respect of nature, our quest for that connection, is why we enjoy stealth camping to begin with.

In certain wilderness areas the authorities require all visitors to camp only in established campsites. The idea is that not all people are conscientious with their camping practices, and for the benefit of the ecology these people are best corralled into known, and therefore more easily regulated campsites, where most of the impact has already occurred. Certainly I do not recommend that anyone practice stealth camping without full awareness of the responsibilities this approach requires, nor where camping restrictions are in effect.

Cooking and stealth-camping

At a stealth-site miles from the nearest water supply, how would one cook the evening meal and wash up? Actually we do not cook at these sites, mainly because of the risk of attracting bears, but also as a matter of zero impact. Instead, we stop at a water source in the late afternoon or early evening, and there we cook, eat and wash. Also we fill our bottles with enough water to meet our needs for that evening and part of the following morning. Refreshed and energized, we pack up and resume hiking. Miles later, we leave the trail and head well into the woods, to make our impromptu stealth camp. With the evening meal out of the way, we could use the extra time for exploring, journal writing, or perhaps simply for quiet observation and connection.

Benefits of sleeping on a gentle slope

While searching for a stealth-site, look for ground that is somewhat elevated above its surroundings, so that it does not pool rainwater in a heavy storm. If you cannot find such ground, then look for ground that is sloped. Rain cannot pool on sloped ground, and only in the heaviest rain will it actually run downhill. Usually the rain is simply absorbed.

Once you find a sloping stealth-site, you must give some thought about which way to situate your shelter. The tendency when camping on a slope is to sleep with the feet downhill. This is not a good idea. It allows gravity to pool the blood into the lower extremities, and in so doing it restricts circulation and greatly reduces the restorative benefits of an otherwise good night's rest. Or one might decide to try sleeping laterally on the slope, only to spend the night clutching their bedding, trying to keep from rolling sideways down the hill.

The way to sleep on sloped ground is with the feet uphill. This obviates pooling, and it even draws the day's swelling from the lower extremities. It is excellent therapy for the hiker's legs and feet.

Which way is down?

Judging which way is downhill is a simple matter when the ground is steeply sloped, but it can be more problematic when the ground is barely sloped. Especially after a long day on the trail, with fatigue interfering with one's sense of equilibrium. In such cases you might pitch your shelter in what *seems* the proper orientation, only to spend the night trying to prevent yourself from rolling down to one side.

The solution is twofold. First, walk around the potential site and examine it from all directions. While looking at the ground from one vantage it might appear sloped toward you. Don't be fooled by this, because when you walk around and view the ground from the opposite side, it may again appear tilted toward you. Nevertheless, this walk-around is the first method of determining which way is *probably* down. That done, spread your groundsheet and lie down, with your feet pointed in the direction that seems uphill. If the slope *feels* uphill toward your feet, then it most likely is, and you may then pitch your shelter with confidence.

This inability to judge slope manifests itself on the trail as well. When fatigued, the hiker often gauges downward slope as being far more gradual than it is. Jenny and I hiked the PCT northbound twice, and were very familiar with certain switchbacks where the trail's downward gradient seemed far too gradual. We were surprised, during our ensuing southbound journey, to find those same switchbacks amply graded while hiking them the other way—uphill rather than down.

How steep a slope can stealth campers sleep on? I have found it best not to rule out a more steeply sloped site until I have checked it by feel, lying on my groundsheet. Jenny and I joke that if we awaken the following morning and find that we have slid out of the shelter, then the terrain was a little too steep.

If the area of your site is hardly sloped at all, look for a place on a slight rise that would provide runoff in the event of rain.

Warmer, softer bedding

The surface layer of a typical forest floor is called litter. It consists of needles, leaves, cones, sticks and other natural materials. Beneath the litter is a layer of decomposed and compressed litter called duff. In some areas this duff can be several feet thick. If you have never stretched out on a pine needle or leaf carpeted forest floor, you are missing one of nature's softest beds. It is more comfortable than a foam pad, and it provides excellent insulation from the cold soil and rocky substrate. And those thick layers of litter and duff will tend to absorb any rain, wicking it down and away from your groundsheet. Of course, while this natural insulation is of considerable benefit to the hiker traveling lightly, it also necessitates extreme caution with fire.

Minimizing impact

When establishing a stealth-site, we would exercise the utmost care, especially when it comes to altering the landscape and its flora. One might hand-preen any twigs, pine cones and sharp-pointed cone scales that would poke into the bedding, but we never brush away the beneficial layers of forest materials—the long-fallen leaves and pine needles. We avoid breaking away green limbs and yanking out plants or saplings that might occupy the prospective site. If we find such obstructions, we search elsewhere for a place naturally free of them.

Another kind of impact is noise. When stealth camping we remain reasonably silent, to avoid degrading someone else's wilderness experience (human or animal) while pursuing our own. And this way we are more likely to see and hear wildlife at closer range, and less likely to attract any unwanted human attention. In short, we respect the quiet of the wilderness as though in a house of worship, for in many ways the wilderness is a sacred temple of creation.

Climb high, camp low

High, exposed areas tend to take the brunt of any blustery weather. With this in mind, we can greatly reduce any weather-related problems by avoiding the storm-whipped heights. Instead, we descend to the lower regions at night—but not all the way into the katabatic valleys—and there we look for small stealth-sites that offer protection from the elements.

During our Continental Divide Trail thru-hike, Jenny and I met only one other distance hiker; this was in the remote mountains of western Montana. He was going north, and we were headed south. The day was late, and after an enjoyable conversation we went our separate ways. The fellow resumed his ascent of the mountain we had just come down, and we continued our descent. A short ways along the trail we made a comfortable camp nestled in the pines. Our evening was very pleasant, highlighted by a pair of owls flying round the tent and landing on a branch within a few yards of our open doorway. In the morning we awoke to find the mountain enveloped in cloud, and we felt concern for our new friend, since he had indicated that he wanted to camp up there. Months later he sent us a few pages photocopied from his journal describing how he had endured that harrowing night on top of the peak hanging on to his tent in a savage storm. Our camp and his were only half a mile apart, but ours was protected snugly in a vale while his was fully exposed to everything the elements could hurl at it. This is just another example of the wisdom in the adage "climb high, and camp low"—to which I would add: but not so low that you are in the katabatic zone.

If the wind is blowing, try to position your stealth-site behind sheltering trees, brush, logs or rocks. However in heavy wind, keep a safe distance from trees, in case one comes crashing down, or in case a large branch snaps off. In clear weather you can camp beneath the sheltering branches of a tree; they will greatly reduce the accumulation of the early morning's dew on your shelter. In rainy weather it is usually best to camp away from the branches, since they continue dripping long after the storm's passing. The exception to this is mature spruce, which can shed the rain very nicely.

Animal visits at our stealth-sites

Most animals are opportunists. If they happen upon your food bags while you are asleep, they will usually help themselves. And when it comes to marauding animals, bears can be the most formidable. So let's discuss bears first.

In the human-populated areas of the "Lower 48" backcountry, black bears focus their perpetual quest for food in the more productive regions, and these are usually the established campgrounds. Picture those over-used lake-side campsites, and how attractive they must be to bruin. Night after night they fairly bristle with signaling campfire smoke, irresistible odors of cooking food, the sight of bags of food and trash. The hiker will find it very difficult to elude the bears at these locations. At our far-removed stealth-sites we avoid the bear hassles by avoiding their nightly haunts. Read more on this in the Bear chapter.

A question that commonly comes my way goes like this: "Granted, at a stealth-site you are not camping in an area that bears go to regularly, but if a bear happens to travel by, how close must it get to smell food or any other smell which might entice it to roam into your camp?"

The number one bear attractant is the odor of cooking food. This is a signal odor, and it lingers at a campsite and is detectable by bears for many miles, and even for several days after the camper has gone. This suggests the folly of imagining that by not cooking at an established campsite, the bears will not be attracted to it. And it suggests the benefits of stealth camping far from where anyone has cooked. Lacking that one signal odor, our sites are already about 90% safe.

Bears have mediocre eyesight but an extraordinary sense of smell. This of course helps them locate food in areas of poor visibility, for example in thick timber and heavy brush. If they can smell it, then they can find it. At the same time, virtually all bears here in the Lower 48 are very familiar with people. And in the wilds, outside of the National Parks, bears are generally suspicious and wary of people. So even though they may smell your deodorant, sunscreen or mosquito repellent over a mile away, this does not mean that they will automatically make a bee-line for you. If you or your camp do not smell like something they cannot resist, namely food, then they will probably give you a wide berth.

And as I mention in the Bear chapter, if a black bear does wander into your stealth camp and shows reluctance to leave despite your mild provocations, simply pack up and move on.

At the other end of the spectrum are the mice and their rodent cousins. In established campsites these creatures are well versed in associating humans with food bags, and are bound to invade your domain. This does not mean that they are being pests; it means only that they are responding to the temptation of the food you place at their disposal. At the stealth-sites, these creatures will rarely associate you with food. Squirrels and chipmunks may be your neighbors, but usually they will be practicing stealth themselves, trying to avoid detection. So they will rarely venture close enough to investigate.

Jenny and I once enjoyed a wee visitor at one of our stormbound camps on the banks of the Yukon River. A redback vole skittered out of the brush and made a hasty inspection of our front porch area. Not too surprisingly it found a hearty snack in the form of a few crumbs of spilled cereal. And with that we became friends. The little vole proved itself very well behaved, not once did it nibble at a plastic bag or nylon gear bag. It did, however, have the audacity to crawl into one of our cups, from which we had just eaten, and proceeded to lick the cup clean. Within a few hours our friend became almost tame, paying us little mind as we watched at face-close range. It reminded us of a miniature brown bear, little more than a wispy ball of cinnamon fur with a rusty brown stripe down its back. It had a short, fuzzy tail and two beady, coal-black eyes. We often name our camps for their more salient features, and this was our "vole camp."

Not all nocturnal creatures are out to plunder your camps. I find it amazing how much animal activity there is at night. Depending on the geographic locale there might be deer, raccoons, boar, porcupines, skunks, owls, fox, coyotes and a wide variety of rodents. These animals will normally avoid human presence. Still, they may amble past your stealth-site in the night, which can be disconcerting if you hear their shuffling but cannot see what is making the noise.

Forever new and fresh

Our wild lands are fast becoming over-trodden, and now is the time to start practicing a more respectful and sensible approach to wilderness camping—the stealth-site. The world out there is forever fresh and new, so why not spread out, enjoy it, and take care of it?

A small island of bare ground in a sea of snow-covered terrain. One of our stealth-sites in the North Cascades during our PCT southbound trek.

Campfire and Cook-Fire

By the trails my feet have broken,
The dizzy peaks I've scaled, the campfire's glow;
By the lonely seas I've sailed in ...
I am signed and sealed to nature—be it so.

— *Robert Service*

The traditional hearty campfire impacts its surroundings enormously. It greedily incinerates the natural supply of firewood, and sends dangerous sparks into the night—sparks that could start an uncontrolled burn. It scorches the subsoil deeply, sterilizing its microbiology while greatly suppressing regeneration. Many backcountry campsites and shelters feature large fire pits, and these only engender the old mindset by inviting campers to construct large fires. Even in less visited areas we often find visible evidence of the impact: the tell-tale ring of blackened rocks, the mound of ashes mixed with bits of aluminum foil and half-burned rubbish, and the charred and sooty ground. These are unsightly reminders that our numbers and carelessness may be threatening our wild lands more than we might care to admit.

During our five thru-hikes, totaling more than eighteen months in the wilds, Jenny and I built a total of eight campfires. Each was small and utilitarian, solely for the purpose of drying clothing after a particularly wet day on the trail. We enjoy evening campfires as much as anyone, but during these treks we were trying to limit our effects on the land.

Any kind of fire, large or small, will have some degree of impact, and our utilitarian fires were no exception. But in times of genuine need I think a small campfire is appropriate. For instance, should the hiker find him or herself deeply chilled, and with clothing and sleeping bag hopelessly wet, then a small, warming and drying campfire is well justified.

Fire safety

As discussed in the previous chapter, the rich layer of needles, leaves, twigs and other natural materials that make up the surface layer of the typical forest floor is called litter, and beneath this is a layer of decomposed litter called duff. Duff vaguely resembles dirt, and campers commonly mistake it for such and often build fires on it. Even if they recognize it as duff, they might incorrectly assume that it is non-flammable because of its high moisture content. What they may not realize is how quickly their campfire will dry it.

On a winter mountaineering trip in the Colorado Rockies back in the 1960's, my partner and I trudged into "base camp" and pitched our tents. Digging through several feet of snow to the ground, we built a modest fire and cooked dinner. Afterwards we buried the fire under what seemed like a ton of snow, and packed it down with our boots. The next morning we left camp and climbed our intended mountain. Returning in the late afternoon, we were aghast to find a small hole in the snow bellowing smoke. For an hour we dug into the smolder, following a few spreading arms, one of which was heading for a nearby tree. This was an unforgettable lesson on the flammability of "wet" duff.

Fire is not always a negative element. Nature has used fire to maintain her ecology for eons. Lightning triggers most wildfires, and these are both beneficial and necessary. They burn away the downed trees and branches, along with the forest's accumulation of undergrowth. This keeps the flammable materials to a minimum, and prevents a future fire from burning so hotly that it kills all the trees and scorches the subsoil. Regular, small fires merely expose the forest floor to sunlight, giving saplings and new plants the chance to flourish.

All was in balance until the Forest Service started fighting fires in order to protect its timber "harvesting." The forests started accumulating downed trees and underbrush in unnatural quantities, to the point where our second and third growth "tree farms" have become immense tinder boxes. Now when they burn, they sweep the land in an inferno of destruction. Policies are beginning to change, but meanwhile our National Parks, forests and wild lands are extremely vulnerable to devastating fires. This is why we hikers have to be so careful, keeping our campfires few, and giving them much forethought, constant tending, and thorough extinguishing.

Obviously our stealth-sites are not safe places for campfires. When we need to build a drying fire we would default to the established campsites and their fire pits. Only in an emergency would we build a campfire in a pristine location. And then, only after scraping the duff away to expose a wide circle of bare dirt—of course restoring the site afterward.

The utilitarian campfire

To make a small, drying and warming campfire, begin by collecting dry tinder. Again, I consider it wise to carry a small bag of tinder in the backpack, as an emergency item. Dry tinder is difficult to find naturally when the woods are wet. Pine needles, dry leaves, seed heads, birch bark, certain types of dry moss, even old bird nests—any of these would make suitable tinder. If you are not carrying a supply, you could look for natural tinder under fallen trees, under pieces of bark, in the hollows beneath rocks or boulders, and at the base of trees. Some trees, such as spruce, protect their lower branches from rain; the thin, dead branches still attached are very flammable. If dry tinder is unavailable, you could use a knife to cut into a wet stick. The larger the stick, the drier it will be inside. A small pile of extremely thin shavings will usually ignite very readily. Look also for a bit of hardened sap, chipped from an old wound of a conifer. You can use this to encourage your initial flames.

Next, collect the kindling: pencil-size twigs. On wet days, look for this wood on the lower branches of trees, and possibly under blowdowns and large rocks. Once a fire is burning well, it will accept damp or wet kindling collected from the ground. But to get the fire going, use only dry twigs. After amassing a small pile of dry kindling, collect larger pieces of wood, but nothing larger than perhaps ¾" in diameter.

If not using an existing fire pit, then you will need to prepare the fire site by scraping away all ground detritus to bare dirt. That done, lay down two short platform sticks about ½" in diameter. These will hold your tinder off the wet ground, and provide it with ventilation. Lay a few pieces of kindling across them to make a bed, then onto that add the dry tinder. Atop this, place more kindling, one piece at a time. Remove a single match from its container, and replace the lid. Strike the match with your thumbnail, or across the dry bottom of a rock. The instant the match ignites, place it under the materials, and hold it carefully there until it is nearly spent. At that point, withdraw it from under the materials and insert it down into them, head down. There it will assist the wee flames and act as dry kindling itself. Blow *gently* into the fire to feed it oxygen, adding more kindling between breaths.

If the fire dies, set aside all partially burned materials. Build a new pile of tinder and kindling as before, strike a second match, but this time light a birthday candle. Hold the candle over the materials, dripping hot wax on them. The wetter the materials, the more wax needed. Then place the burning candle under the materials, which themselves will then act as candles.

The cook-fire

In addition to the eight small campfires that Jenny and I built during our thru-hikes, we also crafted dozens of cook-fires on our fifth trek. The cook-fire is an open flame, but that is about the extent of its similarities to a campfire. It does not qualify as a drying and warming fire because it is not large enough. Rather, it uses only pencil-size kindling. Fed into the tiny fire at regular intervals, this kindling heats the bottom of a single pot. The cook-fire is an art form, a low-impact means of cooking a meal. We craft it to cook the meal quickly and then to consume itself. Its tiny pile of ashes is then easily eradicated. The cook-fire leaves no scar, and no blackened rocks.

The cook-fire technique is a good backup should one's stove break down or run out of fuel. It is a way of cooking that affords the greatest Connection.

The cook-fire requires proper technique and finesse. Those who do not care to learn the correct form should not attempt the methods in the wilds. The cook-fire is also illegal anywhere open fires are banned. And it is unsafe at the stealth camps where pine needles and duff have accumulated deeply, or where dry leaves and grasses might be present—regardless of whether the woods are dry or wet. It is unsafe in high wind, and it may be entirely inappropriate in areas of heavy use.

Building a cook-fire

A good place to build a cook-fire is in an established campfire ring. If you are stopping to cook dinner in the late afternoon, you will usually find

such rings near water, which you will need anyway. Never build a cook-fire at your stealth-site where marauding bears might be a problem, or where the duff or forest liter is so deep that you cannot scrape a fire circle down to bare dirt. In the photo nearby, Jenny is using a cook-fire on an area of bare dirt.

When searching for a suitable place to build a cook-fire, take into consideration the direction and strength of any wind. Select a cooking area that is free of vegetation, and wide enough to prevent any shooting sparks from reaching the flammable brush or forest litter. Carefully scrape away all litter and duff so that the fire will sit on dirt or sand. Nothing else will do. Safety necessitates a circle of dirt at least 2½ feet in diameter; the cook-fire will go in its center. Rather than scattering the materials re-moved from the site, save them in little piles off to the side. These will be spread back over the area once the cook-fire is extinguished and the ground has cooled.

Tinder for igniting a cook-fire could be any of the small, dry materi-als like those found in your emergency fire starter kit. However, save your kit for an emergency, and instead look for dry tinder in the field. As for kindling, the only wood suitable for a cook-fire is again about a pencil's diameter. Anything larger will not incinerate completely, and will prevent you from restoring the site back to its original condition. To prepare the "fire sticks," break dry sticks and twigs into 6-inch lengths, and pile these neatly and conveniently to one side. By amassing all your fire sticks ahead of time, you will avoid any interruption to the cooking process, and will be able to monitor the fire at all times, for safety's sake.

Using a cook-fire

Since antiquity, people have been devising all manner of ways to support pots over cooking fires. I think I have tried most of them, and have settled on the one that works best for me. This is the tripod, made of three sticks lashed together at their tops, suspending the pot over the fire.

Suitable tripod sticks are about four feet in length, and perhaps about 1½ inch in diameter. If you start looking for them while hiking along the trail, before stopping to cook dinner, you will save yourself that much hassle at the dinner stop.

With all three tripod sticks in hand, you can begin looking for your cook-fire site. Once you have located and determined it to be safe for a small fire, lash the three tripod sticks together at one end, using a short length of cord. Then stand the tripod upright, not over the fire site just yet, but off to one side.

In order to suspend the pot from the tripod, the pot will need a bail. This is a wire, or a strip of metal, fitted to the pot near its top. If your cookpot lacks a bail, you can easily make one. Using a drill or hammer and nail, bore or punch two small holes—one on each side of the pot, just below the rim. Stainless steel pots are more resistant to drilling, while aluminum and titanium pots are very easily drilled. Into these holes, thread a length of wire. Optimally, the wire would be about half the thickness of an ordinary coat hanger. Finally, crimp or twist the ends of the wire so that they will not slip out of the holes.

After filling the cookpot with enough water for the meal, fit its lid in place. The lid will keep the water clean, and it will help retain heat. Then suspend the cookpot from the tripod. For this you will need a hanger, and this can be a notched stick or a length of cord. Either works well, but the cord is easier to adjust, raising or lowering the pot as needed. The flame is quite small and does not reach the cord, which is why the cord does not burn through. Tie the suspension cord to the tripod, now—before starting the fire. Use overhand knots, then feed the lower end under the bail and secure it back onto itself with a taut-line hitch. The hitch allows the adjustment in height. The pot is now suspended from the tripod, which is standing off to one side of the fire site.

Start the cook-fire, and begin feeding it with fire sticks. As the cook-fire comes to life, place the tripod over it and press the base of the tripod sticks gently into the ground to prevent them from shifting. Adjust the length of the suspension cord so that the pot hangs about an inch off the kindling. This distance is important. We want the pot *in* the fire, not so closely that it suffocates the fire, and not so high above the fire that the flames dissipate before reaching the pot. Ideally, the cook-fire should engulf the entire bottom of the pot, without reaching high enough to burn the suspension cord, nor wide enough to ignite the tripod sticks. Keep the fire small, yet focused. Done correctly, this little cook-fire will boil water as fast as any stove. And with experience the entire procedure can be very quickly done.

If a draft is sweeping the heat away from the cookpot, you can block it by situating yourself upwind, or by placing a few rocks upwind of the fire. However, avoid placing the rocks so close to the fire that they would blacken with soot. If they do blacken, leave them in dirt, blackened side down. The soil will transform the carbon faster than would the atmosphere.

Once the water reaches a boil, remove the lid and stir in dinner. Stirring with a spoon would place your hands and fingers too close to the fire, so instead use a longer stick. After cooking the meal, lift the tripod carefully away, then lean it over to bring the pot to rest on the ground. Then untie the suspension cord and set the tripod aside.

Baking bread or dessert

As soon as the cook-fire has generated a few small coals, you can use them for baking a dessert. Jenny and I use the term "scones" to refer to any kind of baked dessert. We usually mix and package our own scone ingredients at home. An alternative for those who do not object too seriously to the white flour and chemicals, is the store-bought "just add water" muffin-type mix. Even the type of mix that requires egg and oil will bake nicely without these ingredients. Jenny mixes the batter inside a resealable plastic bag, or inside the commercial packaging, adding water a few dollops at a time while stirring with a small stick. The idea is to use as little water as possible; the drier the batter, the faster and more thoroughly it will bake.

For a baking sheet, Jenny uses a simple piece of aluminum foil about 12 inches square. She scoops the batter onto the middle of the foil, then folds the foil over it—as though wrapping a loaf of bread. Then she seals the ends to contain the steam. Handled carefully, this foil will endure several bakings. Scoop a small bed of coals out of the cook-fire, and place the foil-packaged batter on them. Then scoop a few more coals over the top of the foil. Coals that are quite hot will tend to burn rather than bake. Cool them by spreading them out. Turn the packet over mid-way through the baking process, for better heat distribution, and continue adding a few glowing coals to the top of the packet as the old ones cool. Properly baked, the scones will be nicely browned on the outside, and cooked all the way through.

Even simpler than the scones baked in aluminum foil are "ash cakes." Mix a stiff bread or scone dough, press it flat, and place it directly on a bed of fine coals. Turn occasionally to ensure even baking. Once the ash cakes are cooked you can brush away any small bits of ash that remain on the crust.

The monster mash

As you are finishing the meal, rebuild the cook-fire just a little, and place all the unburned ends of the sticks into the tiny fire, as well as any paper trash. Tend the little fire very carefully, encouraging the flame to consume the last of its embers. When only ashes remain, use a stout stick to stir in water, dirt, or both. This extinguishes any remaining traces of fire, and cools both the ashes and the ground.

Now it is time to do the Monster Mash. This erases any indication of the cook-fire. Step on the cooled ashes with the ball of your shoe, and twist. This grinds the ashes to powder. Kick in a bit of dirt, and continue stepping and twisting, one foot after the other as though dancing some sort of ceremony. Call it the cook-fire-monster-mash-leave-no-trace ceremony. A few *minutes* of this will work the last traces of carbon into the earth.

If you are planning to camp within range of the cook-fire area, then you could return to the site the following morning and restore it to its original condition. For example, the cook-fire site could be in a dry creek bed, and the stealth-site a few hundred yards away in a glen. However, in bear country you would want to put several miles between your dinner site and your stealth-site. So if you will be moving on after cooking, you will need to "zero-impact" your fire site before heading out.

Place your hand on the ground at the cook-fire site, and make sure it has cooled. The possibility is slight, but if the ground is too hot to hold a hand on, then an unseen ember under the ground could possibly ignite the surface debris long after you have gone. If you detect any heat at the site, pour more water on it, mix and mash some more, and wait until the site is cool. That done, restore the original debris back over the site. Thoughtfully done, this light scattering of debris will erase any hint of the cook-fire's presence. And this is exactly the effect we are looking for.

Lastly, disassemble the tripod sticks and place them where they cannot possibly start a fire. By now, these sticks will no longer be hot to the touch, nor should they be charred if you constructed your cook-fire properly. If the tripod sticks are hot, rather than simply disperse them into the forest, for safety's sake carry them a ways until they have cooled.

The cookpot will be coated in soot from the fire, and this actually hastens the cooking process. There is no sense trying to clean the exterior. Instead, stow the pot in its own stowbag, so that the soot does not blacken everything it touches.

The beauty of the bow drill

The cook-fire offers a more natural means of cooking our meals, and with a much closer sense of connection. But the depth of that connection will also depend on how we ignite the fire. If we use a match or butane lighter, then the fire will be utilitarian and useful. However if we start the fire using a bow drill or hand drill, then that fire will be much more than simply heat for cooking. It will be sacred in some ways.

When we carve the bow drill parts—the fireboard, spindle and socket—from pieces of wood, we are investing our energy into them. And when we place the spindle to the fireboard, and use the bow to spin it with vigor enough to generate sufficient heat, we produce a glowing ember. That ember is an extension of ourselves. It is connected to us by virtue of the muscular energy we used to generate it. We place the ember on the tinder bundle and feed it oxygen with our life breath, and if all goes well the tinder bursts into flame. But the fire itself is not our creation. It is a gift of the Creator for our use in cooking the meal and warming ourselves. It is in that sense that the fire is sacred.

The techniques for using the bow drill and hand drill are beyond the scope of this text. Many books on wilderness survival describe the techniques; one of my favorites is *Tom Brown's Field Guide to Wilderness Survival* (Bibliography).

Physical Conditioning

Making light of toil

In a scene from Lewis Carroll's *Through The Looking Glass,* Alice and the Queen were running through the wilderness hand in hand as fast as they could go:

> The Queen kept crying "Faster!" but Alice felt she could not go faster, though she had no breath to say so. The curious thing was that the trees and other things round them never changed their places at all. However fast they went, they never seemed to pass anything. Just as Alice was getting quite exhausted, they stopped, and she looked around her in great surprise. "Why, I do believe we've been under this tree all the time! Everything's just as it was!" "Of course it is," said the Queen. "What would you have it?" "Well, in our country," said Alice, still panting, "you'd generally get to somewhere else—if you ran very fast for a long time, as we've been doing." "A slow sort of country!" said the Queen. "Now, here, you see, it takes all the running you can do to stay in the same place. If you want to get somewhere else, you must run at least twice as fast!"

Lewis Carroll was poking fun at his contemporaries caught up in the material world. Today's society spins at an even faster pace, and Alice would probably still see our chasing after the golden fleece of so-called success and security as just as futile.

But Carroll's metaphor speaks to me in another way. With more than 20,000 miles of hiking experience, one might imagine that I would be in peak physical condition. But this is hardly so. The summer's hiking and adventuring is wonderfully conditioning, but at season's end the leanness is soon lost. I have found that it takes all the hiking I can do to stay in the same place, fitness-wise. And unlike Alice, when I stop for the season I soon find myself sliding back downhill.

Why train?

My dictionary defines training as "exercise in order to prepare for an event." The event might be a summer's thru-hike, or perhaps a long-anticipated multi-day outing. Either way, the pre-hike physical conditioning is extremely beneficial. By strengthening our bodies we become more capable in handling the exertion of hiking. And with stronger muscles, tendons and ligaments, we become less susceptible to injury, especially to the knees, ankles and feet. Thus, we reduce the hardships and discomforts, both physical and mental, and we increase our chances of success. In effect, the pre-hike conditioning shortens every mile and flattens every hill.

The training forays also help us develop patience and persistence, and they go a long ways in helping us overcome lethargy. They allow us to spend considerably more time outside than we otherwise might, thereby providing respite from the daily rut and from any beleaguering pressures and worries. And the exercise, fresh air, and increased blood circulation will stimulate vitality and productivity back at our jobs or studies.

Methods of training

Wherever you can walk, you can train. It might be several blocks to a city park, or perhaps a loop through the forest. In any case, the idea is to begin your conditioning exercises far in advance of the summer's outings, giving your body a chance to adjust to the heightened activity and strengthen to the task. My recommendation for hikers planning to cover more than 2,000 miles in a single season is to start their training five months prior to the start of their journeys.

Whatever your hiking goals, begin your conditioning by walking a comparatively short distance, every-other day over gentle but irregular terrain. Do this initially without a backpack. If you are starting from ground zero fitness-wise, you might start by walking around the block. Or if you can handle a twenty minute walk, then start with that. Regardless of your specific approach, keep the training hikes moderate. Walk only until you become a little tired, then turn around and walk back. Resist the temptation to set geographic goals for yourself. Instead, stay tuned to your body, and regulate your outings according to your present abilities.

Limit your training forays to three or four times a week, giving yourself a rest day between every hiking day. This is beneficial for proper strengthening. At the beginning of each new week, add a little mileage. Continue with this until you can walk five miles without tiring to any significant degree.

When you can manage the five miles with no backpack, it is time to start carrying a small pack. Remember that you are not trying to condition yourself to carrying the standard elephantine load. The lightweight pack is the hiker's best friend. So don't concern yourself too much with added packweight. You can add a bit of weight week by week, but you would optimally begin with a small pack that is very lightly loaded. Carry things you might need, like water, snacks and extra clothing. Depending on your familiarity with the training region, you may need a map and compass, as well as perhaps a small knife, matches and tinder, flashlight and first aid kit. Again, add these items gradually. If the weather is cold, you could also carry an insulating pad to rest on, a warm jacket and hat to wear during the rest stops, and perhaps even a thermos of hot soup or hot chocolate.

When you are ready to increase the load further, add a few bottles of water. Water works well because you can dump some of it should you find yourself tiring, mid-way. Pour it on plants that could use the water. When training for a thru-hike, my target load is thirty-five pounds, with a distance of twelve miles.

Consider keeping a log of your conditioning mileage. The amount of mileage you will log depends on the nature and extent of your summer's hiking goals. For a two-week trek you might try for a hundred training miles. For a summer's thru-hike, I have found five hundred training miles about right. This may seem like a lot, but the training miles add up fast when the forays are regularly done.

The more you train, the easier

A widespread misconception about training is that it becomes progressively more strenuous as miles and packweight are added. Not so. As you build strength and stamina you become more capable. With the passing of weeks you will find that you can walk farther with less fatigue. Although the differences between the first training jaunt and the last one can be monumental, you do not feel those differences.

The further you progress with your training program, the greater your need for nutrition. As much as possible, eat wholesome and fresh foods. And remember to drink plenty of water, and to stretch out your calves every day. (See the Stretching chapter.)

Training for steep grades

Some trails have a reputation for steep climbs and rough tread. The Appalachian Trail certainly comes to mind, but although this trail does climb and descend a great deal, it is reasonably graded along most of its length. When Jenny and I were preparing for our AT thru-hike, only a portion of our training involved climbing and descending the local buttes. We concentrated mainly on mileage. And just as importantly, we spent a lot of time developing lightweight gear and our abilities to use it effectively in all sorts of conditions. We knew that the ultralight gear would benefit us immeasurably in terms of surmounting those hundreds of hills along the AT. And this certainly proved to be the case.

Still, "hill" conditioning can be beneficial. If you do not have access to a steep hill, you could incorporate some stair climbing and barbell squats (described below) into your training routine.

Train on irregular surfaces

On his second hike across the country, Robert Sweetgall walked 11,208 miles of roads through all fifty states in 364 consecutive days. George Meegan spent seven years on a continuous trek from the tip of South America to the top of North America, walking mostly roads. Both of these walkers have written books about their accomplishments (Bibliography). Peter Jenkins and numerous others have journeyed long and far on roads. And as any pavement pounder will tell you, roads are very tough on the feet and legs. But they are not the best surfaces for conditioning yourself for trail hiking. This is because they do very little to strengthen the lateral muscles, tendons and ligaments of the ankles and feet. So your training is best done on uneven ground. The idea is to gently work those ankles. Make them rock and roll.

Training in inclement weather

I enjoy beautiful weather as much as anyone, but on my training days I go, no matter what the weather's mood. On a sunny day I enjoy the sunshine. On a rainy day I enjoy the rain for how it scents the air with its promise of life—as I hike beneath my umbrella. If snow is falling, I enjoy the beauty of the crystals and their whitening of the landscape—again beneath my umbrella. On a cold and windy day I simply wear warmer and more protective clothing.

The more time you spend hiking in various weather conditions, the more confidence you will gain and the more you will tend to shed weather-related anxieties. In fact, during your training hikes you can use inclement weather to your advantage by testing your clothing and equipment to see what works best.

The overconfidence syndrome

One of the greatest myths in all of hiking has to do with some magical trail quality that supposedly buoys the hiker along. In reality, when we head into the wilds we are in for some real exercise. And the more ambitious our trail objectives, the better conditioned we will need to be. At the far end of the scale is the long-distance hike, which comprises walking day after day, climbing and descending interminably, and forging ahead in all types of weather for months on end. This is an intense physical challenge, and the prospective thru-hiker should not underestimate the demands and difficulties, or overestimate his or her abilities. With the proper training beforehand, the journey will likely proceed as a matter of course. Without the training, it can be very difficult.

Be aware, also, of the fitness overconfidence syndrome. Basically, in this scenario the hiker feels that he or she is in pretty good shape to begin with, and does not need to train. Granted, a person might get away with this on a short trip. And even if carrying a heavy load, the poorly-conditioned hiker will often manage to trudge along for a few days without major problems. But beyond that, the problems of being out-of-shape can begin to manifest themselves.

Another common misconception is that the hike itself will be the training. The usual plan is to start out slow, take it easy for the initial several days, gradually building strength and endurance. This approach has a serious flaw: it omits the needed rest day between each day's hiking. During the training phase, this rest day is vital to the renewal of energy and the building of strength. When well-conditioned hikers arrive at trail's beginning, ready to commence their hikes, they no longer need the every-other-day rest periods. But when out-of-shape hikers begin their journeys, they normally try to hike day after day. This places enormous strains on their bodies because it affords them very little time for recuperating, let alone for building endurance. The continuous day after day push very often leads to stress injuries. Meanwhile, most of the fun goes out of the journey. Miles of beautiful, stimulating country pass by, and all the poorly-conditioned can think about is how much they hurt. They are not conditioning or adjusting to the rigors of trail life; they are surviving.

For the most enjoyable, injury-free trek, condition yourself well, and well in advance.

Training time reduces trekking time

Let's say that two hikers set off on a two-week trek at the same time. One is well trained; the other is not, but intends to use the journey itself as the training. The first day the un-trained hiker manages eight miles. The well trained hiker is able to cover twice that, and with less overall fatigue. However, the main benefits of training become apparent not at the end of the first day, but at the beginning of the second. The out-of-shape hiker will probably struggle out of the sleeping bag—mid morning—feeling stiff, muscle sore, and needing a rest day. The well conditioned hiker is apt to arise early, and in excellent condition despite the previous day's exercise—enthusiastic to continue the trek.

For those with their sights on thru-hiking a big trail, every hour spent conditioning can shorten the journey's duration. Spend five months training beforehand, hiking maybe five hundred miles in the process, and rid your packweight of every needless ounce, and you should be able to cut a couple of months off your overall time. This reduction in duration might be an attractive option for those with limited time off from work or classes, or for those who want to avoid harsh weather at the start and end of the summer hiking season.

Of course, hikers-in-planning often want to make their journeys last as long as possible. For them the journey is what matters, rather than the destination. But the fact remains that any journey will be that much more enjoyable and risk free when the hiker begins it properly conditioned.

Supplementary exercises

Most gyms are well equipped with stair climbers, stationary bicycles, Nordic tracks and so forth. But these machines are not the best way to train for hiking, because they isolate certain muscle groups, and exert them in very singular ways. This is completely unlike the motions of hiking, which works all major muscle groups in a wide variety of ways.

Still, two leg-strengthening exercises can be very beneficial. These will help you climb out of snowpack postholes and moats, surmount steep terrain, and climb over wind-felled timber blocking the trail. And they can easily be done at home.

• When performed correctly, the barbell squat is generally considered a safe and effective thigh strengthening exercise. The technique is to stand upright, hold a barbell across your shoulders and behind your head, squat down, then rise back up. If you are new at this, use a broom handle with no added weight. Or simply hold a bottle of water in each hand. As you squat, keep your chin up and your spine upright. Most importantly, avoid squatting below the comfort level. Any knee pain indicates that you are squatting too low.

- The second recommended exercise is the leg extension, which helps strengthen the muscles supporting your knees. Sit in a chair and place the leg to be exercised over the chair's armrest, letting the foot hang free. Loop a small weight, suspended by a short length of rope or webbing, over the foot. Slowly straighten the leg, then ease it back down. Exercise gently, and use very little weight (one or two pounds) to begin with. If your knee makes grating noises, reduce the weight and merely hold the leg out horizontally, rather than raising and lowering it.

Back pain or headaches, during or after the conditioning forays, are almost always a sign of dehydration. The exercise tends to be dehydrating, and calls for an increase in water intake.

Developing a sense of balance

Another exercise of great benefit during your training program is one designed to improve your balance. A well developed sense of balance will help you walk across logs spanning small creeks, step from rock to rock, and scramble over rough terrain. And it will help you stand one-legged, for example while dumping gravel out of a shoe. None of us is born with good balance, we have to learn it, and practice it. Simply stand on one leg for a few minutes every day, looking ahead and upward. Switch legs and repeat.

Keep the training hikes fun

Avoid making the training routine so difficult that it ceases to be fun. Motivation is fueled by positive feedback; frustration by negative. If your training is not fun, then you are extremely likely to abandon it. The key here is patience. Build the miles and packweight gradually, without overextending. Also, eat a few snacks during your conditioning forays, to boost energy and uplift your spirits.

Remember that you are not just conditioning, you are developing your particular hiking style. If you go about your conditioning in a gentle way with a positive attitude, then once you begin your actual journey you will tend to adopt that same easy-going, positive manner.

"Weston the Pedestrian"

In 1909, Edward Weston walked 4,500 miles across the U.S. in 105 days. The following year, at age 72, he repeated the journey in the opposite direction in 76 days, for a remarkable average of 59 miles a day. One of the most accomplished walkers of his time, Weston believed that walking was as healthful and natural as sleeping. Throughout most of his life he walked 12 to 15 miles every day of the week except Sunday. He disdained the notion of "training" and considered his daily walking merely a part of his lifestyle.

So if you disdain the notion of training as well, consider making your pre-hike walks a regular part of your lifestyle too.

Hiking Pace

When I was on the Yukon trail,
The boys would warn, when things were bleakest,
The weakest link's the one to fail—
Said I: "By Gosh! I won't be weakest."
So I would strain with might and main,
Striving to prove I was the stronger,
Till sourdough Sam would snap: "Goldurn!
Go easy, son; you'll last the longer."

— *Robert Service, Take It Easy*

Walking with lightness and economy of motion

Top runners may cover 20 miles a day when training for competition. Yet backpackers can consistently surpass that mileage while carrying backpacks and gaining and losing thousands of feet in elevation. During our southbound PCT trek, Jenny and I hiked a 1,322 mile stretch averaging 33.9 miles a day, unsupported, for 39 consecutive days. This was from Elk Lake in central Oregon, down into northern and central California, through the High Sierra, to Kennedy Meadows. An ordeal and a struggle? Hardly; it was more like a pleasure cruise, and was one of our most memorable and connected trail experiences. The difference between a 20-mile-a-day runner, exhausting him or herself, and a higher-mileage hiker taking life easy, is little more than a carefully regulated pace.

In any type of running competition, the longer the race, the slower the pace. Over the long haul at least, it seems that the human body is capable of accomplishing only so much work each day. We can expend most of our energy in a few minutes, as do sprinters, or we can apportion it over the entire day. So if footraces and athletics teach us hikers anything, it is the trade-off between speed (or physical exertion) and endurance.

The more we exert—by carrying a heavy load, wearing heavy boots, and by hiking too fast (elevating the heart rate to extreme levels)—the fewer miles we will be able to travel each day. Yet simply putting one foot in front of the other is not the answer either. To optimize daily mileage, as well as health, comfort and enjoyment, we ensure that for each mile of hiking, we expend the least amount of energy. We accomplish this by maintaining an efficient hiking pace. And whether our trails are long or short, we can all benefit by walking with more vitality and less fatigue.

Trail running

I once met a fellow who said he was "running the PCT." Receiving extensive assistance from load carriers, shuttle drivers and resupply helpers, he and his companion carried no packs but wore a few extra garments wrapped around their waists. They were the epitome of fitness and almost military organization. However, they seemed to require one or more days of recuperation between nearly each day's travel. And because they needed so much recovery time, these fellows were actually among the season's slowest travelers. I don't mean to take the gentleman's approach out of context. His goal was to "run" the trail. But I do feel that the other hikers passing him, heavy packs and all, demonstrated that the slower but steady approach gains the better mileage.

Running is good exercise, but it is an inefficient means of travel. Running elevates the heart and respiration rates far above their most efficient levels. The result is a greater waste buildup in the muscles, deepening fatigue, and longer recovery times—to say nothing of the discomfort. This is why at the end of a marathon race, 26.2 miles of extreme effort, the runner is exhausted.

Power hiking: Hurry up and stop!

When Jenny and I hiked the Appalachian Trail in 1993, we shared the trail with more than a thousand other thru-hikers. Of course, everyone was spread out over many hundreds of miles, so we rarely saw anyone while hiking. I do not remember passing anyone who was actually moving along the trail; but a great many hikers passed us. As we ambled along at our usual, strolling pace, someone would go shooting past and disappear around the next bend. Then at the next trail junction to a shelter, we would often see where their tracks left the trail. Or sometimes we would find them resting alongside the trail, and as we strolled by we knew that we would soon be passed once again. And sure enough, varroom! They would race ahead. These were not all young, athletic types; we had a wide variety of people passing us, both young and old.

Why were these people trying to hike so fast? Perhaps like driving a car on a turnpike, they were going faster to get there sooner. Or maybe it was a reflection of our aggressive, fast-paced society. Of course, some of it could have been for show. Jenny wondered (in jest) whether there might have been an ice cream truck parked up ahead. If there was, we never found it—maybe because we were so slow. But in the late afternoons when these "power hikers" (as we started calling them) were spreading their sleeping bags in the shelters, Jenny and I were still moseying enjoyably along, making more miles. Our lack of fatigue is what allowed us to continue far into the nights. Then the following mornings we would rise early, and had usually hiked another ten miles before the others got going again.

Power hiking is like running; it is deeply fatiguing. And once the exhaustion catches up with the power hiker, it is time for a long rest. It's the hurry-up-and-stop approach. Like a series of sprints.

This is not to depreciate AT hikers by any means. In fact, the diversity of people is what makes the AT the unique experience that it is. Jenny and I delighted in the trail camaraderie. And we believe that everyone should "hike their own hike." But there were differences in style that I found interesting, those involving pace and the associated degree of fatigue.

Years earlier I had begun to wonder: what is the optimum hiking speed that will gain us the best mileage? Or the least fatigue? Of course the answer depends in part on the terrain, and the load on our feet and backs. But mainly it is a matter of listening to our bodies, and striving for the optimum cardiovascular rate. Once we have this under control—and this does not take a great deal of effort—then we will realize a considerable reduction in our per-mile energy expenditure.

Cardio-awareness

Power hiking is a matter of striving for maximum leg rate while disregarding the heart rate. My method is just the opposite. I ignore the urge for speed, and concentrate instead on the heart rate. I keep the heart beating at a moderate but efficient rate, slowing or speeding my walking pace according to the slope of terrain. This is a conscious exercise in whole-body control, not merely leg control.

The development of better cardio-awareness is best begun at home, with contemplative exercises in deep breathing and body awareness. These exercises can teach you to listen to the beating of your heart. Find a quiet place where you can sit undisturbed. Block out the surroundings and distractions, and concentrate on the inner workings of your body. Close your eyes, and feel the blood pulsing through the arteries in your neck and upper arms. Feel your heart beating and your lungs expanding and contracting. Once you have developed a better cardio-awareness, you can start putting it to use on the trail.

Developing a controlled pace

Physiologists describe aerobic exercise levels in terms of percentage of maximum heart rate, but I find this too mechanical. We are not on laboratory treadmills monitoring our electronic pulse meters and varying our pace accordingly. But we can achieve the same results by developing our natural sense of body awareness. By focusing inward and carefully avoiding over-revving our hearts, even for a moment, we will expend the least amount of energy per mile of hiking. This will take you a bit of experimentation to find the heart rate that is most efficient for you. But it will pay big dividends. And again, the key is inner awareness.

In effect, cardio-awareness is a stepping stone to a deeper wilderness connection, since it helps us flow across the landscape in a smoother and more energy-economical way. Released of the distracting fatigue and discomfort, we are free to tune into the more subtle details of the natural world all around us.

Going uphill and downhill

Although the gangbuster's pace is typically counterproductive, sometimes the circumstances might prompt us to hike at a more elevated pulse rate.

Suppose we hike 10 miles on level ground at 3 miles per hour. Excluding any periods of rest, we would cover the distance in 3.3 hours. Now instead of hiking level ground, let's say that we have a hill to climb. We hike slower uphill for 5 miles, and reaching the top we hike faster 5 miles down the other side. Will we still travel the 10 miles in 3.3 hours? For an answer, let's examine the following table. In each case, we subtraet a certain speed from the 3 mph going uphill, then add it back double on the descent.

Steepness of hill	Speed while hiking 5 miles uphill	Speed while hiking 5 miles downhill	Time required to hike the 10 miles
flat	3 mph	3 mph	3.3 hours
moderate	2 mph	4 mph	3.8 hours
steep	1 mph	5 mph	6.0 hours
very steep	0.5 mph	5.5 mph	10.9 hours

So we see that scurrying downhill at a fast clip does not even begin to recoup the time required to hike slowly uphill. This is because while hiking uphill we are traveling slower for a longer period of time, and the two effects multiply against each other. These numbers illustrate the advantages of hiking uphill at a slightly elevated heart rate, and the futility of trying to make up for lost time by surging downhill.

The rest step

I learned the rest step at a Sierra Club mountaineering class back in 1964, and have used it ever since for climbing steep slopes, particularly snowpacked slopes. You can experiment with it on a flight of stairs. Start with both feet together at the foot of the stairs. Place the right foot on the first stair tread. Lean forward but keep the right knee bent. With your weight now on the bent right leg, straighten and lock that right knee. Rest for a moment, then repeat the motions with the left leg. This technique uses a different set of leg muscles than the more typical uphill walk, and is an excellent way to moderate your pace and control your heart rate when climbing a very steep slope.

Going easy on the leg muscles

The steepness of the slope, the ruggedness of terrain, and the weight on your feet and in your pack all affect your degree of leg fatigue and muscle tightness, particularly in the calves. Your gait—the actual sequence of individual foot movements—can also influence muscle tightness. If you pull your heels off the ground prematurely with each step, and if you shove off too hard with the ball of your foot and toes, you are overworking your calves. These exaggerated motions waste effort. They tend to stiffen the muscles and increase their susceptibility to injury. And they can encourage blisters.

Take a moment occasionally to critique your shoe tracks in soft ground. Craters at the ball of the foot and toes indicate an over-energetic push-off. When walking on soft sand or crusty snow, the push-off will actually retard progress. In this case practice *lifting* the toes at the end of the stride, rather than shoving ahead with them. When walking on firm ground, a certain amount of toe push is beneficial. How much is a matter of terrain and personal style. Too much is entirely counterproductive.

Here is another easy test. Walk on soft ground a ways, then turn around and look at your line of tracks. Are the toes turned out? This is "duck walking," and for most people it can be hard on the knees. For the most efficient stride, make an effort to keep the feet tracking straight ahead.

Hiking with the brakes on

Learning to properly coordinate the muscles used for walking is another way to reduce fatigue. For example, most of us do not completely relax the muscles not being used for forward progress. During a step, certain muscles draw the leg rapidly ahead. Then those muscles must quickly relax to allow opposing muscles to draw the leg back. If the forward muscles fail to relax fast enough, they resist the rear muscles. This inadvertent braking action holds true with a multitude of opposing muscle groups throughout the body. Yet we may not notice all this as we hike along the trail. To relax and coordinate the muscles, try what I call the "robo meltdown." Without breaking stride, tense all of your muscles like a robot, then slowly decrease the tension until achieving the bare minimum of stiffness required to carry on.

Cruising

In his book *Maximum Performance* (Simon & Schuster: 1977), Laurence E. Morehouse describes a technique he calls "walking in cruising mode." The technique he describes is very similar to the smooth and flowing rapid walk—slow run technique used by native South American Indians for no doubt thousands of years. The method is to walk with the knees slightly flexed and the head held steady with minimal bobbing up and down. Crouch a few inches lower than you normally walk, lean back slightly, and pretend you are carrying a jug of water on your head. Start slowly, then build a little speed. Cruising requires an ultralight backpack, and sufficient conditioning of the muscles involved with these specific motions. Experiment with it gently to prevent pulling a hamstring or giving yourself shin splints.

Once you have tried cruising, you will see how it differs from power hiking. Cruising is a flowing, fluid-like motion, with little energy expenditure when your leg muscles are sufficiently conditioned to the movements.

Jenny and I normally walk at a very moderate pace. But when we need to cover a few quick miles we sometimes switch into cruising mode. This might be to descend to more protected ground in the event of a threatening storm, or to reach a resupply station before it closes for the weekend.

Interludes

The motions of hiking are very repetitious, but this is not to suggest that we must march along like soldiers. To break a monotonous walking rhythm, go into cruising mode for a short distance. Or turn and walk several steps sideways, or turn completely around and take a few steps backward. I know this sounds nonsensical, but try it. When you vary your step, you use different muscles in different ways. Your body, and particularly your feet and legs, will benefit from the brief interlude. So be creative with your hiking style. Strive for efficiency, but season it with a little variety. Variety is the spice of life. And it is also the spice of hiking.

Optimum resting

Frequent rest stops throughout the day will help keep the weariness from setting in. And while resting, we should keep in mind that the restorative effects are critically dependent on ample circulation. As the blood flows through the body it carries nutrients and oxygen to the tired muscles, and it carries away the waste products of metabolism. As we hike along the trail, the muscles in our legs actually help pump blood back up to our heart. When we stop and rest, our leg muscles relax. And if they are very tired, then they actually hyper-relax and allow their blood vessels to enlarge. This is known as "vaso-dilation." If we are resting on a rock or log as though sitting on a bench, then gravity will pull the blood down into our lower legs and feet, and pool it there. This is an extremely inefficient way to rest, because the pooling hampers circulation in the legs and feet, and therefore it hampers their ability to recover from exertion. A much better resting position is to sit on the ground with the legs extended, preferably with the legs also elevated a ways.

The best resting position, however, is to lie down and elevate the legs and feet to heart level or somewhat above. Rest them on a log, rock, or backpack. As a resting pad you could use your foam pad, your groundsheet, or an open jacket or shell jacket. In jest, I call this "power resting."

A restorative night's rest

Optimum circulation is equally vital for a restorative night's sleep. The greater the fatigue at day's end, the more the blood will tend to pool in the legs and feet during the night if they are even slightly below heart level. The blood pooling in the legs at night will also reduce the body's warmth, since this blood is not being circulated throughout the body. It is the proper circulation of blood, warmed by the heat of metabolism, that in turn warms the entire body. And this is true even while at rest. For the warmest and most restful night's sleep, sleep with the legs elevated. To facilitate this, look for a stealth-site on a slight grade.

The easy-going approach

Jenny and I appreciate how our lighter loads and moderate pace allow us longer days on the trail. This is important because we enjoy the hiking. To us, hiking means more than walking along passively, blocking out what is happening all around us while the mind is a thousand miles away, dwelling on some problem or memory that has nothing to do with the present moment. Rather, we try to travel in a more active, tuned-in mode. Tuned into nature, rather than to a pair of stereo headphones. We would rather listen to the constant stream of messages emanating from the landscape and its creatures—a bird's chattering, a tree's whisper of an approaching cloudburst, the tinkling of a hidden trickle of water along a dry stretch of trail. And when the ears are tuned into the natural environment, the other senses tend to follow suit. It is a matter of integrating with the setting, rather than simply passing through it en route to somewhere.

With our moderate pace, frequent rest stops throughout the day, and a rejuvenating late afternoon dinner break, we can easily continue into the evening hours, perhaps long past when other folks have pulled off the trail to make their camps. We hike on, watching the sky fade into night, absorbing the cooling night air, and listening to the nocturnal sounds of nature. When finally we do stop, it is with a feeling of satisfaction with the day's experiences. And yes, it is also with a good aura of tiredness, making for a very sound sleep.

Even though the day might have been long, it was not hard since we did not overexert. So we can rise early the next morning to greet the dawn, without feeling the need to sleep late. We enjoy the early morning hiking tremendously, soaking in the stillness and the freshness of the new day. All this is made possible by a moderate, well-controlled pace.

A bed of pine needles makes for the ultimate in power resting.

Foot Care

Keep walking and keep smiling.

— *Tiny Tim*

Why is it that we tend to neglect our feet during regular personal hygiene? Perhaps because they are so far away—out of sight, out of mind, as it were. Yet these distant members deserve our very best care and attention, since we depend on them every step of the way. After all, if our feet are suffering pain or injury, then we may not be hiking far.

Imagine the complexity: each of our feet has some 250,000 sweat glands, which altogether exude about a pint of sweat per day. And this is when at rest—the sweating is much more extensive while we are hiking, especially in hot weather. This perspiration serves to keep the skin moist and supple, but mainly it helps cool the hard-working feet. This cooling is meant to be evaporative, and heavy boots and thick socks largely prevent this. In terms of foot care, this is one major advantage with highly breathable running shoes and lightweight socks.

The ravages of athlete's foot

Athlete's foot fungus is always present on everyone's skin. This fungus consumes callus, to our benefit. Without the fungus, our calluses would grow thick and crusty, especially on the soles of our feet. Yet when we wear heavy footwear that restricts ventilation, we encourage the fungus to multiply unchecked, and this can lead to the removal of nearly all foot callus. This is bad news for the hiker, who needs a certain thickness of callus on the feet to protect them from abrasion. Stripped of callus, the feet are much more likely to blister.

The surest indication of a moderate infection is a notable lack of foot and toe callus. In this condition the skin on the bottom of the feet and toes is paper thin. The indication of a serious infection is the itching, blistered surface layers, and in more severe cases the oozing pustules. In such a condition the fungus has consumed the callus and is now feeding on live skin.

Whether you think your feet are infected or not, begin treating them for athlete's foot infection long before you head into the wilds. Distance hikers would start the foot treatment at the beginning of the pre-hike training program.

The first step in the treatment of this infection is to wear shoes that provide ample ventilation. If you could wear no footwear at all, and assuming you could avoid stepping on infective substances, then your fungal "flora" would not develop into an infection. But since going shoeless is rarely possible, your best option is probably to use an over-the-counter antifungal medication. And I might note that the liquid, or liquid spray, varieties are much more effective than the powders and spray powders.

Be careful about stepping barefoot on infective surfaces, such as bathtubs or showers, not only in motels or at the gym, but even in your own home. Protect your feet with plastic beach thongs or the like, and disinfect them occasionally. Although these precautions may seem excessive, they will go a long way in helping you avoid the pain and difficulties of blisters.

When showering in a public campground or motel, Jenny and I wear home-made shower booties. These are like inverted shower caps for the feet, with elastic around their tops. Lacking those, one could use plastic bags, or perhaps lay a spare towel over the stall floor. After showering, dry the feet well and apply antifungal medicine, carried in a small vial in the backpack.

Another hazard associated with showering barefoot in public stalls is that of contracting a plantar wart. This feels like a sharp pebble on the bottom of the foot, and it can make walking painful. It is viral in nature, and is normally transmitted on floors that someone else with such a wart had walked barefooted on.

On-the-trail foot care

Pre-hike foot care will go a long ways in eliminating problems. And the same holds true during the outing itself.

An important part of on-journey foot care involves resting, ventilating and cooling the feet during the trailside rest breaks. Depending on ambient temperature and personal fitness, these stops should normally occur after every 20 to 60 minutes of hiking. At each stop, remove your shoes and socks, shake out the gravel, and pull the insoles out of your shoes for better drying. Rest with your feet and legs elevated to encourage good circulation and the reduction of swelling. If the day is hot, then you might be able to cool your bare feet by placing them flat against a shaded rock. Or wiggle them down through the top layers of dirt to the cooler soil underneath.

The ultraviolet component of sunlight is very effective at reducing athlete's foot fungus. To this end, distance-hiker Karl Diederich suggests spreading the toes apart to the drying and healing sunshine.

Before setting off from the rest stop, tie your recently removed socks to the outside of the pack, where they can air. Brush the dust and debris from the feet and toes, massage them encouragingly, tape any sensitive areas, and put on fresh socks. Then stretch the toe area of the socks lengthwise and widthwise to give your toes more space. Before putting the shoes on, check for wrinkles in the socks. Wrinkles can induce blisters in short order. Lastly, put on your second pair of shoes or sandals, if you are equipped with them. These will be drier and cooler than the shoes you had been wearing, and a genuine pleasure to change into.

Carry at least three pairs of thin socks at a time, and for maximum foot comfort wear a pair of socks for no more than a third of the day before swapping them for fresh ones. This means that you will need to wash your socks often. With thin nylon socks this is easily done, using the "dundo" method (see the Hygiene chapter). Collect water from a natural source, move away so as not to pollute that source, and wash the socks by hand. Also wash your feet often, dry them thoroughly, and apply antifungal solution to the bottom of the feet and between the toes. Try to go barefoot at your stealth-sites, where possible, allowing your feet the fresh air and the chance to toughen.

Hot spots

Pay particular attention to your feet as to whether they are chafing inside your footwear. An increasing pain warns of a blister in the making. The minute you feel one of these "hot spots," stop and remove your footwear, and try to figure out what is causing the problem. Most of the time these hot spots stem from lack of callus, in combination with shoes or boots that fit the feet too tightly.

As mentioned, you can prevent most blisters and other foot pains by treating the feet for athlete's foot infection well in advance of the hike, and buying shoes sized larger than what you normally wear. But sitting there alongside the trail with hot spots making your feet tender, you can at least air your feet for temporary relief. If you are carrying a spare pair of sandals, change into those to reduce the heat and the friction causing the hot spots. Another option is to revert to your thinnest pair of socks, or you might be able to wear no socks at all inside your shoes or boots, giving your swollen feet a little more room. And remember that you can toughen your feet by walking a short ways along the trail barefoot each day—being careful where you step, of course.

The point is to experiment with possible solutions and find a remedy, rather than carry on and endure the pain of blisters in the making.

Blister first aid

Once a blister has formed, wash and dry it, and cover it with a *breathable* fabric adhesive strip: Band-Aid® or its equivalent. Avoid applying the adhesive part to the blister, as this could tear the skin when peeling the adhesive strip back off. If the strip fails to adhere, the skin is probably moist. Dry the skin better, then apply a new adhesive strip.

A blister is the skin's response to damage caused by heat and chafe. By filling with fluid, the blister lifts the injured layer of skin away from the underlying layers, cushioning and protecting the healthy tissue. I find, though, that the fluid actually slows healing. If you have to walk many days on a blister, then it is often helpful to drain the fluid. This reduces the pain and speeds healing, provided you do it properly. The procedure is to dab the area with antiseptic, and then to lance the blister with a flame-sterilized needle. Blot the oozing fluid with a square of clean toilet paper, dab with antiseptic, then apply a layer of Spenco 2nd Skin™ or the equivalent. The main risk with the lancing procedure is that of introducing infection. This is why keeping the area clean and sterile is important.

The product 2nd Skin consists of a sheet of moist gel, and a thin sheet of breathable, adhesive knit. To apply it to a blister, cut out a piece of gel only as large as the blister itself. The gel comes sandwiched between two layers of plastic cellophane. Remove the cellophane on one side, apply the raw gel to the blister, then remove the cellophane on the outside.

Finally, secure the gel in place using a larger strip of the adhesive knit. At day's end, remove the entire dressing—gel and knit bandage—and dispose of them in your litter bag, along with any other tape and bandages. If your blister needs protection again the following morning, apply fresh dressings.

I rarely use moleskin; it sticks so tenaciously to clean, dry skin, that it can tear the blister and pull away small chunks of healthy skin as it is being peeled off.

Duct tape is supposed to be the ultimate blister bandage, since it is more friction-free. But because it does not breathe, it greatly inhibits healing. The best way to reduce the friction is by reducing the crowding inside the footwear, again by wearing hiking shoes larger than what you normally wear at home.

Another blister-related myth is that tincture of benzoin acts as a skin toughener. I used TB for many years while climbing, as a taping base. It makes the protective tape stick better to the fingers and hands. But my skin never toughened from using the tincture.

While hiking I carry a partial roll of this white adhesive tape (also known as athletic tape). This tape is breathable, and it works well for covering hot spots. Again, I do not apply it directly to blisters because it could tear the damaged skin when being removed.

One gains little if any benefit by over-taping in an attempt to protect especially troubling blisters. Too much tape can actually worsen the situation by increasing the crowding. Jenny and I discovered this during our first thru-hike. It was only our third day when we found ourselves hobbling along blister-footed, and needing a layover day. We took the layover day, and it did wonders for our feet, and got us going again. In the next few weeks of hiking my feet gradually improved, but Jenny's feet worsened due to an athlete's foot infection and lightweight boots that fit too tightly. So there she was, bravely mincing along with blisters festooning every toe and the heels of both feet. Every morning she treated the athlete's foot infection and applied fresh bandaging, yet every day our progress diminished, despite her best efforts. Finally it became obvious that we needed to leave the trail for a few days, to allow her feet time to heal. We stopped for a rest by a cold brook, and there she removed the several layers of bandages. As an experiment, she put her shoes back on without the bandages. We plodded on, and to our surprise her pace began to improve. By mid-day her gait was back to normal. What we discovered was that all that bandaging, intended to protect the blisters, had actually been aggravating them.

I remember one time on our fifth thru-hike when a sizeable blister formed on the side of my heel. What was unusual was that it persisted for days on end. Finally I cut a hole in the shoe, removing the part that was causing the irritation, and this solved the problem.

Blisters are caused by the footwear. The moment you remove your shoes and socks, and all the tape you have applied, the blisters will begin to heal. Three days of such airing, while staying off your feet, will make your feet nearly as good as new. Even one day of bare-footed rest can work wonders. Keep this in mind should your blisters become so painful that they threaten to send you home. During the rest days, keep your feet clean and well aired, and apply antifungal liquid twice daily. And remember that when you start out again, your feet will likely re-blister if you fail to rectify what caused the blisters to begin with. Namely, athlete's foot and cramping footwear.

Cracks in dry skin

Adequate ventilation in our footwear is very beneficial, but too much can actually work against us. The person wearing sandals all summer with no socks, or someone who walks barefoot all summer, is prone to developing thick calluses that are deeply cracked, at least in drier climates. These cracks cannot heal because callus is dead skin. Yet they can be quite painful because the cracks pull the live skin apart and keep it that way.

Hiker James Lofton suggests using superglue as a temporary fix for these painful cracks. I have tried this myself and find that it does provide relief from the pain, and keeps the cracks from deepening. It also works great for cracks in the fingertips. Whether the crack is on the finger or foot, clean both the crack and the surrounding skin well, then lay a bead of adhesive over the crack. Pinch the cracked skin together, and hold it that way until the glue has hardened. Interestingly, superglue was invented during the Vietnam War era, specifically to close lacerations. Yet the packaging now warns against applying it to the skin.

Superglue on the feet is a temporary "fix," allowing the hiker to continue walking less painfully. It does not prevent new cracks from forming. The solution for the person hiking in a dry climate while wearing sandals is to wear a few pairs of thin socks also. These hold in just enough beneficial moisture to prevent the cracking.

———

Our feet deserve all the attention and meticulous care we can give them, both before and during the hike. With a good balance of fresh air and sunshine, ventilation and protection, comfort and roominess, cleanliness and care, our feet will carry us as long and as far as our minds can dream.

Walking-Related Stress Injuries

> Creativity can solve almost any problem.
> The creative act, the defeat of habit by originality,
> overcomes everything.
>
> — *George Lois*

Prevention and treatment

The natural world beckons us to come and explore. And one of the best ways is to travel on foot. Walking is extremely beneficial to health, and it affords greater freedom and more time to savor the glories of nature.

Yet walking for any distance is contrary to today's urban way of life. We rely on vehicles and other labor saving devices, and as a result are generally in less than ideal physical condition. So when heading into the wilds, the tendency is to turn to modern equipment to make up the difference. Today's "advanced" backpacks are purported to carry heavy loads in comfort, so they encourage people to carry big loads. But they do nothing to assist the hiker's knees, ankles and feet in sustaining those loads. Trekking poles are supposed to relieve the stress of walking, but in reality they do very little. Stout boots are often advertised to take a person virtually anywhere on earth in perfect comfort, but their greater mass and stiffness only add to the problems.

Regardless of the type of equipment carried, (or in many cases because of it) the rigors of wilderness trekking can sometimes overtax the hiker's body. The result is discomfort at best, and pain at worst. Pain is a natural warning signal, telling of an impending injury. It is the body's way of saying, "Please stop this, because something inside me is being stressed in the wrong way." If the hiker ignores the pain and continues ahead, the overexertion may indeed lead to a stress injury.

Causes of injury

Let's take a look at a few of the more common hiking pains, their causes, prevention and treatment.

• **Carrying too heavy a load**

Imagine a normally sedentary person driving to a trailhead, then reaching down and picking up a heavy backpack. Crack! The back lets go, and this person is now suffering a "slipped disk." Or imagine that the person manages to shoulder the pack without incident, and proceeds to follow the trail leading steeply uphill. The hiker reaches the top, sweating and breathing hard, and all is apparently well—until descending the far side, which is also steep. Grind! The knees let go, and that person now has "blown out" knees. Let's say that, fortunately, neither accident happens and our heavily burdened, ill-conditioned hiker manages the steep climb and descent, and proceeds along the trail without incident—until accidentally stepping on a protruding rock with the edge of his boot. Snap! The ankle twists sideways and cartilage breaks loose. The person has sprained an ankle.

These accidents happen almost every day of the summer. But does this mean that the wilderness is inherently risky, or that hiking is dangerous? Or might it suggest that these people are carrying loads far too heavy for them?

• **Inadequate physical conditioning**

For trips lasting weeks or months, pre-hike training will be important to success. But even for the occasional day-hike we benefit by conditioning our bodies ahead of time with regular exercise. Short but regular "training" walks with a small pack would suffice for a weekend outing, at least if that outing will be done with lightweight gear. A multi-month trek would require a more definitive training program. In addition to the training walks, certain exercises can benefit specific areas of the body. The foot-lift exercises, described previously, will go a long way in mitigating knee problems. Certain other exercises can raise fallen arches and help straighten pronating ankles. Even old injuries to bones, tendons and cartilage can be strengthened with exercise.

• **Wearing boots that are too heavy**

Heavy footwear increases the exertion and reduces the hiker's overall progress. It also subjects the hiker to greater risk, since it makes the walking more clumsy.

• **Wearing any kind of footwear that is stiff-soled**

Boots or shoes with steel shanks or other sole-stiffeners restrict the legs, ankles and feet from flexing naturally. These devices can lead to soreness, pain and eventually to injury.

• **Wearing footwear that is ill-fitting or broken down internally**

Based on my own experiences and the feedback from many other hikers, I estimate that the chances are about 70% that any pair of shoes or boots will eventually cause pain. The person who tries to ignore this pain is heading for a debilitating injury. The two most common shoe problems are improper fit, and worn-out internal materials—even though the shoes or boots may appear fine on the outside. Either of these problems can create unbalanced forces with every step, and lead to pain and injury. Proper fitting footwear in serviceable condition goes a long way toward reducing this type of injury.

• **Dehydration**

Adequate water intake is essential for health, particularly while hiking. Our joints need water for lubrication and cushioning; our muscles, tendons, and cartilage need water as well. Deprived of adequate fluid, they lose their elasticity and become increasingly brittle. This can happen to our bones also, making them more susceptible to stress fracture. In any pain-injury situation, acute dehydration almost always plays a role.

• **Neglecting hourly calf-stretching exercises, while training and on journey**

Strenuous hiking places great demands on the calf muscles. In an attempt to "guard" themselves, these muscles tighten, becoming less elastic. Gentle but regular calf stretching encourages these muscles to relax, and helps restore their suppleness. Read more about this in the next chapter (Stretching).

On longer journeys, tight calves can be more of a problem. The stiffness and pain can be accompanied by swelling, discoloration, and sensitivity of the skin of the lower leg and ankle. I have experienced these symptoms while wearing certain shoes and not while wearing others. The usual causes are dehydration, lack of regular calf-stretching exercises, a stride that places undue strain on the calves—such as an overly aggressive toe push-off—and faulty footwear. When I stop a few times each hour to drink water and stretch out the calf muscles, the swelling reduces and the symptoms subside. And with new shoes the symptoms vanish.

The pain that stabs with every step

Another foot condition specific to hikers, particularly long-distance hikers, is the stress of repetition. It is caused not by the hiking itself, but by the repetition of taking step after thousands of steps in poorly fitting or broken down footwear. The shoes or boots may not fit properly. They may have some small manufacturing defect, unnoticed at first but worsening with wear. Or they may have broken down internally over the course of many miles. I have hiked a great many miles in scores of different shoes and boots, and nearly every one of them has ultimately broken down and started causing problems. Footwear of any type is artificial, and the technology is still a long ways from perfection. This is why virtually any shoe or boot has the potential to cause a stress injury if walked in for too many miles.

Footwear-related stress problems are characterized by a pain that stabs with every step. While the budding injury itself may be in the foot, the pain can be elsewhere: in the ankle, leg or knee, or even in the hip or lower back. Regardless of the location of the stabbing-type of pain, it almost always signals a dire problem calling for prompt attention. This is one instance where determination will work against us. I know runners who have tried to "run through" various stress pains, only to undergo multiple surgeries in the lower extremities that left them permanently injured. But the good news is that normally we hikers do not have to endure these pains for long. A few minutes is about my limit. How do we stop them? By realizing that our footwear is causing them, and by taking the appropriate corrective measures.

A pain that stabs with every step may be gradual in its onset, or it may be sudden. Either way, the alarms are sounding and the red lights are flashing. First and foremost is to say a requiem for the shoes or boots you are wearing. It does not matter how many miles you have hiked in them, or how few—or how expensive and widely advertised. Nor does it matter how terribly fond of them you may have become. If you are walking with a stabbing pain, then those shoes or boots are threatening your health and the continuance of your journey. Many hikers have not recognized this simple truth, and have left the trail and returned home. Yet the solution is straightforward. Remove the offending footwear, place it in your pack, and carry it out to civilization. There you would send the broken-down shoes or boots home, or if they are well worn, you would deposit them in a rubbish bin. Either way, the key is to recognize the footwear as the source of the problem.

After removing the offending shoes or boots, your next step is to begin rehydrating in earnest. The more water you can drink, the speedier will be your recovery. Chug down as much water as you can, then change into your spare pair of shoes or sandals and hike to the next water source. There, start drinking water by the quart.

Rest and rehydration can be very beneficial, especially if you elevate the painful foot or leg. But no amount of rest will remedy faulty footwear. If you put those offending shoes or boots back on and continue on your way, they will probably disable you once again.

If you are not carrying spare shoes or sandals when the stress pain strikes, then you will have to experiment. After resting, try walking barefoot a ways, assuming that the terrain is accommodating. If the pain continues to stab while walking barefoot, then you need a longer rest and lots of water. Haul off the trail and make camp, and try again in the morning, but not before stretching the calves ever so gently. Since the cells of the body take two or three days to rehydrate completely, continue your hydration efforts for that period of time.

If the pain is less severe, and if you have no spare footwear, then you could experiment with ways of modifying the offending footwear to at least enable you to reach the next town. Jam a bandana or handful of grass or moss into the shoe or boot of the affected leg, placing a sizable wad under the arch. Walk a ways and see if this helps. If not, move the wad under the heel, and try that. If you cannot find a way to continue in the footwear, then try walking in several pairs of socks. Or fabricate a makeshift shoe by wrapping the hurtful foot in a few shirts and lashing them in place with cord.

While experimenting with any of these remedies, place the painful foot down gently with each step. No more tromping. Rest often, and with the feet uphill. Then at the next town, buy a new pair of shoes.

As you pursue your wilderness goals, you can greatly reduce your vulnerability to hiking-related injuries by conditioning your body ahead of time, by drinking plenty of water, and by paring down your packweight to a reasonable minimum. And for the long-distance hiker, the best way to prevent stress injuries is to avoid hiking in ill-fitting or internally broken down shoes or boots.

Stretching

Limber muscles
for safer hiking

The more we use our muscles, the stronger they become. But during vigorous exercise our muscle fibers tend to develop microscopic tears. These produce the typical "muscle soreness," the aching and the stiffness. Of all the muscles in the hiker's body, it is those in the legs that are the prime target for these stress tears. And this is especially true for the long-distance hiker. In an attempt to guard against the associated micro-damage, the leg muscles stiffen. But this can lead to more damage, as the exercise of hiking continues. Regular, gentle stretching encourages the muscles to relax, and can do much to prevent the micro-tears from growing larger and leading to bona-fide injuries.

In *Yoga 28 Day Exercise Book,* Richard Hittleman writes, "[Stretching] requires a minimum of effort to attain maximum results." In other words, the stretch is pressed only until a slight pull is felt, and no more. If overstressed, the muscles contract and shrink in an attempt to guard themselves from injury.

I have completed Hittleman's 28-day program many times and recommend it highly. But I would caution against working the joints away from the axes of normal hiking flexion. Out-of-axis *exercising* strengthens the ligaments; out-of-axes *stretching* tends to weaken them. An example of out-of-axis stretching would be the lotus position (seated on the ground, legs crossed, each foot atop the opposite leg). Hikers should not practice this because it can weaken the knees laterally.

Let's take a look at a couple of stretching exercises that will limber our legs and help keep them injury-free.

The hiker's calf stretch

Before you can stretch a muscle, you must relax it. Otherwise, the stretching could injure it. Relaxing a muscle is not easy, especially after it has been propelling you along the trail for several hours. But with practice, you can relax the muscles quickly in order to stretch them.

The best leg stretching exercise is the hiker's calf stretch. This is a modification of the classic runner's calf stretch. Practice this stretch several times during the day's hiking, as well as in the morning before setting off, and in the evening before retiring.

Stand facing a sturdy object, such as a tree, a rock, or an embankment. Position your feet a yard or more out from its base. Let's use a tree for our example. Lean in and brace the hands against the trunk, elbows locked straight—as though about to do a push up.

Stretch one leg at a time. Let's start with the right leg. Straighten the right knee, and let the heel rest on the ground. Cross the left leg in front of it, toe on the ground and heel slightly elevated. Press the back of the left knee against the front of the right knee, locking the right knee into position. This helps the right leg relax by preventing its knee from buckling, and it shunts most of the balancing mechanisms that would interfere with muscular relaxation. Be careful not to let the right ankle pronate, or roll inward, because this would place great strain on the ligaments. If your ankle naturally pronates, which most do to some extent, place the inner edge of the right foot on a small rock or stick for additional support.

Once in position, slowly bend the elbows, bringing the body closer to the tree. Relax, feel the stretch in the right calf, push away slightly, and hold for twenty heartbeats.

Lift the right leg and let the foot hang limp. If you have been hiking vigorously you may feel a throbbing sensation in the calf muscles. This is caused by the muscle relaxing, the blood vessels dilating, and the blood pooling. This throbbing is a sure indication that you need to pay more attention to the stretching exercises, and to keep them gentle. When the dangling calf has relaxed as much as it is going to (in ten or fifteen seconds) and the throbbing has eased, place the foot back down gently, and repeat the stretching procedure with the other leg.

Do not practice this stretching exercise while standing totally upright, in balance. In this position the many muscles in the legs are constantly flexing, first on one side of the legs then the other, keeping the body in balance. Before a muscle will stretch safely, we must relax it. This is why we lean against a fixed object, to shut off the balancing mechanism and allow the calf muscles to relax.

The hiker's ankle, foot, and toes stretch

Another exercise of particular benefit to the hiker is the ankle, foot, and toes stretch. You can do this stretch using the same tree that you used for the calf stretch. In addition, look for a small platform to rest the foot upon, such as a rock, log, or a sloped embankment; something no more than six inches high. Leaning forward against the tree, position the right foot back, its heel flat on the ground as before, but without locking the knee. Bring the left foot forward and place it on the platform, with the heel hanging off the edge. Without placing body weight on the forward foot, roll it up onto the ball, flexing the toes back gently. Be careful not to pivot the ankle sideways, or in a circular motion, because this would stretch its ligaments out-of-axis. Hold for five heartbeats. Without removing the foot from the platform, relax the forward leg completely. This rolls the foot back down and stretches out the calf muscle. Hold this relaxed position for twenty heartbeats. Repeat this stretch with the other leg.

———

Regular stretching is very beneficial, and will do much to keep you injury free on the trail. Pay particular attention to the calves, and make these exercises a part of your everyday routine. Drinking plenty of water throughout the day also helps. The dehydrated hiker's muscles tend to be quite stiff, and far less capable. When dehydrated, stretch only with *extreme* gentleness.

Hygiene

If you don't have comfort,
you give up the trip for lack of enjoyment,
before you give out for loss of energy.

— *Verlen Kruger*

Backcountry practices for good health

One of the joys of an excursion into nature is the freedom it affords from society's obligations. Incidental niceties and customs—such as hair styling, shaving, the use of deodorant and even toothpaste—are not necessary when we set out on our simpler lifestyles. At the same time, hiking and camping do not offset the need for good hygiene. Regular hygiene will go a long way in discouraging various intestinal disorders. And cleanliness can promote a strong sense of comfort and well being, which in turn can lead to a more positive attitude. Keeping ourselves clean is also a sign of respect for ourselves and those we meet. So while it is one thing to adopt a more natural approach, being a trail tramp is not a mandatory, or even beneficial part of the summer's experience.

Bathing in the wilds, dundo style

Our skin is an excretory organ, in the sense that our pores eliminate toxins from our bodies. This is why doctors call the skin our "second liver." And it is one of the main reasons we need to keep our skin clean.

Most hikers, myself included, take pleasure in the occasional dip, especially in large lakes and natural hot springs. In fact, swimming or dipping in creeks and lakes is the backpacker's standard method of bathing. And while these activities are a way to a higher connection with the natural world, we must also consider that the next person coming along might not care to collect drinking water from that in which we just swam. So we need to respect the rights of others who may be seeking pristine wilderness experiences of their own. This is why swimming and dipping are becoming more controversial, especially in regards to the smaller water sources. More and more we need to consider the adverse ecological impact. The fact is, the residues washed from our bodies are far more polluting than most of us might imagine. Plug the drain at home and take a quick shower, then examine the water—you will see what I mean. Body oils, dead skin, hair, salts and acids from sweat can all have an impact on backcountry water sources, particularly the smaller ones. As can the dirt and grime accumulated while hiking, along with any applied bug repellent and sunscreen.

As we hike along the trail our skin becomes coated with this "trail patina," and we are better off removing it. Fortunately, the "dundo" bathing method makes this easy. With this approach we do not bathe with water only, we can also use soap. This might seem contradictory to the Connection, but consider that many if not most primitive humans used natural soaps, such as tannic acid and saponin-rich plants. Nevertheless, the dundo with soap is more effective than a swim or a dip without, and almost as convenient and refreshing. And correctly done, it has no adverse effects on the water sources.

Jenny coined the term "dundo" (*DONE-dough*) in regards to bathing, during our AT hike. An excerpt from our trail journal describes how this came to be: "After a day of crossing the Skyline Drive, climbing the next hill, thrashing through brush, and descending to the road again, ad infinitum, we passed the turnoff to the Blackrock Shelter and continued a few miles to the Dundo Picnic Area. The place was deserted, so at a drinking fountain we stripped, and ignoring a light rain we filled our water bottles and poured the contents over ourselves, while hastily rubbing on a bit of soap. We had not been long re-dressed when a car drove slowly past, its three passengers gawking at us. Never mind the publicity, one cannot describe the wonderful feeling of the chilly splashes embellished with a small bar of soap after a long, hot and sweaty day." Jenny started referring to this type of bath as the "dundo," and the name stuck.

Regardless of the type of container used, one simply dips it into the water source and carries it to the showering area. Similar to a stealth area, this dundo shower area is used only once by one person, to keep the impact at a minimum. Be sure to locate it far enough away from the water source such that heavy rains would not leach it back. For best results, scrub vigorously with a wet hand towel and a small amount of soap. Collect more water, move well away from the water source again, and rinse off. Repeat as necessary. Wring out the hand towel and use it to dry off with, wringing the towel of excess water now and then. You can wash your hair in the same way.

The hand towel I use is nothing more than a cotton washcloth, approximately eight inches square. For soap I have found that a liquid biodegradable type works well for washing hair, while a very small chunk of bar soap—preferably perfume-free—is adequate for the body.

A shortage of water or a blustery day is hardly an obstacle to bathing. One can sponge bathe while wearing clothing by reaching under and scrubbing with a damp hand towel. The camper can also sponge bathe while inside the tent or under a tarp, again using a damp hand towel.

Oral hygiene

Hard work and good nutrition promote healthy bodies, teeth and gums included. This is because the extra exercise of the hiking lifestyle promotes better circulation, and consequently better vitality throughout the body. Generally speaking, then, distance hikers suffer very few dental problems. Nevertheless, all hikers will benefit from regular brushing and flossing. Some dentists advise that toothpaste actually complicates various gum problems. Toothpaste is an abrasive, and it is loaded with chemicals and so-called natural ingredients—most having nothing to do with oral hygiene. I feel that brushing without these agents makes better sense in the wilds. And who among us appreciates the splats of toothpaste residue around camping areas and water sources? The best way to dispose of toothpaste, once used, is to dilute it with a mouthful of water, and disperse it in a vigorous spray, well away from the more heavily used areas.

If you are in the habit of brushing while you hike, as I am, remember to breathe through your nose rather than your mouth during brushing. Brushing creates a fine mist that is not particularly beneficial to inhale. And of course, you would need to be very careful not to stumble with toothbrush in mouth. I cut off part of the toothbrush handle and often carry my stunted toothbrush in my pocket. I first learned of "adventure brushing" during a climb of the North Face of the Grand Teton, in Wyoming. Peter Lev and I were bivouacked on a tiny ledge that we had chopped at the head of a steep glacier. Sitting there, strapped to the ledge to prevent ourselves from sliding into the abyss, I looked over at Peter, and there he was blissfully brushing his teeth. I asked why in the world he bothered, and he replied, "It's refreshing."

Remember, too, that rinsing the toothbrush in suspect water could introduce giardia into your system the next time you use the brush. Rinse it in treated or spring water (away from the water source). And at some of the resupply stations, or at home after a short trip, consider disinfecting your toothbrush by soaking it in hydrogen peroxide, or by pouring boiling water over it.

The primitive privy

When the wagon trains headed west in the mid- and late nineteenth century, cholera killed more emigrants than anything else. In a bad year, some wagon trains lost two-thirds of their travelers. Cholera is caused by a certain bacterium, and virtually the only means of contracting it is from food or water contaminated by the stools of other cholera sufferers. Prevention of the disease is a matter of sanitation.

Hepatitis A virus (HAV) is another disease spread when infected individuals do not wash their hands after using the toilet, and then handling food. People who eat this contaminated food run a high risk of becoming infected. The virus also spreads in drinking water that is contaminated, even minutely, with excrement.

Traveler's Diarrhea is another malady resulting from poor sanitation and hygiene. It is caused by infection with one of a number of bacteria, protozoa or viruses that are ingested when eating food or drinking water, again contaminated by stool. Dysentery is a particularly severe form of diarrheal disease.

All this suggests the importance of maintaining good sanitation, especially when it comes to the primitive privy.

Along developed and often busy paths such as the Appalachian Trail, we are obliged to use the installed privies, although there are plenty of hikers who do not. Instead, they dig cat holes behind trees and bushes, often somewhere around the perimeter of the shelters and the established campsites because of a reluctance to venture into the darkness of night. Which is only to say: be careful about where you pitch your shelter in these areas!

While hiking less frequented trails we are generally free to head for the proverbial "bushes," as long as we move well away from the trail and any water sources. On the way, collect an assortment of natural toilet paper—smooth stones, leaves, sphagnum moss (going easy on the ecology), evergreen twigs, or Douglas fir cones. Flattened snowballs work particularly well. If well chosen, any of these materials work better than toilet paper. At the selected site, dig a "cat hole" about six inches deep. If the hole is much deeper than this, the microbes will not be able to decompose it. To dig the hole, use a plastic trowel, the adze of an ice axe, or a stick. Or in soft ground simply dig with the heel of the shoe. If stooping is awkward or uncomfortable, try sitting on the edge of a log or rock.

In his book *Chips from a Wilderness Log,* Calvin Rutstrum writes: "You also need to train your evacuation organs. Once trained they will respond by reflex. Don't sit on the seat for long periods straining. Watch an animal. He does it as you should, in one fell swoop. Forget what you can't readily evacuate with the first generous effort, and proceed with the cleaning process. In time you will have trained the bowel to give forth a stool in one single release."

After using natural "toilet paper" (stones, leaves, etc), finish the job with a few sheets of toilet paper if desired. Try to minimize the use of TP, since it can remain intact for a long time, particularly in drier climates and at higher elevations. Rather than leave it lie, or bury it, a better idea is to bag it, and either carry it out or burn it at the next opportunity. Never burn TP at the cat-hole site in the woods; a number of forest fires have resulted from this practice.

On your return from the bushes or established privy, wash your hands with an antibacterial scrub, such as ethyl alcohol gel (recommended in the upcoming First Aid chapter). Otherwise, use an antibacterial soap, not in a creek but dundo style—pouring water from a container, well away from the water's source. Sterilizing your hands will *greatly* reduce the chances of your contracting giardia protozoa and other bacteria and microorganisms the next time you eat from your hands. And remember that not all hikers wash their hands after eliminating, by any means. As a precaution, beware of eating food they have touched, or even touching things that they have touched.

Burying tampons and sanitary pads invites animals to dig them back up. Burning them requires an extremely hot fire, inconsistent with today's no-trace ethic. These materials must be carried out, and one recommended method is to double bag them. An inexpensive and ecological option is the use of a natural (and reusable) sea sponge. Carry water away from the water source, and pour it on the sponge to rinse it, and to wash yourself. A more expensive option is a menstrual cup such as the "Keeper."

Washing dishes

Washing dishes with soap and hot water is a carry-over from home, and that is a good place to leave this practice when venturing into the backcountry. This is not to suggest that we should ignore the job altogether. But dishwashing soap has its problems. It will cut some of the grease and food residue but certainly not all. The grease that remains on the pots and dishes will begin to harbor harmful bacteria. Dishwashing soap does not sterilize the dishes against these undesirable microorganisms. Soap residue left on dishes can cause diarrhea (and soap left in camp-laundered clothing can irritate the skin). Moreover, the entire process is wasteful of treated water, and it introduces unnecessary chemicals into the environment, due to the large amounts sometimes used. Scouring dishes with a nylon scrub pad is particularly unhygienic. The pad collects bacteria and provides an ideal breeding ground for bacteria. In other words, the scrub pad actually contaminates the dishware it is supposed to be cleaning, to say nothing of the water sources when being rinsed out. If your camp dishes are greasy or oily, water by itself will clean them very little, particularly if the water is cold. And unless you first purify that water, it could expose you to giardia and other undesirable protozoa. Even long after the dishes have dried, a percentage of the microorganisms can remain active.

Jenny and I use a different approach. First, we eat from our cookpot. Leaving the plates and bowls at home obviates the incessant chore of washing them, and then having to sterilize them. After eating from the cookpot we clean it. Depending on what we have cooked, we might pour water into the pot, then after scraping and stirring with a spoon, we might drink the resulting gruel if we are low on water. Or if not, we simply disperse it—far away from any water sources. We then wipe any remaining grease or residue with a handful of weeds, dried fern, leaves, or pine needles. Any persistent spots we scrape with a stick. Afterwards, we disperse these materials, leaving no indication that we had cooked and eaten there. The next time we boil water in the pot we are automatically sterilizing it. And we can dip our spoons into the boiling water also.

We do not normally carry drinking cups. Hikers who do would be effectively sterilizing their cups every time they pour boiling water into them, when making hot drinks.

Sterilizing water bottles

For proper hygiene we must also sterilize—or replace—our water bottles on a regular basis. This is especially important if we use the bottles for mixing flavoring powders. To sterilize a water bottle, one method is to boil some water for a hot cuppa, and pour it first into the empty water bottle, swishing it around a bit, before pouring it into your cup (or discarding). Another possibility is to zap your water bottles in a microwave oven, as long as the bottles have no metal parts. And while at it, you could zap your plastic spoons as well. Or you could soak your water bottles overnight in a strong solution of water purification chemicals or household bleach. On longer journeys you could include such products in the resupply parcels. An attractive option is to dispense with commercial water bottles, and use recyclable beverage containers as water bottles. By replacing them once every two weeks you obviate the need to sterilize them.

Incidentally, one should never mix powdered milk in a plastic water bottle. The pores in the plastic will absorb some of the milk, making it impossible to remove. Such a bottle will never again keep water fresh.

Incinerating trash

When finding bits of litter along the trail, candy wrappers and so forth, it is always a good idea to pick them up. Not only will this small deed help to keep our wild lands litter free, it will also avoid the problem of the hikers coming along behind you thinking the trash was yours.

Your own accumulating trash (usually empty food wrappers, plastic packaging, and used toilet paper) can become bulky and heavy, especially when hiking for many days between wayposts of civilization. Along some of the more developed trails you might find trash receptacles at trailheads and road crossings, but when these are not available you will need to carry your litter out and dispose of it properly, even if that means carrying it for several days.

In remote regions, burning might be an option, if carefully done. Burning plastic is never a good idea, since most types emit toxic fumes when burned, and breathing those fumes can make you very ill. On a windless day you might be able to burn paper, toilet paper, cardboard, and cellulose (a wood product), but only if you can manage it in a low-impact way. Remember that hastily burned trash leaves an ugly mess.

If you decide to incinerate your burnable trash, here is the best way. Select a place on bare dirt or sand. Make certain the ground is not humus or duff. And stay away from tree roots, since a smolder could work its way underground, consuming the sap-rich root until eventually reaching the tree. Build a tiny fire, no bigger than 4 inches in diameter and 4 inches tall. Use matchstick-size twigs. Into this fire feed the paper and cardboard, small bits at a time. Add more kindling as required. Without the kindling, the fire will not burn hot enough to consume the trash. As the ritual is winding down, place the unburned shards of wood back into the little fire. When the flame self-extinguishes for want of fuel, do not simply bury the ashes. Instead, stir them into the earth. The more you stir them, the more you grind them into powder, and the more the admixture of dirt will cool the particles and distance them, rendering them incapable of rekindling. Sufficient stirring will erase the little fire site altogether. Lastly, "monster mash" what remains, as described earlier in the Campfire and Cook-fire chapter.

Restaurant sanitary measures

Restaurant meals are sometimes few and far between, but when available they are valuable. They have a way of lifting our spirits, filling our stomachs with plenty of fresh foods, and injecting our hikes with more enthusiasm. But they do require certain precautions in terms of hygiene. This is because they are potential sources of colds and flu, the result of germs left behind by infected customers. We hikers are particularly vulnerable because we tend to lose some of our immunities while living in the wilds, which are relatively free of these types of germs. Once we become infected, our trek can lose much of its luster while these ailments run their course.

The best defense is to keep from touching the usual infectious objects—doorknobs, table tops, etc.—and to eat with your own spoon rather than the house silverware. In fact, one should view all house tableware with great suspicion, particularly the forks because the spaces between the tines are well known for harboring microbes. The laws pertaining to sterilizing dishware are loosely interpreted and rarely followed. To keep your health intact, drink water from your own water bottle, or ask for a straw. Also, remember that the table top is almost never sterilized, which is why it is not safe to eat bits of food that you might have dropped onto it.

> (According to FDA Model Rule, which most states adopt but few restaurants follow, the rinse cycle of a dishwasher must reach 160°F. Dishes washed by hand must be by the 3-sink method: wash, rinse in 160°F water, and sterilize in 75°F water and chlorine bleach @ 50-200 ppm.)

These precautions may seem extreme, but most hikers who have become very sick would no doubt endorse this advice heartily. They, like myself, have learned the hard way that when hauling into town, the hiker needs to be diligent about not handling things that other people have. This holds true not only at the restaurant table, but in the restrooms.

And by the way, don't forget that you could order a second meal "to go" and carry it with you to your next camp. It will make a great dinner.

First Aid Supplies

The subject of wilderness first aid is beyond the scope of this book, so I can only refer you to a first aid manual or two. Some of the more prevalent ones are very well done (Bibliography). By studying these you will gain confidence in your abilities to handle most first aid situations.

The hiker's first aid kit is somewhat more specific than the ones described in the manuals. A kit containing enough first aid items to meet every contingency would be impracticably heavy, bulky and expensive. So we compromise by including only the basic items intended to handle some of the more possible situations.

Prior to embarking on a longer hike, consider getting a physical exam. In addition to alerting you to any potential problems, the physician can prescribe medication you might need for your first aid kit, such as that for giardiasis, poison oak / ivy, and bee stings—and can caution you in their use. During the visit, explain that you will be hiking in the wilds. Some types of medication can lessen a person's capacity for strenuous exertion. And some types can cause photo-sensitivity of the skin.

A few items carefully chosen

My first aid kit contains only a few items, but each is carefully chosen. Certainly you may find the need for more (or different) items, in anticipation of your needs.

- **Gelled ethyl alcohol** characterized by the stationary bubbles, and sold under many brand names (such as Purell®), and used as a waterless hand sanitizer. Contains about 60% ethyl alcohol in a glycerin-like base. Compare brands to avoid the strongly scented ones. Carry in a small vial and use mainly as an antibiotic scrub for the reduction of giardia and cryptosporidia protozoa on the hands after eliminating. Use also for sterilizing blisters and superficial cuts and abrasions, and decontaminating the skin after contact with poison ivy and oak. Replenish on longer journeys by including more in the resupply parcels.

- Small bar (or vial of liquid) **antibacterial soap** for bathing dundo style. Whether biodegradable or not, do not use this directly in a natural water source.

- **Betadine®** for use in more serious cuts and punctures, where alcohol would damage the underlying tissue.

- **Antiseptic salve**. Alcohol is a flash sanitizer; Betadine is the same but also leaves a protective film. Use either when you want the wound to breathe. For more lasting protection use an antiseptic salve. My favorite is Campho-Phenique® Antibiotic Plus Pain Reliever.

- Small vial of **antifungal solution** for the treatment of athlete's foot infection.

- A small, partial roll of **white adhesive tape**, also known as athletic tape. Useful for bandaging hot spots and blisters. You can also use this tape to wrap a sprained ankle, although a properly tied bandana would also suffice.

- A half dozen (or more) **adhesive strips** (such as Band Aids®), and a couple of small, **sterile gauze pads**.

- One or two sheets of **Spenco 2ⁿᵈ Skin™** or the equivalent, for blisters and burns. Include a small knife with scissors to cut this material, and a small needle for lancing blisters.

- A small pair of **tweezers** for the removal of ticks, thorns, stickers, cactus spines and wood slivers.

- **Aspirin** or other mild pain reliever.

- In venomous snake country: a **suction device** such as the Sawyer Extractor™.

- Poison ivy / poison oak preventatives and/or medications.

A simple first aid kit containing a few well-chosen items will suffice for most hiking endeavors. Of course there is no substitute for knowledge, and one would be wise to review a first aid manual every now and then. Remember, too, that serious accidents requiring major first aid treatment are often the result of carelessness. Safety in the wilds depends mainly on common sense, alertness while hiking and camping, and an awareness of potentially risky situations.

Photography

A man must carry knowledge with him
if he would bring home knowledge.

— *Samuel Johnson*

Camera, contrast and the art of seeing

Photographs can capture the magic of the moment, and they are a great way to foster enthusiasm for the outdoors and to encourage wilderness preservation. The photographs we take during our hiking and camping adventures can help us share what it was like "out there" with family and friends. Some hikers may want to give more formal slide presentations to groups, and others will need pictures for articles and books. And almost everyone who takes photographs enjoys reminiscing over his or her pictures, refreshing the memories and reliving the experiences.

———

Regardless of our individual motivations for taking photographs, we can greatly improve their quality with an understanding of the basics of photography. Excellent books on the subject abound, and the more we read and study a few of them, the better our pictures.

The hiker's camera

If you are interested in high quality, professional images, then you will need to carry more expensive camera gear, and this can add considerable weight and bulk. But do not assume that the cameras, lenses, tripods, flash attachments and reflectors will automatically guarantee masterful photos. This equipment is truly useful only in the hands of someone well versed in the art and science of photography.

Those of us who are not accomplished photographers might be better off selecting a camera for its simplicity and ease of use. A quality point-and-shoot model has fewer features and settings to keep track of, yet it is capable of producing very satisfactory photos. The main advantage of the point-and-shoot camera is that it will probably weigh a good deal less than a more sophisticated single lens reflex (SLR) camera and lens. It will also allow more spontaneity, due to its ease of use.

Lens quality varies greatly among brands and models, and has a tremendous effect on the quality of images the camera can produce. Check with your local camera shop and ask which point-and-shoot cameras have the sharpest lenses. Other desirable features include the self timer and the built-in flash. Equally important is the type of film used, and the quality of film processing. For best results, study the camera's many functions, as described in the product guide. Then practice by shooting a few rolls of film. This will give you a better working knowledge of the camera, and once you see the resulting pictures you will know how well the film is performing, and whether the processing lab work is to your satisfaction.

Several of today's small point-and-shoot cameras are 'weatherproof' or weather resistant. These features can extend the life of the camera, and they permit taking pictures during inclement weather, allowing the hiker to capture a more realistic impression of the expedition. Still, one must be careful not to introduce moisture and grit inside the camera when changing film. Water can damage the electronic and mechanical components. Regardless of your camera's type, stow it in a waterproof bag until needed.

A single particle of dust can scratch the film acetate or its emulsion as the film advances from frame to frame, and again later as it rewinds. The result is what appears to be one or more telephone wires traversing each scene. You can minimize the problem by cleaning the camera's interior with a small bulb brush, one that blows air when squeezed. Do this before inserting each roll of unexposed film. And be sure to brush off the film canister before placing it into the camera. For convenience, carry the bulb brush with your spare film.

Shadows: the photographer's nemesis

As we gaze at a scene to be photographed, our eyes constantly adjust focus as we look from one part of the scene to another. Our pupils constrict and dilate, adjusting to the varying intensities of light coming from objects in sunlight and shade. And most importantly, our brain interprets the image by automatically compensating for harsh contrast and filtering out extraneous detail. The result is a pleasing rendition, perceived via an unimaginably complex battery of faculties.

Even the most technologically advanced camera, lens and film are severely limited when registering the same image. Therefore, the photographer must select scenes that lie within the capabilities of the photo equipment.

Today's cameras and film are generally not capable of accommodating scenes of high contrast. The term "high contrast" denotes the harsh differences in light, for example between objects in direct sunlight and those in shade. So it is up to us to avoid situations of high contrast when composing our photos.

When you look through the viewfinder, examine the scene carefully for shadows. In direct sunlight, even mild shadow will render as darkness or even blackness on the print. The shadow does not appear nearly so dark to the human eye because the brain smoothes the contrast. The camera and film cannot do this, which is why photos taken mid-day in bright sunshine are unlikely to turn out well. Depending on how the camera adjusts its settings, the areas in sunlight might be properly exposed, but those in shade will probably turn out much too dark. For best results when taking pictures in a forest setting, try to shoot at times of lower contrast, meaning early or late in the day, or on a cloudy day when the light is diffused and the shadows are subdued. Or when a patch of sunlight fully illuminates the subject.

The same holds true of a photo taken of someone wearing a shading brim hat. In direct sunlight, the hat might turn out great, but the face shaded by it will be lost in darkness. Portraits and close-ups often produce better results—with or without the hats—when illuminated by a manually-activated fill-in flash. The flash helps even out the contrast. However, if the subject is wearing eyeglasses, they can reflect the flash. Ask the subject to turn his or her head slightly, or to remove the glasses. And while the flash on a small camera seems extremely bright to our eyes, keep in mind that it is not capable of properly exposing the film beyond six or eight feet. Use the flash feature only within that range, day or night.

Most point-and-shoot cameras do not offer direct control over the f-stop (size of the aperture) and shutter speed settings. This is one reason that most photo buffs do not use these types of cameras. Another reason is that the smaller lens captures much less light, resulting in less photo definition. However, we can gain some measure of control by centering the viewfinder on darker or lighter areas, depressing the shutter release half way to lock the settings, (in cameras that have this feature) and then framing the photo the way we like and snapping the picture.

The self timer

I have seen many hikers' slide shows, and by far the best pictures were the ones in which the photographer took the trouble to set up the camera, activate the self timer, then move into the picture. Scenery shots can be very pleasing, but to capture the essence of the journey you need to impart a sense of presence. It might be a hiker walking along the trail with an interesting view in the background, for example, or a hiker at camp. Both are effective at drawing the audience into the experience.

A tripod enables a wider variety of shots, but is too heavy and bulky for most of us. In its place you can set the camera on rocks, tree stumps, or on the occasional fence post. You can even tie it to a tree with a length of cord. For an interesting angle, try placing the camera directly on the trail.

A touch of humor

Photo Jeff Robbins

Photography can be a great medium for exercising creativity. And while thinking of the possibilities, remember that hiking is not *all* serious. Be sure to include some humor. Some of the funniest hiking pictures I have seen were by Jeff Robbins, who has a penchant for making his slide show audiences laugh uproariously. One of his shots, shown here, has a hiker ambling along a logging road with this massive sign lashed to his backpack. It had obviously fallen from the back of a truck. Another of Jeff's pictures shows a group of hikers imitating a rock band, but in a snowy, alpine scene. They carried toy instruments and strange costumes for the occasion. Another time he had placed a plastic golf club in the hands of the Walt Whitman statue along the Appalachian Trail. "Look for humorous situations," Jeff advises, "and you'll find them just about everywhere."

Digging for something to eat.

The film

Whether to use slide or print film is a matter of preference. Most photographers striving for quality use slide film. If you are intent on publishing your photos in books or magazines you would normally render them from transparencies (slides). For computer scanning, gloss finish prints work well. The recreational photographer interested in simply compiling a photo album may prefer print film, since prints are quite handy for casual viewing. Print film can accommodate greater differences in contrast. This means that it maintains better detail in the shadows, while minimizing glare.

Among the huge variety of film, some types produce far better results than others. Select your film carefully. Currently, my favorite transparency film is Provia, made by Fuji. Ask for recommendations at your local camera shops.

When preparing for a longer journey afoot, estimate (based on previous trips) how much film you will need, then contact a few firms that advertise in the national photo magazines. Ask their price for the amount of film you need, for the same number of pre-paid processing mailers, and for the shipping and handling. Equipped with this information you could then telephone a few local photo shops, and tell them what you need. You could also mention the mail-order price, saying that you would rather do business locally if their prices are reasonably competitive.

On average, Jenny and I shoot a 36 exposure roll of film every 3½ days. At home we include the film and pre-paid processing mailers in our resupply parcels. For example if we are planning for a 7 day stretch between resupply stations A and B, we place two rolls of film in box A, and two processing mailers in box B. Once we have reached resupply station B, we mail the exposed film to the processing lab, using our home address as the return address. As a further precaution you could use the address of a relative or close friend as the return address, and ask them to examine the photos and alert you to any problems with the camera.

Spare battery

I have met hikers unable to use their cameras due to dead batteries—casualties of high altitudes and cold temperatures. In fact I once improvised a battery replacement on my own camera by wiring a couple of AA flashlight batteries to it. The AA batteries were much larger than a camera battery; they would not fit inside the camera. So I simply taped them to the outside. For electrical hook-up wiring I used a pair of twist-ties from a plastic bread bag. I stripped the paper coating from the thin wires, then led the wires from the batteries, inside to the battery contacts. AA flashlight batteries are normally 1.5 volts, so two of them wired in series supplied the 3.0 volts the camera needed. My camera looked pretty odd, but it worked fine and took some great pictures that I otherwise would have missed. This is an option, but a better one is to carry a spare camera battery. If you are planning a summer-long journey, place an extra battery or two in your resupply parcels or drift boxes.

If your camera has a motor-driven zoom lens, you will need even more spare batteries due to the increased electrical drain.

Artistic rendering

The hiker wishing to avoid higher technology while still capturing the journey's essence could carry a small sketch pad and pencils or pens. For those so inclined, sketching various scenes would be an excellent way to spend some of those trail-side breaks.

Whether you choose to capture the scenes on paper or film, your images will be a unique combination of sights and emotions from that moment in the journey. Both drawing and photography can sharpen one's powers of observation, and bring the artist or photographer to a closer connection with the natural world.

———————

When photographing the beauty of untouched wilderness areas along the way, consider yourself recording the scenes for posterity. I think it is a mistake to imagine that the National Park and Wilderness designations will protect the enclosed lands and forests forever. These are nothing but political boundaries, easily changed in response to increasing demand for resources. As just one example of such pressure, consider that the non-recycled portion of America's Sunday newspapers consumes some 500,000 trees, on ten thousand acres every Sunday.

Knots for the Hiker

This chapter details the knots I use while hiking and camping. They are the most simple yet functional. And they are easily learned.

Clove hitch

Use the clove hitch whenever you want to secure something mid-way along a length of cord or rope. I use it for attaching tarp ridge lines to support sticks. And to attach tarp guylines to stakes. The clove hitch does not slip, yet it is quickly untied by slipping it off the end of the stick or stake.

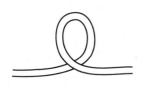 Hold the cord in both hands, thumbs pointing toward each-other, but at a 45 degree angle away from you. Without letting go, make a rabbit-ear loop as shown by twisting the cord in the right hand. Pinch the loop's cross-over point with the left thumb and index finger.

 Slide the right hand along the cord to the right. Twist and make a second loop. Pinch its cross-over point with the right thumb and index finger.

 Pass the right loop behind the left loop. The clove hitch is complete.

Run your tent stake through the loops, and tighten the line. Press the stake into the ground where you want it.

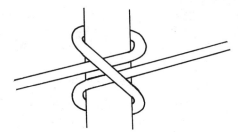

Tie the clove hitch in your tarp's ridge line, using the method described, then place it over your tarp support stick.

If using extremely thin cord on a tent stake, the clove hitch can sometimes grab so hard that it is difficult to slide off. In this case you can tie the clove hitch with a quick release. When you pull the free end, the knot unties itself.

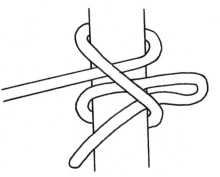

Taut line hitch

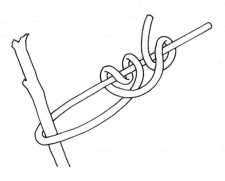

The taut line hitch is an adjustable knot. Use it for tensioning a tarp guyline around a stake, bush or tree.

The taut line hitch is also useful at one end of a clothesline running under a tarp or inside a tent. In this case one would cinch it only tight enough to take up the slack, without distorting the shelter.

I use the taut line hitch also to suspend my cookpot over a cook-fire. Thin nylon cord (1/8") works best for the suspension cord. Tie one end of the cord to the tripod with a couple of overhand knots (see below), then feed the lower end under the pot bail and secure the cord back onto itself with a taut line hitch. The taut line hitch enables you to adjust the height of the pot over the flames.

Sheet bend

Use the sheet bend to secure a line to the corner of a sheet of fabric. Its main use is for rigging the plastic tarp, as described in the Tarp chapter. This makes an extremely strong attachment.

Overhand

The overhand is the first knot most people learn. When we tie our shoe-laces, we start by tying an overhand.

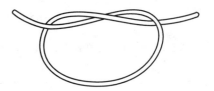

Overhand on a bight

The working end in a cord is called its "bitter end." When you fold it back on itself to create a loop, you make what is called a "bight." If you then tie an overhand in that doubled line, you make an "overhand on a bight."

I use this knot to secure the ends of the guylines to the tarp. Run one end of the line through the webbing loop, bring it back alongside itself several inches, and then tie the overhand on the doubled line.

I also use the overhand on a bight to attach lanyards to items such as the ice axe and pocket knife. For the ice axe I use a piece of parachute cord about three feet long. One end of the cord feeds through a hole in the head of the axe and attaches with the overhand on a bight. At the other end of the cord, tie another overhand on a bight, making the bight just large enough to slip your hand through it. This will keep the ice axe secured to your wrist when in use.

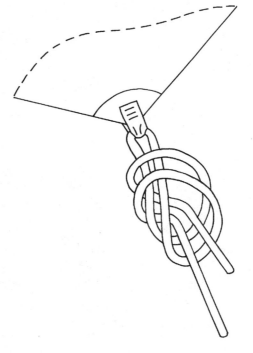

On smaller items such as the pocket knife I simply loop the parachute cord (a ten-inch length) through the small ring at the end of the knife, bring the cord back so that both ends are even, then tie the overhand on a bight right near the two ends.

Two half hitches

Use the two half hitches to secure a tarp guyline to a rock, log, bush, or tree. Use this knot in the same way as the taut line hitch, but secure the knot right against the object, to prevent the object from sliding out of the loop. Add a quick release to the second half hitch if desired.

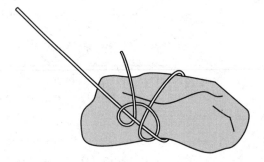

Section 3

Obstacles

The Avalanche
of Adversity

Obstacles are those frightful things you see
when you take your mind off your goals.

— *(Author not known)*

Projecting one's consciousness
through—and beyond—obstacles

One of the more powerful forces of nature is the climax avalanche. When one comes crashing down a mountain slope, it snaps even the largest and strongest trees like match sticks, hurling them into the air, and driving them far down into the valleys. And there it piles them in acres of tangled heaps. And as we try to pick our way across one of these tangles, we are humbled by the awesome natural power that placed it there. Yet gazing up the slopes we see that the avalanche does not strip the mountainside bare. When the mass of snow smashes into willow, young aspen and other types of supple vegetation, it cannot exert its power on them. They simply bend over until the avalanche has passed, and spring back upright.

When we venture into the wilderness, we are bound to meet with various obstacles and adversities: wet brush on the trail, dry brush on the trail, incessant rain or driving thirst, trails too steep or too gradual, tread too muddy or dusty, deep snow or sweltering heat, bridgeless torrents or dry, thirsty creek beds, slippery roots and rocks, mosquitoes, blackflies and bears, resupply stations too far from the trail or towns too close to it—and other hikers complaining about same.

We cannot prevent these obstacles, but we can temper our reactions to them. Like stalwart trees we could let the avalanches of adversity mow us down, or like the willow we could bend and spring. Nature has perfected her ways throughout the eons, and in most cases we humans can benefit by accepting those ways. When we enter the woods with unrealistic ideals born and bred in Urbania, we may instead expect nature to cater to us. Haven't we all heard someone say, "I'm going hiking today, I hope it doesn't rain." Well, what if it does rain? Our sodden hiker returns home, expectations unfulfilled, rebuffed by the Avalanche of Adversity. When we expect things of nature, we weaken ourselves with our own inflexibility. Our hiker could have said, "I'm going hiking today, and in case it rains I'll carry my umbrella." It is our rigid expectations that make the wilderness seem so hostile. And this is what keeps many people at home.

Interestingly, many times our views of obstacles and adversities stress us far more than the obstacles themselves. Those adversities listed above are not nearly as hostile or life-threatening as they might seem. We build them up in our minds as such, based on imagined possibilities, and our minds then treat the imagined possibilities as real. Our central nervous system has no way of distinguishing the difference between real and imagined, and this is why adversities can stress us so greatly. Only after thousands of miles on the trail did I finally learn that I could surmount these obstacles simply by projecting my consciousness through them. In other words, I accept, adapt, and focus my attention beyond the current difficulty.

Citified thinking

In order to focus beyond the difficulties confronting us, we need to set aside certain parts of our citified thinking. As an example, when people go into restaurants, they expect the service to be punctual and polite. They expect the food to be fresh and hot. If they are non-smokers, then they expect their dining experience to be free of second-hand smoke. If each of these conditions is not met, then they might become upset. Granted, the customers are paying for these services, and for the most part these expectations are justified. But it is this mentality of insisting that things meet our expectations that we should leave behind when we venture into the wilds. Out there, this mentality works against us. And when the conditions fail to meet our expectations, we may become more than upset, we may become subject to great danger—like the trees in the avalanche.

Rigid thinking

Rigid thinking is something else best left behind. We find some of the best examples in sports and the military. The football coach hammers his team into delivering absolute maximum performance. The Marines teaches its recruits to "do-or-die-trying." This approach might be effective in defeating an opposing team or a hostile army, but in all my experience I have not seen it succeed against the vastly superior powers of nature.

Jenny and I once met a hiker wearing camouflage-type clothing and clasping a cigar stub in one corner of his mouth. Nearby was his backpack, a gargantuan affair loaded with all manner of what appeared to be Army surplus gear. It was not surplus we soon learned. "One hundred and twenty five pound's worth," the soldier informed us, adding that he could carry it only fifteen minutes between rests. I asked why he didn't lighten his load by sending a few things home. "I started with it," he replied, "and by god I'm gonna finish with it. I come from the military and that's how we operate." I do not mean to paint a grim picture of this fellow, he was actually quite personable once we got to know him. But I think his inflexible approach increased the labors of his journey unnecessarily.

One of the great benefits of hiking is how it allows us to pursue our goals however we like. Each of us has our idiosyncrasies, personal ambitions, hiking parameters and philosophies. But when it comes to dealing with natural obstacles along the way, known or unknown, real or imagined, our best approach is to remain flexible, changing our ways when necessary, and accepting nature as she comes.

The positive aspects

When encountering brush overgrowing the trail, we do not have to take it as a personal affront. We can simply accept the brush and proceed cautiously ahead. Rarely will the brush physically stop us, or even slow us down. The brush is not what causes the struggles and frustrations, but our unrealistic demands.

Wet bushes on the trail? Proceed ahead wearing nylon shell pants and running shoes. They will dry soon enough. Rain? Anticipate this by carrying an umbrella. Driving thirst? Carry more water. Trails too steep or too gradual? Accept these as the reality of the moment. Deep, residual snow? A potential problem for those who neglect nature's timetables and venture into the high country too early in the season. Haul off the trail for a couple of weeks and allow the snow to melt. Searing heat? Wear the minimum of clothing and make it lightweight and loose-fitting. Carry plenty of water, and hike beneath a mylar-covered umbrella. Bridgeless torrents? Try heading upstream in search of a fallen tree bridging the creek, or turn around. Dry creek beds? Again, carry more water. Mosquitoes? Wear mosquito-proof clothing. Bears? Practice stealth camping away from their nightly haunts. Resupply stations too far from the trail? Minimize off-trail hiking by choosing resupply stations carefully ahead of time. Towns too close to the trail? Accept the trail routing as it is, and value its diversity of both landscape and culture. Other hikers complaining about all the above? Point out the positive aspects of the moment.

Of course, these are not the only solutions, but my point is merely that we can learn to deal with adversity in ways that do not weaken us. And remember that fatigue can make an obstacle seem far more foreboding. Often a good rest will reduce what seems a monumental obstruction to easily manageable proportions. Keep in mind, also, that colossal backpacks, heavy boots, deep dehydration, and poor nutrition are sure ways to fatigue.

───────────────

If we confront the Avalanche of Adversity with rigid expectations it will surely weaken us. It will also distract us from any kind of wilderness connection, and deprive us of the moment's happiness. Yet adversity is mostly imagined. So look for ways of operating within the parameters of nature, and then of projecting your consciousness through the inevitable obstacles. The key is to remain flexible, like the willow.

Rain

May the warp be the white light of morning,
May the weft be the red light of evening,
May the fringes be the falling rain,
May the border be the standing rainbow.
Thus weave for us a garment of brightness.

— *Song of the Sky Loom (Tewa Indians)*

Picture yourself hiking up a long, uphill grade while carrying a heavy backpack. A cold rain is falling, but you have come prepared with the latest and most sophisticated technology. You are wearing a $120 thermal wicking shirt beneath a $350 rain jacket. The farther you progress up the hill, the more heat your muscles generate and the more you sweat. You unzip the jacket's front opening, but still you sweat. You open the pit zips, but with no improvement, since heat rises and the zips are under your arms. The sweat is soaking your shirt, and the rain jacket is dripping with condensation inside. And there you are, slogging along in the rain, nearly as wet inside as outside, and feeling like a $3.25 poached Wienerwurst. Surely there must be a better, more comfortable way to hike in the rain.

In more than twelve thousand miles of hiking together, Jenny and I have spent a lot of time in the rain. Rain that is hardly more than a falling mist, to rain that pummels in a deluge. Rain that lasts but a few minutes, to rain that continues for days and even weeks. Through it all, our best protection has been our umbrellas.

The umbrella

The umbrella's most salient feature is the ventilation it provides. This eliminates the typical clamminess of a waterproof-"breathable" rain jacket and the associated sweat-soaked clothing. Even in heavy rain, the umbrella allows the hiker to dress for the temperature rather than for the rain, which means that normal hiking clothing can be worn. And because it keeps the rain off one's face and from running down the inside of the jacket and shirt, the umbrella makes rainy-weather hiking a lot more comfortable. See the Umbrella chapter for more details.

The rain jacket

The optimum rain jacket would not be insulated. Even in cold weather, the hiker would sweat-soak the insulation, adding to the jacket's weight and reducing its usefulness when at rest. A full-length, front opening zipper allows the jacket to be opened wide for improved ventilation when possible. The full-length zipper also permits wearing the jacket backwards, the advantages of which are described in the Cold chapter.

The rain jacket should fit large so that several layers of insulating garments can be worn under it, if needed. The sleeves should extend beyond the wrists, permitting the mittened hands to be withdrawn into the sleeves to keep the rain off the mittens. The jacket itself should extend below the waist, covering the lower torso amply.

Undesirable features in a rain jacket include pit zips, a plethora of cargo pockets and their zippers and storm flaps, mesh liners, and designer seams crisscrossing the fabric. And remember that the rain protection does not come from company logos.

Particularly for the long-distance hiker spending the entire summer afoot, the rigors of the journey can wear out even the most expensive rain jacket in a single season. The pack straps pressing against the jacket will, over time, abrade the inner membrane. This is another reason I encourage the use of the umbrella in all types of rain except those driven by strong winds. An umbrella used instead of the jacket will extend the life of the rain jacket considerably.

My home-made waterproof-breathable rain jacket weighs six ounces, and occupies very little space in the backpack when not in use.

Leg wear

Rain pants can complement the rain jacket, but I see them mainly as an emergency item, to be kept in the pack for an unexpected storm that brings rain, gale-force winds and lower temperatures. But of course on a rainy day they can also be handy for someone ambling along at a slow pace or sitting around camp.

The rain pants—like the rain jacket—should be made of waterproof-breathable or vapor-permeable fabric. If instead you opt for rain gear made of waterproof-nonbreathable materials, you will quickly soak them in perspiration. While the vapor-permeable materials are not highly breathable by any means, they do allow at least some moisture to pass through them. How much moisture? Enough to keep the wearer's legs reasonably dry while merely ambling or resting.

But while hiking at an average pace, we perspire much more than while resting, and this is likely to sweat-soak even these modern weather-proof-breathable fabrics. Once wet on the inside, the pants may start binding at the knees with every step. This can retard forward progress and reduce comfort and energy. The result can be a sweaty, unenthusiastic hiker. And once wet on the inside, the rain pants become less suitable for wearing at the rest stops and at camp. And remember that sitting around in wet clothing of any kind can lead to hypothermia. So in other words, rain pants might be nice to have, but they may not be the best garb for hiking at a reasonable clip.

My personal preference in rainy weather is to hike beneath an umbrella whenever possible, and to wear highly breathable legwear. My legs do not mind being wet, as long as they are warm. Arriving at camp, I wring out the wet shorts and/or pants, and hang them beneath the tarp. And without delay I don dry clothing and slide comfortably beneath the quilt.

In rain where temperatures are mild, I usually wear spandex shorts. If I am hiking in cold rain I wear the shell pants over the shorts. Even though these pants are made of lightweight, breathable nylon, they offer considerable warmth and wind protection. And when wet they do not bind at the knees as much as rain pants. When the rain eases, the shell pants dry within ten or fifteen minutes. This means that during intermittent rain the shell pants will be dry most of the time. In continuous rain the shell pants will be wet when I reach camp, but once again I simply hang them on the clothesline under the tarp, knowing that by morning they will be at least reasonably dry and ready for another day of hiking. In very cold and wet conditions I wear thermal pants under the shell pants.

In any kind of wet conditions, my focus is always on staying comfortably warm. My selection and use of garments works well for me, but certainly your needs may differ, depending on your preferences and hiking style.

Mittens for rainy weather

Hiking in pouring rain while wearing a rain jacket, but without an umbrella, you cannot raise your hands, for example to hook your thumbs in the pack straps or thumb loops. Otherwise, the rain would funnel into your sleeves. And you cannot hike with your hands in your pockets, because the rain would channel into those pockets. So you hold your arms down and withdraw your hands up into the jacket's sleeves for better protection—assuming the sleeves are long enough. In such a case, your mittens do not need to be waterproof. Simple fleece mittens will suffice, and this is true also if you are carrying an umbrella. However, if your jacket sleeves are not long enough to cover your hands, you may need a pair of waterproof shell mittens to go over your fleece ones. So when trying on jackets, pay attention to sleeve length. If and when the fleece mittens become wet, you can take them off, wring the water out, and put the mittens back on.

Footwear appropriate for wet conditions

In the Footwear chapter I discuss the fallacy of trying to keep your feet dry while hiking in rainy weather. Even the most expensive boots fall short in stopping the pervading wetness, both from the rain outside and the perspiration inside. Lightweight, highly-breathable shoes worn with nylon socks or wool-synthetic blend socks, work very well in cold, wet weather. Yes, the shoes and socks will become wet, but the exertion of hiking will keep your feet surprisingly warm. And once the rain has stopped, your shoes and socks will soon dry.

Keeping gear dry inside the pack

Pulling sopping wet clothing and sleeping gear from a backpack can be dispiriting. We would like to think that our pack should keep its contents dry, but from a manufacturing standpoint (in terms of weight and appearance) making a pack waterproof is very impractical.

The standard way of keeping a pack "dry" is to fit it with a rain cover. This method has serious drawbacks. A rain cover cannot be adjusted to fit a pack that starts out fully loaded with supplies and then gradually becomes smaller as the food is eaten, day by day. When the pack is at its smallest, the pack cover will be excessively baggy. If the bagginess occurs under the pack, which it usually does, then it will act as an unwanted water bag as the rain channels into it. Moreover, a rain cover leaks all around its perimeter.

For decades I hiked with external pack covers ranging from plastic garbage bags, to commercial pack covers, to home-made ones that I designed to suit the packs. None of these kept the packs, or their contents dry. And this is why I also used waterproof stowbags inside the packs, to protect spare clothes, sleeping gear, and so forth.

Finally, I abandoned the idea of trying to keep the pack dry, externally. Internal stowbags are the answer, and in severely wet conditions one can augment them with a waterproof pack liner, placed inside the pack. This could be a plastic garbage sack, twisted at the top and folded over. Or it could be a waterproof, pack-size stowbag that is more durable and lightweight.

Camping in the rain

With the right gear, techniques and attitude, camping in the rain is hardly more problematic than camping in dry weather. The most common mistake is that of choosing an unsuitable site. This can put the wetness into one's wilderness experience in a big way, should the rain intensify during the night. Rather than look for a level clearing without paying attention to surrounding terrain, look for a protected location that slopes gently away on all sides, providing good drainage. In other words, one that is slightly elevated above its surroundings. As the rain runs off your shelter, you want it to course away from you rather than drain back toward you.

The tarp in wet weather

The tarp is particularly suited to wet weather camping, since it affords much more living space with far better ventilation. In the Tarp and Tent chapter I described how and where to pitch a tarp, but let's review the specific rainy weather considerations here.

As you search for a site with good drainage, look also for natural protection from wind, such as behind trees, rocks, logs or tall bushes. If you cannot find a site that is a little higher than its surroundings, look for one on a slight slope. And if rain starts falling so hard that water courses down that slope, you could use a stick to dig a shallow V-shaped groove uphill of your tarp to divert the flow. As mentioned back in the Tarp and Tent chapter, however, the V-groove should be used only in times of real need.

The harder the wind is slanting the rain, the lower you will need to pitch the tarp, streamlining it aerodynamically. In any kind of wind, try to orient the tarp with its ridgeline perpendicular to the wind and be sure to lower the tarp's windward side flush to the ground. Keep in mind the possibility of the storm intensifying in the night, and make certain that you have secured the guylines to sturdy anchor points and tensioned them well—before crawling under the tarp. Exercise that extra bit of care while still in your wet clothing, so that you will not have to emerge from your cozy shelter in the night to make adjustments.

Wet ground does not automatically necessitate a tent with a "bathtub floor." Where the ground is pooled in water, one would be ill advised to pitch a tent or a tarp, regardless of floor construction. But if the ground is merely wet, then the tarp should work just as well. Once you pitch a tarp over wet ground, that ground begins to dry. And your groundsheet will start to drive the moisture into the earth. If this seems unlikely, think about the times you have pitched a tent on wet ground, and the next morning packed up to find that ground dry.

If rain is still falling by morning, you may be reluctant to break camp. But the ability to pack everything but the tarp, while still under the tarp, makes the prospects of setting off a lot more appealing. All you have to do is deploy your umbrella, step outside, take the tarp down and give it a few shakes to remove some of the wetness, and stow it away. Then off you go, still comfortably beneath your umbrella.

Should the rain subside during the day, you can withdraw the wet tarp and spread it to dry. Even if the sun is not shining directly, the tarp will normally dry fairly quickly if you spread it on ground that slopes generally toward the sun. But if the rain continues and you cannot dry the tarp, then rest assured that it will perform just as well when wet as it does when dry.

The tent

The key to pitching a tent in rain is to plan ahead. The quicker you can get the job done, the less rain the tent will absorb.

Locate a suitable site that affords good drainage and hopefully protection from wind. Preen the site of any sticks and pine cones, etc. Pull out the tent fly and spread it on the ground to one side of the site, right-side up. Remove the tent poles from their bag, section them together and place them under the fly. Try to keep them dry, since the shock cord inside them will absorb moisture and would be slow to dry. But be extremely careful not to step on the poles. Breaking one could put the tent out of service.

Pitch the tent and quickly throw the fly over it. If the tent is free-standing, move it to one side, spread the groundsheet onto the site, then position the tent quickly back over it. This minimizes exposure of the rain-catching groundsheet to the elements.

Use the tent's vestibule or rain awning to house your backpack. If your tent does not have one of these, you may have to leave your pack outside, preferably under some kind of a cover. Inside the tent a small hand towel will be quite handy, for mopping the wetness incurred during the pitching process and from your wet clothing.

For a description of my tent awning, see the Tarp and Tent chapter.

The tarp-tent combo

Using a tarp over your existing tent might be an option when camping in persistently wet conditions, and when you are not hiking far and thus are not too concerned about the extra weight. The tarp pitched over the tent will keep the tent dry and will allow you to keep the tent door wide open for the best ventilation and enjoyment of your surroundings—even when rain is pouring. An awning allows this too, but the full tarp gives all the more coverage. Pitch the tarp only high enough so that the tent fits snugly underneath. A simple and inexpensive option is a sheet of 3 mil plastic, cut about three feet larger than the tent all around.

Care of sleeping gear

No matter what kind of quilt or sleeping bag you use, you will need to keep it dry. The best way to do this is by keeping it in a waterproof stuff sack, inside the backpack during the day. For added insurance, as I mentioned above, use a pack liner, such as a plastic trash bag, inside the backpack.

In periods of heavy rain, a synthetic fill quilt or sleeping bag that has become wet will still keep you adequately warm, but a sodden down-filled bag may not. This is why synthetic fill is usually the better choice for use in persistently wet weather. Should your quilt or bag become wet, whether it is down or synthetic, you can dry it—as long as you can strike a campfire. If rain is falling you will have to shelter both you and the sleeping gear beneath an umbrella, or sit under the tarp or tent awning. The idea is to keep the sleeping gear out of the rain, yet close enough to the fire to absorb its radiant heat. If you try this, be careful to keep the fire small and at a safe distance from your shelter.

Care of the clothing

The more garments you bring with you, the more time and effort you will spend in rainy weather trying to keep them all dry. This takes us back to the idea of the synergistic system, discussed in the Clothing chapter. In wet weather, carry only what clothing you need.

Keep your spare clothes in a waterproof stuff sack for use once you reach camp. When you stop hiking for the day, your wet clothes can quickly begin to chill you. Remove them and crawl into your shelter, and put your dry clothes on. If you have no dry clothes, then the quilt or sleeping bag will still keep you warm, even had you intended to use it with your clothing.

Your hiking clothing must be fast drying, and this is particularly true in wet weather. Except for wool-blend socks, this means 100% synthetics. I do not recommend clothes made of cotton, not even a very small percentage of it. Cotton is much slower drying, since its individual fibers themselves absorb moisture.

In extended periods of very wet and cold weather, don't be reluctant to build a small campfire to dry things out.

Resting in the rain

While hiking on a cold and wet day, the best plan is to rest often—perhaps hourly—but to keep each rest stop brief. The inactivity at those rest stops can invite a penetrating chill. Consider the rest stops little more than snack stops. This frequent snacking will assist your energy and metabolic warmth. And where the rain is prolonged, keep the day's hiking fairly short. Then at day's end, avoid puttering around camp, because that, too, can sap body heat. Pitch your shelter, change into dry clothes, and crawl into bed to preserve warmth.

Cooking in the rain

When not in troublesome-bear country, your rainy weather cooking might best be done at camp. Beneath a sheltering tarp you can safely use a stove as long as you take precautions to ensure that the stove does not flare up. If you decide to cook a reviving mid-afternoon meal before stopping to make camp, plan the meal ahead of time to help smooth the process. Think about what you want to cook and where it is in your pack. Consider also the whereabouts of your pot, matches, fuel and stove. Such forethought will help eliminate the inevitable digging through everything looking for this and that. Also, fill your water bottles ahead of time so that you will not have to interrupt the cooking process to collect more water. In rainy weather, the less time you spend at the open meal stop the better. So keep the meal simple. Save the more elaborate dishes for a drier day. And remember that a familiarity with the idiosyncrasies of your stove will greatly expedite the process.

Rather than stopping just anywhere to cook, look for a naturally sheltered area or objects that will deflect some of the rain and wind—perhaps in the lee of a hill or a cove behind a cluster of boulders. Even trees will offer some protection, as long as their branches are not dripping heavily. Put on a few extra clothes, a warm hat and your rain jacket. Position yourself so that the rain and wind are at your back. The umbrella can also provide shelter for both the stove and yourself. You can tuck the umbrella shaft under one arm so that both hands remain free, or you can set the umbrella on the ground such that it protects the stove.

Ample hydration

On a very rainy day you might not imagine that hiking would dehydrate you, and you might be even less inclined to drink a lot of water. But the exertion of hiking in any kind of weather can be very dehydrating. The more dehydrated you become, the worse you will feel and the colder you will become. Good hydration improves blood circulation, and this brings energy, warmth and vitality.

One rainy afternoon on the Appalachian Trail, Jenny and I stepped into a shelter for a short respite. There, we greeted a lone hiker lying in his sleeping bag, brewing tea and listening to a weather forecast on his radio. "My trail name is Fairweather," he said. "I got it because I never hike in bad weather. Been here for two days."

After a pleasant chat we wished the fellow good luck, deployed our umbrellas and stepped back outside into the "bad" weather. And while rambling cheerfully along I recalled my own reactions to rain years ago, when I, too, had been intimidated by prolonged wet weather and had endured most of it inside my tent. The contrast made me appreciate my lightweight, more functional gear, in terms of how it had freed me of those weather-related concerns.

With the right choices in clothing, gear and attitude, we begin to realize that nature has a beauty and rhythm in all her moods, and a cleansing, purifying aspect to the miracle we call rain.

Drying gear after a few days of rain, on the PCT in 1991.

Lightning

Go forth under the open sky,
and list to Nature's teachings.

— *William Cullen Bryant*

The white-hot sledgehammer

Lightning plays a fascinating and important role in the ecology of our planet. As a bolt rips through the sky it releases nitrogen; twenty million lightning storms annually deposit some 100 million tons of nitrogen on soil and plants, carried to the earth by rainfall. Nitrogen is sustenance to the world's flora. Have you ever stood at the base of a big tree and wondered where all that mass came from? Not from the earth, otherwise the tree would have made an equal-sized hole in the ground. Rather, the mass came mainly from the nitrogen (and carbon dioxide) in the air, created in lightning storms and brought to the earth by rain.

Lightning is also beneficial to old-growth forest ecology. It starts fires that clear away dead undergrowth and make way for new plants and seedlings. But sometimes it also injures and even kills animals and people.

Avoidance—Western U.S.

In much of the western United States, lightning tends to be most active on the higher mountain ranges during afternoon thunderstorms. These thunderstorms come in cycles and are fairly predictable. Let's look at how this works:

The cycle can vary from five to ten days. It begins with a day or two of cloudless skies. Then, little puffy cumulus clouds will develop in the late mornings, and clear off in the evenings. These clouds will generally grow more extensive each day, but they do not produce rain. Each day they start to form sooner in the morning. They grow more extensive, and they break up later in the evenings. Then one day they "over-develop" and fill the sky. Still, they dissipate at night. The next day the clouds re-form, but more quickly, and they may grow very dark and start spitting lightning. After a few days of this, a front will pass through and fill even the morning sky with clouds. Rain may or may not fall, but the lightning will have ceased. Then, after the front has passed, the weather cycle will begin anew, initially with clear skies throughout the day.

Observing these cycles can help you predict the weather. For example, if the previous afternoon brought thunderstorms, then the present afternoon may do the same. And should another afternoon thunderstorm appear to be building, you would be very cautions about following the trail up into the rocky heights. Instead you might choose to pitch your shelter and enjoy an early camp. And there you may indeed hear the clapping of thunder echoing from the ridges above.

Avoidance—Eastern U.S.

Eastern weather patterns do not give such specific clues, day to day, as to where and when lightning may strike. A stronger, more active jet stream combined with an abundant source of moisture in the Gulf of Mexico provides the necessary ingredients for thunderstorm activity, but it also complicates matters of prediction.

Eastern summers are frequently humid, even in the mountains. The more humidity in the air, the greater the chances of thunderstorms during the day. If the air feels humid at dawn, and if the sky is at all clouded, or even hazy, then we know that thunderstorms can develop any time from late morning through late afternoon, with or without rain. In any event, one day a front will pass through, bringing drier air behind it. As it passes over the area, short-lived but sometimes violent thunderstorms can erupt. At places along the trail where you can see the horizon, look generally west and north for an approaching line of black clouds. If they are pro-gressing steadily toward you, and if the sound of thunder grows louder and more frequent, then for safety's sake you would make a hasty descent from an exposed high point.

Lying in the ditch

During our CDT thru-hike, residents of the Wyoming flatlands warned Jenny and me not to take chances with the lightning, saying that it could be deadly. We were hiking across the Red Desert when tremendous thunderstorms began developing in the afternoons. The terrain out there is featureless and flat, offering nowhere to descend. The storms treated us to some spectacular shows of nature's raw power, with great bolts of lightning and even a few tornado funnels. Then one time the sky blackened directly overhead. We were following a seldom-used dirt road at the time, and there was nothing for it but to lie down in the roadside ditch. Rain started hammering down, so we covered ourselves with the tent fly. Mighty explosions all around kept us pinned down for an hour, while our ditch gradually filled with cold rainwater. By the time the storm had passed, we were drenched and covered in mud, but thankfully no worse for the wear.

Descending for safety

Thunder is the supersonic shock wave, caused by the lightning bolt ramming air away from the discharge. Thunder travels approximately one mile in five seconds. Watch the flashes and count the seconds until hearing their thunder. To estimate the bolt's distance from you in miles, divide the number of seconds by five.

But don't wait for a lightning storm to develop before taking action. If you find yourself in the high, exposed regions with black clouds approaching, begin an immediate descent. Below treeline, take refuge in the trees but do not sit beneath a tree as shelter from the rain, due to the danger of lightning striking that tree. The rule is: be among the trees but not too near any one of them.

If you cannot descend, perhaps because of cliffs, and if the lightning storm overtakes you, remember that lightning tends to strike the highest grounded object in the vicinity. Make yourself as low as possible by descending as far as you can. Remove your pack, then assume the lightning defensive position: crouch low on both feet (taking advantage of the shoe or boot sole's dielectric insulation), keep your knees together to lessen the spark gap between them, and keep your mouth open slightly to reduce the pressure differential in the ear canals. Crouching on a foam pad might provide additional protection from ground currents. Members of the group should spread out; if lightning strikes one person, the others would not sustain injuries from the "splash," and would be available to administer CPR (cardiopulmonary resuscitation) to the strike victim. Also, set aside any metal objects, including backpacks with metal stays, umbrellas and ice axes.

Jenny and I were thru-hiking our first big trail, and had just surmounted snowbound Forester Pass in the Sierra, at 13,000 feet. Snow was falling heavily, accumulating on our jackets and packs, and obscuring the descent ahead of us. Trudging in deep snow and grappling in the fog, we descended to a long, rocky buttress until finally coming to a cliff. Obviously, the trail had switchbacked somewhere behind us. Cliffs dropped away from us on three sides, and at that point lightning started hammering all around. We needed to descend to safer ground, but could not. We climbed down to the brink, removed our packs, and were just sitting down when our clothing started making ripping sounds—the effects of electrostatic discharge. As long as we remained sitting down, all was well; but each time we tried to stand up, our rain jackets started making those ominous ripping sounds again. What seemed odd was the combination of heavy snowfall and lightning, which I had never experienced before. The storm gradually moved on, we clambered back along the ridge, and after a great deal of searching found the switchback, and followed the hint of the trail down to safer ground.

First aid

Being struck by lightning has been described as sustaining a total-body blow from a white-hot sledgehammer. The results usually include unconsciousness, a shut down of the heart beat and breathing, rupture of the eardrums, and possible burns. The strike victim will appear dead. In most instances, however, the heart is in a quivering state known as ventricular fibrillation. Usually CPR will restore the heart to its regular beat, though this can take an hour or sometimes much longer. Even after the heart does restart, those giving the CPR must maintain ventilations (artificial respiration) until the breathing restarts also.

Umbrella hazard

Obviously, carrying a deployed umbrella when the air is electrically charged is asking for trouble. If you are holding the umbrella in your hand, it would be best to avoid touching the metal shaft. I credit the plastic handles for saving Jenny and me once. While hiking through New Mexico during our CDT trek, we were splattered by a nearby strike. One minute we were hiking along under our umbrellas in a pouring rain—with no evidence of lightning anywhere—and the next minute an explosion knocked us momentarily senseless. The next thing we knew we were both chasing after our umbrellas, with no recollection of having dropped them.

St. Elmo's Fire

One pre-dawn morning in the Colorado Rockies, my students and I set out for higher regions near the Continental Divide. Unfortunately, in the darkness we had not noticed an approaching thunderstorm. Caught short, we spread out and sat huddled beneath our ponchos, experiencing the usual electrostatic discharge: the buzzing and crackling in our ponchos, the hair standing on end. Some experts suspect that the slow discharge means that lightning is dissipating and is therefore not about to strike. Nevertheless, in such a situation it is best to stay crouched low until the buzzing ceases.

My fellow instructor Joe and I shared a tarp in that storm, and we watched a glowing ball of energy slowly climb his arm, moil about his beard, and descend the other arm. This eerie phenomenon is known as Saint Elmo's Fire, and although it is normally harmless, it is rather unsettling and serves to remind us of nature's mysteries and power.

Cold

In the heating and air conditioning trade,
the point on the thermostat in which
neither heating nor cooling must operate
—around 72 degrees—is called
"The Comfort Zone."
It is also known as
"The Dead Zone."

— *Russell Bishop*

To remain indoors in cold weather is to miss a great deal of what nature has to offer. And when the thermometer dips below 72 degrees, this does not mean we have to be uncomfortable. Nor must we rely on artificial climate controls. Instead, we generate our own warmth, metabolically, and we wear clothing that best retains that warmth.

"Bundle up! It's cold outside." As children most of us heard this well-intentioned advice many times. And granted, during our outings we must not ignore the cold, as children often do, and dress so lightly that we become deeply chilled. At that stage the re-warming can be very difficult. But at the same time we must be extremely careful not to over-bundle while hiking. Otherwise we could be hiking towards an encounter with hypothermia.

Our microclimate

In cold weather our clothes create a microclimate next to our skin that is much warmer than the external ambient conditions. We produce this warmth metabolically and we retain it with clothing. And while our eyes see the chilly, external environment, our bodies "see" the warm microclimate adjacent our skin. And because we tend to be sight oriented rather than skin oriented, we see our needs for clothing, rather than feel them. As a result, we tend to overprotect ourselves by piling on too much clothing for the ambient conditions. All is well while at rest, but while hiking we generate a great deal of metabolic warmth, and this, hampered by the excess of clothing, leads to sweating.

Sweat is the body's reaction to overheating. It is very effective at cooling our bodies, as long as the sweat can evaporate. Without evaporation there is no evaporative cooling.

So not only does the heavy clothing cause us to sweat, but the overabundance of garments also prevents evaporation. And when the sweat fails to cool us, our bodies produce even more sweat.

I liken this to throwing a blanket over a car's radiator. Even in cold weather the radiator needs to cool the engine to help dissipate the heat generated as a normal byproduct of work.

Lumbering along on a cold day while perspiring inside excessive clothing—accepting the profuse sweat as an unavoidable part of the activity—is an extremely inefficient and dangerous way to travel. Not only are sweat-soaked garments uncomfortable, but they will be much less serviceable at the rest stops and at camp when needed most—when we are no longer producing an abundance of metabolic warmth. When at rest, we rely almost entirely on our clothing to keep us warm, yet those sweat-soaked garments will have lost a great deal of their ability to insulate.

This is why, in very cold weather, wearing too many clothes can be as hazardous as not wearing enough. I consider this one of the most fundamental skills of cold-weather hiking—body awareness in terms of our microclimate.

This relates not only to higher-mileage hikers in frigid conditions. It applies to all hikers in chilly to cold weather. No matter the type of hike, be it an afternoon jaunt, a weekend peak climb, or a 10-day trek into the high country, when the temperature starts to drop, pay close attention to the microclimate and regulate it by wearing your clothing dynamically.

Mid-June on the PCT in the North Cascades. The day before we took this picture, poor visibility turned us back here. We descended into the valley and made a comfortable camp. This morning, with the storm relenting we returned to the Crest and continued on our way.

Wearing clothing dynamically

Rather than ignore the cold, or the sweat, we can play a more active role in regulating body temperature. We adopt the layering approach, as described in the Clothing chapter, donning a layer the moment we begin to feel a chill, and removing a layer (and possibly slowing the pace) at the first hint of sweat.

Better yet, we learn to anticipate the condition and make the appropriate adjustments ahead of time. For example, suppose we are facing a long, steep climb, one that is sure to get us sweating. We remove a layer of clothing before commencing the ascent. When approaching a long descent, we anticipate the inevitable cool-down by donning another layer of clothing, and possibly by picking up the pace just a bit. (However, when not going downhill, a moderate pace in cold weather produces the best flow of long-term energy.)

In a way, anticipating the conditions is like balancing a yardstick on a finger. Until we learn to anticipate the stick's leaning, our corrections will always come too late, so they will have to be more drastic. But when we learn to make the corrections in advance, they will need to be only subtle.

Our heads radiate away a fair portion of body heat. So if we begin to feel chilled we put on a warming hat. Feeling too warm, we want to increase heat radiation, so we remove the hat. This is a very effective way to make small, easy adjustments.

In cold weather the hands also act as radiators, due to the relatively large surface area of the fingers. If your hands feel hot, remove your mittens and your hands will cool quickly. But since the blood circulation in the fingers and hands is not great, you must be careful not to let them become cold. Otherwise they will be very slow to warm on their own. This means that even on a moderately chilly day you may want to wear at least a thin pair of mittens.

Clothing for hiking in cold weather

As described in the Clothing chapter, start with an inner layer of light-weight clothing, for example a polyester shirt and spandex shorts. Think of these "warm weather" clothes as your cold weather underwear. You will probably be carrying them anyway, so why not use them? Over them might go a long sleeve thermal shirt and thermal pants. Together, these layers would be your first defense against cold. Then, depending on ambient temperature and wind chill factor, you could put on the breathable shell jacket and pants for added warmth and wind protection. If the day is colder still, you could wear two thermal shirts and pants. And although the insulated jacket is useful mainly at the rest stops, still you could wear it while hiking if necessary. And once again, make good use of your hat and mittens.

When distance-hiking in the cold weather of alpine summer, Jenny and I usually go with one pair of thermal pants each, by themselves or over spandex shorts, and, as an outermost layer, shell pants. For the upper body, we wear shell jackets over polyester shirts. In colder climes we will also wear a thermal shirt each. And of course we wear mittens, and we don and doff hats as needed. Provided we keep moving, this combination keeps us comfortably warm without sweat-soaking everything. However, when merely ambling we of course dress more warmly. Depending on your hiking style and the ambient conditions, you will need to experiment with your hiking wardrobe to determine what works best for you. My advice is to carry plenty of layering garments, but to be careful not to wear too much while hiking. Pay strict attention to your microclimate.

Wearing the jacket backwards

Even on a very cold or wet day you will usually find the back of your shirt and the associated part of your backpack soaked with sweat. The pack is over-insulating your back. And yet the front of your body may be cold, especially in any kind of wind. So you may decide to don your rain jacket to block that wind, and of course that makes your back sweat all the more. Why not put the jacket on backwards and leave it open in the back? This will shield the front side of you where you need the protection, but not the back of your torso where you do not. Before I went to the single-shoulder pack carry, I hiked many hundreds of miles wearing jackets backwards.

To try it, simply run your arms through the sleeves and let the jacket drape over your shoulders and the front of your torso. To pin the backwards-worn jacket in place, put it on before you put your backpack on. The shoulder straps will then hold the jacket down. Or, to provide for easier on-and-off as conditions change, put the backwards-worn jacket on after you shoulder your backpack.

Clothing for resting in cold weather

When stopping for a rest, we cease producing the abundance of metabolic heat, and on a cold day the temperature associated with our microclimate will begin to plummet. Very soon we will need to put on our resting clothing. This comprises thicker garments providing greater insulation and wind protection.

In cold weather, look for rest stops that are naturally sheltered from the wind. Remove your sweat-dampened, lighter-weight hiking clothes and hang them to air. Quickly put on dry garments, such as the thermal shirt and pants, a warm hat, and an insulated jacket with its hood. In blustery conditions you might also want to don your waterproof-breathable jacket and pants. If it isn't raining or snowing and you intend to rest for a while, for example to cook an afternoon meal, you might remove your shoes and socks and change into dry wool-blend socks. And you could pull out your quilt or sleeping bag and use it as a comforter.

At the rest stop, don't try to ignore the cold. That is how people become hypothermic. Should you begin to feel a chill, do something about it. Either put on more clothing or abbreviate your rest stop and resume hiking. Once you get moving again, the exercise will soon re-warm you. And when comfortably warm again, make it a point to stop and change back into your hiking garb and put the more insulating, rest stop garments back into their waterproof stuff sacks for safe-keeping. However, if you become chilled and the day is late or your energy is flagging, then you might be wise to stop and make camp.

Eating for warmth

As you hike along the trail your muscles "burn" fuel and oxygen. In cold weather this "combustion" greatly increases your ability to stay comfortably warm. But it depends on your muscles being fed a constant supply of fuel. So your food intake—the fuel—must be ample and nutritious.

High in nutrition does not mean high in calories. The science of nutrition is yet in its infancy. In the decades to come no doubt scientists will learn a great deal more about it. But for now, the way calories in food are measured is simply by burning that food (in a device called a "bomb calorimeter") and then measuring the heat output. They could do the same thing with a piece of wood. Wood is loaded with calories, but that does not mean we can eat wood and stay warm. And by the same token, just because we can eat high-calorie junk foods, that does not mean they provide us with energy and warmth. They do not. So for the highest octane fuel, think nutrition rather than calories.

Substances such as capsicum (chili peppers, cayenne, and tablets) and alcohol give the impression of creating warmth. And indeed they can warm the extremities slightly, but certainly not enough to prevent frostbite. But rather than create heat, they merely "borrow" it from the body's core. In severe conditions they can accelerate the onset of hypothermia.

Real food—as opposed to junk food—is preferable, and hot food can be especially warming, if only psychologically. But not every day will you want to stop and cook along the trail, especially when in exposed terrain. When the temperature is frigid and the weather continues to be gnarly, you might prefer to cook and eat a hot breakfast before starting out for the day, to snack regularly throughout the day, and then when arriving at your next camp, to cook a well-deserved dinner.

In very cold conditions, keep the day's travel relatively short. This ensures maximum hiking energy and therefore the greatest safety margins. And be sure to snack at least every hour, for example on dried fruit and nuts, home-made snack bars or any other ready-to-eat, nutritious foods kept handy in your pack. On a cold day, one option is to cook a double-sized breakfast and after eating your fill, to stow the remainder inside your pack, still in the cookpot with its lid secured. Insulated with clothing, the meal will still be at least somewhat warm by mid-day, at which time it will provide you with the afternoon's supply of energy for hiking and maintaining metabolic warmth.

Drinking water for warmth

As discussed in the Water chapter, dehydration thickens the blood and reduces its volume. This hampers circulation which in turn affects the body's ability to transfer the warmth generated by the working muscles to the extremities and to the body's core—where that warmth is not only desirable but vital. Dehydration also slows metabolism, which decreases energy. And it robs a person of rational thinking and decision making.

Cold weather does not reduce your need for water, yet on a cold day you may not feel like drinking much water. At such times, just the thought of drinking cold water can make you shiver. And what cold water you do manage to gulp down can indeed physically chill the stomach. Fortunately there is a way around this. Unlike in warm weather when the best plan is usually to chug the water in order to ensure an adequate intake, in cold weather it is best to take frequent but small sips. This allows your body to warm the water, gradually, which it will. To facilitate frequent sipping, carry your water bottle in a mittened hand, and while hiking along the trail, take a sip every few minutes.

Hot drinks such as home-dried soups, hot cocoa, herbal teas and re-constituted milk might be warming, but you should not rely on them to re-hydrate your body since they are diuretics. Drink them in addition to pure water, if you like, not instead of it.

Camping in cold weather

In cold weather avoid camping in areas where the trees are stunted or entirely absent. This is often a sign of strong wind or katabatic pockets—places where frigid air from the mountain heights settles in the evenings. If these environments are too cold for trees to flourish, they will be less than suitable for comfortable camping.

If the wind is blowing, try to situate your camp behind natural wind barriers such as rocks, logs, tall brush or trees. However, in strong wind it is usually best to avoid trees due to the danger of one crashing down or a large branch snapping off.

Once you have chosen a protected site and set up your shelter, don't squander precious body heat by fussing with unnecessary camp chores. Collect a generous supply of drinking water ahead of time and have it handy for filtering so that you will not have to leave your warm bedding. If the temperature is sub-freezing, place your water bottles under the edge of your ground pad so that you will still have water in the morning, rather than ice.

Situate your pack next to you under the tarp or inside your tent, giving yourself access to whatever you might need. And before you retire into the sack, double-check your shelter's guylines, making sure they are well secured.

For more information about choosing the warmest and most secure campsites, see the Stealth Camping chapter.

Hypothermia

The term hypothermia ("hypo" meaning low, and "therm" meaning heat) refers to a dangerous reduction in the body's vital core temperature. Dr. James Wilkerson's *Medicine for Mountaineering* (Bibliography) contains an excellent discussion on the subject. Wilkerson describes the progression of deepening hypothermia in stages from mild—with shivering, chilliness and loss of dexterity in the fingers, to severe—resulting in unconsciousness and death. And he points out that what makes hypothermia so dangerous is that it impairs a person's ability to detect the condition as it progresses through the stages.

The threat of hypothermia is ever-present in cold weather, yet we can take definitive measures to ensure the upper hand—staying aware of the microclimate versus the ambient temperature, wearing sufficient clothing while being careful to not overdress, eating nutritious foods and drinking lots of water—all of which we have just discussed.

However, there is something that can work very much against us, and that is overexertion. Overexertion will prematurely deplete a person's energy and heat production. It also promotes sweat, and we have already seen how sweat-soaked clothing becomes far less serviceable. In cold weather the prudent hiker will do anything and everything to minimize sweat. Sweat can be a killer.

Overexerting is usually associated with someone carrying too heavy a load, trying to hike too fast, and particularly with a lack of pre-hike conditioning. Obviously then, a lighter weight pack and a moderate pace will go a long ways in insuring long-lasting energy and warmth.

What to do if hypothermia strikes

Hypothermia is a subtle malady. Unless you know what to watch for you may not notice its effects. Most importantly, if hiking with a partner, watch him or her for signs of physical or mental sluggishness. These might include slow and incoherent speech, uncharacteristic clumsiness and apathy. You can also test yourself by monitoring the dexterity of your fingers. Extend each finger straight, then touch it to the thumb of that hand—one, two, three, and four, and repeat quickly. You can perform this test without removing your mittens.

If your partner is behaving sluggishly or indifferently, or if your own fingers are "stiffening," this is a good time to consider an expedient descent to lower, more protected terrain, for making a sheltered camp. If your partner is becoming less coherent, or you find that you can no longer touch your index finger to your thumb, then you need to stop immediately and build a warming fire. For this, use your emergency fire-building kit, so that you don't waste precious time and body heat searching for dry kindling. Where you cannot build a fire, make camp. And don't be reluctant to pitch your shelter right there on the trail, or next to it, but preferably in a place protected from the wind and with adequate drainage.

If using a tarp in strong wind, pitch it low-lying, with its windward edge flush to the ground, and with its ridgeline perpendicular to the wind. But don't pitch it so low that it would rest against your quilt or sleeping bag, because it's condensation could dampen them.

Remember that even if your hiking clothes feel dry, they are probably at least somewhat damp from the hiking and therefore they can sap your warmth if you leave them on. So once inside your shelter, remove the damp garments and change into dry ones. Crawl into your quilt or sleeping bag, and eat a few snacks. If not in bear territory, fire up the stove for a hot beverage and a reviving meal. If you are in bear territory, eat snacks and heat some water and drink just that. Actually, sipping heated water will do you far more good than would sipping a heated beverage. Under a tarp, cooking will be easy and convenient. If you are inside a tent you will have to reach outside to use your stove.

———————

The information in this Cold chapter can bolster your cold weather hiking and camping skills, and lend greater confidence in your abilities. With this confidence you may no longer view the cold as an adversary, but as an interesting facet of nature. And when you awaken to a frosty morning you can put on the right combination of clothing and resume your journey in safety. And you may find, as I have, that a crisp day has a way of quickening the spirit and filling the heart with resolve.

Snow

Calvin: Wow, it really snowed last night! Isn't it wonderful!
Hobbes: Everything familiar has disappeared!
The world looks brand new!
Calvin: A new year... a fresh clean start!
Hobbes: It's like a big white sheet of paper to draw on!
Calvin: A day full of possibilities! It's a magical world Hobbes ol' buddy...
...let's go exploring!

To trudge or not to trudge that is the question

For many, the thought of hiking across a snowpacked landscape brings to mind a scene of bitterly cold winds, interminable knee-deep trudging, with no trail to be found anywhere. In a word, something to be avoided. Yet with knowledge of when and where the risks lie, and the skills for safe, three-season travel, snowpack can be a wonderful, magical part of a trek, full of possibilities and new realms to explore.

A matter of timing

This chapter does not deal with wintertime snow travel. Yet the snowpack is not a wintertime phenomenon exclusively. In fact, the higher regions of the western states are often snow-laden nine months of the year, while the lower alpine terrain usually harbors snow into late spring and early summer. And, as this photograph shows, winter-like storms can happen at any time. I took this picture in Colorado, on August 25 at nearly 13,000 feet during our thru-hike of the Continental Divide Trail.

The amount of snowpack at any given place will depend on the region's elevation and latitude, the amount of snow deposited there the previous winter, and the springtime melt rate. We hikers have no control over these variables, but we can choose the time of year we plan to visit a certain region. And this choice alone can determine whether we hike in snow or on bare trail.

Obviously, to avoid snow, one would venture into the high mountains only during the summer months. In a normal year this would be from late June to mid September.

However, many of us enjoy snow travel; the beauty and the solitude to be found in these pristine, whitened landscapes are unparalleled. Of course, to hike safely through those snowbound regions requires a certain amount of experience, preparedness and determination. But we can study the theories and techniques, and with the help of a qualified instructor we can gain the necessary skills.

One of the most important techniques has to do with timing. The key is to wait until the snowpack has coalesced, meaning that it has hardened into a compact mass. Before then you will flounder deeply in the soft snow. After coalescence you will walk mostly on its hard surface. Jenny and I learned this during our first thru-hike, while trudging for a month through the soft snow of the High Sierra. A few years later we traversed that range a second time, and because we were there a month later in the season, we walked on the snow's surface almost the entire way. So your timing will determine whether you wallow or you walk.

Remember, too, that the springtime snowpack usually melts very quickly once the summer sun starts bearing down upon it. Many hikers have told me of encountering a great deal of deep snow, and that they had heard from others coming along a few weeks later who found that same terrain largely snow-free.

Being bitten by the bug of impatience when preparing for a longer journey is a common syndrome. But the fact remains that a too-early start is much more likely to put you into the snow. If you are planning a major thru-hike, then naturally, you may feel the need for more time in order to complete your trip, and that therefore an earlier start date would be justified. I have been there, and know the feeling. But I learned, through a great deal of toil, that a later start date can greatly reduce the effort, and thereby improve one's chances of success. My recommendation is to equip yourself with lightweight gear and footwear, and to condition yourself according to the procedures in the Training chapter. This will give you more confidence in your abilities, and it will then ease the pressure from the inevitable urge to start too early.

The only hikers who should start their journeys early are those with considerable snow travel experience, and who are looking for that extra challenge. For them the snowpack is not a hindrance to wilderness travel, but an additional element to be richly savored.

Avoid camping on snow

Camping on snow necessitates the use of a thick foam pad or air mattress as insulation from the cold. But just because you are hiking in snow does not mean that you have to camp on it. With a little forethought you should be able to find patches of bare ground to pitch your tarp or tent. This tactic will allow you to carry only a thin foam pad, saving you weight and bulk in your pack.

As mentioned earlier, during our five hiking journeys Jenny and I spent weeks at a time walking on snow or wallowing through it, but not once did we camp on snow. We always managed to find snow-free terrain to sleep on. The photo at the beginning of this chapter would seem to contradict that, since it shows our tent in snow. But this is not an example of us camping *on* snow. We pitched the tent on snow-free ground, and the

On the PCT in 1987, in very early season we hiked for hours in snow while traversing Mt. San Jacinto and the Fuller Ridge. Then we found this patch of bare ground, which made for very comfortable camping.

next morning awoke to the wintry wonderland, as deposited by the sudden mid-summer storm. Had we been hiking during that storm, we would have descended out of the snowfall and made camp on bare, if wet, ground.

Even in very early season, the lower mountain regions usually harbor patches of bare ground here and there. In the higher country, look for small stands of trees, tall brush or rocky outcrops; you can often find snow-free ground along their south-facing edges.

If you are forced by a storm to camp on snow-covered ground, try clearing away the bulk of the snow by scraping at it with your shoe or a stout stick. If the snow is too deep for scraping, tromp it down as much as possible before spreading your groundsheet. If snow continues falling during the night, tap the ceiling of your tarp or tent occasionally with the palm of your hand to knock off the accumulating snow. This will prevent the weight of the snow from over-stressing the shelter.

Protective clothing for snow travel

When snow is falling heavily, the umbrella makes a wonderful portable shelter. It keeps the snow off your head and upper body, and away from your face. And it shields most of your pack as well. It is equally useful at rest stops and meal breaks. But if a strong wind begins driving the snow sideways, then you may need to stow the umbrella and bundle up, to guard against loss of body heat.

If snow begins falling while I am hiking, I usually pull on my shell pants over my spandex shorts. In colder conditions I wear a pair of thermal pants under the shells. As described in the previous chapter, I normally do not wear waterproof pants. If my legs are going to be wet or damp from internal condensation, I would rather be wearing breathable nylon pants, since my legs can move much more easily in them. Still, a pair of waterproof-breathable or vapor-permeable pants might be nice when I am generating but little body warmth, for example while exploring around camp, or sitting out in the open. And they might be very handy in a severe storm. Stowed away in the backpack, they would make a very appropriate emergency item.

The bomber hat keeps one's head nicely warm, while its waterproof-breathable outer covering sheds snowfall. This hat is much less restrictive, compared with the hood of a rain jacket or insulated jacket.

The extremities are especially susceptible to cold, so in a snowstorm one should wear mittens, and pull the hands up into the jacket sleeves to protect them from the wind and wet. You will also need to keep close tabs on your toes and feet, making sure they are not growing cold and numb. If you are hiking briskly, you will rarely find cold feet to be a problem. Especially if you are wearing medium-weight wool-blend socks, in layers if necessary. When walking on snowpack, the footwear must not fit too tightly, otherwise it restricts circulation and this can chill the feet rapidly. When hiking on snow, wear lightweight boots that are slightly oversize to allow for extra socks. When buying boots for snow travel, keep in mind that the feet will not be nearly as swollen in cold conditions as they normally are in hot. If you find that your lightweight boots are too loose, snug up the laces.

In snowy, blustery weather it is often difficult to keep one's hiking clothing dry. This calls for staying in camp, or hiking with a minimum of the extraneous. As long as your body is producing enough metabolic heat, you are in no danger of hypothermia. "Wet and warm" is fine, as long as you keep moving. If the wind starts blowing with more force, put on your rain jacket over your wet shirts and shell. The rain jacket will help you stay warm by blocking the cold wind and by adding a bit of insulation. When your shirts are wet and you stop to rest, in a sheltered place, remove your wet garments and put on dry ones.

Once again, in stormy weather it is usually better to remain at camp. But if hiking in such conditions you must continually assess your situation. Ask yourself whether it is wise to continue ahead, or whether it would be more prudent to leave the trail and descend, to make a sheltered camp. Study your maps ahead of time, so that you will know at all times whether the trail ahead of you climbs to a more exposed position. Stay alert, and never cross your Rubicon—meaning don't overextend beyond your capabilities. If you exhaust yourself by forging ahead, you could find yourself with insufficient energy for descending and making a safe camp.

Existing snowpack in fine weather

Imagine that the day is sunny, and that you are crunching your way across a snowy landscape. Rather than protect you from cold, your clothing in this situation needs to protect your skin from the sun's ultraviolet radiation. This is true whether the sky is clear or cloudy, because much of the UV penetrates the clouds. And the snowbound alpine terrain, in all its white, featureless glory, acts as a giant mirror, reflecting the UV powerfully. With radiation coming at you from all directions, it can be very burning, particularly in the mountains of the western U.S. where the higher elevations and dry air offer less atmospheric protection from solar energy. At eleven thousand feet, for example, the sun is four times as intense as it is at sea level.

In any event, the snow-tromper needs to cover virtually every square inch of skin. Using an umbrella or a hat is not enough, because of the powerful reflection from the snow. Protect your face with a bandana, and wear dark glasses to shield your eyes. Apply a high SPF sunscreen to the ears, nose and to any other exposed skin. Apply the sunscreen inside the nostrils a ways, and hike with your mouth closed to prevent a painful sunburn to the roof of your mouth.

If you do not want to carry a long sleeve, lightweight shirt in addition to the much cooler short sleeve one, you could carry a pair of long sleeves, cut from an old button-up shirt. Simply attach them to your short sleeve

shirt with small safety pins. This arrangement works well also for desert travel.

I have worn many different types of boots and gaiters in winter mountaineering conditions, and I do not recall a single time when I removed them at day's end and found my socks dry. Fortunately, on most of our outings here in the contiguous U.S. we do not need to worry about keeping our socks and feet dry. The conditions here are fairly mild compared with, say, the Alaska Range, the Andes, or Himalayas. Freezing our feet during the summer months in Colorado or New Hampshire is very unlikely. So, for summertime hiking, rather than trying to keep the feet dry, a more important quality in our mountain footwear is mobility. This means lighter-weight boots. And in my experience it matters not if those boots remain dry or become soaked. The more easily I can cover the miles in them, the happier I am. I prefer lightweight boots for snow tromping, and find that even very lightweight ones keep my well-exercised feet at a comfortable temperature.

While running shoes are very well suited for making miles on bare ground, they are wholly out of place on steep, hard snowpack. Lightweight boots allow you to kick much better steps for greater security.

Gaiters need only keep the snow out of the tops of the boots. This means that they can be short, ultralight, and simple in construction.

Special equipment

Winter mountaineers typically carry skis, crampons, climbing rope and other technical gear designed to facilitate their adventures. And generally, they know how to use that gear safely. In terms of three-season trekking, we hikers rarely if ever need any of these items. For details, refer back to the related information in the Remaining Equipment chapter. However, there is one item of technical gear that is essential to anyone venturing into snowy terrain: the ice axe.

The ice axe and self-arrest

Should you accidentally slip on steep and frozen snow, you would dig the pick of your ice axe into the snow to stop yourself from sliding down into the rocks and trees below. This procedure is known as the "self-arrest." It is not difficult to learn, particularly with the help of a qualified instructor. And once learned it will stay with you for life.

You might imagine that since a trail is *mostly* snow free, then you can travel it safely without an ice axe. The fact is, whether the previous winter's snowfall was massive or minuscule, the snow hazards of early season (spring and early summer) highland travel are about the same. The main

problems are not the expansive, deep snowfields, but the patches and ribbons of sometimes hard and slippery snow lying across a trail—in places where the trail traverses steep slopes. Owing to the steepness of the slopes, these patches can be difficult and even dangerous to circumvent by climbing or descending around. And due to the often compact and slippery nature of the icy patches, especially in early morning before the sun has softened them, they can be extremely risky to set foot on without a safeguarding ice axe.

Granted, many hikers of various levels of experience have hiked snowy terrain without ice axes. Most of these people have met with good luck. But some have slipped and sustained serious injuries. So don't take chances. In early season, carry your ice axe when venturing into the high country, and know how to use it. Think of your axe as a safety parachute. You may not need it; but then again, it could be a life saver.

Schooling in the proper techniques

Once you learn the skills of ice axe self-arrest, your confidence in negotiating steeper sections of snow will soar. This will help you to hike the high and wild places with far greater safety and peace of mind. The safest and best way to learn the self-arrest is under the watchful eye of a qualified instructor, on a gentle practice slope with a safe run-out. So give some serious thought to enrolling in an accredited class in the early spring. Consider the costs of the lessons as a form of insurance: you pay the one-time premium, and you are covered for life. To locate various schools, check with your local backpacking or mountaineering supply shops, or perhaps search the Internet. If you live in a mountainous region, check with any nearby colleges, they may offer winter mountaineering classes, or they might have outing clubs that could point you in the right direction.

Anatomy of an ice axe

The bottom, pointed end of the shaft is called the point, or spike. The top end is called the head. At one end of the head is the spoon-shaped, step-chopping blade called the adze (pronounced "adds"). Also on the head but opposite the adze is the long and narrow blade called the pick, used for self-arrest. To help you remember, think of a gold miner's pick and pan. The adze need not be razor sharp; using it for digging daily cat holes in

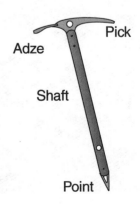

soft earth does not detract appreciably from its ability to chop steps in hard, steep snowpack. In fact, the sharper it is, the more it will tend to get stuck in hard-frozen snow while chopping steps.

The self-arrest described

The accompanying photo shows Jenny in the self-arrest position. She demonstrates on a concrete slab so that the pick of the axe is not buried in the snow, obscuring the important nuances of the position. Note that the body does not lie on the surface, nor do the knees. Rather, these are held up off the surface in order to exert maximum plowing pressure on the pick of the axe and the toes of the feet. Note also that the feet are spread apart somewhat. These three points of contact—the feet and the pick—form a triangle, providing the optimum stability. The strongest hand grips the head of the axe, with the fingers wrapping over the top. The other hand grasps the shaft near the spike, stabilizing the shaft while holding the spike off the snow.

The head of the axe is held close to the body for a secure grip, but safely away from the face. The greatest danger when learning to self-arrest is that of dropping down onto the slope in the self-arrest position and allowing the axe to gouge you in the face. Before dropping down onto a slope, hold the axe firmly in the self-arrest position and focus on one thought: keeping the adze away from your face. On a steep slope you must grasp the head of the axe very tightly, to prevent it from being pulled out of your grip as you slide down the slope. This means holding it fairly close to your shoulder and head.

You can practice the self-arrest position in your backyard. Not by dropping down onto the ground, as you would on snow, but by simply lying in place, thinking about bracing your body off the ground, about spreading your feet, and about holding the adze away from your face. Once you get the position right, commit it to memory. Then later on, go over it in your mind once in a while.

Actual practice

While lying in your backyard, face down in the self-arrest position, you will learn much about the proper stance and technique. But you must also practice on a snow slope in order to coordinate the aggressive movements of jamming the pick of your axe into the snow. Here you must be very careful about choosing a gentle practice slope that offers a safe run-out. The slope must be very forgiving of any mistakes. Remember to keep a tight grip on the axe, and to keep the adze away from your face. With every practice fall, concentrate mainly on the adze.

Once again, always hold the head of the axe with your strongest arm. If you are right-handed, grasp the head in your right hand, and vice versa if you are left-handed. Should you suddenly slip, you will not have time to think about which hand goes where. The action must be reflexive, and the best way for beginners is to hold the axe the same way every time. Resist the temptation to switch hands when facing the other way on a steeper slope.

In the event of a slip, you would most likely land on your knees or stomach, and this is the most favorable position for the self-arrest. Should you land on your backside, roll over onto your stomach—in the direction away from the spike of your axe to prevent the spike from catching the snow. If you are right-handed, roll to your right. If you slip and land head-downhill, go into the self-arrest position and dig the pick in gently but well off to one side. This will swivel you around. If you land head-downhill on your back, go into the self-arrest position but reach out to the side with the pick and grab the snow with it. This will swing you around, during which time you would roll over onto your stomach. For more information refer to a book on winter mountaineering skills, such as *Freedom of the Hills* (Bibliography).

The hiker's ice axe

Self-arrest ice axes do not have drop point heads, such as those used for ice climbing. They curve only moderately from adze to pick. They are available in aluminum or steel. The aluminum types are lighter in weight and more expensive, and some (but certainly not all) might be of dubious strength. The steel types are heavier but tend to be much stronger. The shaft length

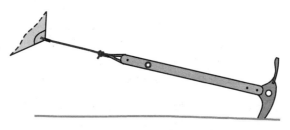

Place your best tent stake to windward

of the hiker's ice axe is not a function of the user's height. The axe I normally use is 20 inches long and 9 inches along the head, which is a good all-around size for most hikers.

Stow your ice axe on the outside of your backpack in such a way that the axe will not snag overhead branches, and that it will not inflict injury should you accidentally fall down. I stow my axe by passing the shaft behind a horizontal strap on one side of my pack, and down through a special loop near the pack's bottom. This allows me to grab the axe and withdraw it without having to unshoulder the backpack, even when I am using both shoulder straps.

When hiking on level and compact snow, either stow the ice axe or carry it by the shaft in one hand, and in such a way that the pick points away from you, to avoid injuring yourself in the event of an otherwise uneventful slip. When climbing a steeper slope, hold the axe in the self-arrest position. It is also a good idea to attach a lanyard (cord or thin webbing), about three feet in length, to the head of the axe for securing to your wrist during use. The lanyard prevents the loss of the axe should you accidentally drop it, or reflexively toss it away during a sudden slip.

Climbing a snow slope

Walking on compact or frozen snow on level or moderately sloped terrain is no more difficult than hiking on bare ground. This type of snow contains irregularities and grit. It is not ice-rink slippery, and you can negotiate it without slipping and sliding. Even so, footwear with a deeper "waffle" pattern tread will give better "purchase," meaning that the tread will bite into the snow with a better grip.

As the snowfield leads more steeply uphill, you will reach a point where you rely less on the waffle-tread of your boots for purchase, and more on their edges. The edges of the boots should be parallel to the slope, and they should bite into the snow in the same way as would a pair of metal-edged skis. For a better bite, stomp the edges of your boots aggressively into the snow, making small footholds. If the snow is so hard that it resists, kick repeatedly until you can make an adequate step.

As mentioned earlier, the adze of the ice axe can be used to chop steps, and you can chop a series of steps straight across the slope (a traverse), or diagonally up it. However, one must never chop steps in snow that is frozen so hard that the most vigorous kicking fails to produce a usable toe hold. Snow is often this solid early in the mornings of late spring. When the snow is that hard, you are better off staying off it. Should you slip and have to self-arrest, you might be able to stop yourself from sliding, but you would not be able to stand back up. While lying in the self-arrest position, you would not be able to kick adequate steps into that frozen snow, nor could you release your axe from the snow in order to chop steps. Short of a rescue from your partner, only the most violent kicking would save you. If you can see safety below, then you might be able to descend in a controlled slide using the ice axe as a brake. However a far safer and smarter move is to avoid the situation altogether. Either traverse around that patch of rock-hard snow, where safe and practical, or wait until it softens, which it probably will as the day warms.

Only if you can kick at least barely adequate steps with your boots should you consider chopping larger, more secure steps with your ice axe. Chopping steps can be laborious, due to the need to make the steps large enough to stand on in comfort and security.

Descending a snow slope

The snow conditions on either side of a major mountain pass can be as different as day and night. As you climb to a crest and gaze down the far slope, bear in mind that the slope could be frozen. And do not be fooled by deeply imprinted boot tracks leading down. The hikers who made them may have descended the previous afternoon, when the snow was mushy. Test the snow by taking a few very cautious steps, prodding ahead with your axe. If the snow is too hard to plunge step (see below), or if it resists the kicking of adequate steps, do not be tempted to chop steps with your ice axe. Trying to work below you is very awkward, and you could easily lose your balance. Instead, return to the ridge and enjoy a long rest, allowing the snow to soften. Otherwise, if the snow is already sufficiently soft, then proceed ahead cautiously while assessing the avalanche hazard.

Remember that wilderness snow slopes are not groomed bunny hills at ski resorts. Very often they are pockmarked with invisible soft spots, and possibly rocks that you cannot see from your higher vantage. So do not be tempted to slide down the slope. Above all else, never sit on a groundsheet and zip down a slope as though riding a sled. In a flash you would be traveling at breakneck speed, while completely out of control.

Sliding while seated in the snow, and using the pick of the axe as a brake is called "glissading." You may read about this in other books, or hear other hikers talking about it. I consider this technique too risky, unless you have first climbed that slope and know its condition. As with any other kind of slide, it affords very little directional control. And it soaks the seat of one's pants.

If you are confident on your feet, you might try "boot skiing." Simply pretend that your boots are skis, and head on down, carving your turns. This works well because you can steer clear of any rocks, and you can keep your speed to the very minimum. Never build speed while boot skiing. Should your foot suddenly break through the crust, your leg could jam into a hole between underlying rocks, and your body's forward momentum could snap that leg.

The safest descent of a steep slope—again, one that is not frozen hard—is with the "plunge step." As you take a step, lock the knee and let the weight of your body pile-drive your heel down into the snow. This creates a solid and secure platform for your foot that will hold your weight. For the safest descent, slow down and make each plunge step deliberate and forceful. And as with boot skiing, hold your ice axe at the ready so that if you lose balance you can drop into the self-arrest position.

Avalanche!

When the high peaks are deeply snowbound, avalanches can pose a real danger to the backcountry traveler. To increase your margins of safety, learn to recognize the conditions of greatest peril, and avoid the danger zones. Unfortunately, your chosen trail may sometimes lead straight through avalanche-prone regions. For this reason you should never follow a snowbound trail heedlessly. When the route ahead looks unsafe, turn back. No journey is worth the risk of tangling with an avalanche.

Snow slopes frequently offer clues as to their avalanche "disposition." The steeper a slope, the more gravity tugs at the snow covering it, and the more that snow is liable to cut loose. Also, a winter's snowpack is like a multi-layer cake, with each layer consisting of the snow deposited by a particular storm. And because each storm is different in moisture content, duration, and ambient temperature, so is the snow it deposits. The greatest avalanche danger occurs on a steeply inclined slope where a heavier layer rests upon a lighter and less cohesive one.

So, if you find yourself hiking above treeline when the terrain is still snowbound, avoid traveling across or beneath steep snow slopes. Many times a trail will switchback up a steep slope to gain a high ridge or pass. But this trail can be difficult to locate when covered deeply in snow. And the steep slope can present a real avalanche hazard. The safest way to climb such a slope is along one edge, away from the likely path of any avalanche. Before starting the ascent, examine the slope carefully to determine the best route. Part way up, you might check the slope's consistency by carefully digging a slot a couple of feet deep with your ice axe, and examining the layers. If you find that all layers are compact, then the slope is less likely to slide. But if you find an icy layer, or a layer that lacks cohesion—called "corn snow" because the flakes have metamorphosed individually without bonding together—then however thin that layer might be, do not proceed. Even your body weight could trigger the slope into motion.

Climb a slope one person at a time, while your companions stand well to one side. And keep your backpack's hip belt unlatched. The unfortunate hiker caught in an avalanche should quickly shrug off the backpack, roll over onto the back, and "swim" frantically and continually for the surface. When avalanche alluvium comes to a stop it tends to set like concrete. A friend of mine was once overtaken by a small avalanche that buried only his head and one shoulder; the rest of him remained above the surface, yet still he could not struggle free. After his buddies had dug him out they had to administer artificial respiration.

Those hikers wishing to test their mettle in very early season would do well to study a few books on avalanche safety, and to carry transponders and probes. But of course the best way to avoid avalanche hazard is to plan the hike for summertime.

Brain lock

One of the most dangerous aspects of snow travel is a phenomenon I call "brain lock." Remember the cartoons of the coyote forever chasing the road runner? Road Runner zooms off a cliff into space—for after all, he is a bird—and Wile E. Coyote unthinkingly pursues. Suddenly realizing that something is dreadfully amiss, the coyote stops. Suspended in mid-air, he ponders the enormity of the situation for a few moments before giving the audience that look of resignation. Then he plummets.

The coyote's reaction is not so far removed from our own tendencies. Despite the actual circumstances, the hiker on a steep slope will not drop until his brain tells him that he must. As an example, I was leading a group of students across a snowfield in which our boots were barely imprinting. I was so accustomed to walking on steep snow that I could easily secure myself when needed by stomping the edges of my boots aggressively into the snow. The slope gradually steepened, but we were doing fine until one fellow piped up, "Hey, this is really steep!" Suddenly five of them went down like bowling pins and slid a few dozen feet to the bottom of the snowbank. Fortunately none of them landed hard enough to sustain any injuries. The others held their mental timbers tight, and together we safely traversed off the slope.

This is an example of brain lock. I have witnessed it many times, and have noticed that once it happens, the effect is very difficult to reverse. The situation must resolve *itself*, for better or worse. Brain lock is the result of irrepressible fear leading to panic. It is a natural mechanism designed to relieve us of having to deal with a frightful situation. Yet the consequences of not dealing with it can be fatal.

I was cruising solo near the Continental Divide in the Colorado Rockies, planning to meet with students farther along. I came to a snow slope and found it in excellent condition, so I began boot skiing on down. The slope soon steepened and I happened upon a most unexpected scene. Someone was lying in the middle of the slope, clinched in the self-arrest position. Three others were seated safely off to one side in the talus fifty feet away. They were afraid to risk their own lives to help the person in trouble, even though all of them had ice axes and wore stout mountaineering boots. The person on the snow was brain locked. I sped to her assistance and escorted her safely off the slope. My point here is that her brain lock was caused by the *possibility* of her plummeting down the slope, not by any certainty of doing so. Once I had her safely in my grasp, the possibility of her slipping disappeared. The situation resolved itself immediately, her brain unlocked, and together we easily walked across the slope to join her friends. Had she kept her cool from the beginning, she could have traversed off the slope just as easily by herself.

How do we anticipate brain lock, and how do we prevent it? Early one mid-August morning during our second PCT hike, Jenny and I were descending Fire Creek Pass on the slopes of Glacier Peak, not too far from the Canadian border. A hundred miles earlier I had consigned my trail-ragged shoes to a trash bin, and to avoid a hitchhike out to buy a new pair, I had appropriated Jenny's spare shoes. These were three sizes too small for my feet, but since we had only a few hundred miles to go, I had slit those shoes all manner of ways, managing to enlarge them just enough to walk in. Part way down from the pass we came to a steep, frozen slope that dropped far below. This slope was inconvenient to circumvent, as often they are. So, exuding confidence despite our lack of safety gear, I led across and Jenny followed. The farther we traversed, the harder was the snow's surface. Yet my shoes were so tight that the uppers bulged far over both sides of the soles, rendering the soles useless for edging. To hack each minuscule step, I slashed repeatedly with the blunt shoes, and

How to fit into your wife's well-worn shoes: slit
them in several places, and cut your socks off
below the ankles.

in retrospect I probably could have done better wearing roller skates. A few dozen feet from the far side I judged the ever-steepening slope too dangerous for further progress. Feeling a brain lock hovering menacingly overhead, I clinched my resolve and very calmly, very matter-of-factly, told Jenny that we were, ho hum, turning around. Unaware of how insecure my footing was, she easily walked back across our small footholds.

I prevented brain lock in myself by keeping a level head. And I prevented it in Jenny by projecting calmness and confidence. We circumvented the snow slope by climbing around it, and I went away with an increased distrust of those shoes.

Should you find yourself in dire straits, realize that the dangers lie primarily in your own mind. Use foresight to keep yourself out of trouble, and clear, prudent thinking to get yourself out of trouble when you do get into it. Remember too that where the mind leads the body follows. If you find yourself in a dubious situation, focus on a positive outcome.

Differing types of snow

To the casual observer, both soft snow and hard snow look about the same. Yet despite similarities in appearance, the differences in texture can be profound. And to mistake one for the other can be dangerous. Stepping out onto a patch of steeply-inclined snow—thinking that it is soft—could be a serious miscalculation if that snow is frozen as hard as an ice-skating rink and almost as slippery.

I have been hiking and climbing on snow for decades, in all sorts of snow conditions, and still I cannot judge with complete accuracy whether a patch of snow is compact or compliant just by looking at it. I have to physically test it in some way. If I am hiking a bare trail that traverses a steep slope, and if I come to a patch of snow covering the trail, I do not test it by simply walking out on it. That could prove disastrous. Instead, I probe with my ice axe, or by kicking at it, with one foot on solid ground. Also, snowpack is softest around its margins; invariably it is more compact and slippery farther from the edges. So even though my initial few steps go well, that is no assurance of the snow's condition farther along. It could be much more compact. This is why it is a good idea to withdraw the ice axe before starting across, and to hold it in the self-arrest position, just in case.

The coalescing snowpack

Winter snowfall in the high mountains is usually soft and fluffy, depending on ambient temperatures. Traversing this powder snow requires the use of skis on steep terrain, or snowshoes where it is less steep. Otherwise, the boots alone would sink in too deeply with each step. Week after week, the snowpack begins to coalesce—from the surface down. And as it does, it begins to support the hiker's weight better. Meaning that the feet do not sink in quite so deeply. As summer approaches, the warmth of the daytime sun accelerates the melting of the upper layers of this snow. And when the nighttime temperature plummets, those upper layers freeze. Generally, the clearer the sky at night, the harder the freeze, since a clear sky allows maximum heat loss through radiation. The problem for the early-season hiker is that this upper layer of snow is not yet thick enough to support body weight. So when taking each step, most of the weight is applied, and then suddenly the foot will break through the crust and drop deeply into the soft underlying layers. This is called "postholing," and it can be exhausting. You are forever climbing out of holes, and immediately falling back into new ones.

As the weeks pass and the snowpack coalesces further, it will support more of our weight, until finally it becomes so compact that it will barely indent. Yet even this very compact snow will conceal soft spots. So while walking on its surface we must be very careful where we step, particularly while hiking steeply downhill.

In light of this coalescing process, it is obvious that the snow conditions we encounter are not a matter of chance, but of timing. Much too early in the season and we will flounder in it deeply. A few weeks later this snowfield will have a crusty surface and we will posthole laboriously. Several weeks later still, and we will walk on its surface. Moreover, the snow's depth is of little concern. Walking on consolidated snow that is twenty five feet deep is no different than walking on consolidated snow that is five feet deep. What does matter is the snow's condition—and that, once again, is a matter of our timing.

Plying the transition zones

Snowpack melts in three ways. On the surface it sublimates, meaning that it simply evaporates directly from the solid state. Sometimes on a crisp morning you will see the snowfields steaming. This is the vapor of sublimation condensing into visible form. Snowpack also melts on the surface, from the heat of the sun and the sun-warmed air. Puddles do not form because the underlying snow absorbs the water. And thirdly, snowpack melts from the heat of the earth, rocks and vegetation. It is this latter effect that most concerns the hiker. Snow deeper than about three feet absorbs the moisture of melting and remains structurally intact, able to bear the hiker's weight. Less than this, and it typically becomes slushy and saturated, or as we say: "rotten." Saturated snow is a much better conductor of heat, and this accelerates its melting.

I refer to this rotten, fast-melting snow as transition snow. It is soon to vanish, and for the hiker descending from the mountain heights it is the transition between relatively solid snow and bare ground. Transition snow occurs mainly near a snowfield's lower boundaries. Depending on the depth of snowpack, the transition zones can be from one to several hundred feet in width, as measured from the margin toward the middle of the snowfield. And usually they provide many clues as to the best routes through them. Not all of the snow in the transition zones is rotten. Once you learn to read the clues, you will travel across snowpack far more quickly and easily, simply by avoiding the soft spots.

How to read the snow

The following clues apply only to the coalescing snowpack typical of late June and early July, mainly in the highlands of the western states. It does not apply to winter and early spring conditions when the transition zones are minimal, or to autumn snow when they are entirely absent.

- While crossing the transition zones, look for bushes or other twigs and branches barely protruding above the surface. Also scan ahead for a darkened hint of a buried bush. The heat of these plants has probably desiccated the snow's substrate and weakened it considerably. Give these areas a wide berth. They are booby traps.

- In meadows and open areas that are gradually sloped, the transition zones can be hundreds of yards wide. As you make your way through these areas, pick a line that keeps the farthest from rocks and trees, and try to pass uphill of them. These objects absorb more of the sun's heat, and conduct it beneath the snow's surface. This sub-surface heat slowly melts the surrounding snow. The resulting moisture flows imperceptibly downhill, not near the ground as one might expect, but as a horizontal effusion throughout. This saturates and weakens the snowpack as it goes. To step onto this weakened snow is to posthole suddenly into it. Recognize it in two ways: by what objects are uphill of it, and by the subtle sagging or depression in the snow's surface, running downhill from the object causing it.

- In any type of snow, avoid the margins around protruding, or notice-able underlying rocks. Rocks radiate heat, even when deeply buried, and they melt the snow surrounding them. The resulting void, often covered, is known as a moat. Generally, the larger the rock, the more cavernous its moat. Whimsically, those who have not inadvertently fallen waist deep into hidden moats at least ten times have not yet qualified for the cosmos-is-avenging-me merit badge. Those who have seen gaping moats as large as dump trucks might not care to try for this badge. Either way, it's usually best to stay away from underlying rocks.

- Finally, as you descend a snowfield and are about to reach its lower margin, watch for very subtle lines indicating the boundaries of the transition zone. The rotten snow is often a little more crystalline in appearance, and sometimes slightly more yellow. If you step only a few inches to one side of a crystalline margin, (and to one side of someone's posthole) you will probably avoid sinking in.

No matter how assiduously you adhere to these recommendations, you may still find yourself wallowing and postholing a fair amount. Faced with acres of unavoidable, rotten and thigh-deep snow, it is time to change priorities. Switch off the speedometer. Banish the urge for forward progress. Mitigate your pace and concentrate solely on your heart rate. Think of a soft snowfield as a steep hill. If you feel that you are clawing ahead at a mere snail's pace, then you are struggling with your own impatience. Using brute force will deplete you very quickly. Instead, proceed thoughtfully and in control, striving for the proper balance of pace and mental serenity. Once you have found that balance you will cruise ahead with far less effort.

Following a snowbound trail

When snowbound in early or late season, alpine trails can be difficult to follow. This is particularly true where they are not blazed at regular intervals. A GPS receiver, coupled with a microchip containing the trail's coordinates, can pinpoint a hiker's location and specify (depending on the unit's accuracy) where to look for the trail. Although this technology would simplify route finding through snowpack, it would do nothing to simplify the physical labors of trudging, or to alleviate the dangers of avalanche and snowmelt run-off. So it might be helpful to learn a few trail sleuthing techniques.

Before entering a region of snowpack, study your maps. By examining the topographical features you will know what landmarks and features to look for. At each of these features, note your location on the map, and check your wristwatch for the time of day for the purposes of dead reckoning (described in the Compass section of the Remaining Equipment chapter). And most importantly, study the map's line of the trail, noting the general location of any switchbacks. It is the switchbacks that cause the greatest route finding difficulties. At one of these the trail suddenly changes direction, often without any indication above the snow's surface. And since you cannot see the trail buried beneath the snow, you certainly cannot see where it switchbacks. Beyond the switchback you will be heading one way and the trail the other.

A trail does not lead directly through a tree. Therefore, where you see a tree, you know the trail is not there. Conversely, where you see no tree, the trail *might* be there. And developing this logic: where you see a line of no trees in an area of otherwise thick forest, the trail is *probably* there. The trail builders likely felled that line of trees. In areas of dense timber,

Traversing a slope to reach the trail, seen here as a line of no trees. On the PCT in 1994

these treeless corridors are common, and they are your best clues. However, in areas of large trees the trail builders usually route the trail around each one, leaving no evident corridor.

Even where corridors are lacking, the trail crew may have left clues. When Jenny and I hiked the PCT southbound we traveled a deeply snowbound trail much of the way through Washington. I reckon we navigated about 60% by snipped tree branch stubs. You do not see them much while hiking a bare trail because you do not need to see them. In winter-like conditions, you need to see them, since they might be the only part of the trail there is to see. When hiking through the forest with no hint of a trail, if you find a tree that has only a stub of a snipped branch with a clean edge that appears to have been cut with a saw or nippers, you have almost certainly found the trail.

A log that has one end cleanly sawn off is sometimes an indication of the trail and sometimes not. When the trail crews saw an offending log, they discard the part blocking the trail. They might give it a shove and send it rolling down the slope, or they might carry it a ways into the forest, out of sight of the trail nice and tidy like. And there you may find it, protruding above an ocean of snow. What you have not necessarily found is the trail. Still, you are probably near the trail.

In addition to snipped branch stubs, Jenny and I navigated about 20% of the way by shovel cuts. Look for these on steeper terrain, in the vicinity of large trees. Each large tree normally has a snow-free moat around it, melted away by the tree's relative warmth. Very often where the trail comes close to a tree on steeper ground, the trail crew's shovel cut will lie close enough to the tree to be visible in the tree's moat. The shovel cut will not look like fresh-cut dirt. But it will look like dirt. Exposed dirt is rare in timber country, especially near trees. If you find even a little, the chances are it was shovel-cut.

Following a snowbound trail is much easier while hiking in a northerly direction. As you scan the terrain ahead, you are looking at south-facing slopes. These slopes are exposed to the sun's warmth, and are far less snowbound than their north-facing counterparts. By continually looking ahead, you can often locate at least a small piece of the trail on a patch of snow-free, south-facing ground. As you climb over a rise and start down the other (north-facing) side, the trail may again disappear beneath unending snow, but by looking far ahead you may see at least another piece of it leading up the next south-facing slope.

If, on the other hand, you are traveling south and looking ahead at north-facing slopes, as Jenny and I were that year in Washington, you would need to look for other clues. One such clue is a faint but straight line, like a depression in the snow, leading across a snow slope. Jenny and I navigated about 10% of the time by studying the terrain far ahead for these faint lines. Straight lines leading across slopes are unnatural. Each time we saw one, we memorized where it started and where it went. Even though apparent from a distance, these lines are rarely visible at close range. So rather than search for the trail at our feet, we searched for it well ahead of us.

The remaining 10% of our navigating was a combination of map study and logical assessment, familiarity with the trail and relying on memory, with a bit of "by-guess-and-by-golly" thrown in for good measure.

Where the land is covered in tall but patchy snowdrifts, it is best to resist the temptation to walk around them. You might save energy, but you can easily become disoriented as to the trail's directional trend. Follow the trail up and over every snowbank. If they are five or ten feet tall, then so much the better because they will allow you to see that much farther ahead.

On the PCT in 1994

When trying to follow a snowbound trail through dense forest, do not strike out cross-country unless you know exactly where you are, and where you are going. In difficult conditions you have only so much trail-searching time in one day, and this time is best spent near the trail rather than far from it. If you lose the trail, search the area repeatedly, always coming back to your last known point, until eventually you find the snowbound trail a short ways farther on. Remember that in dense timber the trail will lead you to your destination, or out of the wilderness, in the easiest and usually the most expedient manner. Stay with it.

Hidden lakes and creeks

Lakes, ponds and tarns can be very dangerous to cross when they are covered with snow. You have no way of accurately judging the solidity of the underlying ice. And should you break through an invisible soft spot in the snow and plunge into the frigid water, and if that water is deeper than you are tall, then you may not be able to extricate yourself. Rather than shortcut across, it is usually much safer to go around.

Creeks are a different matter, at least the small, shallow ones. In the early season they will often be bridged with compact snow that you can safely walk across. But again, it depends on the depth of the water. If you break through and land in water only ankle deep, then what you get is wet feet. But if the water is over-the-head deep and running swiftly, then the risks could be considerable. As a general rule when crossing snow bridges, listen for the creek's muffled gurgling at your feet. If you hear it, turn back immediately. The noise means that the snow bridge is thin. Otherwise, make sure to unbuckle your pack's hip belt, so that you can shed your pack quickly if you do break through.

Autumn snow travel

To this point we have considered snow that has spent the winter consolidating, and which we encounter in spring or early summer. Now let's say that the summer has passed, and that you find yourself hiking the high country in very late season. So late, in fact, that pre-winter storms are starting to play over the landscape. These storms are well known for bringing sudden and severe conditions, with strong winds and freezing temperatures. As such, they call for extra clothing, including wool-blend socks, shirts and pants, an insulating jacket and a rain jacket. If the storms persist and the route ahead begins to look intimidating, consider descending out of the high country. Remember that if a major snowstorm catches you at a higher elevation, it could present you with a real challenge. The new-fallen snow will not bear your weight, since it has not coalesced. And if it is deeper than what you can wallow through, then it can fairly immobilize you—unless you happen to be carrying snowshoes for the occasion. So in the event of a major snowstorm, it is better to descend out of it, rather than make camp and wait it out.

In closing this chapter I would like to recommend an excellent book called *A Snow Walker's Companion; Winter Trail Skills from the Far North*, by Garrett and Alexandra Conover (Bibliography). The Conovers do not go lightweight, but they do provide wonderful insights into the possibilities and the joys of extended wintertime hiking.

———

Snow travel can open up new worlds of hiking adventure and excitement. It will test your knowledge, your skills, and your mettle. In return, it will reward you with great feelings of accomplishment. Remember that snow is a part of the Grand Scheme, another facet of nature's many wonders. When you come to terms with it, you will be that much more balanced as an adventurer, and that much better connected. So learn to appreciate the snow. Respect its power, and gather strength from the challenges it poses.

Creek Fording

Setting out on the voyage to Ithaca
You must pray that the way be long,
Full of adventures and experiences.

— *Constantine Peter Cavafy*

Exercising sound judgement

Picture for a moment a stretch of mountain trail, climbing the flanks, dipping into valleys and crossing streams and creeks, and leading ever onward. Now imagine what that terrain would be like without its waterways coursing through it, providing water to animals and vegetation, shaping the land, and carrying rain water, snowmelt, and sediment to the lakes and valleys below. Where our trails cross these creeks we can observe firsthand the dynamic processes of the watershed in action, and can better appreciate the equilibrium of the mountain ecosystems. And of course where these rivers are bridgeless, they sometimes confront us with dangerous crossings.

In my years of adventuring I have gained considerable experience in fording creeks and rivers. The result has been an enormous respect for the power of moving water. I have come to realize that nearly every unbridged creek of size poses risks to those who try to ford it. This chapter is about assessing those risks and "reading" a river, so that you will better know where and how to cross safely—and most importantly, when not to attempt a crossing at all.

Trial and error

Working as wilderness instructors years ago, my colleagues and I experimented with every technique we could think of for using ropes to safeguard creek crossings. Then, as now, there was no fail-safe method, and certainly none that were widely agreed on.

Initially, we waded our groups across the rivers as "human chains," in lines parallel to the water's flow, elbows locked together. The idea was that the person upstream takes the brunt of the current, while the second in line offers support, and so on down the line. With enough people in the chain, the technique worked fairly well, except when someone became frightened and let go. At that point the group broke apart, and people would be swept away at great peril.

So we instructors rigged a safety line angling obliquely across the river, on the surface but out of sight downstream. The next student to let go of the gang jettisoned predictably downstream and onto our rope. But to our dismay the rope only entangled him and threatened to drown him. The director swam to the student's rescue and pried him free of the rope. That was our first and last experiment with such "safety" ropes, and our last use of the human chain method.

In ensuing years we experimented further. We tried wading individually while holding onto a rope fed from a belayer ashore. But the drag caused by the water's flow pressing against the rope compromised the wader's concentration and balance, and threatened to pull him into the water. Realizing that the rope could not be in the water, we installed "sky-lines" over creeks, tree-to-tree, and experimented with rigging these at various heights and tensions. Initially we secured the students by their climbing harnesses to a sky-line using long lanyards and carabiners (metal snap-links). But this, too, proved dangerous, because the stretching sky-line offered little balance, and its tension tended to drag the wader face-first into the river. We then tried using the sky-line as a hands-on support; but with the same results.

In an attempt to avoid the water altogether, we set Tyrolean traverses—pairs of taut ropes—across which students hauled themselves bodily, suspended in mid-air by harnesses and carabiners. But the weight of even one person hanging on the ropes stretched the ropes beyond their elastic limits, and ruined them for future use. We also constructed complicated rope lattice-works in the form of Burma bridges. Both these techniques required that someone first swim across the river while towing a pilot line, and this was very dangerous.

I mention these "trial and error" experiments to illustrate how firmly we believed the myth that ropes are a viable means of safeguarding river crossings.

A roped drowning

A friend of mine and his climbing partner had completed a technically difficult, multi-day ascent of the Leaning Tower, in Yosemite. Descending the Tower's back side, these two decided to return to the valley via a shortcut that led across Bridalveil Creek. The precipitous falls lay immediately downstream, so my friend waded in with his climbing rope attached to his harness and leading back to his partner seated on the riverbank in the standard belay position. In an instant the wader became not just a swimmer, but a submarine. The torrent's force, countered by the strain on the rope, submerged the victim and pinned him to the riverbed. Yet his belayer could not pay slack because of the nearby waterfall. The belay rope, intended as a safety device, now acted as a drowning device. The belayer later told me that the force on the rope was unimaginable. After struggling to secure the rope to his anchors, he rigged a haul system commonly used to hoist bags of water, food and bivouac equipment up rock walls. After a protracted struggle he finally managed to winch the body out of the water.

Every year, dozens of hikers across the nation drown in their misguided attempts to ford creeks and rivers, often while using "safety" ropes. These accidents happen, in part, because the water is usually deeper than it appears (due to refraction of light), more swift than it appears from the bank, and far more powerful. And, too, because no matter how swift the current, or how cold and clear the water, algae will usually be growing on the riverbed. This algae is often invisible, and can be extremely slippery.

Trails leading across bridgeless creeks

The creeks and rivers of summer are oftentimes benign, with stepping stones leading across them. This is the condition that the trail builders normally work with, when planning their routes and constructing the trails. But early in the year the snowmelt runoff and heavy rains can turn those waterways into raging torrents. The same can happen in summer, following a downpour. Therefore, when hiking a trail that leads into a creek

only to emerge from the far bank, do not assume that this is a standard, safe crossing.

The natural bridge

Obviously, the easiest and safest way to cross a sizeable creek is on a man-made bridge. Unfortunately, backcountry bridges have a way of disappearing, victims of floods and avalanches, or simply of time and decay. So where a map indicates a footbridge, this does not guarantee that the bridge is still in place and usable. Where no bridge exists, look for rocks or fallen timbers spanning the watercourse. Searching upstream is usually best, because the main creek and its feeder creeks get smaller in the direction of their source. If you hike downstream along the banks, the feeder creeks enlarge the main creek. Also while hiking downstream, you are more likely to come to an unfordable feeder creek barring further progress.

Fallen logs often provide the only safe crossings, and walking across one usually requires a good sense of balance. Good balance is a skill; none of us is born with it. In the chapter on Physical Conditioning I describe an easy exercise that can greatly improve your sense of balance.

However, before walking across a log spanning a creek, consider the consequences of falling off. If the water is shallow and easily waded, then falling from the log into the water might not be serious. But if the water is deep and swift, don't risk it. Instead, remove your backpack and lay it on the log in front of you, then sit down and straddle the log. By removing the pack you lower your center of gravity and improve your stability.

Your feet dangling on both sides contribute greatly to balance, and if necessary you can squeeze the log between your legs for added security. In this position, scoot across a few inches at a time, shoving your pack ahead. One caution with this technique, gained from experience: make sure the log cannot roll.

The fording staff

Where the map shows your trail crossing a creek, and where you assume wading will be necessary, perhaps half a mile from the creek you may need to start looking for a stout stick to assist with your balance. If creekside campers would cease from burning these fording staffs as firewood, we would no doubt find a number of staffs on both sides of the creeks. So after wading the creek with the aid of a staff, carry it well beyond the campsites and deposit it along the trail for the benefit of hikers traveling the other way.

In shallow water, trekking poles or hiking staffs may suffice, but in deeper water you need a single, longer staff, one that you can grasp with both hands for better stability. This fording staff should be chest high, and at least two inches in diameter. It has to be strong enough to withstand your weight and the force of the water without buckling.

Unlatch the hip belt

Before stepping into any creek, large or small, remember to unlatch the buckle of your backpack's hip belt. Some hikers may be reluctant to do this, concerned that the pack could shift and throw them off balance. Or that should they slip into the water, they might lose their pack. But the hiker's safety comes first, and one cannot swim very well, if at all, encumbered by a heavy backpack, particularly in rough water. The pack will remain on your shoulders as you walk carefully across the creek, and should you slip and plunge into the water, you need the ability to shrug off the shoulder straps in one quick motion. For this reason you should also unclip the sternum strap if you are using one. I am not giving this advice based on theory, but again on the tragic experience of losing a friend who slipped on algae while crossing Bubbs Creek in the Sierra, in water less than knee deep. Unable to shrug off his backpack because of the hip belt and sternum strap, he was swept over a waterfall.

So make a habit of unlatching the hip belt when tackling any situation where a heavy, bulky object strapped to you might increase the danger. This applies when balancing across fallen logs, stepping from rock to rock, and also when traversing precipitous terrain and steep snowfields.

Where to ford

As a general rule, if the flow is swift and knee deep or deeper, do not attempt the wade. Rather, scout the bank for a natural bridge. Jenny and I have hiked as much as five miles along creeks in search of safe crossings.

If you find a place to wade where it appears safe right there, but where whitewater lurks downstream, don't take the risk. One slip, and the current could sweep you into the rapids. Also, if the creek bed is solid rock, look elsewhere. In all likelihood that rock is polished by grit and coated with a translucent layer of algae that can be unimaginably slippery.

For the safest ford, look for an area of the creek that is wide and shallow, rather than narrow and deep. Be cautious, too, about mid-channel boulders; some offer safe resting places partway across, but others create turbulence that can form holes in the creek bed and deep water around them. Finally, examine the opposite river bank, and make sure it will not be too steep to climb.

Fording techniques

If all looks well, and you decide to wade the creek, proceed slowly while clutching a stout fording staff in both hands. Rather than shuffle ahead facing the opposite bank, turn sideways and face upstream. "Streamlining" your feet in this way reduces the water's force on them, and gives you more control and stability. Keep the feet about a shoulder width apart, and lean forward, upstream, using the staff for balance. This creates a more stable tripod with the feet and staff. Do not face downstream; you will be much less stable.

If the riverbed feels dangerously slippery, reverse direction, still facing upstream, and shuffle carefully back to shore. If the river itself is flowing more swiftly than you had expected, exerting more strain than you can safely manage, return to the bank and look for a safer crossing elsewhere. Do the same if the water proves much deeper than it appeared from shore.

If all is well, then proceed ahead, step by cautious step. With each step, avoid placing weight on the foot until it has explored the bottom by

feel and found secure footing. If you step too quickly, a rock could roll out from underfoot and send you sprawling. Rivet your eyes on the far shore to prevent the water's motion from upsetting your equilibrium, but do not lock onto the far shore as your goal at the expense of judgement. Gaze ahead, but anchor your mind on your present situation. Feel the current pressing powerfully against your legs, trying to wrench each foot as you lift it free of the bottom while preparing for the next step. Keep a cool head and maintain control, never allowing brain lock to take hold. If you feel insecure, reverse course and carefully work your way back. Returning is generally easier, because you will be more familiar with that part of the riverbed you have already covered.

Before reaching the halfway point, assess your strength. If you find yourself tiring, consider turning back, since fatigue can greatly undermine composure. At the same time, do not let the numbing coldness of the water dissuade you. The biting cold is uncomfortable, but it is only temporary. Your feet will begin to re-warm after you have stepped ashore.

Drawing closer to the far shore, you may find the water becoming deeper and more swift than expected. This is often the case at the outside bend of a river, where the water's centrifugal force drives it into the far bank. In such a case, do not let the nearness of shore tempt you into a careless bolt for the bank. If prudence suggests turning back, then do so.

Of all the safety precautions for creek crossings, the most important

Looking for a safe crossing

is to remain on your feet. Do not assume that you can swim in a torrent. If the water is too swift and deep to wade, and the bottom too slippery, then it is extremely dangerous to assume that in a last ditch effort you will be able to swim across. Strong turbulence can make swimming impossible.

Foot protection

For any substantial creek crossing, it is best to wear some kind of protective footwear. This might be running shoes or sandals. Either way, tighten the laces or straps for added security. Or you can protect your feet with just a few pairs of socks and no shoes. If the water is deep, then do not try to ford it wearing heavy boots. Boots create a lot of drag, but more importantly, should you slip and fall headlong into the water, the boots will make swimming impossible.

During our CDT trek, Jenny and I hiked for a month in extremely wet weather through northern Montana. In the process we often waded dozens of creeks every day, a few of them quite formidable. We rarely bothered to remove our socks or shoes, because the rain and wet brush had them continually sopping wet anyway. But the exercise of hiking kept our feet warm.

Wet shoes are acceptable for hiking, but dry ones are better. In situations where the wade will be minor, I normally ford barefoot, after tying my shoes to my pack and stuffing the socks into an outside pack pocket. Where the creek bottom is rocky and irregular, I might wear a few pairs of dirty or wet socks. Once at the creek's far side, I remove the wet socks, wring them out and hang them on the pack to dry. Then I slip back into dry socks and shoes, and continue on my way.

Jumping small creeks

Sometimes the trail may cross creeklets too wide to step over, yet small enough to tempt a leap. Think twice, though, before you try it. The rocks or logs on the other side could be coated in slippery algae. Or in early morning, the diffused light may not reveal the glimmer of verglas—condensed and frozen dew. Either way, you could land off-kilter and pull a muscle or sprain an ankle. In such circumstances wading is usually best.

———————————

Safety in creek crossings is mostly a matter of exercising sound judgement. And a big part of that judgement comes from somewhere inside, some part of us that has nothing to do with logic and reasoning. It is a sixth sense, innate in us all. So when standing at the bank of a swift creek, assess the situation, then pause for a moment and pay attention to those inner feelings. If things just do not feel right, honor that intuition and look elsewhere for a safer crossing.

On the CDT, early season in Glacier NP

Hot

I walked in a desert.
And I cried:
"Ah, God, take me from this place!"
A voice said: "It is no desert."
I cried: "Well, but—
The sand, the heat, the vacant horizon."
A voice said: "It is no desert."

— *Stephen Crane*

Crisp mountain heights, shaded forests, lakes and cascading streams: these are the usual mountain idylls, drawing us into the high country for relief from the sultry, dog days of summer. Yet as we explore a closer connection with all wild places, we may find ourselves also in the foothills, dense woodlands, and deserts—places where the temperatures can soar. We are fortunate to have access to so many climatically diverse regions. And if we learn to adapt to them, then we will be much less limited in the scope of our ramblings.

―――――――

Desert dwellers thrive in their torrid environments, traditionally by wearing heavy clothing to shield them from the strong ultraviolet radiation, and to insulate them from the parching heat. But we hikers cannot emulate them in hot weather. The metabolic heat we generate while hiking would build inside the heavy, insulating garments, and practically parboil us. Instead, we need protection that offers the best possible ventilation.

The mylar-covered umbrella

First and foremost we need shade. If hiking beneath natural shade, such as cloud cover or trees, then all is well. But if we are out in the open, we will need to provide our own shade. Normally the best way is to carry a shading umbrella, since it provides ventilation nearly on par with the clouds and trees. If the day is positively scorching and the sunshine is intense, then we can cover the umbrella with reflective mylar. The mylar is extremely effective at reducing the sun's thermal radiation.

During our fifth mega-trek, Jenny and I traversed the desert-like regions of southern California in late August and early September. These regions see very few hikers at that time of year, due to the intense heat. Yet our mylar-covered umbrellas allowed us to hike those eight hundred miles without difficulty. Beneath the umbrellas we dressed as lightly as possible, and of course we drank plenty of water. This combination facilitated the greatest cooling effect through evaporation of perspiration.

The umbrella offers no additional cooling to the person hiking beneath the cover of clouds or forest. In very windy weather, the umbrella cannot be used at all. Overall, though, it is an indispensable piece of gear for hot weather hiking. For details see the Umbrella chapter.

Clothing considerations

Back in the Clothing chapter, I detailed my clothing suggestions for hiking in hot weather, so I will mention them only briefly here.

Whether the humidity is very high or low, the clothing should be loose-fitting, light in weight and fast-drying. Most importantly it must provide maximum ventilation, allowing the hiker's sweat to evaporate.

In hot weather my usual hiking attire is very simply the spandex shorts, and the short-sleeve, button up shirt when necessary. Jenny wears nylon shorts, and a light polyester shirt, or in very hot weather, a tank top.

In warm to hot weather we wear lightweight socks with shoes that provide good ventilation. We also carry sandals as spare footwear, and often wear these for several hours each day, usually with thin socks. And when not using the umbrella we wear wide-brimmed sun hats to keep the sun off our scalp, face, ears and neck.

Cotton for hot weather?

Wearing cotton clothing can be dangerous in cold and rainy weather, but what about lightweight cotton shirts and shorts on a hot day? Unfortunately, the same problem applies. The individual fibers of cotton absorb the moisture and salts of our perspiration, making the garments very slow to dry. Wearing wet clothing is, for most people, rather unpleasant, and can lead to chafing where the fabric rubs against the skin. Summertime cotton garments are fine for those hiking casually enough so that they do not sweat much, but that is about as far as it goes.

What about wearing cotton clothing in desert environments, where wet clothing would help cool the skin? I have certainly tried this, and found that—here again—cotton fails to perform. The warmer the conditions, the more we need the cooling effects of evaporation. Cotton clothing wicks the sweat from our skin, and tends to hold onto it. And as the wet fabric slowly evaporates, it cools. But it is not cooling our skin, it is cooling only the clothing. We may have slightly cooler clothing, but what good is that if we are fairly broiling inside it? The reason we are broiling is because wet cotton is more restrictive of ventilation. You can demonstrate this for yourself. On a hot day, hike in a cotton shirt until it is quite soaked. Remove the shirt, deploy a shading umbrella unless you are hiking beneath shading trees, and continue on your way bare-skinned. The cooling you will experience will be immediate and dramatic. And this is as nature intended. For best results you need the evaporative cooling to take place on your skin, not on your clothing.

On the AT in Maine

Minimize clothing

When sweat evaporates from the skin, it cools the skin in an effect known as the "latent heat of vaporization." Each gram of water evaporating from the skin reduces the skin's temperature by about 540 calories. Therefore, the evaporation is all important. Any breeze moving across the skin accelerates evaporation, thereby improving the cooling. Clothing of any type—thick or thin, cotton or synthetic, light or dark—hampers evaporation.

Jenny and I thru-hiked the Appalachian Trail in mid summer, and along the southern half of the trail often encountered both temperature and humidity in the 90's. At these times our pace on the uphill grinds was often limited less by our heart rates than by our inability to dissipate metabolic heat fast enough. Many were the times we had to slow way down in order to keep heat exhaustion at bay. A week into the journey we discovered that by minimizing our clothing we stayed far cooler, and could hike closer to our normal 2.75 mph pace. After that I went shirtless most of the way, except in towns. I found that the bare skin made an enormous difference in comfort. And for those unfamiliar with the AT, I should note that the vast majority of it is protected beneath a magnificent forest canopy. Generally, it is very well shaded.

Sunburn

If the day is excessively hot and the sunshine intense, you will remain much cooler if you can keep the sun off you and your clothing. Trees overhead will do this for you. Or lacking those, you could use a shading umbrella.

Another option of defense is lightweight clothing. Although the clothing is heated by the sun, and therefore it can be quite hot to wear, it at least keeps the intense ultraviolet radiation off your skin. Or mostly so; for according to dermatologist and long-distance hiker Tom McGillis, the SPF (Sun Protection Factor) rating for most lightweight fabrics is 8 to 10. And when that clothing is wet, for example with sweat, its SPF is theoretically much less.

SPF (sun protection factor) ratings indicate how much longer than normal you can remain in the sun without getting burned. So for example, lightweight clothing boosts our bare-skin exposure tolerance 8 or 10 times.

Another option is of course sunscreen with a high SPF. So for example, if you normally tolerate only 20 minutes of sun before you start to burn, then an SPF 30 sunscreen would boost your sun tolerance to 20 x 30 = 600 minutes, or 10 hours. If you use sunscreen, apply it in the morning as soon as the sun emerges, and reapply a small amount two or three times a day, as needed. Pay special attention to the backs of the fingers and hands, the nose, forehead, ears and the back of the neck. I much prefer covering or shading these areas with clothing. I have even used adhesive tape on my ears, which are especially sensitive to the sun. The reason I prefer the shading and covering methods is that the cremes can clog the pores, they can wash away with sweat, and they can affect the skin chemically. For example, PABA and benzophenone, the two active ingredients used in most sunscreens, can produce allergic reactions, one of which is photodermatitis.

Photodermatitis

When hiking in intense sunshine, you may experience the unpleasant effects of photoallergenic and phototoxic contact dermatitis. Unlike sunburn, this type of skin damage is characterized by raised, pus-filled blisters that usually itch like poison ivy or oak. This photodermatitis is caused by the application or ingestion of certain chemicals that increase the skin's sensitivity to solar radiation. The responsible agents might be something in a food or drink, soap, shampoo, hand lotion, insect repellent, or ironically even in sunscreen.

To treat the affected area, rinse repeatedly and gently in cold water without soap, then apply a hydrocortisone cream or dab the area liberally with antiseptic. If left exposed to the sun, the rash can rapidly worsen, so it is important to cover the affected area. But at night, it is best to uncover it for better ventilation. Photodermatitis most often occurs on the back of the fingers and hands, so it is a good idea to cover these with some kind of lightweight, breathable "sun mitts." These could be home-made sun mitts, or thin gardening gloves. Or they could be bandanas wrapped around the hands, or even an old pair of socks. For better ventilation, cut the fingertips off the mittens or gloves, or cut the toe section off the socks.

Another type of sun-related reaction is the itchy rash that often develops on bare arms and legs, and even under the socks. This is "heat rash," and is also known as prickly heat. It looks like tiny clear or red bumps on the skin. These are actually sweat glands plugged with accumulated dead skin cells, trapping the sweat. The remedy is to scrub the area gently with soap and water.

Water is life

In late April during our first PCT trek, Jenny and I experienced the hottest temperatures of our hiking career. The nearby town of Palm Springs was recording 120 degrees Fahrenheit. This was a dry, desert heat that sapped body moisture. The available water sources along our route were from five to twenty miles apart, and initially we each carried only two or three quarts of water between those sources. With our packs already overloaded with excessive gear, we were not too inclined to load up on water also. So our method was to hike with determination from one water source to the next. Unfortunately, this did not work well. Typically we would reach the next source only through sheer will. After one particularly demanding jaunt we arrived at a distant source and drank five quarts of water each, on the spot. In the ensuing days we tried other strategies, but finally decided that the weight of water is inconsequential compared with its value in sustaining life. And with this realization we resumed hiking in reasonable comfort and health, despite the extra weight of water and the extreme temperatures. By the time the heat had eased to 110 degrees we were each consuming three gallons of water a day, including what we used for cooking. On our most recent PCT journey we hiked that same stretch of trail in late summer, and in 100 degree temperatures we averaged two gallons per person per day, which again included water used for cooking the evening meals.

In humid heat, such as that of the eastern states, water consumption is equally important although the quantities might not need to be quite as high. During our AT thru-hike, Jenny and I found water amply available along most of the trail, or at least within easy reach of it. So even in the hottest weather we could usually set off from a source carrying no more than a quart each.

Remember that the hotter the weather, the more detrimental are diuretics like coffee, sports drinks and alcohol, since these cause a net loss in the body's fluid.

Heat exhaustion

Heat exhaustion is a comparatively minor disorder, but if not treated it can lead to heat stroke, which can be fatal. The symptoms of heat exhaustion are gradual weakness, dizziness, nausea, anxiety or faintness. The remedy is to lie in the shade, remove extraneous clothing, and drink large quantities of water.

Far better is to prevent heat exhaustion in the first place. Do this by hiking at a moderate pace, wearing minimal and lightweight clothing, and drinking plenty of water all along the way. Use an umbrella in intense sunshine, and eat fresh (or low-temperature dehydrated) uncooked fruits and vegetables for their minerals and electrolytes. And for a most refreshing experience, where water is abundant you can pour it on yourself and the clothing you are wearing.

Hiking at night

In very hot weather, hiking in the cool nighttime hours is sometimes an alternative. In order to maintain a decent pace, you will normally need a flashlight to avoid stepping in holes, tripping on rocks, and possibly treading on a snake. The problem of batteries should not be limiting if you are using one of the new, bright LED flashlights.

Granted, in desert-like regions the use of a mylar-covered umbrella usually obviates the need to hike at night, since it allows one to carry on in reasonable comfort throughout the day. But sometimes night hiking is just plain fun, and well worth the effort. Where snakes are absent, you might even prefer to hike without a flashlight. Naturally, your pace will slow as you step more cautiously to remain on the trail while avoiding obstacles. Yet when you slow down and allow a simple shift in consciousness, lessening your reliance on your vision, the night becomes a fascinating realm. I find that occasional night hiking is of great benefit to the outward journey—to beat the heat, and the inward journey—to widen one's perspectives.

Mosquitoes
and Biting Flies

Never kill a mosquito or blackfly.
If you do, a million other ones
will come to its funeral.

— *Verlen Kruger*

Guardians
of the wilds

Venturing into the wilderness, we seek the richness of the landscape, the peace it affords, and the life it sustains. Well, maybe not all life, since hoards of mosquitoes, blackflies, and no-see-ums can be discouraging. But like the rain and snow, the wind and the heat, to say nothing of the glorious sunsets and endless views, the proliferating insect life has its place in the grand web of creation. This does not mean, however, that we have to remain beneath the bugs on the food chain. By taking a few simple precautions we can do much to thwart their aggressions.

Blackflies

In the western states and north country, blackflies are known as gnats. By whatever name, they resemble small house flies but with slightly venomous bites. They cause a small loss of blood, but in very large numbers they can kill birds and animals both wild and domestic. More often, they are merely a nuisance, although in tropical regions they can transmit a disease that causes blindness.

The blackflys' active season extends from the spring thaw through mid-summer. They tend to be least active in the early mornings, gaining momentum as the day wears on. Late afternoons, particularly in hot and humid weather, they can come out in force. A cool, dry breeze will usually discourage their presence.

Unless they are truly swarming, blackflies tend to lose interest in us when we enter any kind of enclosure, such as a tent, even with its doorway wide open. Nor can they bite through even the thinnest clothing. However they are very adept at crawling beneath the gaps in our clothing to get at the bare skin beneath. And once there they inject a natural anesthetic that eliminates any sensation of their bites, making us unaware of their presence—until we remove the clothing and discover the bloody welts.

On a canoe trip across the Barrenlands of the Northwest Territories, Jenny and I were wearing our shell jackets and pants to thwart the swarms of gnats. We always tucked our shell pant legs into our socks, to prevent the bugs from crawling under the pant leg cuffs and getting at our bare legs. But sometimes the river's current would pull a pant leg free of a sock, as we waded the canoe in the rocky shallows. One evening I crawled into the tent, removed my shell pants and found hundreds of bloody welts on both legs. From then on, I was a good deal more careful about keeping my pant legs tucked in. And interestingly, the welts healed quickly and never bothered me, mainly because I did not scratch them.

Deer flies, horse flies and no-see-ums

Deer flies and horse flies are fairly ubiquitous across North America, and are most prevalent during the warm months. Their bites are instantly painful, but since they are large (two or three times the size of common house flies) and rather noisy in flight, they give us plenty of warning of their approach.

No-see-ums, on the other hand, are so small that a person can barely see-um, let alone hear-um. They are also known as midges and punkies. They are common across most of North America, and are particularly numerous in the northern regions, appearing from time to time during the warmer months, with no particular pattern. Chemical repellents are not as effective against these tiny insects, but adequate clothing easily rebuffs them, as does no-see-um netting, which is a much finer mesh than mosquito netting.

Mosquitoes

Mosquitoes breed in water. Their eggs and developing larvae are food to fish and other aquatic species. Male mosquitoes have small mouth parts designed to feed on nectar; they cannot suck blood. The females are the ones that buzz around like little hypodermic needles, seeking blood for reproduction. During feeding, they inject some of their salivary fluid into the wound, not accidentally, but specifically to dilate the capillaries and to prevent the blood from clotting. The result to the mosquito is an increase in the local flow of blood. The result to us is the inflammation and itching.

Currently, most mosquitoes here in the U.S. do not carry disease. However, the common house mosquito of the United States is sometimes a carrier of encephalitis. The Asian tiger mosquito, arriving in the U.S. as a stowaway aboard cargo ships, can also spread a type of encephalitis, as well as dengue fever and other disease. Also, when swatting a mosquito, we sometimes find it contains old, darkened blood, not our own. Obviously, mosquitoes and other bloodsucking insects like ticks are capable of spreading disease organisms picked up elsewhere.

I think most of us are disturbed by the sight of a mosquito on someone else's face. The tendency is to want to tell the person, or to slap the mosquito ourselves—perish the thought. Or maybe we simply wipe our own face in hopes that the person will get the idea. But the person being bitten feels nothing. The sight of the mosquito is what disturbs us, not the actual bite. Or the sight and sound of a number of them swarming around us. So I suppose there is some merit to the philosophy of mosquito forbearance: "Just ignore them, it's all psychological." At least in regions where mosquitoes do not normally carry disease.

But the idea of dismissing mosquitoes as though they do not exist does not appeal to me. Partly this is the result of being stricken with malaria. For a decade after that fateful visit to the jungles of Panama I experienced almost yearly relapses, each one being more severe than the original onset. These came at the worst of times, invariably when we were on journey. They were also very sudden, meaning that Jenny and I had to make hasty camps in some very unlikely places. From this I learned to take mosquito and other insect-borne diseases seriously. Especially considering that they kill millions of people annually in various parts of the world. I finally eradicated the malaria in my own body using Robert Beck technology (Bibliography).

Protection

Anyone who spends time in the backcountry would do well to protect themselves from flying insects of the biting and bloodsucking kind, not only for the peace of mind, but for the surety from possible disease as well. We have a number of options, and one of the most effective is clothing (and if necessary, a bit of repellent). Just as we wear clothing that protects us from rain, cold, strong winds and harsh sunlight, we can wear clothing that blocks the mosquitoes and blackflies. With bug-proof clothing and head-netting—and the right attitude—we can hike and camp very comfortably in the wilds.

Clothing

What about the "bug-proof" shirts and pants made of mosquito or no-see-um netting? I have used such garments extensively, and find them less than ideal. In places where the netting contacts the skin—for example at the shoulders, elbows and knees—a mosquito can insert its proboscis through the mesh, and easily reach the underlying flesh.

Which is what led me to develop my shell garments, described back in the Clothing chapter. These are the same, ever-adaptable jacket and pants for use in wind and brush, rain and cold. And because these insects cannot pierce the material, we need not worry whether it lies pressed against our skin. At the same time, the material is very breathable, allowing us to wear these garments while hiking, even in warm weather.

For protecting the hands and feet, shell mittens and booties can be constructed of the same tightly-woven material. In their most simple form, the mittens are nothing more than large, loose-fitting cylinders, closed at one end. They cover the hands and extend half way up the forearms for added protection. Elastic cuffs hold them in place. The mitts can be used while resting or hiking. The booties cover the feet and lower legs, and are normally worn only while seated or lying down with the shoes off—for example at the rest stops and at camp. They are also useful while sleeping beneath a tarp on nights too warm for a quilt or sleeping bag.

To keep the bugs away from my face, I use a loose-fitting head-net made of no-see-um material. This extends below the shoulders with a pair of flaps. One flap extends about eighteen inches down the back, and the other down the chest. These flaps are tucked inside the shell jacket to secure them in place and to seal out the bugs. The head-net fits quite loosely, otherwise the mosquitoes would insert their mouth parts through it and into the skin. A wide brim hat or baseball-style cap worn underneath the head-net, although not essential, will help protect the scalp and keep the netting draped away from the face.

Color

Many times in buggy regions I have noticed that as Jenny and I sit together, one of us in light-colored clothing and the other in dark, the person wearing the darker garments is the one the mosquitoes and blackflies are most interested in.

The head-net should be dark in color, at least the part covering the eyes. Black netting absorbs more of the scattered light reflected by its fibers, and is therefore a little more transparent when close to the eyes.

DEET repellent

I have tried most types of chemical repellents, and have always gone back to DEET, the active ingredient in the majority of commercial insect repellents. However I prefer to keep its use to a minimum. Purportedly, six hours after application about half of it will have absorbed into the skin, and most of that will have entered the blood stream. Ten to fifteen percent of each dose can be recovered from the urine. Studies have shown, and my experience has verified, that concentrations of 35% DEET are as effective and long-lasting as those of 100%. I have found that concentrations below 25% do not work as well.

Spraying DEET on clothing, rather than on the skin, is ineffective. The chemical does not actually repel the bugs, as the term "repellent" would imply. Instead, it masks the human essence, essentially hiding us from the insects—at least what parts of our skin we have treated. I have on a number of occasions found mosquitoes squeezing beneath my watch band to get at the untreated skin there.

At day's end I always try to wash the repellent off, at least what remains. For this I use the dundo method away from the water source. Still, I find that after a few weeks of using DEET in the wilds, I start to lose my tolerance of the chemical. The very thought of it becomes nauseating. Many other hikers have reported similar effects. And when we reach this point, we also lose a great deal of our tolerance for the buzzing hordes. They start to *seem* far more tormenting—such is the chemical's impairment of our mental processes. These effects may not be cumulative; at least they appear to subside after we have not used the product for a few months. Still, I do not consider DEET my main protection, especially on more lengthy trips.

B vitamins as repellent

Jenny and I experimented with B vitamins in the Arctic one summer, as protection from mosquitoes and blackflies. At the beginning of the trip we took one B vitamin pill a day. This enabled us to stand out in the open, mosquitoes swarming everywhere but not landing on us. This was a big help, especially while bathing. Except that after bathing we were typically attacked. Apparently our skin was exuding a B vitamin related chemical that acted as a repellent, and the bathing washed this chemical away. With the passing of weeks we found that we needed greater quantities of the vitamin to achieve the same results. Eventually we were up to three pills a day, and even then the mosquitoes were starting to break through our defenses. And it was about that time that our bodies and minds began rejecting the intake. The vitamin started making us nauseous and prone to seasickness. Our bodies also reeked of the vitamin chemicals. We stopped taking the vitamins, and from then on used shell clothing and head-nets, with a little repellent on our hands.

Natural repellents

Tom Brown, Jr. (Bibliography) advises that scented soaps attract mosquitoes, as do certain foods, including bananas, peanut butter and sugar. Tom also recommends eating the pods of plantain (*Plantago spp.*) to repel mosquitoes and blackflies. Other people suggest eating large amounts of garlic. Yes, it does repel insects, to a degree, thanks to its toxicity; but purportedly it also kills brain cells. Others recommend crushing a few fresh yarrow (*Achillea spp.*) leaves and rubbing them on exposed skin. Jenny has tried this and finds that it does repel mosquitoes, but that it requires frequent applications.

Self-generated repellent

A far more advanced type of repellent, and one that I have been learning about and experimenting with, is a type that we create ourselves. This is a long way from passive forbearance, in which a person tries to ignore the bugs and allows him or herself to be bitten. Rather, it is a more active and dynamic approach, a type of protection that we generate internally. A beautiful example of the method comes from a book entitled *Rolling Thunder*, by Doug Boyd (Del Publishing: 1974).

"I recalled Rolling Thunder standing in that cloud of mosquitoes, stooping over the herbs, without a mosquito on him. 'There is a certain attitude you can have about yourself. Mosquitoes won't bother you— might not even touch you—if you know how to maintain your good feelings. These attitudes make vibrations, and they have a smell to 'em. That's what keeps the mosquitoes away. You can make a smell they don't care for. One reason they put that poison in your blood is to make you nervous so the others can smell you. When the chemical works you feel irritated, but if you don't feel irritated the chemical isn't working. So if you do get bit you don't have to let yourself get all swelled up and itchy. You can control your whole situation by the smell you make—by the vibrations you make. It's not easy, that kind of control. But it's not impossible because you do it yourself. It's all done from the inside."

Ticks

It is better to travel alone
than with a bad companion.

— Senegalese proverb

Ticks are parasites, relying on warm-blooded animals for their food. Adult ticks measure about ¼-inch across, about like the one wandering around on this page. As I watch one of these little bloodsuckers crawling through the hairy jungle of my arm, I am amazed at how tenaciously those stubby legs can propel the creature along. I have to admire its single-mindedness, that driving desire to find a meal. Not that I intend to provide that meal.

Juvenile ticks are called "nymphs," and are only pin-head in size. And even though they are more difficult to detect, they are equally capable of transmitting disease. Actually, relatively few ticks carry disease; only about twelve percent of ticks worldwide.

Tick-related disease

Tick-related diseases can be serious, and anybody who spends time outdoors should be able to recognize the early symptoms of at least the two most prevalent types.

Lyme Disease

Currently, some 10,000 cases of Lyme Disease are reported in the U.S. annually. The cause is a bacterium carried by certain types of ticks. In most cases of Lyme Disease, the earliest evidence of infection is a skin rash at or near the bite. If the rash does appear, it will most likely do so about a week after the bite. In the next several days the rash might expand, growing into an ever-widening red splotch. Along with the rash, or sometimes in its absence, the person may experience flu-like symptoms: fever, malaise, headache, and possibly deep fatigue. Even if not treated, these symptoms usually disappear within a week or ten days. But the disease generally progresses unperceived until it resurfaces later, possibly leading to serious health problems.

Doctors can treat Lyme Disease at any stage, but the earlier, the better the patient's outlook for a full recovery. The diagnosis is usually based on the symptoms, because in the disease's early stages blood tests rarely confirm the presence of Lyme. Antibiotics are generally the most effective treatment. A vaccine called LYMErix is available against Lyme Disease. The drug is said to help prevent Lyme, but not with 100% effectiveness. For precautions about vaccines of all types, see Len Horowitz (Bibliography). As a possible alternative against Lyme and other tick-borne disease, see Robert Beck technology (Bibliography).

Rocky Mountain Spotted Fever

Rocky Mountain Spotted Fever is perhaps the most serious tick-borne disease. And despite the name, the majority of the cases reported are in the eastern and southern U.S. The initial symptoms usually include high fever, headache, chills, muscle pain and deep fatigue. A few days later a spotted rash often develops—hence the name—initially on the hands and feet, but spreading. This disease is considered a medical emergency.

Thwarting ticks

Tick bites are fairly common in the backcountry, and because of the associated risks we need to take certain precautions. We do not have to avoid tick habitat altogether, even during prime tick season, which is usually spring and summer. Instead we can wear protective clothing, and apply insect repellent to the skin around the margins of that clothing where the ticks might crawl under it. Most importantly we must inspect the skin under the clothing on a regular basis.

The tick cannot fly or jump; it merely waits on vegetation for a host to happen by, then it reaches out and grabs a hold. But rather than feasting right away, it usually wanders around, sometimes for several hours as though looking for just the right spot. If we are inspecting ourselves at least that often, we will usually find the tick before it bites. If we are not making these regular inspections, then we are giving the ticks carte blanche, since their bites cause no sensation that might give them away.

However, the wandering delay does not always hold true. While hiking through Glacier National Park in mid June, Jenny and I passed through an area where the ticks were large and voracious. We would stop on the far side of a large clump of brush to inspect ourselves, and find one of these ticks already bitten in.

In parts of southern California in late spring, the brush can be so teeming with ticks that a hiker can find fifty or more on his or her shoes, socks and pant legs after scraping through a single clump of brush. Even so, proper clothing and repellent constitute perfectly adequate protection, as long as they are backed with regular inspection. Late in the season, these western ticks tend to be less a problem. While hiking the PCT southbound, Jenny and I passed through its notoriously heavy tick areas in early September and found not a single tick.

Since ticks are dark brown, they are more visible on light-colored clothing. Back in the Clothing and Mosquitoes chapters I discussed the benefits of the light-colored, nylon shell jacket and pants. Ticks seem to find these garments very slippery, and in fact Jenny and I have never found a tick clinging to ours. Temperature permitting, we always wear these shells when hiking through brush and other common tick environments during their peak season. We protect our ankles and feet with some kind of insect repellent, DEET if necessary. Socks alone are not sufficient protection; ticks can force their mouth parts through the weave of a sock and get at the underlying skin.

Despite all the precautions, ticks can sometimes still find their way under the hiker's clothing. And at that point the clothing only serves to conceal the ticks. Very important when in tick country then, is to inspect your bare skin every few hours, and particularly before you retire at day's end. If hiking with a partner, inspect each other's underarms and backsides. If hiking alone, self-inspection will be necessary, by sight where possible and by feel otherwise. Before retiring for the night, run your fingers over every square inch of your body. A tick feels like a little mole that you did not know you had. During the night, should you feel something crawling on you, do not simply scratch it and go back to sleep. Rather, sit up and shine a flashlight on the area, and see whether it is a tick. If so, do not kill it, because doing so could spread any disease-causing bacteria inside it. Nor would you simply flick it away, since the tick can follow your trail of carbon dioxide back to you. What I usually do is place the tick on a small rock or piece of bark, and give that a hearty toss. In the morning, before donning clothing, shoes and backpack, check them for ticks.

Tick removal

Ticks attach themselves by inserting their mouth parts into the host's skin. To remove a tick, grasp its head with tweezers. Pull very gently and steadily, without twisting, until the tick lets go. Pulling too hard can break the mouth parts and leave them embedded. Take great care not to crush or puncture the tick's body, or to contaminate your skin with its fluids. Remember that if you find a tick embedded in your skin, this does not automatically mean that you will contract a tick-borne disease. Not all ticks carry disease. And even if your tick is carrying a disease, it will rarely transmit it within the first eight hours of attachment, seldom even within the first eighteen hours. So if you remove it carefully before then, you should be alright. If you squeeze its body, and if the tick is carrying disease-causing microorganisms, then you will probably cause the tick to regurgitate under your skin and inject some of that. So the most important aspect of tick removal is to avoid squeezing its body.

After removing the tick, disinfect the bite site with an antiseptic such as alcohol, and scrub your hands with an alcohol gel or antibacterial soap. Remain watchful for several days. If signs of illness develop—flu-like symptoms, headache, fever, lack of balance, skin rashes, muscle or joint pain, or nausea—see a physician.

Like mosquitoes, blackflies, and the rest of the insect world, ticks are part of the intricate cycle of nature. So don't let a fear of ticks keep you out of the backcountry. Take an active role by following the preventative measures outlined above. Then carry on enjoying the wilds.

Poison Ivy and Oak

Itching for knowledge, or lack of it

Each species of plant we find in the wilds offers new insights about our wondrous ecology, and about some of the unique ways it has adapted for its survival. Some plants rely on chemicals that impart a foul taste to discourage browsing animals. Other plants defend themselves with spines or thorns. Fiddleheads, for instance, have hair-like needles. Holly has sharp leaf tips. The tiny needles of stinging nettle inject formic acid, a painful toxin. Despite their many forms of defense, these plants are nonetheless beautiful to behold: cactus in bloom, wild roses scenting the air, succulent berries borne on thorny stems. In the fall, fiddleheads tint the hillsides in glorious shades of yellow and gold. The leaves of stinging nettle lose their sting after a light boiling in water, and are highly nutritious. From their stem fibers we can make strong and supple cordage.

The more we walk our path toward wilderness connection, the more we come to understand the intrinsic value of each and every plant found along the way, even the toxic varieties. And so it is with poison ivy, poison oak and poison sumac—poisonous to the touch, and known collectively as the toxicodendrons.

Distribution and identification

The U.S. is home to five different toxicodendrons. The poison oaks and poison ivies are closely related, and their leaves grow in distinctive clusters of three. Poison oak leaves are serrated or lobed, whereas poison ivy leaves have smooth edges, but the patterns frequently overlap. Poison sumac has a different leaf pattern altogether.

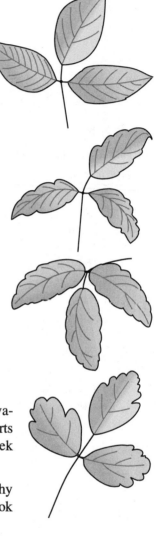

- Eastern poison ivy (*Rhus radicans*) is found in parts of New England, in certain areas of the mid-Atlantic states, and despite its name, throughout most of the Rocky Mountain states. It grows as a small plant or climbing vine, and is ubiquitous in temperate forests, along creeks and on mountain slopes.

- Rydberg's poison ivy (*Rhus rydbergii*) grows in the Rocky Mountain states as a small shrub (up to three feet high). It prefers moist, sunny areas. Watch for it in creek drainages below 6,000 feet.

- Eastern poison oak (*Rhus toxicodendron*) is found throughout the southeastern states, as well as portions of the Midwest. It grows in sandy soil, and in areas devastated by fire.

- Western poison oak (*Rhus diversiloba*) grows as an isolated plant, a thick bush, or a climbing vine, from sea level to 5,000 feet. It is most prevalent in the lower elevations throughout much of California and parts north. It prefers shaded slopes and creek banks, even where the creeks are dry.

- Poison sumac (*Rhus vernix*) grows in marshy areas east of the Mississippi. To identify, look for toothless leaves and drooping clusters of small white berries. Non-poisonous sumac (*Rhus spp.*) has toothed leaves, and dense, upright clusters of red berries growing from the ends of its branches.

The poison content

Despite differences in appearance and habitat, all five species defend themselves in the same way. They rely on a toxin called urushiol, (ou-ROO-she-all) which causes the blistering, itchy rash we commonly experience after inadvertently touching these plants. This toxin is present in all parts of the plants: the leaves, stems, berries and roots, regardless of whether the plant is dead or alive, and even in the smoke of the burning plant. When the hiker touches the plant—even brushing against it lightly—it deposits some of this toxic oil, or sap, on the skin, clothing and footwear.

The disguise of bare stems

During our first PCT trip, Jenny and I met a hiker who had recently hitchhiked out for medication. The doctor treated him for a severe case of poison oak, yet this fellow was adamant about not having touched the plant. I explained how toxic even the leafless twigs can be, and pointed them out all around us, including some small ones he happened to be sitting on.

Avoiding contact with these plants is our most effective preventive measure. And to do this, we must learn to recognize them in all seasons and stages of growth—including when still leafless in early season.

Poison ivy and poison oak tend to grow in small, scattered communities. In early season look for bare, thornless stems standing one or two feet tall. The hallmark of these stems is their characteristic curve, and each stem will be capped with a small, pointed bud—the coming season's new growth. Bare vines pose the same risk; look for these growing on trees and rocks. To be on the safe side, avoid touching, sitting on, or placing clothing or equipment on *any* bare stems or vines found along the trail, especially in drainages. If bare stems drape unavoidably across the trail, shove them aside with a stick, or else circumvent the area altogether. Be especially cautious at night, whether you are searching for a stealth-site or just getting up for a quick trip outside.

In late spring, the bare stems of poison ivy and poison oak begin developing their foliage. Normally growing in clusters of three, the young leaves are beautifully colored in reds and greens, and are notably shiny or greasy-looking. By summer they turn dark and vibrant green, and in autumn they tend to bright reds and yellows.

Mistaken identity

"Leaves of three, let them be" is a useful adage for poison oak and poison ivy, but in the plant world the trifoliate arrangement is very common. Many berry plants (*Rubus spp.*)—for instance blackberry, raspberry and salmonberry—have leaves grouped in three, and even though the stems of blackberry and raspberry are thorny, hikers and campers will sometimes mistake them for poison oak or ivy. Squaw bush (*Rhus trilobata*) is fairly widespread in the West, and is almost universally mistaken for poison oak, but in fact squaw bush is quite harmless. The key to its identification lies in the center leaf of each three-leaf cluster. The center leaf of squaw bush has no stem, while that of poison oak and poison ivy does. If it lacks the stem, it lacks the poison.

Symptoms

Early Native Americans were largely immune to the irritants in these poisonous plants. They even made baskets of the vines. Here in modern times, about two-thirds of us would be affected to some extent by an "average" contact—for example should a bare leg brush against a few poison ivy twigs reaching across the trail. But nearly all of us would suffer severe skin irritations from a massive exposure to any of these plants.

One to several days after the contact, a small, itchy rash will manifest itself, resembling a mosquito bite. If touching it causes an intense, almost fiery sensation, then it is probably not a mosquito bite, but the onset of the "contact dermatitis" brought on by exposure to poison ivy or oak. This itchy area may enlarge, and soon become reddened, raised, and often blistered.

Scratching will not spread the rash, but it certainly can aggravate it. Scratching can also lead to bacterial infection that in more serious cases can result in blood poisoning. Despite appearances, the rash spreads only by means of the toxic oil itself, not by the oozing and weeping fluid from the blisters. That blister fluid is a product of your own body; it contains no toxic oil. The reason the rash often continues to break out in new areas is that people often re-expose themselves to more toxic sap, usually from their sleeping bag and unwashed clothes, especially socks, shoes and laces. Almost anything that comes in contact with the plant can carry the sap.

Another common skin condition that may resemble a poison oak, ivy or sumac rash is phototoxic dermatitis. As discussed back in the Hot chapter, it is caused by mild sunburn in combination with a skin allergy to a soap or cream, or to some type of food or drink.

Treatment

If you happen to brush against one of the toxicodendrons, it might not be the best idea to ignore the fact and continue on your way. Instead, stop and try to remove some of the toxins. If you are successful, you can spare yourself some or all of the inflammation. Theoretically you have ten or fifteen minutes before the toxic oil begins to chemically combine with your skin.

The best way to remove the toxin is to pour a mild solvent over the exposed area, and then to rinse it copiously with cold water. Do not use hot or even warm water, because this will open the pores and encourage an unfavorable penetration of the oil into your skin. One of the better solvents is gelled ethyl alcohol, the hand sanitizer mentioned in the Hygiene and First Aid chapters. Dab it on, and rinse it away. Virtually any other alcohol-based liquid will work, as long as you apply it to the affected area liberally, and rinse with large amounts of cold water. If you let the solvent evaporate without washing it off, it will leave the toxic oil in place. Water not only flushes the alcohol from the skin, but it also tends to slowly oxidize, or inactivate, the urushiol. Adding a small amount of hydrogen peroxide or bleach to the rinse water will enhance this oxidizing effect. One problem with the solvent is that it removes not only the toxic oil from your skin, but also the skin's natural, protective oils. Therefore, after washing with a solvent, be very careful not to touch more poison ivy or oak, since a new exposure could then be more serious.

Lacking a solvent of some kind, wash the affected skin liberally with soap and cold water. I have used Fels-Naptha® soap with good results. Another product, which I have not tried, is Oak n' Ivy®, which supposedly works by breaking down the active ingredient in the oil. Still, any type of soap will do. Or simply rinse with cold water alone. Even if it is too late to prevent the rash, washing the skin to remove excess plant oil will keep the rash at a minimum by removing much of the remaining transmissible toxins.

After detoxifying, or before, change out of whatever clothing that might have brushed the plants. Place the contaminated garments in a plastic bag and stow them in your backpack. Arriving home or in a town, empty them straightway into a washing machine. This will effectively remove the toxins from clothing and shoes, and without contaminating the machine for the next user, as long as you use plenty of laundry soap.

Once the oil has bonded to your skin, the best possible treatment are the gifts of nature—the aloe vera, or the Jewelweed (*Impatiens spp.*). The Jewelweed, found mostly in the east, is easily identified by its yellow or orange flowers, and seed pods that resemble miniature cucumbers. When mature, the pods pop open when you touch them. Jewelweed is fairly common in damp, shady areas, along roadsides and stream banks, and it often grows in the vicinity of both poison ivy and poison oak. To use this remedial plant, pinch off a few leaves and stems, crush them, and rub them gently on the exposed area. Jewelweed also soothes the sting of nettles and insect bites.

Most pharmacies offer a number of commercial remedies for treating a toxicodendron rash. Drying agents like Calamine or other lotions can be soothing. Hydrocortisone creams or sprays reduce the inflammation, swelling, and itching, however the over-the-counter varieties are too weak to be effective. In my experience the prescription concentrations work extremely well, as long as they are not petroleum jelly-based. In severe cases a physician can prescribe antihistamine creams, tablets or shots.

Lush undergrowth along the AT

Snakes

Hiking with our eyes and ears

Snakes are among nature's most fascinating creatures. We rarely see them, since they spend much of their time hidden in piles of rocks or leaf litter, in decaying logs, tree cavities and underground hollows such as those created by tree roots. Even when resting in the open they usually conceal themselves under at least some vegetation. And depending on temperature, they tend to be most active at night.

Snakes find their prey by sight and scent, and sometimes by temperature. They lack ears, but their bodies are very sensitive to vibrations. Their vision is quite good, as is their sense of smell thanks to a harmless, flicking forked tongue that carries scent to a sensory organ inside the mouth. Some species kill their prey with venomous bites, others with constriction, and others by overpowering and swallowing. Lacking chewing-type teeth, they swallow their meals whole.

All snakes play an important role in the balance of their local ecology. They feed on rodents and other small animals, helping to keep populations in check, and in so doing they help reduce disease. In turn they are fed upon by birds of prey and larger animals.

Sometimes a snake will slither across our path when least expected. But this does not mean that it is being malicious towards us. We can ensure our safety by remaining alert and keeping a safe distance, as nature intended. And I think we all benefit by learning to tolerate and even to appreciate these interesting reptiles.

Common non-venomous snakes

Gopher snake

The gopher snake, (*Pituophis spp.*) is common in drier regions—sandy woodlands, chaparral and prairies—from sea level to 9,000 feet. This snake and its various subspecies are found across the U.S. except in the northeast. In the mountain states it is called the bull snake, and in the eastern states, the pine snake. Some members of this group grow quite large, with recorded lengths in excess of eight feet.

Intimidating as they may appear, they are harmless to hikers who leave them alone. The gopher snake normally behaves passively, but if confronted it may hiss and sometimes flatten its head and vibrate its tail. If threatened it may even lunge at an intruder. And of course if molested it is likely to bite.

Due to the gopher snake's behavior and to the patterns of brown or black blotches on its back, hikers regularly mistake it for the rattlesnake and often kill it. This is unfortunate because the gopher snake is extremely beneficial to the ecology, and to farmers troubled by rodents.

While hiking through the desert-like Tehachapi Mountains of southern California, Jenny and I came to a shading tree and were about to sit down when we noticed a gopher snake there. Over the years we had seen many gopher snakes, often stretched across the trail and looking like sticks from a distance. But we had not seen one quite as large as this six footer. Leaving it ample room we sat down anyway, and soon it slithered behind us, only inches away, before continuing on its way.

Black rat snake

The black snake, or black rat snake (*Elaphe obsoleta*) is related to the water snake. It eats insects, rodents and other small mammals, frogs and lizards. The black rat snake is normally harmless to humans, but when provoked it can bite. These snakes inhabit hardwood forests, old fields, farmlands, and wooded canyons from sea level to 4,400 feet. They range from Vermont south into Florida, and west into Minnesota, Michigan and Texas.

Species such as the black snake consume great numbers of rodents, and their presence around barns is of great benefit to farmers. Hikers reap the same benefits in and around many of the Appalachian Trail lean-tos and shelters, where the black snake helps keep the mice population in check.

This snake can grow quite large also, up to eight feet, and I remember one big fellow who had taken up residence in a shelter along the AT. As Jenny and I were approaching the shelter we saw it slithering through the rafters. Realizing that it meant us no harm, we took its picture, then sat inside, appreciating the creature while eating our lunch and signing the register book.

King snake

The many subspecies of the king snake (*Lampropeltis spp.*) are distributed widely across the U.S. They range in size from two to six feet, and are adaptable to a variety of habitats, including woodlands, chaparral, brushy and rocky canyons and talus slopes, from sea level to 9,000 feet. This is generally the same elevation range as for the gopher snake, although the king snake is not nearly as common. King snakes are constrictors; they feed on rodents, birds, and even on other snakes, including venomous ones. Curiously, they are immune to rattlesnake venom.

Several types of king snakes have beautiful bands along the length of their bodies, in red or orange, black, and yellow or off-white. These color patterns are similar to those of the venomous coral snake. Such "mimicry" is thought to be nature's way of discouraging predators. And of course these similarities often lead people to mistake the king snake for the coral snake. See the description under "Coral snake," on how to tell the difference.

Venomous snakes

North America is home to only four types of venomous snakes: the rattle-snake, copperhead, cottonmouth (also known as the water moccasin), and the coral snake. The bites of these snakes rarely cause human fatalities.

Coral snake

Two species of coral snakes are found in the United States: the Eastern coral snake (*Micrurus fulvius*), of the southeastern states; and the smaller Western, or Arizona, coral snake, (*Micruroides euryxanthus*) found from the southern regions of New Mexico and Arizona to northwestern Mexico. The eastern coral snake lives in many habitats, including pine woods and hardwood forests. The western coral snake is found mainly in dry habitats. Both are timid and seldom seen by hikers. They spend much of their lives underground in cracks and crevices, feeding on small lizards, snakes, reptiles and amphibians.

The coral snake tends to be small, averaging only twenty-four inches in length. It is not a pit viper like the rattlesnake, copperhead and cotton-mouth (see below). Rather, it is an elapid, related to the Asian cobra and many Australian snake species. It has a small mouth, and tiny, fixed fangs. It is not normally aggressive, but like any snake it will bite if handled or accidentally stepped on. Coral snake bites are rare in the United States, only about twenty-five bites a year by some estimates.

Almost all subspecies of the coral snake are brightly colored, and have regular patterns of red, yellow and black bands. Many subspecies of king snake are marked in similar ways, but the arrangement of the colors differs between the two species. The king snake's red bands are bordered on both sides by black bands. The coral snake's red bands are bordered by yellow bands. "Red and black, friend of Jack. Red and yellow, kill a fellow." This is an easy way of remembering the distinction between the two.

Cottonmouth (water moccasin)

The cottonmouth (*Agkistrodon piscivorous*) lives in streams and swamps of the south and southeast United States and parts of Illinois, Kentucky, Missouri, Oklahoma and Texas. Like all vipers, the cottonmouth has hollow fangs that inject toxin. The bite is rarely fatal, although it can be painful and can cause local tissue damage. The snake is brown or olive, with broad black bands across its body. Growing to four feet or more in length, it feeds on fish, amphibians, reptiles, birds and small mammals. The term cottonmouth derives from the color of the snake's mouth lining, which is white, and from the snake's mannerism of holding its mouth agape when threatened.

Copperhead

Another venomous member of the pit viper family, the American copperhead (*Agkistrodon contortrix*) is identified by its regularly spaced bands along its length, and its flattish, triangular head. The adult snake is from two to three feet in length and occasionally larger. It is copper in color, but this can vary from light brown to pinkish, helping camouflage it among leaves and forest debris. It prefers rocky, forested hillsides and wetlands for habitat, and ranges from Massachusetts to northern Florida and westward to Illinois and Texas. It is gregarious, and hibernates with other snake species.

Small mammals and frogs account for most of the copperhead's prey, as do birds and insects. This snake, in turn, serves as food for red-tailed hawks, possums and even bullfrogs.

When approached, the copperhead will either move away quietly, or lie motionless, relying on its camouflage for protection. Like all snakes, this one prefers to be left alone, but it may exhibit a tenacious personality when approached. It can jump twice its length, and if aggravated it will strike with vigor. Bites usually occur when someone unknowingly steps or reaches too close, unaware of the snake's presence in the leaf litter, the hollow of a log, or a crevice in the rocks. We hikers therefore need to remain vigilant when in copperhead territory. At least the snake's venom is milder and less dangerous than that of other venomous snakes; its bite is rarely fatal.

Rattlesnake

In our many miles of hiking, Jenny and I have encountered snakes of all kinds: rattlesnakes, copperheads, gopher, king, and many others. And no doubt we have walked past many without noticing them. But it is the rattlesnake that seems to be the most prevalent, especially on or alongside a trail.

Both eastern and western rattlesnakes (*Crotalus spp.*) have many subspecies. The eastern diamondback (*C. adamanteus*) tends to be the largest; it is found in some of the southern states. The timber rattlesnake (*C.

horridus) can also grow quite large, up to six feet and more in length. It is found from southern Maine to northern Florida, and west to Minnesota and Texas.

Several species of rattlesnake inhabit the mid-western and western states. Along the CDT they are common in Wyoming and New Mexico. Along the PCT they occur throughout much of California, but are almost unknown along the trail through Oregon and Washington, except in the Columbia River Gorge.

Rattlesnakes prey mostly on small rabbits and rodents such as ground squirrels, chipmunks, rats and mice—creatures that tend to reproduce prolifically in years of abundant food. So we are most likely to see rattlesnakes (as well as copperheads in the East) in areas where rodents feed, namely along streams, in rock piles and stands of grasses, and under brush and wood piles. In warm weather, rattlesnakes are active throughout the daylight hours; however, during the hottest months of the desert Southwest, they limit most of their activity to the cooler hours, generally from twilight to dawn. Rattlesnakes hibernate in dens shared with other rattlesnakes and also with other snake species. They are also excellent swimmers.

How to recognize the rattlesnake

The rattlesnake, like all pit vipers including the copperhead and cottonmouth, has pits on each side of its head, between the eye and nostril. These pits house its infrared sensors, which allow the snake to detect its prey at considerable distance. Once the rattlesnake finds the heat signature of a mouse, for example, it simply follows the heat trail leading to the creature's den or nest.

The pupils of the rattlesnake are vertical and thinly elliptical, rather than round like those of non-venomous snakes. But if you are close enough to see this, then you are much too close. Rather, what you will notice from a safe distance is the stout, heavy body with a flattish, triangular-shaped head, wide in the jowls and fashioned improbably onto a thin neck. This is the viper look.

And you will probably see and hear the jointed tail rattles, although in some cases these might have broken off. The rattlesnake is normally marked with brownish "diamonds" (actually hexagons or ovals) along the midline of the back. And hikers should remember that the harmless gopher snake has somewhat similar markings.

In desert regions of the Southwest lives a particularly venomous rattlesnake, known as the "Mojave Green." It is common, and the chances of a PCT hiker seeing one are good. Fortunately, the ground cover in these regions is sparse, so with even a modicum of attentiveness on the hiker's part, the chances of being bitten by a Mojave Green are very slim. This snake has much the same markings as other rattlesnakes, and is further identified by its pale green hue, similar to the dusty sage-green color of the surrounding scrub brush. The reason it is more dangerous is that its type of venom can affect the brain or spinal cord.

The snake's primary defense

Being exceptionally sensitive to ground vibrations, snakes can sense our approach from quite a distance. They may slither for cover, but only if this will increase their chances of remaining unnoticed. Otherwise, their primary defense is to remain motionless and inconspicuous. And this is why copperheads and rattlesnakes can be hazardous to hikers, especially as the snakes' camouflaging helps them blend into the surroundings. The hiker can unknowingly approach within striking distance, and only after the rattlesnake's primary defense has failed will it buzz a warning.

When so threatened, the snake will rarely retreat. This is because it cannot turn from danger without increasing its vulnerability. Nor can it travel fast. So it usually stands its ground, mouth agape in an intimidating manner. This defensive mechanism is ineffective against people, who can throw rocks, but it works very well against birds of prey, the snake's usual predator.

I once stopped to drink from my water bottle and a rattlesnake buzzed me from behind. I turned and saw it coiled at the edge of the trail. I had just walked past it without noticing. The snake had buzzed only when I stopped, undoubtedly interpreting my stopping as a threat.

Hiking in snake country

Before setting out on any hike, find out what venomous snakes inhabit the area, and learn to recognize them. Walk attentively, scanning the trail ten or twenty feet ahead. Where the trail is overgrown in brush or grass, probe ahead with a long stick. Trekking poles are much too short for this. As far as clothing is concerned, shorts and sandals obviously offer no protection from a snake bite. Long pants, socks and shoes are preferable but still vulnerable. The more layers, the better the protection. Those hikers wishing to take every precaution could wear snake chaps. A more economical option in remote areas of particular snake danger would be to wear pieces of cardboard or foam wrapped around the lower legs and ankles, and taped in place. If hiking at night, use a small flashlight held low to illuminate the ground just ahead.

Jenny and I were ambling along the AT in Connecticut when we heard the characteristic buzzing of a rattlesnake. Jenny was in the lead and the buzzing was coming from somewhere between us, and off to one side. I stopped, and she continued ahead, out of range. I scanned the brush-covered ground for a few long moments, then saw the source of the rattling—the tail of the snake. I was relieved to see that it was about six feet away. But imagine my chagrin to then discover the head of this large timber rattler fairly at my feet!

A coiled rattlesnake can strike out to about half its body length. If the snake is not coiled, which is how we usually find them as they are trying to remain undetected, then its range is far less. I have inadvertently stepped within as little as a foot or two of a few rattlesnakes, fortunately without being bitten. This illustrates not only the difficulty of avoiding venomous snakes and keeping a safe distance from them, but that they don't always strike when presented the opportunity. In my observation, it seems to depend on the timing, distance, the snake's posture (coiled or outstretched) and how great a threat the snake perceives in us.

One time Jenny was walking behind me, when she stopped abruptly and called out that I had just stepped *over* a rattlesnake. I turned and saw a 24-inch rattler slithering off into the surrounding brush. On the trail we found a circular indentation in the dirt, apparently where the snake had been resting or possibly sleeping.

The rattlesnake's warning is exactly that. And this suggests the danger of hiking with earphones on. One fellow told me about an encounter with a timber rattlesnake. Apparently two other hikers in front of him had walked past the snake, and were watching it from a distance when this earphoned hiker happened along. "I noticed their stern faces and wild gestures apparently aimed at me, but I saw no need to stop, until my eyes finally registered on the snake a few feet ahead." And he went on to say that he never again hiked with headphones.

Before you stop to rest alongside a trail in areas known for venomous snakes, probe the nearby bushes with a long stick. If later a snake crawls out of the brush near where you happen to be sitting, your best course of action would be to sit perfectly still and wait for it to leave—if it appears inclined to do so, which it probably will—or if not, then to back slowly away. Never try to swat a rattlesnake with a book or short stick, as one hiker I know of did. These creatures can strike in one one-hundredth of a second—far faster than you could ever swing at them.

Every time Jenny sees or hears a rattlesnake, she dashes away. And every time I assure her that a couple of snake-lengths away from the creature's head is perfectly adequate, as long as she remains on guard and leaves plenty of room to retreat. On the final stages of our fifth thru-hike a rattler buzzed her, and this time she merely moved aside and studied the area for the snake's whereabouts. I was coming along behind at the time when I heard a shriek. Lesson learned: do not stand a couple of snake-lengths away from where you *think* the snake might be. It could be much closer.

Snakebite first-aid and protocol

Every state but Alaska and Hawaii has venomous snakes. According to the American Red Cross, about 8,000 people a year receive venomous bites in the United States, and about ten of these bites are fatal, mostly to the very young or infirm. I asked Dr. Anthony Manoguerra, director of the San Diego Regional Poison Center, about the incidence of rattlesnake bites to hikers. He said they are fairly common. How serious are they? He explained that the damage depends on the amount of venom injected, its potency, (which varies considerably) and the amount of time elapsed en route to the hospital. In cases of heavy envenomation, the patient may spend a couple of days in the hospital, or a week at most.

According to Dr. Manoguerra, the most important thing to do if bitten by a venomous snake is to stay calm. In nearly half the cases of venomous bites, the snake injects little or no venom. So we should remember that weakness, sweating, nausea and fainting are not signs of poisoning. Rather, they simply reflect the mental trauma of being bitten. The person will usually know within five minutes whether or not venom was injected. The signs are swelling and increasingly severe pain. More serious bites will also cause a tingling sensation, accompanied by a gradual discoloration of the skin.

Envenomation by a Mojave Green rattlesnake does not produce these early symptoms. Only after six to twelve hours will the neurological symptoms become apparent, and by then treatment is long past due. The chances of receiving a bite from a Mojave Green are remote, but such a bite is considered a medical emergency.

If bitten by a snake of any kind, keep your wits about you. If you are carrying a snake suction device such as the Sawyer Extractor, (recommended in the First Aid chapter), then apply it. But do not cut slits in the skin and do not suck with your mouth; these out-dated practices can lead to a serious infection at the bite site, since the traumatized skin there is much less able to defend itself against bacteria. And do not apply a tourniquet. Some authorities recommend a lightly constricting band, and while this may reduce the danger to the body, it could increase the risk to the affected limb; so rely on your own judgement. Whether the signs of envenomation begin to manifest or not, as a matter of personal safety you will have to decide whether to walk out for help or send someone to summon medical assistance. If hiking alone, then you would have to go for help yourself, not at a run—which would increase the heart rate and thus the spread of toxin—but at a normal walking pace.

Camping in snake country

The chances of encountering a snake—venomous or non-venomous—at your campsites are slim. On warm nights, snakes are busy looking for their meals, and at the same time they are being wary of becoming a meal for some larger creature, especially one as large as you.

Seen at an outpost along the PCT:
"BEWARE - BABY RATTLERS"

A tent with its netting doorway closed might seem to provide necessary protection, but Jenny and I have slept many nights beneath our open tarp, and also under the stars in the mountains and beautiful deserts, and have not been bothered by snakes.

————————

Part of the allure and excitement of wilderness travel is the unknown or unforeseen encounters with the natural world, including, every now and then, snakes. And the more we learn about snakes of all kinds, the more we may find how much they have to teach us about ourselves, about the way we perceive all creatures in nature and how we react to them.

Bears

When a man wants to murder a tiger he calls it sport;
when a tiger wants to murder him he calls it ferocity.

— *George Bernard Shaw*

Wild Blackie
Park Blackie

Some Native peoples of North America hunted the bear for its meat as food, its fat as lamp oil, and its hide as clothing and rugs. Other Indians considered the bear to be a reincarnated relative, or sacred in other ways, and left it strictly alone. As settlers moved west and started clearing land for their towns and agriculture, the wolf, cougar and wolverine lost habitat. So the populations of these carnivorous predators dwindled. But the bear is omnivorous: its molars are flat-topped, allowing it to eat plants as well, and this has helped it adapt.

Even so, we have pushed the bear into a few remaining enclaves of wilderness. And when we visit those areas and bring food with us, we give the bear a food opportunity it cannot ignore. And we call this "a bear problem."

———

The black bear is less aggressive and far more predictable than the grizzly, and therefore not as greatly feared. So it continues to flourish in the mountainous regions. But with keen senses and an opportunistic behavior, the black bear tends to gravitate to clusters of civilization in search of food. Once there, it inevitably loses in its confrontations with humans. Mankind is gaining a better understanding of the bear and its role in the web of life, and although our suburbs are still shrinking its habitat, the black bear is beginning to expand its range. At present, we hikers are likely to encounter "Blackie" as far afield as the thick woods of northern Maine to the mountains and arid lowlands of southern California. So let's get to know a little more about our backcountry neighbor.

The black bear

The black bear (*Ursus americanus*) is not always black. It can be brown, reddish, cinnamon, blond or cream-colored. It is powerfully muscled, equipped with claws and incisors, and forever in search of a meal. However, it does not view humans as food. Most of its diet consists of vegetation, grubs, fish, and small mammals. Black bear attacks on humans are quite rare, especially in light of the many thousands of black bears that humans encounter all summer long.

In the early 1960's I worked in Yellowstone National Park, and part of my job entailed picking up campers' trash that the bears had scattered. This was the start of my relationship with bears. Later, I coexisted with bears for eleven years in Yosemite National Park. I have also observed bears while hiking many thousands of miles through the varied backcountry of North America, both east and west. From these experiences I have come to recognize the black bears in two distinct types: the "wild" bear and the "park" bear.

Wild Blackie

The "wild" variety of black bear is found mainly outside the National Parks, where every hunting season it becomes prey to big-game hunters and their hound dogs. For the wild black bear, these encounters with man and dogs reinforce the notion that humans are to be feared and avoided.

In our many outings together, Jenny and I have encountered hundreds of "wild" black bears. Almost without exception they have fled into the woods upon our approach. Cubs and yearlings will sometimes run away with mother, but often they will stop and stare curiously for a few long moments before scurrying up a tree, or running in a different direction into the forest. The point is, left alone the wild black bears pose very little danger to hikers who treat them with prudence. Yes, they are big and powerful and fully capable of harming us, but they virtually never do. My only advice with regard to wild black bears is to leave them alone. In all likelihood they will reciprocate.

Park Blackie

Inside National Parks, where hunting is usually illegal, the black bear is an entirely different animal. Whether it wanders across the park boundary as an adult, or whether it is born and reared inside the park, it tends to gravitate to the nearest black hole of humanity—namely the campgrounds. Once there, park blackie becomes "habituated" to people. So it raids campsites and vehicles for food, or objects resembling or possibly containing food. And being remarkably intelligent, the bear devises all sorts of clever tactics to get the food, including unlatching locks on coolers, prying open car trunks, and even unscrewing lids on jars.

When the park bear's havoc-wreaking becomes intolerable, the rangers bring out their dart guns and bear traps. Once captured, "bruin" is typically drugged and ear-tagged or body-painted, and removed to some far away forest. But the bear does not forget its associations of humans with food. Using its remarkable homing skills it will often return to the scene of the previous crimes, however far away—only to be caught again and tagged on the other ear. Or it might simply descend to the nearest outpost of civilization and resume its pillaging there, only to be shot, as likely as not, on sight. And when the landowner reports the incident to the authorities, the reply is sometimes "shoot, shovel, and shut up."

Park-type bears are also found in a few places outside National Parks, particularly in the East, and usually in areas of backcountry that are very popular with campers and hikers. These are "wild blackies" that exhibit "park" bear behavior. Even though hunted, the temptation of food is so powerful that it overrides the animal's fears. Suffice it to say that if there is food and rubbish strewn about irresponsibly, the black bear is soon to appear.

Dangerous to campers?

Rarely, a park bear will injure a tourist teasing it with food. Even though the bear may appear tame, it still requires a certain amount of personal space. Normally it will only growl or act defensively if someone ventures too close. But instincts can surface, for example when a park visitor instructs his or her children to pet the bear or its cuddly-looking cubs for a photograph.

As with all creatures wild or not so wild, most of the park bear's time is spent in search of food. Yet it has no appetite for the flesh of campers. Bruin wants only their food. And when the bear wanders into a campsite in broad daylight—inside a National Park—only rarely will the campers defend their supplies. Most people flee in terror, leaving the bear to feast at the picnic table, and reinforcing the bear's intimidating behavior. The smart campers quickly gather their food, load it into their car, and drive away. And smart hikers do much the same, packing their food into their backpacks, and hiking on—leaving the bear to try its luck elsewhere.

Traditional methods of food protection

National Park authorities have implemented various schemes to solve the "bear problems." First, they instruct us to camp only in designated camp-sites. This is convenient for the rangers, and ironically for the bears as well. I do not mean to depreciate backcountry rangers; only after we have walked a mile in their moccasins will we begin to appreciate the problems these hardy souls face. In the more popular Parks, Monuments, and Recreation Areas they are inundated with campers who every night of the summer season leave their food scattered all over their camps.

Food bags hung from tree limbs

Because the rangers cannot fine the bear when it steals our food, they fine *us* when the bear steals our food. And these fines can be stiff. Official literature depicts various methods of suspending food from tree branches, so many feet above the ground, and so many feet out from the tree trunk. Unfortunately for the tree, these methods often damage the branches, due to the sawing action of the taut cords. And, unfortunately for the camper, they rarely work.

It seems that many bears in our National Park backcountry owe their livelihood to well-intentioned hikers who trust the food-hanging system. Nocturnal bruin is incredibly resourceful at retrieving food bags, and the nights are long. I have seen the results of scores of bags plucked from remarkable heights. Even lost one myself many years ago, hung so high that the bear would have needed a step ladder to reach it. But reach it, the bear did; and the massive branch supporting my bag narrowly missed smashing my tent. So while new bear-bagging techniques come up into vogue as fast as they go down, the food bags, and the branches support-ing them, mainly just go down.

Metal boxes, wires, hangers and fences

Finding a suitable tree with a strong and convenient branch can be a time-consuming chore that most experienced campers forego. Realizing this, the rangers supplied many backcountry campsites with metal storage boxes and overhead wires from which to suspend food. In some areas we find other devices like "coat hangers" (tall metal poles with angled racks at the top for hanging food bags), fenced-in shelters, such as those found in the Smokies, and bear poles as found in the Canadian Rockies. Recently, however, the authorities have removed some of these contraptions in an attempt to restore the area to a more natural condition. And in the process they have of course discouraged many visitors from venturing into the backcountry, perhaps by intent.

Either way, the Park Service is now recommending the use of personal bear-proof canisters, and in some areas they require them. These canisters are heavy, but on short trips they may be an acceptable option. For distance hikers they are not always practical, owing to their weight and limited capacity. And while the canisters may keep our food from disappearing, they will not prevent bears from prowling through our camps, pawing through our gear, and disrupting our nights. Once bears have learned to associate hikers with the food they carry, they usually try to obtain that food, no matter how many times they meet with failure. If they perceive an opportunity, they will tend to pursue it.

I feel that under the present system, everyone loses. The campers lose their food, the rangers lose their fondness for campers, and when the bears become overly habituated they often lose their lives. I recommend a method where the hiker, the bear, and even the ranger usually win. I call it stealth camping, detailed back in the Stealth Camping chapter. In terms of the bear "problem," it works like this:

Typical camper behavior

Backpackers and campers almost universally exhibit certain practices that attract park blackie. These practices include:

- Camping in designated sites, every one of which lies on the bear's nightly marauding route. (No coincidence there.)

- Advertising one's presence with campfires, the smoke of which sends an olfactory signal clearer than any siren.

- Cooking food at these camps, the aroma being a thousand times more alluring than campfire smoke.

- Hanging their food in sight, as though advertising it.

- Acting terrified by the bear's intrusion and fleeing, leaving Bruin free run of the food.

Of course, campers are not entirely at fault in these scenarios. They are simply following the generations-old rulebook of camping practices. But for today's bruin roving in search of plunder, it is hard to imagine a scenario more conducive to success.

Avoiding park bears

We hikers depend on our food supplies, and therefore we need to turn the tables. Otherwise, the results, as thousands of backpackers have learned, are not likely to fall in our favor. To avoid park bears, first and foremost we need to stay away from the places they frequent, at the times they frequent them. During the summer, and in the backcountry, the park bear roams almost exclusively within range of the designated campsites. These, in turn, are predictably located near lakes and streams. And backcountry campsite marauding in the presence of humans is almost exclusively a nighttime activity.

Jenny and I avoid park bears by camping well away from their zones of activity, and by taking measures to remain undetected at our stealth-sites. By "well away," I mean several miles from the nearest designated site. We are very careful to preserve the stealth-camping legacy by leaving our sites in pristine condition. And of course, we avoid cooking at them. The bears' eyesight may be poor but their sense of smell is extraordinary. In the right conditions, they can smell lingering food odors, as well as other odors such as deodorant, sunscreen, and mosquito repellent miles away. So when in the National Parks, where marauding bears can be a problem, we cook many miles away from where we camp. My personal preference for storing food when in black bear country—and it is only that, my personal preference—is to sleep with my food bag just outside my tarp or tent, and with my flashlight near at hand. Many wild creatures are nocturnal, and a shuffling or scratching around outside could be deer, porcupine, mouse or vole. Or it could be a bear. But so far I have not heard or seen a bear at one of my stealth-sites. If and when I do, I will simply rise, pack up, and move on.

Of course, none of the methods in this book come with any guarantees, particularly those in this chapter. If you emulate my stealth-camping methods and Blackie grabs your food anyway, the tables are irrevocably turned. In the interests of your own safety, do not attempt to steal it back.

The grizzly bear

The grizzly bear, (*Ursus arctos*) also called the brown bear, is the California state animal. However a grizzly bear has not been seen in that state since 1924. Completely eradicated from its former habitat across the western and southwestern states—ostensibly for sport, but in reality out of fear—the grizzly now roams freely only in Alaska and Canada. It also occurs in very limited numbers in Glacier and Yellowstone National Parks and to a much lesser extent, the Bob Marshall and Scapegoat Wilderness areas of Montana.

On average, Glacier N.P. sees about two mauling incidents a year. This is appalling, as are the many more deaths and serious injuries in that Park caused by falling off the trails and down cliffs, by auto accidents, heart attacks and so forth. City life is even more dangerous; thousands of people die annually from shootings, violent crimes and lifestyle-related illnesses. But of the tens of thousands of hikers who frequent grizzly country every summer, most never even see a grizzly bear.

Old timers protected themselves with guns, but today we must protect the animals as well as ourselves. We must do everything possible to preserve the magnificent grizzly bear, and it is up to us to develop methods of coexistence. So before you venture into grizzly bear lands, contact the ranger district, park headquarters, or land management office for the current status on grizzly bear activity and warnings in that area.

Hiking in grizzly bear territory

Since the grizzly can be unpredictable, we need to remain alert when hiking in its domain, not only with our eyes, but with all our senses. Another very effective measure is to hike with companions. On the trail, avoid—absolutely—startling a grizzly as you round a bend. Forewarned, the bear will in every likelihood move away. Thick brush and tall vegetation can conceal bears, and they often do not pay attention to what might be coming. Making lots of noise, then, is the order of the day. In grizzly country (and only in grizzly country) consider carrying cow bells, "bear bells," and singing and making regular call-outs. Finally, in grizzly territory each person might carry a spray canister of oleoresin capsicum. Keep it immediately accessible, both on the trail and in camp.

Cooking and camping precautions

When hiking in grizzly country, you might find it beneficial, for the peace of mind if nothing else, to carry food that does not need to be cooked. Despite your desire for a hot meal and a mug of hot soup, consider that they may not be worth the risk. Keep your garbage tightly sealed and well away from camp. Keep all food (and cooking utensils if you carry them) sealed in at least two plastic bags, again well away from where you sleep. Though bears have rather poor eye sight, they are extremely smell sensitive. And many items that at home you might consider odorless, or pleasantly perfumed, are very attractive to bears. This is one reason Jenny and I do not like to use mosquito repellent in the Arctic. We use it on occasion, but only in areas where bears are few. Other sources of "signal odors" include sunscreen, deodorant, toothpaste, body lotion, the perfume of laundry soap in your clothes, and the perfume from the static-free sheets used in the clothes dryer.

Bathe often and thoroughly, but not with scented soap. Remember also that the odors of cooking can linger in your clothing. As a precaution, consider sealing your hiking clothing, shoes, socks, rain jackets, etc, in a plastic bag at camp, and wearing clean, unscented clothing while sleeping. Be cautious as you search for a stealth-site. Stay away from dense brush and thickets; instead look for an open area where you will have a wide view of your surroundings. And once again, when in grizzly country, consider carrying bear spray.

Bears are neither ferocious man-eaters lurking in the brush, nor real-life stuffed teddies waiting to be petted. A naive attitude toward bears can lead to trouble, yet by following the above precautions we do not have to let their presence discourage us from exploring the remote and pristine lands they inhabit.

Cougar

Like winds and sunsets,
wild things were taken for granted
until progress began to do away with them.
Now we face the question
of whether a still-higher standard of living
is worth its costs in things natural, wild and free.

— *Aldo Leopold*

Stealth and survivability

Just the thought of the cougar strikes fear into the hearts of many hikers, but in the vast majority of cases this fear is completely unjustified. In my thousands of miles of hiking, and many years spent in the wilds, I have seen only one cougar, and that was only a fleeting glimpse. So the notion that cougars are out to attack us on the trails and at our campsites is nonsense.

The early settlers, and even the more recent ranchers often considered the cougar to be "vermin" and tried to eliminate it. The common excuse was that livestock—which the ranchers were importing into the cougar's domain—needed protection. Fortunately for the cougar and the rest of the intricately balanced natural world connected with this magnificent animal, its stealth and adaptability have enabled it to survive.

━━━━━━

The cougar (*Felis concolor*) ranges from central Canada to Patagonia, and survives remarkably well in a variety of environments, including swampy terrain, jungles, deserts, forests—from sea level to alpine regions. Depending on location, it is known also as the mountain lion, puma, panther, catamount and American lion. Thanks to the protection that many states are finally beginning to grant this animal, it is starting to make a comeback, mainly in the western states where natural habitat is more extensive. By current estimates, some 5,000 of these animals inhabit California, a figure that comprises about a quarter of the cougar population for the western states combined. The eastern cougar's distribution is limited to only a few scattered areas. The Florida panther population is estimated at only 30 to 50 animals.

The cougar is very skilled at living and traveling in stealth, which is why we so rarely see it. And it is an accomplished predator. It can spring eighteen feet straight up into trees, and can cover distances of twenty feet in one leap—a skill that comes in handy when hunting. Although it can cover short distances nearly as fast as a cheetah, the cougar prefers to creep up on its prey until close enough to leap onto the prey's back and break its neck. The cougar feeds mainly on deer, but its diet may also include small mammals, wild turkeys and very occasionally, domestic livestock.

Risks to hikers

Statistically, the cougar endangers people in two very isolated scenarios. One: a juvenile cat, seeking its niche and new hunting territory, wanders into an encroaching suburb and finds easy prey in a family pet or lone child. And two: a mother cougar lashes out in defense of her kitten when "threatened" by someone walking or jogging heedlessly along a trail or back road.

Jenny and I were hiking the PCT in Washington when suddenly we heard a nearby growl. We backed away, and saw the animal flash through the nearby brush. Then we heard a soft "meow" from a nearby kitten. The mother cougar had apparently given us warning, as any protective mother would.

Concerning the many wild and colorful stories about cougars stalking and confronting hikers, I tend to discount the vast majority of them. In the one or two reports that seemed credible, the person easily frightened the cat away by throwing sticks or rocks at it.

===

When modern man devastated the cougar's niche, he eradicated most of the animal's natural food sources and introduced livestock instead. The cougar had no choice but to prey on livestock. I liken it to placing bags of candy in a hungry child's bedroom. The temptation for the child would be to gobble as much as possible, and to take possession of the rest before it got away. This is how the cougar sometimes behaves around sheep. But as Edward Abbey pointed out (mainly in jest): "Any animal that eats sheep can't be all bad."

Personal Security

Awareness

In the past several chapters we have examined some of the vicissitudes of trail life—the obstacles and challenges both expected and unexpected. The more time we spend in the wilds, the more we can hone our skills, building competence and confidence in meeting those challenges. Snow travel becomes something to look forward to rather than something to dread. Wild creatures are more fascinating and less abhorrent. Shifts in weather are less troublesome as we change our attitudes and adjust our clothing and equipment to suit. In short, the so-called hazards of the natural world take on more manageable proportions, although they will never lose their potential to develop into dangerous situations.

And so it is with our personal security. Both on the trail and off, the potential for theft and personal threats by other people will occasionally exist. But rather than carry on down the trail with the nonchalant, careless attitude of "it couldn't happen to me," a safer approach is to maintain an awareness of what could happen, and then to take the appropriate measures to prevent it from happening. This allows us to enjoy our outings with much more confidence.

Vehicles encountered on the trail

Bicycles, Motorbikes, Horses

Many of our popular hiking trails are open to bicycles, and even the trails that are not are still subject to renegade cyclists who pride themselves in tackling such challenges. Actually, I find it quite amazing to see what these hardy souls will sometimes attempt. Jenny and I once followed a pair of bicycle tracks many miles through the deeply snowbound Sierra. So even though you may be hiking a trail closed to bicycles, do not be surprised if you suddenly encounter a cyclist hurtling toward you.

Whenever I hear or see a bicycle coming I stand aside, nod a friendly greeting as they wheel past, then continue on my way. Cyclists are forever crashing into things and injuring themselves, such is the price of their rapid technology. But in terms of our own safety, our ears are our allies and any stereo headphones are enemies. We should always listen for sounds of a fast-approaching bike: the telltale whir of freewheel and the squeaking of brakes. And remember that when one bicycle flashes past, others could soon follow.

Off Road Vehicles (ORV's), All Terrain Vehicles (ATV's) and the rest of their motorized ilk present similar problems to us hikers. Luckily, we can hear these machines long before their arrival, giving us ample time to stand well aside. Still, when in known ATV country one should refrain from resting on the trail, let alone camping on it.

Speaking of camping on the trail, remember that in some areas, particularly on trails leading to popular mountain summits, hikers such as myself can come bumbling along at night without flashlights. I have stepped on people sleeping on the trail, unseen. I remember one such incident, when suddenly I tripped on someone and went down onto this poor person, full-body, face-to-face. This shocked me half senseless, as undoubtedly it did the other person. But as I stumbled away I began to see the humor in it.

I have, in turn, been nearly run over by motorbikes traveling the trails at high speed, so I know that the dangers posed to hikers can be real—as can those of bicycles, motorbikes and ATV's. But in my experience these pale in comparison with the dangers of horses and mules. Having to suddenly scramble off the trail to prevent being trampled is not the usual image of relaxing in the wilderness. One problem is that many equestrians expect hikers to scurry out of their way—or else. One afternoon Jenny and I heard a pack train coming around the bend, but we had no idea that the lead horseman would try to run us down. Eight heavily-loaded horses and big mules came charging down on us, at a place where the trail was narrow and the hillside steeply sloped. We barely made it out of their way.

Most of the time, hikers can move off the trail well in advance of approaching equestrians. If the terrain is friable and exposed, then logically it would be up to the equestrians to stop and wait until you can decide what to do. Which they may not do. But when stepping aside, always leave the trail by climbing the slope, rather than descending it. The animals will probably be nervous, particularly the closer you are to them. If one should suddenly bolt, and you are down slope of it, then it could fall on you, or buck its rider or panniers onto you, or dislodge rocks onto you. Or the horse could kick out and knock you down the slope. So remember that the highest position is by far the safer, so long as you take care to ensure that you yourself do not fall. And once again, do not get close to these animals. They are well known for kicking and inflicting serious injuries.

Miscreants

Fortunately for us hikers, the criminal element in society rarely braves the natural world. Isolated incidents have occurred, but compared with the cities, our wild areas are very safe. Even so, a certain amount of caution is always in order.

In general, troublemakers travel by vehicle, and they tend to remain near the roads. So it is usually not the best idea for the hiker to linger at the road crossings, or to camp near roads—especially four wheel drive roads in more remote areas. If you want to camp near a resupply station or trailhead, move well away, make a stealth camp, and remain inconspicuous. While moving away, be alert to any onlookers. If you notice someone watching you, it may be best to change your plans.

To increase your safety, you could hike with friends, or at least camp with them. If traveling alone, you could act as though you are part of a group whenever meeting strangers. If questioned, speak collectively, using "we," rather than "I." Say something to the effect that the rest of your group is right behind you, that they will be along momentarily. When speaking with strangers, never give details about your hiking and camping plans. Trust your instincts; if they urge you to move along, even as the person is persuading you to talk awhile, then follow your instincts and bid a firm farewell. If you feel vulnerable when by yourself, consider carrying mace or pepper spray. In every likelihood you will never have to use it, but if it gives you that added peace of mind, then it is worth its weight.

Hitchhiking

In the right company hitchhiking can be an expedient means of travel and a great way to meet friendly and interesting people. In the wrong company it can be disastrous. Hitchhikers are vulnerable, and the lone woman hitchhiker is all but asking for trouble. One of the most sobering incidents in my experience came after an Outward Bound course, when one of our students was hitchhiking home from her month in the mountains. She never made it.

When planning your hikes, try to minimize your need for hitchhiking. The usual way is to park at the trailhead and hike a loop, returning to the vehicle. A less common, but also less restrictive way is to leave a vehicle at each end of a longer trail. An even better method, where possible, is to use public transportation, or arrange a ride with a shuttle driver. On longer treks involving resupplying, you can avoid many of the longer hitchhikes out to towns by carrying more food and skipping those detours altogether. When this is not practical, you might simply figure in an extra block of time for walking out to the distant towns. This takes longer, but it also preserves more of your wilderness connection, especially if you are on a longer journey.

One cannot plan for every contingency, and occasionally you may find yourself with the need to leave the trail and travel to a distant town. The safest way to hitchhike is to choose your drivers, rather than to submit yourself to their choice like a cow at an auction. One method is to head for the nearest parking area, and ask any likely looking motorists for a ride. This can be particularly effective at popular trailheads, where other backpackers may be loading their vehicles and preparing to drive out of the hills. If they appear to have room, introduce yourself and tell them of your needs.

Various other strategies will improve your chances of getting a ride— such as combing your hair and removing your sunglasses, and making a large sign telling your destination—but they will not increase your chances of getting a safe ride. In holding out the hitchhiking thumb you are relinquishing much of your control. Be wary, don't be afraid to make quick decisions, and don't allow impatience to override common sense. Even though you may have been trying to hitch a ride for hours, if someone pulls to a stop and appears or acts in any way suspicious, decline the offer and move away.

Road walking

Hikers have been struck by cars while road walking, and some have been killed. I remember one heart-stopping incident that occurred to Jenny and me along the PCT. We were walking along the busy paved road below the Hat Creek Rim in Northern California, back in 1987 before the trail along the rim had been developed. We were on the left shoulder of the road, facing the oncoming traffic. And since we could see what was coming at quite a distance, we felt safe. Unfortunately we were not thinking about the cars coming from behind. And we had not imagined that if one of those cars were passing another, then the overtaking vehicle would come quite close to us. Which is what happened. As the two cars flashed past us together, peddles to the metal, the overtaking vehicle missed us by inches.

From that we learned to stay well off the roads in the presence of any vehicle, regardless of which direction that vehicle is traveling. Especially because every now and then a motorist will use pedestrians as sport, steering straight at them then jerking away at the last possible moment.

That same year, Jenny and I were road walking along Whitewater Creek in Southern California, before that section of trail had been built. We stopped for a rest beside the creek, hidden from the road in an area of thick brush. A vehicle passed by and a beer bottle whizzed past our heads. I doubt whether the person who tossed the bottle knew we were there. But it does suggest the risks of even being close to a road.

Hang onto those valuables

Trailside towns and resorts normally offer the usual assortment of amenities, including stores, restaurants, laundromats and lodging. The ambience in these places is often very welcoming and relaxing, and may encourage the hiker to let down his or her guard. But these are hardly the best places to become negligent about leaving backpacks and various items of gear strewn about unattended.

First and foremost, I suggest you carry your valuables (money, credit card, identification, journal and exposed film) in a small bag, and that you keep this bag with you at all times. In town you could place the bag inside a ratty-looking sack that looks like it might hold a half-eaten sandwich from the deli, or something equally non-tempting. Or you could make the bag very small and flattish, secure it to a sturdy strap, and wear it under your shirt. Either way, carry this bag with you whenever you must leave your backpack, for example when going into a post office to pick up a resupply box, or into a store to buy groceries. However, when I say "leave your pack," I am not suggesting that you leave it unattended. Numerous hikers who have done so have returned to find their packs missing. At a post office, leave your backpack inside the building where you can keep an eye on it, and even then, carry your bag of valuables with you.

When you go into a grocery store, set your pack inside the doorway, and keep an eye on it. And yes, carry your bag of valuables with you. It helps if you greet the cashier and ask if it is ok to leave your pack there. Some stores have a "no backpacks or bags inside" policy. If you are with hiking companions, then one of you might have to wait outside with the packs. The lone hiker who leaves a backpack outside a store, unattended, is tempting someone to grab it and speed away.

When entering a restaurant, ask if you may bring your backpack with you. If the answer is "yes," then you might request seating near the door, so that you will not have to lug your pack through the dining area and risk bumping both tables and customers. If the answer is "no," ask to be seated by a window, then place your backpack outside that window where you can watch it. And once again, keep your bag of valuables with you. If all else fails, simply place a take-out order.

Take caution, also, in public facilities like restrooms and showers. When showering in a public stall, leave your backpack close by, just outside your shower stall, and part the curtain just enough so that you can watch your pack. Keep your bag of valuables inside the stall but out of the spray—and out of reach of anyone using an adjacent stall.

Leaving a vehicle at a trailhead

One must not assume that because a parking area exists, it is safe to park a car there. Vehicles parked at such places are easy targets for any vandals who happen along. The basic scenarios include theft of possessions left inside the vehicle, vandalism of the vehicle and/or its contents, and out-right theft of the entire vehicle. Unfortunately, these scenarios happen all too often, and I suspect that concern for a person's vehicle is what keeps many people from venturing into the wilderness, at least for any length of time. Cars are supposed to provide us with freedom, but sometimes they can reduce our freedom by increasing both our dependence on them and our reluctance to leave them. And they can greatly affect the quality of the outing also, when our minds remain anchored—consciously or not—on the vehicle parked at the trailhead.

A much better idea is to leave the car at home. Figure out a way to reach the trailhead without it, even if it means more walking. Jenny and I lived for about a year in Salt Lake City, and we often rode the city bus to the edge of town. From there we hiked far into the Wasatch Mountains. Even on our two-week trips here in the Northwest we usually take the

Greyhound bus to our chosen area, and then hire a driver to shuttle us to the edge of the wilderness. At journey's end we spend the final day walking back out to the bus station for the ride home.

To locate a shuttle driver for your chosen area, telephone the nearest Chamber of Commerce, or any guide services for backpacking or river rafting. Or phone someone locally, for example a small store, and ask whether they know of anyone who might be willing to drive you to such and such a place for a specified amount of payment. With a little effort this almost always works. Jenny and I sometimes pay someone locally to drive us to the nearby mountains, since our small town lacks any kind of public transportation. One time we hired a friendly chap who, on reaching our trailhead, was so taken by the natural beauty of the area that he said he was going home for his fishing pole, and was coming right back. So the arrangement worked very well for all three of us.

Dogs

Opinions vary widely on the dogs-in-the-wilderness issue. Most hikers do not mind seeing the occasional dog on the trail, provided its owner is acting responsibly. By this we mean keeping the animal on a leash so that it cannot chase the wildlife, jump on other hikers, or snoop around their camps. And cleaning up the dog poop and burying it a safe distance from the trail and any water sources, or carrying it out.

This is not to suggest that all owners act so responsibly, nor that all dogs encountered in the wilds are friendly. While I certainly would not wish harm on anyone's pet, I feel that the hiker's safety comes first. My advice is this: Whenever you see a dog at a distance—*any* dog off its leash—pick up a few hefty rocks. Ninety-nine dogs out of a hundred are well-intentioned, and you will know by the way they charge at you. The bark and tail wagging mean only that the dog is excited. The ears are the best indicator of intent: if the ears are upright, then the dog is probably friendly. If the ears are pinned back and the teeth are bared, then that could indicate danger.

Section 4

Longer Journeys

> Thousands of nerve-shaken, overcivilized people
> are beginning to find out that going to the mountains
> is going home.
>
> — *John Muir*

In the next several chapters we take a look at topics particularly applicable to long distance hiking. A summer-long trek, whether it is a thru-hike on a famous trail, or any other kind of long journey, is not so different from the many day and weekend hikes you may have done. It requires the same basic gear, food and water. But a longer trek will require something beyond all of this. And it usually starts with a dream.

Forging Dreams
into Goals

The way you activate the seeds of your creation
is by making choices about the results you want to create.
When you make a choice, you mobilize vast human energies and resources
which otherwise go untapped.

All too often people fail to focus their choices upon results,
and therefore their choices are ineffective.
If you limit your choices only to what seems possible or reasonable,
you disconnect yourself from what you truly want,
and all that is left is a compromise.

— *Robert Fritz*

As we press into the 21st century, our lives encompass the new and the old: the new science and technology, accelerating us into the future; and our old genetic make-up as Homo sapiens, anchoring us in the past. The new strives to create a sophisticated society where progress is determined by how far nature is bulldozed away. But the old was designed to function in that natural world, where physical exertion and exposure to the elements were a part of life. Technology has freed us from those pressures of raw survival, but its freedom is not without great cost. The industrialization and luxuries that shelter us from labor and discomfort also prevent us from connecting with the natural world, and with ourselves.

When we address our primal aspects we become more attuned, more alive. And about the only way we can do this, in this day and age, is to invent goals for ourselves. These goals must take us back into the natural world where we can once again test our grit, exert our bodies, experience a measure of discomfort, and come face to face with uncertainty and risk. For it is only by confronting these challenges that we can even begin to realize our capabilities as human beings.

Yes, we must contrive our goals. Of themselves they do not exist. What may exist are our dreams. But dreams are like electricity without wires: ineffective despite tremendous potential. Everyone has dreams, but not everyone forges them into goals. The usual approach is to wait for opportunities, but this dissipates energy. Self-wrought goals, on the other hand, beckon us ahead of our own volition.

Dispersed campfire coals extinguish themselves, but scooped together they can ignite the kindling to produce a heartening blaze. And so it is with dreams. Scoop them carefully and purposefully together, fan some life into them, and they can engender a blaze of resolve and purpose. And scoop together the disparate but glowing fragments of our lives: the innate talents, abilities and courage within us all, and we become far more capable.

Virtually anyone can take a dream and forge it into a goal. As a friend once confided: "Having been lazy and laid-back most of my life, I was amazed at my ability to set an objective and totally commit myself to it."

Making dreams come true

How many times have you said: "some day I would like to..." or "I've always wanted to..." But someday comes too late. And ignoring your dreams is like locking yourself in a jail and ignoring the key. Give yourself something special to be excited about, to plan for, and to live for. It does not have to be grand or impressive. But when you have decided on a goal, an immediate goal, your life will become more dynamic and meaningful. Your free time will be filled with the preparations, the physical conditioning, and the moving ahead with the plan.

We tend to pattern our lives according to our highest wishes. Those who enjoy watching tv more than anything else, do that. But those who dream of hiking a long trail, and who want to do it very seriously, then that is what they do. Whatever we focus on becomes our reality, regardless of physical make-up, the job, financial situation, age, and level of experience. So don't limit yourself. Your only genuine limits are the ones you make for yourself.

I think Sir Arthur Conan Doyle said it best in one of his dialogues: "My life is spent in one long effort to escape from the commonplaces of existence."

———————————

Society views physical labor as a personal indignity—something to be avoided. But for the hiker, the exercise of moving along the trail is an expression of life itself. And when we direct this expression toward a goal, the journey becomes a pilgrimage and we become pioneers, exploring the realities of the human experience and the glories of nature.

Financing the Journey

There is no more fatal blunderer than he who
consumes the greater part of his life
getting his living.

— *Thoreau*

In-come
versus out-go

For the hiker who dreams of spending a summer on the trail, the chances
of a successful journey can be quite good. This is true regardless of the
person's finances, be they lavish or paltry. To succeed at long-distance
hiking, the adventurer needs to have, first and foremost, an uncompro-
mising sense of motivation and perseverance. Without these, a check-
mate is very likely. But with motivation and perseverance, the adventurer will make whatever compromises might be necessary, financially.

Regardless of income, our financial situation depends mostly on our "out-
go." As a case in point, high-salaried individuals may seem "well-off,"
but those individuals could be practically broke if they spend most of
what they earn, and if they have gone deeply into debt. Debt is rampant
these days, and while it allows for a "higher" standard of living, it also
deprives people of their freedom—freedom to spend more time in the
wilds, in this case.

People often consider their luxury possessions as "essentials," and
they accept the recurring payments as necessary. In reality, the payments
are necessary only because of the debts entered into. And the reason that
modern life is so expensive is because of the size and number of a person's

expenditures: house payments or apartment rent, furniture payments, insurance payments, repair bills and property taxes, utility and telephone bills, health and life insurance, luxury-car installments and the associated insurance premiums, licensing fees, and gas and maintenance costs. And there might be entertainment expenses, vacations, credit card interest, and so forth. Money in the bank equals deposits minus all of these expenditures. Little wonder that money can be such a problem!

Most of us could easily afford a summer's journey by eliminating or at least minimizing some of these expenses. Rather than drive a new car, we could drive an older one. Consider that the monthly payments and insurance premiums on a new car could easily grubstake a thru-hiker all summer long, year after year for the duration of the debt. One very good way to cut expenses is to move to a less expensive town. Granted, the standard of living might not be as upscale, and the job might not pay as well, but the costs of living could be far less. And I think that the prospective adventurer with sights set beyond the ostentatious might be just as content, and that this person's savings would grow.

Many distance hikers finance their multi-month excursions by working long hours during the winter months, while spending the absolute minimum. Even though their income may not be great, their expenses are relatively few, so their savings grow.

Some of my happiest times were those early, penniless years in Yosemite when I lived in an old car. Every summer I saved just enough money from wilderness instructing to get me by. Those three months of employment allowed me to focus the remaining nine months on my rock climbing pursuits. And that focus was so strong that the comfortable, extravagant lifestyle held no meaning to me. I think it is still true today that without all the frills, the human body is quite economical to operate. On the trails this is particularly true, so let's consider the costs of a journey afoot.

Style dictates cost

Obviously, the costs of a summer's jaunt will vary widely among individuals. At one end of the scale is someone who sinks a small fortune into a load of overbuilt equipment. And at the other is the hiker who shopped at army surplus stores years ago. I remember meeting one hiker who carried an odd array of rustic, well-worn equipment tied haphazardly to his pack frame. For a trail staff he was using a mop handle. Despite all this he appeared to be enjoying his trek immensely. Even thriftier was a fellow eating rice cooked over a fire, and making bracelets to sell to the other hikers. This person was so frugal that he did not detour into the trail towns, but spent most of his summer on the trail. So the style we choose will have great bearing on the costs of our journey. The trip will be as expensive or as cost-free as we make it.

Lost income

The largest expense of the summer will be the forfeited wages. But these would be largely offset by the reduction in the high costs of a city lifestyle. I have known people to go overboard with this idea, however, doing things like selling their homes prior to departure, getting rid of pets and a good portion of their worldly belongings. Burning all bridges might not be the best idea, in case you decide to leave the trail well ahead of schedule.

Travel

Travel to and from the trail, by airline, train or bus, certainly factors into the costs of the journey. Hitchhiking would obviate most of the travel expense, but for safety's sake I would not recommend it. You might be able to arrange a ride with college students: check the Ride Boards on campus. Another option is to find a "drive-away" that will take you to or near your destination. Companies that arrange drive-aways are in the business of delivering vehicles to their owner's new locations, for example when the owner moves to a different state. And of course, the owner pays the expenses. Check in the yellow pages of your phone book under "auto transporters." A go-anywhere bus ticket, purchased well in advance, is another affordable alternative.

If planning to travel by air, research the flights well in advance of your departure. Contact a travel agent, or find out what airlines travel to your destinations and call them directly for fare information. In most cases, advance purchase will be much less expensive than buying at the last minute. Also, the travel sections of large newspapers often run announcements of fare discounts.

Food

Buying a large supply of food for several months of hiking can seem like a giant expense, but only because you buy it all at once. Were you to remain at home all summer you would still have to eat. Granted, hungry hikers eat more than they would at home, but their food on the trail tends to be less epicurean. So I do not think the costs of eating while on journey are any greater than at home—unless one decides to eat a lot of freeze-dried food, perish the thought. And because you will be buying most of your food all at once, you can save money by purchasing much of it in bulk, and by watching for price reductions.

The costs of mailing your boxes of food to resupply stations will be greater, the farther you live from the trail. If these costs are prohibitive, you might try my suggestion in the next chapter—purchasing your food in the general vicinity of the trail, in six-week increments.

Shoes

Scrimping on footwear is one area of false economy. The shoes or boots you purchase will be your *modus operandi*, and on them will hinge your entire journey, along with the bulk of its associated costs in money and time. After several weeks of hard use, your footwear will begin to wear out, internally if not externally. And when it does, it may start causing an injury that could sideline you, or even send you home. So in addition to your primary hiking footwear, consider buying spares. I suggest one spare pair of running shoes for each five hundred trail miles hiked. In addition, a pair of lightweight sandals makes a nice reserve. And a pair of light-weight fabric boots would be needed in snow country.

Gear

One of the best ways to reduce the expenses of hiking is to limit the amount of equipment you carry, and to simplify what remains. Making your own, which I describe in the Sewing chapter, is an extremely effec-tive way to reduce the expenses of any hike.

Reducing your packweight will enable you to complete your intended mega-trail in much less time, if needed. By shortening the duration of the trip, you can reduce your time away from your income-producing job. And you can do this without compromising your goals.

Expenses at trail-side towns

The more towns and resorts you visit, and the longer you remain in the company of their goods and services, the more money you are likely to spend. Lighter-weight gear and the associated improvement in the outing's continuity will enable you to bypass some of the trail-side towns. And this can save you money.

Restaurants and fresh foods

Restaurant meals and fresh food from grocery stores along the way can provide valuable nourishment as well as a welcome break from the typical trail fare. These will probably not be extra expenses, since you would likely have eaten in restaurants occasionally and purchased fresh foods from grocery stores had you remained at home.

Accommodations

Unless you are strapped for funds, you might consider planning for an occasional motel room, cabin or B&B. Relaxing and sleeping indoors may not be the focus of your journey, but it can provide a refreshing interlude now and then. To reduce the expenses, look for a hostel, or share the costs of a room with hiking friends.

Other necessities

Food and accommodations are the main expenses in town, but the small items can add up: showers, laundry, phone calls, postage on drift boxes, post cards and stamps. And you may need a bit of extra cash for unforeseen expenditures such as bus or shuttle rides to distant services, and other purchases like books, extra camera film, even emergency medical treatment.

Cash is the most convenient way to pay for these, but there is the risk of losing that cash or having it stolen. Far safer are traveler's checks, which if lost can be replaced. Most restaurants, grocery stores and motels accept traveler's checks, but this may not be true in the small towns and resorts along the way, in which case you should carry some cash in addition to traveler's checks.

───────────

When dreaming of setting off on a journey, do not limit yourself by a lack of funds. Granted, money tends to rule the game in today's culture. But when you temporarily leave society and step onto the trail, the rules will change. In the wilderness your ability to succeed will depend not on your financial situation, but your attitude and determination. So cast your vision outside the city limits, to the wilderness beyond and the glories of nature.

Resupply

I journeyed fur, I journeyed fas';
I glad I foun' de place at las'!

— Joel Chandler Harris
Nights with Uncle Remus

Turning our backs on the distractions of urban life, we follow our chosen trails deep into the wilds. And there we may remain for days on end, reveling in the independence and the freedom; the "tonic of the wilderness" as Thoreau so aptly put it. Until we start to run out of food.

Running out of food does not mean that we have to return home. Nor does it mean that we need to resort to air drops, at least here in the Lower 48. Our wilderness areas are more conveniently situated, giving us walkable access to places that sell food, or places to which we can receive food mailed to us. Along the more well-traveled trails, these "resupply points" are spaced normally no more than five or six days apart. And when we reach one, we can load our backpacks with provisions, and set off again into another stretch of backcountry. On a longer trip we can repeat the process for weeks or even months at a time.

The resupply points usually consist of stores, post offices, or resorts. Seldom are they in the wilderness, or even close to your chosen trails. Most often you have to hike a ways to reach them. Maybe a mile, sometimes much more. But if you are carrying a reasonably light pack, then that extra walking will be little trouble. And if you have been in the woods a while, you may be looking forward to a grocery store, hot showers, laundromat, restaurant, telephone, post office, and perhaps even a motel or hostel room for the night. Some resupply points offer all these amenities and more, while others offer only the bare minimum.

Food for your next stretch of hiking will usually be your greatest need. But many of the small stores and resorts may not sell the types of nutritious foods you prefer; particularly as your hard working body requires quality food, and lots of it. Also, you may need new shoes or a few items of equipment or clothing to replace things worn out.

For these reasons you may decide ahead of time, while planning your hike, to amass most of your supplies in your home town, and then arrange to have those supplies mailed to the "resupply stations" so that they will be there when you arrive.

The resupply station

I use the term "station" not to suggest a large building of brick and stone, like a train station, but an ordinary post office, or a small store or resort with postal facilities. It is a station in the sense that, during the course of a long journey, the hiker stops there for a short while before moving on. However nondescript, it is a place where a friendly postal worker or proprietor will receive your box of supplies and hold it until you arrive.

The types of resupply stations available vary from place to place. Along the popular and well-used trails, most are small U.S. post offices. Along more remote trails, or at least within walking distance of them, the resupply stations might be small stores or resorts that agree to receive hiker parcels.

Each station has its own way of operating, with different hours, availability of services, and restrictions on holding parcels. Based on these differences, we can group the resupply stations in three types:

- **Post Office**: offering the usual receiving and sending services. Typically they are housed in their own buildings. They do not accept parcels sent by the United Parcel Service (UPS). Many are closed on weekends, though some have limited hours on Saturdays. And they are normally closed during national holidays. In the standard three-season trekking season these holidays are: Memorial Day (the last Monday of May), Independence Day (July 4), Labor Day (the first Monday of September), and Columbus Day (the second Monday of October).

- **Resort or store featuring a small post office inside the building**: These offer hikers the best of both worlds. They accept parcels sent via both U.S. Postal Service and UPS. They will usually hand over parcels anytime they are open, which is typically seven days a week throughout the summer season. And they can handle outgoing parcels, at least during their postal hours.

• **Resort or store with no post office**: These are commercial enterprises that receive and hold parcels, sometimes for a fee. On the plus side, they will normally hand over a hiker's parcel anytime they are open, usually seven days a week. And this is a big plus. On the minus side, they can rarely handle outgoing packages or mail. Since these resorts or stores tend to be fairly remote, they are out of range of the postal delivery service. Instead they must send an employee into town to the post office there. As such, they usually prefer that you send your box to them via United Parcel Service. UPS will deliver the packages to their door, whereas the Postal Service delivers only to their nearest post office. If sending a box via UPS, you may save money if you let the clerk know that the package is headed to a commercial address rather than a residential one.

Be aware that handling dozens of hikers' boxes is a big job for the people running the more heavily used resupply stations. Naturally, some of the private concerns charge handling fees. Those that do not are acting out of generosity. Either way, it is always a good idea to express one's appreciation for their services. Without them, our journeys would be far more difficult, if not impossible.

Selecting resupply stations

To determine the various resupply stations available along your intended route, your first step is to study a relevant guide book. Often they will list towns or resorts near the trail. In addition, examine the appropriate maps, starting with a state highway map for an overview of the area. Also, you might contact other hikers who have traveled the same route, and ask them for information about resupply stations and services.

Depending on the trail and the remoteness of the region it passes through, you might have to walk a considerable distance between resupplies. Jenny and I have hiked a number of 200-mile stretches between resupply stations. Along the CDT we once hiked a 300-mile stretch along the Idaho-Montana border, bypassing one far-off-trail possibility. On the other hand, in some cases you might find resupply stations so numerous and close together that you could skip a few in order to save the off-trail time and expense. This is what trip planning is all about, and in many ways it can be a challenge in its own right. The idea is to plan ahead so well that you encounter the minimum of hassles during the journey.

Once you have located the stations and selected them as pertinent to your trip, contact each one and ask whether they will accept and hold your supply parcel (except in the case of post offices, which surely will). And if so, then what are their hours and fees. Ask how far in advance they recommend you send your package, and find out whether they have any restrictions or other requirements. Once they have responded, you can plan your itinerary and start packing your supplies.

The spreadsheet itinerary

A trip itinerary will help you determine what supplies to send where, and when. A computer spreadsheet can greatly facilitate this, or you can simply tabulate your plans with pencil and paper. Either way, begin with the trail miles between each of your chosen resupply stations. If this information is not given in the appropriate guide books, then you can measure it on your maps. Enter this mileage data into your spreadsheet itinerary. For example, your list will show Station A, then x miles to Station B, then x miles to Station C, and so forth.

Next, estimate the number of hiking days between each station. To do this, divide the between-station trail miles by your estimated daily mileage. For example, if Station A and Station B are 100 miles apart, and you plan to hike 20 miles a day, then you would cover the distance in 5 days. This tells you that you need to place five days worth of food and provisions in the resupply box going to Station A.

Obviously, a higher daily mileage will reduce the amount of food you will need to carry between resupply stations, and therefore it will lighten your pack. If the trail is extremely long and the hiking season comparatively short, then a higher daily mileage is beneficial and perhaps even necessary. But on shorter journeys, when you might be more interested in exploring, climbing peaks, or relaxing around camp, the daily mileage may not be so important. Whatever the case, simply plan that into your spreadsheet by adjusting your daily mileage figures.

Estimating layover days

When reaching a resupply station you may want to spend a bit of time there, showering, laundering clothes, and enjoying a couple of restaurant meals. So for the most accurate plan, you would account for this layover time. In terms of the spreadsheet itinerary, the moment you leave the trail to head for a station you are effectively beginning a "layover." If you plan on backtracking to the trail, rather than short-cutting ahead, then while hiking out to the station, and hiking back to it, you are not gaining trail mileage. Technically then, if you spend half a day walking or hitchhiking out, and the same time returning to the trail, you are expending one full layover day. How long you spend off the trail is up to you; what matters is that you figure this into your itinerary.

Let's say that you plan to start hiking on Day 1, and that you will hike for five days and arrive at Station A in the evening of Day 5. You plan to spend that night there, at Station A, and you plan to spend the next day and night there as well. This means that you would depart Station A the morning of Day 7. The idea is to specify this in your spreadsheet, detailing not only your hiking time but your layover time as well.

This type of spreadsheet is simple to create, and it should work for any trail. Engineering types can take the process further by formulating various mathematical algorithms, and programming them as modules in the spreadsheets. This helps estimate our arrival at the resupply stations more accurately.

With your spreadsheet information in hand, it's time to fill your resupply boxes with food, camera film and other supplies for each trail segment.

Preparing the resupply parcels

Once you have determined the number of resupply stations you will use, you know how many shipping boxes you will need. You could buy cardboard boxes commercially, but usually you can find equally suitable boxes salvaged from recycling bins. Check behind the stores in your area, or ask store managers for their discarded boxes. Bookstores often have particularly strong and durable boxes. Keep in mind that resupply parcels are subject to rough handling en route to their destinations. And unfortunately, paying extra for "Special Handling" is unlikely to help. So be sure to use sturdy boxes. Double-tape all the joints, including those across the tops and the bottoms, and carefully remove any and all previous address labels, to reduce the chances of the box going to the wrong place.

Hopefully by this point in your preparations, your housemates will be enthusiastic about your upcoming trip, and they will not mind the many boxes and sacks of food taking up floor space. If you can appropriate one corner of a room for your preparations, then your line of boxes can begin there. If your journey will be long, then so will your line of boxes. In fact they may extend the full length of one wall, head out the doorway and run part way along a wall of an adjacent room. Onto each box tape a temporary label specifying its destination. According to your itinerary, fill each box with its designated number of days' supplies. These supplies would include food (both for meals during the hiking and possibly for eating at that particular resupply station), camera film for the next section of trail, processing mailers for film shot during the previous section, the appropriate section the guide book (cut from the book and rebound into the appropriate trail segments using staples and adhesive tape), any additional maps, journal paper, flashlight batteries, first aid items, and any replacement or additional articles of clothing and footwear. If the parcel weighs more than fifty pounds, (for example if you are boxing up supplies for two or more people) then you would repackage it into two smaller boxes.

Other than potatoes, be careful about adding fresh produce. As it rots it gives off a terribly foul odor that can spoil much of the box's contents, as well as relations with the resupply station managers. Be careful, too, about how you pack your boxes. A mistake that I made only once was to pack soap next to food. The essence of soap permeated out of its bag and into those of its neighbors. The resulting soap-flavored corn chips had little to recommend them.

The shipping label

Be sure to write your expected date of arrival on the shipping label. This helps station managers organize their parcels. And in the unlikely event of a missing hiker, it could provide useful information. Above all, write legibly. And do not forget to include a return address on every package.

If the box contains supplies for two or more hikers, then the shipping label should include all names, rather than only one person in the group. One person might reach the supply station well ahead of the others. Or a person in the group might be elected to detour to the station to collect the parcel. Or, as sometimes happens, someone might drop out. Whatever the case, postal regulations forbid handing over a box to someone whose name is not on the address label. Regulations also require that you show picture identification when collecting your parcels, so be sure to carry your driver's license or other form of picture ID. And for the same reason,

```
┌─────────────────────────────────────────────────┐
│        John Doe                                   │
│ From:  1234 A. Street                             │
│        Histown, NY 01100                          │
├─────────────────────────────────────────────────┤
│                                                   │
│        JOHN Q. DOE C/O General Delivery           │
│ To:    Steamboat Springs, CO 80477                │
│                                                   │
├─────────────────────────────────────────────────┤
│ PLEASE HOLD FOR CDT HIKER                         │
│ ESTIMATED PICK-UP DATE: _____                    │
└─────────────────────────────────────────────────┘
```

the postal service recommends you use your real name on the shipping label, rather than a trail name.

Mailing the parcels

Most distance hikers enlist the services of a relative or close friend, who "volunteers" to mail the resupply parcels according to schedule. Mailing them all at once might seem like a good idea, but postal regulations state that parcels sent to a General Delivery address (the usual method for hiker's resupply boxes) must be returned if not picked up within four weeks. In more realistic terms, if your box has been in residence for more than two or three weeks, the station manager may be less congenial toward you, since they are usually cramped for storage space.

Leave a copy of your shipping schedule with your home-base person, and carry a copy for your own reference as well. And once on journey, consider telephoning home-base occasionally to relate news of your progress, to adjust the shipping schedule if necessary, and most importantly to encourage your helper and express your ongoing appreciation. Theirs is a lackluster job, driving repeatedly to the post office or UPS center, lugging ponderous boxes inside, and standing in line with them. But the arrangement has decided advantages for you, the hiker. One is that you can leave the boxes open so that your helper can add things prior to sending them. These might include home-baked goodies, fresh potatoes, and any items of clothing or equipment that you might request by telephone.

During the course of the summer, should you change your mind about continuing the trek, do not forget to arrange for your parcels to be returned. If you sent your boxes First Class, then they will be returned without extra charge. If you sent them Third Class, then they will be sent back with postage due. In this case, you can save money by using "Change of Address" forms. Stop by your local post office and ask for a set of these forms. Fill one out and send it along with each request that you mail to a postal-type resupply station for the return of your parcel. The private, parcel-holding establishments work differently. These you would need to call or write, telling them of your wishes. And you would of course send them any money required for holding the parcels in addition to the return postage.

Method of shipment

Over long distances, the difference in cost between First Class (Priority) and Third Class (Parcel Post) is negligible. And Third Class can be quite slow.

Should you find yourself telephoning home from a resupply station, requesting some item be sent to your next resupply station, ask your home-base helper to send it First Class. If you need something there at your present location, have it sent Express Mail. Express Mail postage is more expensive, but in the long run it can save you money. This is money you would otherwise spend in town while waiting the extra three or four days for a First Class parcel to arrive. And by minimizing your time spent in town, the Express option can also help preserve your journey's focus. If you are at a resort that lacks postal services, you might consider UPS Second Day or Next Day delivery, or perhaps even Federal Express Overnight. Check with the resort's management, as they will know the ins and outs of deliveries to their location. The best approach, however, is to plan ahead and include all the needed items in your resupply parcels.

The return parcel

At many of your resupply stations you might want to send items back home, items in your pack that you have deemed unnecessary, items from your resupply parcel that you do not need, journal pages from the previous section's hike, and so forth. The best way to facilitate this is to include a shipping label and a small roll of boxing tape in each resupply parcel. To fashion a small roll of tape, simply wrap a long length of tape around a cylindrical object—such as the cardboard insert from a roll of paper towel or toilet paper. There at the station you can recycle your resupply box by cutting it down to the appropriate size for the items you wish to send home. After filling this modified box with the unneeded items, tape it closed, remove the old label, tape on the new shipping label, and mail the parcel home.

The drift box

On our longer hikes, Jenny and I often use what we refer to as a "drift box," or "running resupply box." This is a small parcel that we send ahead rather than home. It contains items that will probably be needed later, but not presently. These might include spare shoes and fresh insoles, extra socks, a spare water filter cartridge, an extra camera battery, a small whetstone, a utility knife with disposable blades, a tube of seam-sealing compound, a spare spoon, an extra sweater, and a roll of boxing tape. The drift box gives us occasional access to these items without having to carry them. We send it First Class to a station approximately two weeks ahead. And we are careful to write forwarding instructions beneath the mailing address, in case the parcel is delayed and we reach the station first. We also keep with us an itemized list of the drift box's contents, along with such information as the date we mailed it, and where we mailed it to. This helps us remember what we sent where. Coming into a resupply station, it is always nice to know what supplies should be waiting. Before you send your drift box ahead, make sure that the resupply station can handle both incoming and outgoing parcels. To send a drift box to a station that cannot send parcels out, is to be stuck with it.

If you arrive at a station and decide not to open your drift box, but to send it to the next station, then the postmaster may or may not charge you the forwarding postage. Domestic Mail Manual, Section F020.3.3 states that if you pay for First Class postage, then you may forward the parcel or return to sender with no extra cost, if the parcel remains unopened. However, this rule was not intended for hikers with drift boxes sending things repeatedly ahead. So it is the postmaster's prerogative whether or not he or she wants to charge you extra for the forwarding.

Hikers lacking a home base

Hikers visiting from other countries, and those without a home-base helper, could use either of the following two methods for resupplying:

1) Take the parcels en masse to a professional mail forwarding ser-

vice. Be sure they understand your plans and your dependency on those parcels. Also, leave with them your mailing schedule. I have used mail forwarding services twice. The first time was a disaster—the proprietor was so disorganized that I had to return to the office, collect my parcels and mail them to a friend who agreed to handle them. The second service, in a different state and year, was a resounding success. So if you decide to use a mail forwarding service, select it with great care and plan for contingencies.

2) The second method is more complicated, but it gives you better control. The variations are practically unlimited, but the general plan is this: Every six weeks, head out to a town and buy food for the next six weeks. Load your pack with a two-week supply. Send a second two-week supply two weeks ahead. And send a third two-week supply four weeks ahead.

You can shorten the two-week interval by loading two or three larger drift boxes with more than ample supplies, and then leap-frogging them ahead. Remember, too, that certain resupply stations may have at least a modest selection of groceries. You could use these opportunities to stockpile extra food for the next section of trail, or for sending ahead to other stations.

Layover day philosophy

When it comes to making the most of the summer's journey, each hiker will have his or her preferences. Some like to spend a fair amount of time in the towns, sampling the culture, socializing with other hikers, and relaxing in the company of services such as restaurants, libraries and hostels. Others prefer to minimize the distractions of society, and spend most of their time in the woods.

Depending on how far away from home you have traveled, and how new you are to the region, you might find the cultural differences quite interesting. The locals are often eager to talk about the town's history and some of its finer points. The town itself might have historic buildings or monuments, or sites that would be well worth a visit.

One problem with layover time is that it can be extremely volatile. On the trail the clock seems to run at its normal rate, but at the resupplies it races. Hours and even days can evaporate at these stops.

Another problem is that even several extra days of layover time will do little to restore your vigor. You haul into a resupply town feeling pretty beat, and after three to five days of rest you set off again—only to feel that same old deep-seated fatigue creeping back into your bones within the first hour of hiking. The solution to this is simple. Condition yourself properly ahead of time, and carry an efficient, lightweight pack. While on the trail be sure to eat nutritiously, drink plenty of water, and very importantly, stay off your feet while at camp. These measures can virtually eliminate your need for excessive layover days.

When detouring out to a "trail town" or resort, you might consider yourself an emissary of the trail, of sorts, and a representative of the hiking community at large. Some of the townsfolk and tourists may not be impressed by your hiking adventure, and might even view you with suspicion. But others might find your endeavor intriguing. And although their questions can sometimes seem a little ignorant, and you might tire of politely answering the same ones over and over again, remember that any positive feelings you can engender on behalf of the trail and its hikers will be of great benefit.

Minimum impact resupplying

Life in the wilds is largely free of urban responsibilities, so of course after we have been out there a while, we tend to forgo some of the social refinements. Appearances aside, we may fail to realize how strong our body odor can be, and how offensive it can be to the townsfolk. This suggests the importance of bathing in the wilds, ahead of time using the dundo method and a bit of soap. Also we could wash a shirt. And once in town, we would head straight for the laundromat and showers.

Scenes of hiker "anarchy" are best avoided—at city parks, laundromats, and in front of the post offices on Main Street—with dirty clothes and grimy gear strewn everywhere about. Always be considerate of the townsfolk, and practice minimum impact resupplying.

Partners

Friends are as companions on a journey
who ought to aid each other to persevere
in the road to a happier life.

— Pythagoras

Hikers traveling solo have successfully completed every long distance trail in America. And with the right attitude and sufficient experience, most of us could do likewise. Going alone offers the ultimate in freedom and spontaneity. But hiking solo does not mean hiking in solitary confinement. At least along the more popular trails, solo hikers meet other hikers along the way. Sometimes they may travel together a ways, and if the arrangement is amenable then a loose partnership can form. Or the solo hiker might simply stop and talk with fellow hikers for a few minutes. And of course solo hikers meet townspeople when detouring from the trail to collect their resupplies, which on the more popular routes is typically every three to five days.

Solo hiking allows for a greater sense of independence. As hiker Fred Coleman notes, "Those of us who go alone do so of necessity, or perhaps because we enjoy the solitary pleasures of thinking our own thoughts, adjusting to our own schedules and needs, and having total, silent connection with the nature which surrounds us. The price we pay is a slightly heavier pack and perhaps an additional element of risk. But hiking alone also carries with it more excitement and less adjustment to the moods and needs of others."

Over the years I have met a great many solo hikers, and have gone solo myself a number of times. There is virtue in solitude, but companionship is also something we all seek at some time or another. In fact, the majority of hikers I have met have been in various partnerships.

Partnership dynamics

Good hiking partnerships are mutually beneficial. Each member contributes to the experience of others, and also benefits from the others. Partners share in the decision making and lend each other encouragement. They share their thoughts, feelings, fears and hopes. A good partnership leads to a deeper knowledge of oneself, and of one's companions, as well as a better understanding of the journey as a whole, its hardships and triumphs, its daily delights.

A partnership is a dynamic team working together, tramping out the many miles and bringing the distant goal slowly to fruition. Granted, "a chain is only as strong as its weakest link," and each individual member must come fully prepared with the necessary skills and gear, but partnerships can help ensure that a little extra guidance or help is available when needed.

Hiking the trails and exploring the wilds with a friend is a wonderful way to share in the beauties, the mysteries, and the joys of the natural world. A good hiking partner can be a true blessing. But how to find such a partner, and what are the pitfalls?

Finding a hiking partner

My dictionary defines the word "partnership" as "a relationship between individuals or groups that is characterized by mutual cooperation and responsibility, for the achievement of a specified goal." The "achievement of a specified goal" is the key here. Prospective partners must understand what each other's objectives are, and at the same time they must allow for personal differences in style and character. So before you start looking for a suitable partner, you might think about what qualities you are looking for, and just as importantly, what qualities you have to offer.

Are you willing to make the compromises necessary to accommodate another hiker in your plans? Are you a natural leader or a natural follower? Which is more important to you, the goal or the relationship? Along the way, should your partner decide to quit the hike, would you be prepared to continue alone?

As you search for a partner, whether it be by browsing the Internet, perusing hiking group newsletters, or advertising in hiking-related publications, remember that enthusiasm is your best asset. People are attracted to others with genuine plans of action. Before actually teaming up, get to know the other person by at least swapping pictures and talking on the telephone. Do not limit yourself to finding someone who fits a certain mold or ideal. I have seen successful partnerships between hikers of considerable differences in age, experience and background. The hiking, and the distant goal, can often be all the common ground you need.

The inability to locate a suitable partner is no reason for dismay. Long distance hiking is becoming increasingly popular, and the chances of meeting other hikers in the same predicament, once you have begun, are quite good—at least along the more popular trails. Many lasting partnerships have formed in this way. So do not be reluctant to start out on your own. Action is an excellent catalyst.

The less popular trails may yield no likely partners, let alone much humanity. So if locating a partner is a high priority, stick with the more popular trails. The most popular long-distance trail (and for very good reason) is the Appalachian Trail. Your chances of finding partners for that trail, either before or during the hike, are excellent. Contact the friendly folks at the Appalachian Trail Conference (P.O. Box 807, Harpers Ferry, WV 25425-0807; 304-535-6331). Subscribe to their newsletter, and consider placing an ad in the "Public Notices" section.

Many partnerships have split, due to incompatibilities that were not apparent until put to the test. But do not lose heart if your partnership dissolves somewhere along the way. You may find yourself hiking solo for a time, but the possibility of meeting others will always exist.

Close friends as hiking partners

If you and a long-time friend plan to spend the summer on the trail, consider yourself fortunate. Both of you are probably aware of each other's strengths and weaknesses, and with some luck and a little effort you should be able to forge a favorable hiking partnership. Try to stay focused on your common interests, and the likable traits of one another. These are probably what inspired the friendship in the first place, and they will help keep it strong. And as La Bruyere reminds us: "Two persons cannot long be friends if they cannot forgive each other's little failings."

Along these lines, be careful about trying to convince a good friend to join you on a long hike, thinking that friendship alone will produce a workable hiking partnership. Success will require that both of you have that internal fire, the lofty dream and the unwavering focus on the distant goal. Otherwise, the first set of hardships could extinguish your friend's weak flame. This happens with some regularity: differences in focus and intent surface, and the journey's stresses and pressures lead to a parting of ways. Yet this is no universal rule; many times the journey forges even stronger and more lasting friendships.

Spouses as partners

Jenny and I always enjoy meeting other couples on the trail, and one summer we ran into Garrett and Leisha Holmes. They were recently married, and their summer's journey on the Pacific Crest Trail through Oregon and Washington was their honeymoon. At the conclusion of their journey they gave this advice: "If you have a new spouse or a long-term friend, go on a long distance hike with them! Our relationship's strength grew tremendously during our trip. Together we endured snow, rain, sleet, bugs, forest fires, and all the "ups and downs" a trail like the PCT can dish out. When the going was exceptionally tough due to minor injuries or other "inconveniences" we could always hold hands and know that with each other and God's help we would persevere. And we did!"

Spouses can make excellent hiking partners. Granted, some hikers enjoy getting away from their "significant other" on occasion, but as Garrett and Leisha pointed out, the rigors of the trail can do much to strengthen the bond, as mates learn to work together, solve the problems, and go the distance. Sharing the beauties of wilderness trekking with the one you love can be a real joy. And in fact, long distance hiking is usually so all-encompassing that the two of you are actually sharing that part of your lives.

More commonly, though, one mate enjoys hiking while the other views it with certain misgivings. Such trepidation is sometimes based on past outings that may have been less than pleasant. The fact is, most genuinely skilled outdoors-people can easily teach beginners how to enjoy hiking and camping, by ensuring that the experiences will be pleasant. This is a skill, and one that reflects competence in the wilderness setting. The person with this skill will foresee and avoid any unpleasant incidents. For example, he or she will keep from exhausting the partner with a heavy load and a fast pace. This person will also see to it that the partner does not become drenched inside an improperly pitched tent during an unexpected downpour. At the same time, the skilled outdoors person places no expectations on someone of lesser skill. The key is to lend gentle encouragement while extending illimitable patience. Ignore the inevitable mistakes, and give recognition to the many accomplishments.

Remember that partnering itself is a skill, and that the arrangement must be both give and take. And one of the best places to develop this skill is during training hikes and the preliminary shorter outings.

Pigs in a poke

If you have arranged a partnership with someone whose hiking plans align with your own, but whom you have not met in person, the chances of this working out can be quite good. The fact that both of you want to hike the same trail suggests important commonalties. Still, you might be cautious about sharing equipment in order to save weight. Should differences arise a few days or weeks into the journey, both of you would need sufficient gear to carry on independently. Give yourselves several hundred trail miles together before you start sending home redundant gear.

Shared gear

What items of gear partners can share depends on the nature of the partnership, and on the skills of each person. The following is a list of the gear that Jenny and I share. Hopefully this will provide some kind of basis for your planning. Refer to the gearlists (near the end of the book) for our full inventory.

> Tarp, groundsheet, quilt; stove, fuel, lighter and cookpot; pocket knife, compass, first aid (including aspirin and vitamins), foot care, sewing and medical kits, emergency fire starting kit, eyeglasses cleaning kit and No-Fog cloth, comb, can opener, soap, insect repellent, sunscreen, camera, film, spare battery, camera cleaning kit, wristwatch, water bags, water scoop and trough.

Staying together

While instructing wilderness programs in the 1970's, one of my responsibilities was to keep my group of ten students together. Naturally, some of them preferred to hike fast, and some slow. Losing someone, either ahead or behind, was a constant concern, especially since trails have a way of branching and branching again. Losing someone was very rare, but when it happened it constituted a major disruptive event. All course activities had to suspend while we searched, and this was a good way to lose someone else. So although it may seem overly regimented, I had to teach the students to stay together from day one.

To do this, I introduced them to the techniques of glacier travel, where everyone ties to a climbing rope for safety, spacing themselves at regular intervals. Roped-together hiking sounds simple enough, but actually it emphasizes the differences in everyone's hiking style and amplifies those differences all out of proportion. Choreographed hiking is not ingrained in anyone, especially with ten different people from ten different parts of the country pulling in ten different directions. But the students soon learned that if they were to make any forward progress at all with this method, they had to cooperate. What this accomplished was quite amazing. It turned each person's attention to his or her fellow classmates, and brought him or her face to face with everyone's differences. A mere fifteen minutes of hiking this way illustrated the concept of individual compromise for the benefit of the group; that a group travels at a different speed than the majority of its individuals might prefer.

Hiking partners can, and do, experience the same difficulties of staying together. Everyone tends to have their own unique hiking pace and traveling style. As often happens, the partnership may split during the day and reform again each evening at camp. Outwardly, this system might seem to afford everyone the needed freedom. But it can also greatly increase the chances of you not finding each other that evening.

In the late 1970's I was sea kayaking with two friends along the coast of Baja, Mexico. Late one afternoon two of us stopped for spearfishing, but our third partner decided to press on to camp. We reconfirmed where that camp would be—on a prominent finger of land five miles ahead. The two of us arrived there after dark, but could not find our third partner. We had specified a contingency plan, so we all knew where our next camp would be—50 miles farther along. And we all understood that if we did not meet at that second camp, then we would wait one full day for any stragglers. The two of us paddled the 50 mile stretch, glad that from the start we had ensured that each person carried his share of the food and community gear. Still our friend did not show up, so we waited at that second camp throughout the following day, again to no avail. Considering that our misplaced partner was the independent sort, we decided that rather than return to look for him, we would continue to the next town, five days ahead. Four days later we were resting ashore when our friend came paddling past. After a happy reunion we compared notes, and discovered that we had camped nearly together on the first finger of land, he on one side and we on the other; that all three of us had waited the full day within a quarter mile of each other. And remarkably, we had been leap-frogging all the way along the coast without seeing each other.

This scenario can happen almost anywhere, not just in kayaks along a coastline where visibility is practically unlimited. So whether you and your partners plan to hike together or not, realize that you may lose track of one another. Before starting each day, make sure that everyone knows the day's objectives. If actually planning to lose sight of each other, agree on a place and time to regroup. Specify the intended location of that evening's meal-stop or camp. And remind each other what to do if some-one does not show up. Will you wait? And for how long? Or will you continue ahead to your next resupply point? As a contingency, always make sure that each person has the resources (food, equipment, map, etc.) and the wherewithal to carry on alone.

─────────────

Jenny and I stay close together when on journey. The only exception is when one of us detours into "the bushes." And even then the other will continue ahead no more than a hundred yards before stopping alongside the trail and waiting. We know that the chances of losing each other are real, particularly on our more remote ventures. And we consider the consequences far worse than any inconveniences caused by staying to-gether. And besides, we enjoy each other's company.

Finishing the PCT in 1991

Trail Shock

For you never can tell
if it's heaven or hell,
And I'm taking the trail on trust;
But I haven't a doubt
that my soul will leap out
On its Wan-der-lust.

— *Robert Service*

Metamorphosis

Long-distance hikers first starting out on their journeys tend to undergo a number of abrupt changes in lifestyle. Their exertion levels skyrocket, launching their nutritional needs practically into orbit. Yet the types of foods they eat often default to the traditional trail-foods variety, causing their nutritional intake to plunge. The excitement of having finally begun the trek, coupled with the anxieties of confronting the great unknown, tends to suppress the appetite. So rather than eat greater portions of higher quality foods to satisfy their soaring needs for energy and nutrition, they tend to eat less food of lower quality.

Water plays another key role. Full of enthusiasm and ambition, these hikers may travel at an uncontrolled pace for the first few days, despite their loads and any steep hills and mountains along the way. The overexertion causes them to sweat, often profusely, and soon they become dehydrated, often very deeply. Water sources may be somewhat sparse, the job of treating the water in the quantities they need might be too bothersome, and their suspicions about the quality of the water may discourage their drinking much. And during those first few days, the trail may lead to higher elevations, where the atmosphere may be a little thinner than what the hikers are used to. This further upsets their fluid balances by increasing the rate of sensible and insensible perspiration.

Blend in the preexisting fatigue of hectic, last-minute preparations, the weariness of traveling from home to trail, the exhaustion of the overly rambunctious hiking with an assortment of stiff, aching muscles, and maybe a growing collection of blisters, and the result, as many have discovered, is the standard early-trip breakdown. One moment things seem only miserable; the next moment the journey loses every hint of its former luster, and the prospects of continuing can seem utterly impossible. At this point depression sets in, as the mind struggles to accept the new reality of "failure" and its myriad and practically unthinkable consequences.

I call this "trail shock," and recommend that every prospective long-distance hiker plan for it. Basically, the newer the person is to distance hiking, and the newer to the particular environment, the sooner trail shock may hit. And the more out-of-shape, and the more overly ambitious, the harder it will hit. But take heart. Trail shock is not a sign of failure but of adaptation. In every likelihood the journey is not at risk; the hiker is merely going at it too hard. The solution is to throttle back for the initial few weeks, and allow both body and mind the time they need for making the necessary adjustments.

Jenny and I have experienced trail shock in the initial stages of all our long journeys, to greater or lesser degrees. When it happened on our first two treks we suffered the usual misgivings and despondency, but after that we learned to recognize trail shock for what it was, and were able to minimize it. We did this by taking things easy during the first few weeks of the journeys, by paying very careful attention to our nutrition and fluid intake, and by keeping our minds focused on the positive aspects all around us.

A variation of trail shock can strike at other times during a long hike. In these instances it is not so much the body trying to adapt to a new lifestyle, but the mind attempting to deal with a goal that it perceives as impossibly distant. Here again, proper nutrition and adequate intake of water play key roles in preventing—and treating—these little hit-the-wall type burn-outs. If all else fails, give yourself a few days' "vacation" from the trail. These will in every likelihood refresh body and soul, and can usually bring the original goal back into focus.

Hiking Enjoyment

You Can't Afford the Luxury of a Negative Thought

— Book title by Peter McWilliams

"We cannot control the wind but we can adjust the sails"

While planning our outings we have much to consider: Training, a practicable diet, packweight reduction and efficient footwear, matters of logistics and itinerary—along with the many other subjects detailed in this book. It all leads to the ultimate goal of spending more time in the wilds, learning what we can from nature, and finding our path to that closer wilderness connection. And of course we hope that these outings will be filled with enjoyment. To that end I would like to pass along a few ideas garnered from my own experience.

———

The concept of hiking enjoyment would seem, at first glance, to be rather cut-and-dry. You are either having a good time or you are not, depending on the weather, scenery, your encounters with other hikers and townspeople, and a multitude of other externals. You cannot control most of these circumstances, but you can adjust the way you internalize them.

When looked at in this way, we realize that hiking enjoyment is a skill—not a physical motor skill, but an emotional one. And as with any skill, it has to be learned—and then practiced.

In a way this is like riding a bicycle. Before you can ride a bike, it needs to be in good condition. The tires must be properly inflated, the bearings well lubricated, and so forth. If these conditions are not met, then you will not be riding far. And so it is with your brain. If it is not in good working order, due to poor nutritional intake, then your mind will be far less able to interpret things in positive ways.

Once the brain is properly nourished—and this can be a major challenge for some people—it becomes more capable of generating happiness and the feelings of well being. But only that: capable. These positive emotions will not automatically blossom, but at least you can start fostering them.

Water off a duck's back

One major stumbling block to happiness in wilderness hiking has to do with a person's methods of processing "negative" externals.

Let's go back to the city for a moment, and imagine that you are driving along a highway during rush hour, and suddenly someone cuts you off. One reaction is to get angry, shake a fist perhaps, and start driving more aggressively yourself. In so doing you send the whole incident cascading along. Or, you could shrug off the matter like water off a duck's back. Simply let it go. With no effort at all you can ignore the negative impulse and hang on to your happiness.

The same principle holds true in the wilds. The natural world is full of situations and circumstances that could strike you as negative, if that is how you decide to interpret them.

Consider the rain. We know that rain is essential for the well being of our planet. Indeed, the more we ponder the miracle of water, life-blood of the earth and sustainer of animal and plant, bird and fish, the more we may appreciate how precious every drop of rain is. Yet what is our usual reaction when we are out hiking and rain begins to fall? We may feel annoyed, as though it is ruining our day. Or we may hunker down and plod miserably ahead, wishing the rain would stop. Do such attitudes banish the rain? Or do they merely frustrate and weaken us? Does the rain take away the beauties of the natural world, or do our reactions to it take away our enjoyment?

With the right gear (umbrella for rain, shell clothing for bugs, etc) and particularly with a focus on the positive aspects of whatever circumstances or obstacles confront us, we do not have to impose our will on them, or feel let down when they exhibit a will of their own. And we could take this a step further. The umbrella and protective garments are merely tools to help us shift our mental gears.

Positive by choice

I once met a fellow who quit his thru-hike because of brush growing on the trail. It peeved him that much. Brush growing on the trail is a simple fact of life in many regions, on par with mosquitoes and rain. It is not a genuine barricade to progress, but only a minor inconvenience. Annoying or discouraging external circumstances like this call for us to let go of our unrealistic expectations—in this case, the expectation that the trail should be perfectly groomed.

Until we learn to shrug off such externals, they have a way of returning to challenge us time and again. In that respect they are our teachers. Only after we have taken away their power—water-off-a-duck's-back style—will they leave us alone. Every time that hiker saw a bush growing on the trail, it tested him. He reacted by wrestling with the torment. A person can never win such battles. In the end, this fellow's emotions overwhelmed him and sent him home.

In a sense our minds are like radios. When they start playing unpleasant music we can change the station. Assuming we are reasonably well nourished, we do not have to entertain negative thoughts. Such thoughts can be especially compounding to long-distance hikers, who have so much time to think.

Quicksand

We all experience negative thoughts at various times, and to various degrees. And although the idea of banishing them by "changing the channel" sounds simple enough, for many it is not so easily accomplished, at least with consistency. How, then, can we free ourselves of wasteful negativity while tapping into the positive energy all around us?

Jenny and I were hiking cross-country through Yellowstone National Park when we came upon a beautiful meadow. This meadow was lush and green, and far off the beaten track. Nearby flowed a small creek, and as we approached, the ground beneath our feet began to quiver ominously, as though the grass was undermined with quicksand. And sure enough, the minute we stopped walking, our feet began to sink in. With the ground oozing and sucking at our shoes, we struggled to pull them free. As we retreated we found that as long as we kept moving, all went well; but every time we paused, down into the bog again our feet would start to sink.

Pulling our thoughts free of the bogs of negativity can sometimes be a struggle. And just because we have extracted a foot once, that does not mean we have solved the problem. It has to be a conscious and ongoing process, until we can eventually reach firm ground.

Vis medicatrix naturae

(wes med-i-KA-trix na-TU-ri)

The healing power of nature

One way to reach firm, positive ground is to keep the mind on the present moment. When we do that, we may discover that nature can be the cure to the common negative mindset. Even the smallest stimuli such as the singing of a bird or the babbling of a brook can open positive mental channelways, and allow life's simple but often profound pleasures to come flooding in.

When the mind does not travel with the body, it can easily wander off course and into the bogs. So whenever possible, keep your senses open to your surroundings, and tuned to the enlivening sights, sounds and lessons. Learn to live in the moment.

As Thoreau expressed so simply: "nature is our medicine."

═══════════

In his book *Flow, The Psychology of Optimal Experience*, Mihaly Csikszentmihalyi (pronounced CHICK-sent-me-high-lee) details his "...principles to transform boring and meaningless lives into ones full of enjoyment." Happiness, he says, does not just happen, nor is it the result of money, power, good fortune or chance. Instead, happiness must be cultivated from within. And he goes on to say that "the best moments usually occur when the body or mind is stretched to its limits in a voluntary effort to accomplish something difficult or worthwhile."

Happiness in the wilderness experience does not just happen either. Nor is it the result of high-tech equipment, stunning scenery, or favorable weather. Yes, nature has the capacity to enrich our lives, but only the capacity. We ourselves must create any meaningful experiences—and enjoyment—from within.

PCT Thru-hikers; photo by Jenny

The Power of Focus

The secret of happiness is freedom,
and the secret of freedom, courage.

— *Thucydies (B.C. 460-400)*

A study of successful adventurers past and present will reveal that the paramount ingredient for success is focus. Focus promotes determination and strength, but paradoxically it is extremely fragile. It has to be nurtured and guarded carefully.

———————

Like happiness, focus comes from within. And the best time to start developing a sense of focus is in the planning stages of the trek. The more focused you are on your preparations, the more capable you will be once you hit the trail, and the better your chances of achieving your distant goal.

On a particular pre-hike training day you might find the weather not particularly suitable. But rather than let the weather dampen your focus, gather your resolve, think about that distant trail, and head out the door. While shopping for trail food you might be tempted by certain types that you know are less than nourishing, that will not help you along the trail. Focus on your goal and give that junk food a miss.

During your actual wilderness journey, beware of distractions that can drain your resolve. For example, the list of "adversities" is practically endless (bugs, rain, brush on the trail) and any one of these can dishearten you, but only if you let it. Turn the adversities around and look for their salient features. Plan ahead for the inevitable obstacles with proper clothing and gear, and project your consciousness through any distractions.

Remember that where the mind leads, the body follows. Rather than focus on fatigue, focus instead on endurance and strength. And take a critical look at what types of food you are eating and how much water you are drinking. A better diet and more water intake can make you vastly more energetic.

Should body and mind start to grow weary of trail life, you may lose focus and let go of your goal. The mind may start to pester you with thoughts of quitting. "Why should I keep going if I'm not having any fun and enjoying myself?" you may ask yourself. For after all, it's the journey, not the destination that counts. But quitting the journey is not the only way to end unhappiness. In fact, quitting rarely produces the desired results. So rather than letting your focus slip away unchallenged, try to figure out ways to reverse any negative trends. Take a break, seek some interesting diversion. A little variety can often help maintain your focus.

Your goal and focus are linked together. When your focus fades, inevitably the goal will become less important. And without the goal, the journey quickly loses momentum. So to keep your dream alive, live each day to its fullest, and focus your energies on that distant goal.

———————

Remember what you came to the trail for, and what you hope to leave with. Project yourself ahead in time and think about how you would like to look back at the summer's experience—then make it happen now.

Supercharging Mileage

"Come to the edge," he said.
They said, "We are afraid."
"Come to the edge," he said.
They came.
He pushed them…
And they flew.

— *Guillaume Apollinaire*

Hiking greater distances with no extra effort

To this point we have examined ways of reducing the travails of hiking, ways that are applicable to virtually any trail, be it long or short. And while most wilderness enthusiasts are not interested in covering 20 or 30 miles every day, those dreaming of thru-hiking a trail of a thousand miles or more, in a single season, might want to give the matter some thought. So in this chapter I detail a few techniques that can boost mileage. These techniques are not only for thru-hikers; they can help almost anyone heading out for more than a few days.

―――――――

We might imagine that people who hike large daily mileages miss everything along the way. That they are left with nothing but hazy memories of rushed trail experiences. My own thru-hiking has not borne this out. I find that I can connect with the natural world very profoundly while hiking 30-plus miles a day, week after week. At such times the journey tends to expand in many dimensions—outward, inward and upward—as much as it reaches ahead and behind. In addition to my higher mileage trekking

I have been on plenty of trips lasting a week or more while covering very little mileage. My conclusion is that as long as a person is traveling on foot, his or her ability to observe, experience and connect with nature has nothing to do with the number of miles hiked each day.

Avoiding the quagmire

In order for the miles to come easy, we need to take a more critical look at our wants, and distinguish them from our needs. The following scenarios illustrate how strongly such choices in hiking "style" can affect the course of the journey. I am not suggesting that one choice is better than the other, but simply that they produce different results.

More work—fewer miles

Let's imagine that we are planning a wilderness trek, in which we will follow an established trail several hundred miles from one end to the other. Along the way we will detour to a few towns near our route, to replenish food and stove fuel as the journey progresses. And because we have set aside plenty of time for the trip, we are in no hurry. We intend for this hike to be an easy-going vacation.

The trail distance to our first resupply point (Station A) is 48 miles. At a modest pace of 12 miles a day, this initial section will take us four days. Intent on taking our time and enjoying life, we decide to include a considerable quantity of food, along with a few niceties such as a thick paperback and a backgammon set. However, our existing backpack would be crammed with all this, so we decide to buy a larger one.

While carrying this new and heavier backpack loaded with all these supplies, we will have to exert ourselves, granted. But we will allow ourselves plenty of rests along the way. And we will sleep in late whenever we feel like it. For after all, we are in no hurry. So we might as well plan a fifth day to hike the 48 miles. Of course, in order to accommodate that extra day we will need to pack another day's food and stove fuel. These will increase our load once again; but not to worry: the new backpack has plenty of room. The pack is so large, in fact, that we might as well throw in a frying pan. We will never know it is there because the pack is advertised to carry heavy loads in comfort.

Originally the plan was to take life easy; this hike is supposed to be enjoyable. So maybe we should divide this first trail segment by hiking out to another town for supplies, midway. This will lighten our load by reducing the amount of food and fuel we will have to carry. To reach this intervening town from our trail route, we will have to hike a side trail six miles out. And after an uncertain hitchhike into town, and another one back to the trailhead, we will have to backtrack the six miles to the main trail. So we are adding two more days—one to accommodate the extra hiking and hitching, and the other for relaxing and enjoying town life. Adding these two days to the five, we will now spend seven days reaching our original objective at Station A. But during each of the two segments we need carry only three days of food and fuel. This leaves us plenty of room for extras. Let's bring along a backpacker's chair, and a zoom lens for the SLR. And since we have been wanting to try out that nifty baking device, we can bring a number of special dessert mixes.

I think you can see the trend. As we sink into the planning quagmire, we are turning the trek into an ordeal. Not only are we shrinking our daily mileage capabilities, but in the process we are also imposing heavier loads on ourselves, taken as a whole. All this benefits us nothing in terms of comfort and enjoyment. In short, everything we try to do to make the hike more convenient only compounds the difficulties.

Fortunately, we can reverse this trend with only a minor adjustment in style.

Less work—more miles

Let's go back to the drawing board and re-plan this hike with a fresh approach.

We want to hike the original 48 miles to Station A in 4 days. And it would be nice if we could enjoy the hiking, rather than endure that heavy load and its associated grief. Since we would like to hike the full trail, all several hundred miles of it, we can now see how a bit of discipline would prove beneficial. Originally we had planned to hike 12 miles a day. At a modest pace of 2.75 miles an hour, we would need to hike 4.4 hours each day, not including the rest stops. Surely we can hike more than that. Let's get going an hour earlier. Disciplining ourselves into hiking 5.4 hours each day, and still allowing 8 hours of sleep each night, we leave ourselves 10.6 hours of resting and relaxing every day. So maybe we can hike an additional hour in the afternoon. Assuming we travel at the same 2.75 mph, our daily mileage will jump from 12 miles to 17.6. That extra 2 hours on the trail makes a huge difference. At 17.6 miles a day, we would travel the 48 miles not in 4 days, but in a mere 2.7. We just saved ourselves 1.3 days of hiking. So we can remove that much food and fuel from our load. This reduces its weight by several pounds. And we might as well eliminate a few luxury items from our pack, lightening it even further.

And here is where the "magic" in the more disciplined approach begins to take place. Because our pack is less heavy, we will hike—not faster—but with less fatigue. So in terms of endurance, the reduced packweight offsets the extra time spent hiking. Covering the 17.6 miles a day while carrying a lighter pack, we will arrive at the evening camps no more fatigued than had we hiked only 12 miles while carrying the heavier load. We gain extra mileage at no additional cost in effort.

Let's develop this plan further.

Once we reach Station A, we might decide to send home a few more items that we do not need. Some of these we have not been using at all; others we have been using infrequently and with no real advantage. None of this extra gear is facilitating our trip, so why lug it for nothing, six hours a day, every step of the way? Let's rid ourselves of the spare fleece sweater, the cotton t-shirt worn only at camp, the extra nylon pants, two pairs of the most worn (and dirtiest) socks, the down booties, four pads of the moleskin, the two extra tent stakes, the carabiner dangling affectatiously off the pack, the salt and pepper shakers, the candle lantern (saving a few pieces of one of the candles for emergency fire-starting), and the electronic pedometer.

I am not condemning any of this gear, or those who use it; these are only examples. They do make quite a pile, and ridding our pack of them will make the hiking that much easier. With better maneuverability, we will not have such a hard time tromping through deep snow, climbing over blowdowns, and wading swift creeks. Also with less weight on our back we can move ahead with less strain, meaning that we will be less prone to injury.

As we ponder the pile of things on their way home, we have to admit that they were not helping us enjoy the trip. The pile weighs close to 5 pounds, and if we subtract that from our original load, which let's say was 35 pounds, then we have diminished our burden by about 15%. This weight reduction will enable us to hike an additional 2 miles a day with no extra effort, (see chart in Packweight chapter). And the aesthetics of the journey will increase, as we travel less encumbered.

Our daily mileage is now up to 19.6, and this is without hiking any faster. We still amble along at an easy 2.75 miles an hour.

With the extra 2 miles per day gain, we no longer need as much food to reach our next resupply at Station C. And when we remove that food, we are lightening our pack again, and enabling ourselves to hike a little farther each day—still with no additional effort.

We are making some big gains here, but we are not finished.

We have seen other hikers wearing running shoes, and they seemed to be doing very well in them. At home we wear running shoes for kicking around town, and for the daily jog. Maybe we can hike in them as well. Let's send home our boots in favor of running shoes. The running shoes will allow us to hike—not faster—but with less fatigue. Switching from heavy boots to lightweight running shoes gains us another 7½ miles a day, (see the Footwear chapter) again with no more effort (assuming that we had strengthened our ankles by training in the shoes prior to the hike). Our daily mileage capability has risen to 27 miles. We have more than doubled our original figure, and are now hiking marathon mileages.

And of course, this additional 7½ miles a day allows us to remove even more food and fuel from our pack, lessening its weight further, and increasing once again our mileage capabilities.

Since we are improving our capabilities, we might as well use them to best effect. Let's skip resupply station C altogether and press on to Station D. This will save us from hiking out to Station C, and squandering the time while tending to logistics. And by planning to skip the resupply station, we eliminate the chances of arriving there on a weekend when the post office is closed and our resupply parcel is unavailable. Skipping Station C saves us at least a full day of hassles, maybe two or three. And it saves us the money we would have spent there, and the postage on that resupply box.

In skipping resupply station C and continuing on to D, we will need to include more food. How much depends on the distance between C and D. Let's say that this distance is 67 miles. This may sound like a lot, but at our new rate of travel it is only 2½ days. That many days' food at 2½ pounds per day weighs 6¼ pounds. However, that last day of hiking will be quick and easy, since our pack will be down to its baseline weight, which is not much. And we will not need to carry the final day's dinner, because we would arrive at resupply D in time for a hearty dinner there. So out of our pack comes that dinner.

All said and done, we arrive at station D in good stead, literally weeks ahead of when we would have, had we stuck with our initial quagmire-type plan.

Dividing the day into thirds

Now that we have supercharged our mileage, we need a way to better regulate the day's hiking and let us know how we are doing.

A technique that Jenny and I use, when we want to extend the day's travel, is to divide the day in thirds. For example if we want to hike a 33 mile day, we hike 11 miles in each third. Let's look at how this works.

On reasonably graded trails we tend to hike at 2.75 mph, which is a very moderate pace. Let's say that on average we hike for 45 minutes, then stop for a 15 minute rest break. Nothing difficult about that. Each hour we cover 2 miles. So our *average* pace is 2 mph. We want to hike 11 miles, so this will take 5.5 hours.

We start hiking at 5:30 in the morning, intent on covering the eleven miles by 11:00 that same morning. Then we hike eleven more miles by 4:30 that afternoon, and the final eleven miles by 10:00 pm.

Here is how this works. After studying the map we know about where the 11-mile point is, and the 22-mile point, and the 33-mile point. If we reach the 11-mile point by 11 am, then we know that we are doing well. If we do not reach it in time, then we know that we need to shorten the rest breaks. What usually happens with Jenny and me, though, is that we reach the 11-mile mark an hour early, by 10:00 am. This allows us to cruise through the remainder of the day in an even more relaxed fashion, taking longer rests and stopping more often to chat with other hikers.

So although at first glance this system might seem restrictive, actually it is a great way to help regulate the pace. At the end of the day we have spent 12 hours hiking, and 4½ hours resting along the way. So, yes, the 33 miles may be a considerable distance, but by taking regular and fairly lengthy breaks, we are left with plenty of time to snack and drink water, and cook a meal to maintain the needed energy. The beauty of this system is that virtually any well-trained hiker can take a 15 minute break every hour of the day and still pull off some big miles. The secret is to start early and finish late. We do this comfortably by carrying lightweight gear, wearing running shoes, eating nourishing foods, and staying well hydrated.

The table summarizes the triple-segmented day for various daily mileages, at an *average* hiking rate of 2.0 mph. Select a daily mileage and divide it into thirds. Then divide your day in thirds, and you will be well on your way toward higher mileages.

Daily Mileage	Segment Mileage	MORNING	MIDDAY	EVENING
24	8	6 am - 10 am	10 am - 2 pm	2 pm - 6 pm
27	9	6 am - 10:30	10:30 - 3 pm	3 pm - 7:30
30	10	6 am - 11 am	11 am - 4 pm	4 pm - 9 pm
33	11	5:30 - 11 am	11 am - 4:30	4:30 - 10 pm

Seize the day

A good night's sleep brings the dawn of a new day. The birds bestir themselves at the first hint of daylight, and like them, when distance hiking I like to rise at dawn; the early morning hours are my favorite for hiking. In pilot training we learn to take off from the beginning of the runway. "The runway behind you does you no good," as the flight instructors say. And so it is with the hiker's day.

An early start and a late stop, as we have seen, will help you make the most of your day. And you need to make the most of your rest stops also. You do this by staying off your feet, drinking lots of water, and eating hearty snacks. The higher mileage hiker needs to be careful not to spend too much time standing, for example while talking with other hikers. Not because of the delays, but because of the blood pooling into the legs and feet. If you feel like chatting at some length, then consider declaring a rest stop, taking off your pack, and getting off your feet.

Another technique that can help extend the miles is to use waypoints as springboards. Shelters, creek crossings, lakes, and trail junctions can serve to urge us several more miles. The temptation might be to say to ourselves, "four more miles to Green Lake Shelter; I think I'll stop there for the night." This is letting the waypoint dictate progress. Instead, we could say to ourselves: "once I reach the Green Lake Shelter, I will continue for one more hour before making camp." The idea is to use the waypoints as incentives, rather than as destinations.

In the late afternoons, fatigue may prompt you to stop and make camp. But much of that tiredness stems, not from the hiking, per se, but from a lack of food. If you are in shape and traveling lightly, then at this point in your day you probably need a hearty meal. So as though making camp, you stop near a water source and cook and eat dinner. You gather and filter a supply of drinking water, and you clean your pot and spoon. Then you might enjoy a dundo bath, or at least a sponging of the day's dust and sweat. But rather than pitching your tarp or tent, you re-load your pack and press on. If the meal is high in nutrition, then it will re-energize you, and you will probably find yourself hiking buoyantly for several more enjoyable hours. Much farther along you would leave the trail and establish a stealth-site. Your arrival there can be quite late because the camp chores will be mostly done. About all you will have to do is pitch your shelter and crawl gratefully into the sack.

Loading the 8.5 pound pack

Carrying the 8.5 lb pack

On the PCT in '94, we were often mistaken for
day-hikers

The Artistry of Hiking

One must labor for beauty as for bread.

— John Muir

Like the artist who dabs all the right colors of paint in just the right places, the distance hiker paints a canvas with a million steps. Up close you may see only the rough brush strokes: the dust and fatigue, the heat, mosquitoes and rain. But unlike the artist, you cannot stand back to appraise your work. So you must depend on your vision, rather than your sight. And when at last you arrive at trail's end, like the artist you will stand back and admire the labor of love, and suddenly your hard-wrought masterpiece will snap into focus. So do not expect to see much of the work while it is in the making. Maintain focus, and make each step a brush stroke of love.

During the hike, the far border may seem impossibly distant, almost unreachable, and the days may drag on. But in a few short months your hike will be history, and you will be left with memories—of the people and places, and interesting events. Memories of hard-earned vistas, flora and fauna, and new ideas and feelings entertained along the way. Living in the moment ensures the greatest memories and the greatest enjoyment. And on a big thru-hike there are joys to be had every minute of every day.

Many years from now, as you gaze back at your work of art, you will be able to see clearly how much that journey changed you, and how much you learned from it. You will see that nature had awakened your senses, allowing greater discoveries of the world around you, about yourself and who you really are. This is personal growth; and is what the artistry of hiking is all about.

Re-entry

Here I am, safely returned over those peaks
from a journey far more beautiful and strange
than anything I had hoped for or imagined.
How is it that this safe return brings such regret?

— *Peter Matthiessen*

The descent
back to civilization

If you return from your summer's journey feeling a little alienated from society: welcome to the club. Such is the plight of the adventurer. But take heart. That same inner strength you won on the trail will remain with you and serve you well throughout life. One of the greatest benefits of distance hiking is how it builds confidence in dealing with new challenges. So when returning home, keep in mind that you are now that much more capable.

The longest part of the journey is said to be the passing of the gate. But in my experience the passing back through that gate, when returning home, can be even more challenging. With the long trek over, we have said farewell to the trail that has been a constant companion all those weeks and months, and we may find ourselves undergoing a type of end-of-hike shock. The adventure, the challenges, the freedom and the joys of living in nature are suddenly no more. In their place come the all-too-familiar responsibilities of jobs and the hassles of society. How does someone who has just come out of the woods after several months on the trail adjust back to the "real" world? My answer is: only superficially.

When we return to our daily work, home and family routines, we need to keep a firm grip on those valuable lessons and discoveries about ourselves learned in nature. We cannot simply remove those insights, set them on a shelf somewhere and forget about the glories of nature that we so richly experienced. Nor should we turn our backs on the hard-won lessons learned through toil and privation. But while our journeys blessed us with greater independence, they did not wean us from society altogether. So the challenge now before us is to incorporate nature's lessons into our daily lives. Compromises will be necessary, and we need to find ways of blending back in, superficially.

Splashdown

During the final few weeks of your trek, begin thinking about what you would like to do after returning home. Plan ahead. Project yourself forward in time and envision yourself busy with a number of interesting projects. Give yourself something to look forward to, so that you do not simply stumble off the end of the world at trail's end.

Nutrition was important during the journey, and it is equally so afterwards. Eating quality foods will go a long ways in helping your brain cope with the difficult transition back to urban life.

Depending on your degree of re-entry shock, you can keep the summer's adventure alive in several ways. Try to work and relax outside for a few hours every day. Sleep outside if possible. Go on day hikes and consider becoming involved with trail crews—they always need help. Stay in touch with trail companions. Attend a hiker gathering. Give slide shows or speaking presentations. Transcribe your scribbled journal notes and elaborate on them from a retrospective view. Not only will these activities help you ease back into your routine, but they may plant seeds for future adventures.

The uncompleted journey

If you had to cut your journey short, coming home can be even more difficult. Rather than looking at your uncompleted journey as a "failure" though, view it as a valuable learning experience. Before I climbed the Diamond (the East Face of Long's Peak in Colorado) the first time, I "failed" on six attempts. This was back in the late 1960's when this climb was notoriously difficult, mainly due to the era's primitive equipment. But each failure taught me more of what I needed to know in order to succeed. My goal was to climb the face of that magnificent wall, and on the seventh try I finally did. And once I had achieved the skills I went on to scale the precipice several more times.

To the person who is genuinely determined, there is no such thing as failure. Remember that nature allows no shortcuts. You can proceed ahead in your adventures only one step at a time, and only with the knowledge and skills which that step requires. Your trail will still be there, if and when you choose to return. And as I have done many times, you might adopt the saying "Reculer pour mieux sauter." It means, "Draw back in order to make a better jump."

Section 5

Back to Basics

Sewing Your Own Gear

Are most people inept at sewing
because of ignorance or apathy?
I don't know and I don't care.

— *(Apologies to) William Safire*

The machine that pays for itself
its first season of use

Picture the illustrious garments in the backpacking stores and catalogs. These garments began as rolls of fabrics, and in most cases these fabrics are available directly to the consumer. With these materials, active people everywhere are discovering the benefits of sewing their own performance clothing and gear.

———————

In this chapter I describe how to sew your own hats and mittens, ditty bags, stuff sacks, thermal shirts and pants, rain jacket, tarp, and several other items. Granted, sewing these yourself will take a bit of time. Perhaps you could borrow that time from some television watching. Sewing is at least as interesting, and far more productive and rewarding. And it can save you a great deal of money otherwise spent on commercial items. You can also customize the designs to suit your particular body size and style preferences. You can choose your colors and fabric types, add pockets, zippers, drawstring closures, and reinforce stress points to make sure the item will stand up to heavy use. The possibilities of creating and customizing your own clothing and gear are endless. And I like to think that the skills of "sewing your own" foster a more independent attitude, taking you a step beyond the usual consumerism.

A suitable sewing machine

Many older sewing machines are actually more robust and powerful than those of our modern, plastic genre. And they are more than capable of sewing the projects in this chapter. Whatever type of machine you choose, it does not need the confusion of computerized stitches. A second-hand machine will do fine, and it need have only the three basic stitches:

- The straight stitch—for joining fabrics that do not stretch appreciably.

- The zigzag stitch—for joining stretch fabrics. By nature of its geometry this back-and-forth stitch gives, like an accordion, when the material is stretched.

- The reverse stitch—for finishing each row of stitching by sewing backward a short ways, preventing the stitching from raveling.

Almost all sewing machines have mechanisms for adjusting the upper and lower thread tensions, allowing the machine to accommodate fabrics of differing weights and thickness.

If you are new to sewing, ask someone to show you how to operate your machine. Practice on scraps similar to the materials you will be sewing. Sew two scraps together and examine both sides. Are the stitches reasonably similar on both sides? If not, then adjust the upper and lower tensions, sew another row of stitching, and check again. Once you can balance the stitching, you become fully capable of making an entire line of backcountry gear.

Note that we cut the fabrics with scissors or a rotary blade. To protect the edges from raveling we simply tuck them inside the seams.

Needles

Use high quality needles and replace them often. Synthetic fabrics are more abrasive than cotton and will dull the needles much faster. A dull needle will skip stitches and break thread.

For the projects detailed in this chapter you will need three sizes of needles: size 80 for most medium weight fabrics, size 70 for the very lightweight, and size 100 for sewing through many layers of heavier fabrics and webbing, as in the backpack project. Buy one package of each size.

Thread

None of the projects require heavy thread. Ordinary 100% long-fiber polyester thread, medium weight, will suffice. You can also use cotton-coated polyester thread; the cotton content is miniscule, and it helps protect the fabric from thread abrasion.

Fabrics and patterns

Well-stocked fabric stores may sell some of the materials needed for these projects. For instance, they might have lightweight nylons, polyesters, perhaps fleece, thermal fabrics such as polypropylene, and maybe even waterproof-breathable fabrics.

Otherwise, you can mail-order all your fabrics, sewing supplies and patterns. My two favorite suppliers are Outdoor Wilderness Fabrics in Nampa, Idaho (800) 693-7467, and The Rain Shed in Corvallis, Oregon (541) 753-8900. Other choices include Seattle Fabrics, of Seattle, Washington (206) 632-6022, and Quest Outfitters in Sarasota, Florida (800) 359-6931. Ask for catalogs, and compare prices.

One other item of great worth is the book *Sewing Activewear*, published by the Singer Company (Bibliography). This book has great instructions, tips and ideas, and is quite motivational.

When purchasing your fabrics, check to see what weight they are. For example, the 1.9 ounce coated ripstop nylon is quite light, but there are even lighter nylons available. The number refers to ounces per square yard. No-see-um netting is about .8 ounces per square yard.

All of the sewing projects described in this chapter are relatively easy to complete. Some require more materials and more time than others, and I have arranged the projects with this in mind, starting with the most basic. As with hiking, proceed ahead while focusing on the task at hand, and take things one step at a time.

Fleece hat

Let's begin by making a simple skullcap for use while hiking on a blustery day, and while sleeping. I never go on a trip without one. The first step is to select a fabric. You will need two pieces, both 12" by 14". Use thin fleece, sweatshirt fleece, brushed tricot, or any other synthetic with a bit of loft for warmth. Lay the two pieces together with their fuzzy sides facing away from each other. You will be sewing the hat together inside-out. In fact, you will sew all of your projects inside-out. When you turn the finished products right-side out, the seams will be neatly hidden inside. Pin the pieces together, and cut them into a dome shape, leaving the bottom flat. Also, make the hat long, so that it covers the face for sleeping and folds up over the forehead for wearing during the day. Using a narrow zigzag stitch, sew the two pieces together—up one side, arching over the top, and back down the other side. Keep the row of stitching about 1/2" away from the edge. This space is called the "seam allowance." Try the hat on for fit, then if necessary make it smaller, or start over and make a larger one.

Neither the sewing novice nor the expert should expect their projects to turn out perfectly the first time. The seam-ripping tool is the tailor's best friend. And as George Bernard Shaw said: "Success covers a multitude of blunders." Once your skullcap fits snugly and to your satisfaction, trim away the excess seam allowance, leaving about a quarter inch of material outside the stitching. Turn the hat right-side out, and voilà!

Mittens

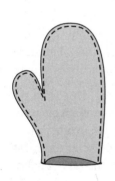

Making a pair of mittens is almost as easy as making a skullcap. Use the same material as for the skullcap, and also make a second pair from thicker, warmer fleece.

Start by drawing your pattern. To do this, simply lay your hand on a piece of paper in the mitt position (fingers loosely together, thumb at a 45° angle). Then trace around your hand and along the wrist a few inches. Cut the paper pattern out, not on the line but half-an-inch outside of it, allowing for a looser fit.

Before tracing the pattern onto a suitable piece of fabric, check which way the fabric stretches. Most fleece and jersey knits stretch more in one direction than the other. When making an item from stretchy material, even slightly stretchy like fleece, align the direction of stretch to cover the body part girth-wise, rather than length-wise. For example, when you lay your mitten pattern down on the fleece, have the stretch of the fabric running the width of the hand, not from fingertip to wrist.

Lay the pattern on the material in the correct orientation, trace around it, and cut the material on the line. You will need to cut out four of these identical pieces to make one pair of mittens. Match two pieces, pin them together, and sew around the outside, leaving the opening for the hand. Use a straight stitch or a very narrow zigzag, with a 3/8" seam allowance. Before you turn the mitten right-side out, try it on. If it fits well, you can trim the seam allowance closer to your stitching to minimize seam bulk. If necessary, re-size the pattern here and there for the best possible fit, then save the pattern. Jenny and I re-use our patterns time and again, year after year. In fact, we make patterns for all our projects, and keep them in a special box. They are very important to us, because we know that whatever we make from them will fit us correctly.

Ditty bag

I like to carry my small, personal items in a ditty bag, one that closes with a drawstring and small toggle. Generally this bag measures 7" by 5¹/₂" with a flat bottom (or 6" by 3" with a square bottom, description to follow). I usually make the bag from silicone nylon, or sometimes netting so that I can see the contents; but the choices of suitable fabrics are many.

Whatever the fabric, cut a piece 11¹/₂" wide by 8¹/₂" tall. Sear the edges lightly with a flame to prevent fraying. Fold the material in half to form a smaller rectangle, 5³/₄" wide by 8¹/₂" tall. The fold will be along one edge of your bag. Using a straight stitch with a ¹/₄" seam allowance, stitch along the other edge and across the bottom. You should now have a small, flat bag, 8¹/₄" by 5¹/₂" open at the top. Its seam runs down one side and across the bottom. Now we will make the drawstring casing, and the hole for the drawstring to exit that casing. With a hot nail held in a pair of pliers, melt a hole through one layer of the fabric, opposite the side seam and

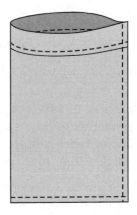

1¹/₂" down from the top edge. Size the hole so that a safety pin secured to the end of your drawstring will fit through it.

Fold the top edge down, to form a 1¹/₄" wide drawstring casing. Stitch

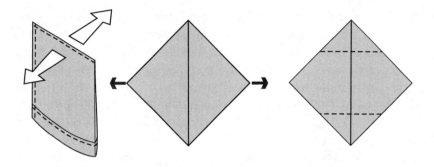

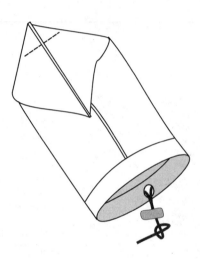

along the edge with a ¼" seam allowance, making a 1" casing. Then turn the bag right-side out. Cut a piece of nylon drawstring 15" long, attach the safety pin to one end, and feed it into the hole, round the bag inside the casing, and back out the hole. The safety pin facilitates this feeding process. Remove the safety pin, attach a toggle to the drawstring, and tie a keeper knot in the end of the cord.

To make a square bottom, begin by turning the ditty bag inside-out. Holding it upside down, pull the sides apart, forming a square bottom. Lay this square bottom flat, and stitch as shown.

Waterproof clothing bag

You can easily test a fabric for waterproofness by pressing it to your lips and trying to suck air through it. If any air passes through the fabric whatsoever, then for our purposes the fabric is not waterproof. Contrary to what one might expect, we cannot suck air through waterproof-breathable or vapor-permeable fabrics to any noticeable extent. This tells us that these fabrics are only infinitesimally breathable.

I invented a waterproof clothes bag in 1986, and about the same time Chouinard-Black Diamond came out with one about like it. A coincidence I am sure. At any rate, you can blow this bag up like a balloon, close the top, and toss it around like a beach ball. It is as waterproof as they come.

Waterproof Stowbag

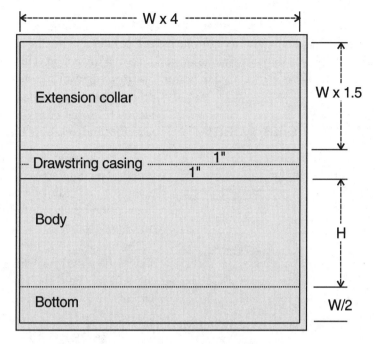

Finished stowbag:
W = width
H = height

Seam allowances:
Left: 1/4"
Right: 1/2"
Top: 1/2"
Bottom: 1/2"

Most lightweight, waterproof fabrics are suitable for this project. My preference is the ultralight 1.3 ounce silicone-coated nylon. Start with a piece 15" wide by 36" tall. Fold it in half (coated side out) to give a 7½" wide by 36" tall rectangle. With this project we will use a stronger seam known as the felled seam. Sew the length of the long edge with a 3/8" seam allowance. Lay the bag—which is actually a long tube at this point— on the table with this side seam running down the middle. Using your finger, push the seam allowance down to one side; this is where the term "felled" comes from. Feed the tube back through the machine, stitching this felled seam allowance down. Stitch only through one side of the bag, the other side goes under the machine's free arm. Stitch a quarter inch away from the first row of stitching, right alongside the raw edges of the seam allowance. As you sew, apply tension to the original seam. When you turn the bag right-side out, you should see two parallel rows of stitching, a quarter inch apart.

Next you will sew the bottom seam. With the bag turned inside-out, lay the tube flat and sew its bottom closed. Rather than using a felled seam, simply fold it over twice and stitch, like making a hem. This clothing bag will have a rectangular bottom, as described in the ditty bag project, so measure down two inches from the triangles' corners for your stitching line.

The Felled Seam

↓ Sew

Fold back

Fell

↓ Sew

After sewing the bottom, turn the bag right-side out again, lay it flat, and draw two parallel lines around its circumference: one 12½" from the opening, and the other 13½". These lines show where the drawstring casing will be. Fold the top "collar" of the bag in on itself, and crease it along the 12½" line so that the raw-edged opening is inside the bag. Sew two parallel lines, 1/8 inch apart, around the bag on the 13½" line. Stitch back and forth across the side seam several times to reinforce that intersection of stitching. We have now made the drawstring casing, one inch wide. Instead of melting a hole for the drawstring as you did with the ditty bag, slit half an inch of the side seam near the top of the casing. Cut a length of drawstring twenty inches long and feed it through the casing. Add the toggle, knot the drawstring, trim the excess cord, and sear their ends to prevent fraying.

After waterproofing the seams (refer to the next chapter: Seam Sealing) you can test them by inflating the stow bag like a balloon, twisting its top closed, and squeezing the bag. Listen for air leaking out a seam.

Load the stowbag with your hiking clothes, then squeeze out some of the air to reduce the size. Close the bag by twisting the collar tightly. Pull the drawstring half way, tuck the twisted collar beneath the casing, then cinch the drawstring tight.

Quilt or sleeping bag stuff sack

When I place something into a bag, I call that bag a stowbag. When I stuff something into a bag, I call it a stuff sack. The quilt or sleeping bag we stuff. And we make their stuff sacks the same way as we did the clothing bag. Here again I like the 1.3 ounce silicone nylon, since it is so slippery that it reduces the stress of pulling the sleeping bag out of the stuff sack. Whatever fabric you use, be sure to start with a new needle, size 70 for silicone nylon, or size 80 for somewhat heavier coated materials. You will have to customize the size of the stuff sack for your needs, but for a general guideline start with a piece of material measuring 37½" by 17". The finished size will be 8¼" by 20", with an 11½" collar. The drawstring casing needs to be slightly wider, 1½". Be sure to seal the seams well.

Spandex hiking shorts or pants

When sewing spandex (Lycra®), use a sharp, size 70 needle and a narrow, short zigzag stitch with a quarter inch seam allowance. I use the Kwik-Sew Pattern #1567, which gives patterns and sewing instructions for both long pants and mid-thigh shorts. Choose your material carefully. There are many different kinds (avoid the cotton ones), and weights, all with different stretch characteristics. For spandex shorts and pants, choose a lightweight nylon spandex with good stretch in both directions. Remember that the direction offering the greatest stretch goes around the body.

I modified the Kwik-Sew pattern in a couple of ways. I do not make the leg cuffs that wrap under the feet, and I have never found the need for elastic in the leg hems, so on both the long pants and the shorts I simply fold the material once and zig-zag stitch it to form a hem. I also reduce the width of the waistband casing and elastic in order to minimize absorption of sweat.

Thermal shirts and pants

Today's thermal fabrics include polypropylene, Thermax, Coolmax, Poly Lycra Jersey, and the polypropylene-fleece blends, to name but a few. Each has its own weight, thickness and stretch, and you will need to make sure that the type you select for shirts and pants has the appropriate characteristics. Most importantly, make sure that the fabric will stretch at least as much as that shown on the pattern you intend to use. For making thermal pants and shirts, you might try the Kwik-Sew Pattern #1295. This pattern is for long underwear, so the fit will be snug. Simplify the design by omitting the fly. When sewing thermal fabrics, use a size 80 needle and a short zigzag stitch set to medium width.

Fleece jacket

Fleece jackets are comfortably warm when we are sitting around camp, but they are also rather heavy and bulky, which is why I designed an ultralight insulated jacket for GoLite. Nevertheless, a lightweight fleece jacket is very functional and not difficult to make. The patterns for these are many. I use SewEasy #163 with some modifications. For example I omit the waistband and the sleeve cuffs. Instead, I make the jacket and sleeves longer, and finish off the bottom edges and sleeve cuffs with a spandex binding. (For instruction on how to do this, see the book *Sewing Activewear*, mentioned earlier.) I also reduce the bulk in the collar by using a lighter-weight material for the collar facing, for example a thermal fabric. For the front zipper I have found the 1-way separating, (rather than the 2-way separating) to be the best choice. The 1-way zipper is easier to start and more durable. I use a 29" zipper and Jenny, a 27". When purchasing your zippers, stay clear of the metal tooth type, which are too heavy and bulky for our clothing and gear projects. Use either the plastic molded tooth or the nylon coil types. On pockets I prefer lighter-weight coil zippers.

When sewing non-stretch fleece, use a straight stitch. When sewing stretch fleece, use a zigzag stitch with a short length and width.

On these jackets I like front pockets for warming the hands, and zippers on those pockets for containing things. To install a zipper, slit the front of the jacket where you want the pocket opening. Sew on a 6" or 7" coil zipper, following the directions on the zipper package. Cut a piece of thermal fabric for the pocket liner. Hem all the edges, pin the liner to the inside of the jacket against the zipper, and stitch it around its perimeter.

Shell jacket

The shell jacket is an invaluable addition to the hiking wardrobe, protecting us from mosquitoes, blackflies and no-see-ums, and from sunburn, wind, and brush. Jenny and I carry shell jackets and pants on all our outings, even in the Arctic. These are made quite easily from tightly-woven, uncoated nylon. The material should be breathable, but not overly so. You can test the breathability of a fabric the same way you tested for waterproofness: by pressing it to your lips and sucking air through it. If you can breathe through it quite easily then it is probably not mosquito-proof. On the other hand, if sucking air through it is difficult, then you are likely to sweat in it. I prefer the lighter colors for these garments because they are cooler while hiking under direct sunshine, and they are less attractive to flying insects.

Patterns for shell jackets and pants abound. One option is the Kwik-Sew pattern #2066, which is designed specifically for non-stretch nylon. Be sure that the pattern you choose has a hood. And consider adding zippered front pockets. Remember that the emphasis with all your sewing projects should be on simplicity and lightness of weight.

Shell pants

For the shell pants, try the Green Pepper pattern #128. I omit the side zippers, as they add unnecessary weight and bulk. However, you might want to add a chafe patch, approximately 6" wide by 5" tall, stitched to the bottom of the pant legs, where your shoes brush against the pants every now and then. I also use a narrower (half inch wide) elastic waistband and elastic in the leg cuffs to keep the mosquitoes out. The fabric for the shell pants should be breathable yet bug-proof, same as with the shell jacket.

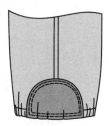

Mosquito mitts & booties, and sun mitts

Mosquito mitts and booties weigh almost nothing, and they take up very little space in one's backpack. And they provide welcome relief when mosquitoes or blackflies are swarming. I prefer to use them in lieu of chemical repellent. I wear the mitts while hiking, and both the mitts and booties while resting alongside the trail, when I normally remove my shoes for airing.

Make the mitts pattern by simply tracing around the hand in the same way as you did for the fleece mittens. The mosquito mitts fit very loosely, so this needs to be a separate pattern. To keep the bugs from crawling in at the wrists, make the mitt wrists several inches longer so that you can tuck them way up inside the sleeves of your shell jacket. For fabric, use scraps left over from your shell jacket and pants projects. Do not be tempted to use no-see-um netting; mosquitoes can bite right through this fabric wherever it presses against the skin. The booties are nothing more than a couple of curved, loose-fitting tubes, long enough to tuck up into your pant legs.

Although these bug mitts will also protect the backs of your hands and fingers from strong UV, I find them too hot in those intense sun conditions. And I like to have my fingertips free of any covering. For sun mitts, I prefer a simple tube made of breathable nylon that fits over the hand, open at the fingers but still providing effective cover for the backs of the hands.

Mosquito head-net

A mosquito head-net completes the bug-proof ensemble. This we make out of no-see-um netting, which is a much finer weave than mosquito netting. No-see-um netting comes in white, black or gray; black absorbs more of the sun's heat, but it is easier to see through.

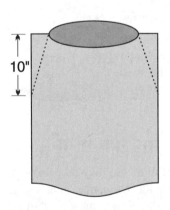

Start with a round piece of netting, 15" in diameter. This will be the top of the head-net. Make the side walls from two pieces, 30" wide by 24" tall. Lay out these rect-angles, and along the 30" edge make a mark 3" in from each end. Place the round top piece on top of one of the rectangles, and with a 3/8 inch seam allowance, stitch the two together between the two marks. The result looks like the accompanying illus-tration. Then sew the second rectangle to the other side of the circle. The 3" marks that you made should meet up at the sides of the head-net. You will eventually trim away the excess seam allow-ance, but first sew the two side seams, starting at the round top edge and stitching 10" down. Stop at 10" and stitch back and forth several times to keep that stress point from tearing out. That 10" point will sit on top of your shoulders, and the remainder of the material will hang down inside your shell jacket, one flap in front, the other flap in back. Now you can trim off the excess 3 inches from both sides, leaving a nice 3/8 inch seam allowance down both sides of the head-net.

A broad-rimmed hat, or baseball cap worn underneath the head-net will keep the netting off the top of your head and away from your face.

Rain jacket

Jenny and I make our rain jackets usually of 2-ply Gore-Tex or other waterproof-breathable fabrics, as opposed to coated waterproof fabrics that do not breathe. We make these jackets from the same patterns as the shell jacket, but we make them somewhat larger to accommodate a few more layers underneath. You can skip the hand pockets unless you also want to sew protective covers over the zippers. Again, make sure you start with a new needle, size 70 or 80. Use the felled seam where possible, since it is stronger and easier to seal. Use a quality seam-sealing compound, as you did on the waterproof clothing bag. See the following chapter on seam sealing.

Tent awning

(See illustration in Tarp and Tent chapter) To make a tent awning, choose a lightweight, waterproof fabric such as silicone-coated nylon. The awning's shape and attachment will depend on the shape of your tent fly and its doorway configuration. The idea is to shelter that doorway to prevent rain from entering when the doorway is wide open, which it normally should be for optimum ventilation.

I will describe here how I make an awning for a tent that is symmetrical about its long axes, head to foot. To ensure a proper fit, make the awning from two pieces: a left and a right, each piece measuring approximately 35" by 45". You can customize this for your own tent. After pitching the tent and fitting its fly, tape each awning-half along the 35" edge onto the fly above the doorway, and overlapping half an inch where the two pieces meet in the middle. This overlap will become the seam allowance, although you will need to trim it to the right shape before sewing that seam. When you lift the two pieces and hold them outstretched and slightly downward in the finished awning position, you can see how the pieces will overlap. Mark where the two halves cross each other at the front edge, then remove them from the fly. Trim appropriately, and stitch them together using the felled seam. The awning is now one piece, and ready to sew onto the tent fly. Mark the fly where the awning will attach to it, then remove the fly from the tent and sew the awning to it, and seal the seams.

Next, sew three guyline attachment loops and reinforcement patches, one at each corner and one in the center along the front edge. When you do not need the awning you can fold it back over the tent or you can roll it up and secure it with webbing ties sewn through the fly and seam sealed.

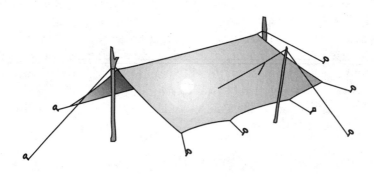

Tarp

The tarps that my students and I used for many summers of wilderness travel back in the 1970's were made of ordinary clear polyethylene plastic, 3 to 6 mil in thickness. We hung them over ridge lines strung tightly between two trees, and fastened lines to their corners with sheet bend knots. For a neater appearance one could apply duct tape to both sides of the plastic in the vicinity of the attachment points, then sew on small loops of °" webbing. The duct tape serves as reinforcement, preventing the stitches from pulling out of the plastic. One would then tie the guy lines into these loops.

The tarp that Jenny and I used for many years is made of 1.9 ounce coated nylon. This material is quite strong and reasonably light in weight, and it is a good step up from clear plastic. Today we use 1.3 ounce silicone-impregnated nylon, which is the lightest and most waterproof for its weight, but at a slight sacrifice in strength—meaning only that it requires handling with a bit more care. For the reinforcement patches at the guy points, one would use scraps of tarp material. And for the attachment loops (pulls) use very thin nylon webbing.

My two-person tarp is 106" (8'10") square (not including the beaks). To customize a tarp's length to your own needs, simply add 36" to your height. To make a one-person tarp, reduce the finished width to 86". The

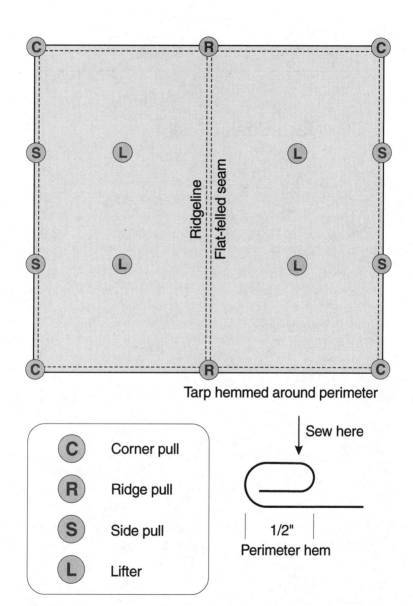

Ridgeline

Flat-felled seam

Tarp hemmed around perimeter

C	Corner pull
R	Ridge pull
S	Side pull
L	Lifter

Sew here

1/2"

Perimeter hem

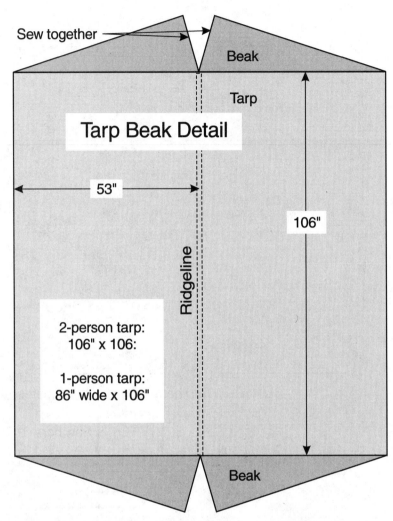

Sew together

Beak

Tarp

Tarp Beak Detail

53"

106"

Ridgeline

2-person tarp:
106" x 106:

1-person tarp:
86" wide x 106"

Beak

To make one beak, cut two halves from a single rectangle.

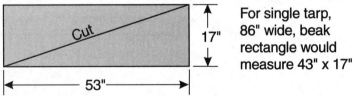

Cut

17"

53"

For single tarp,
86" wide, beak
rectangle would
measure 43" x 17"

Side Pull

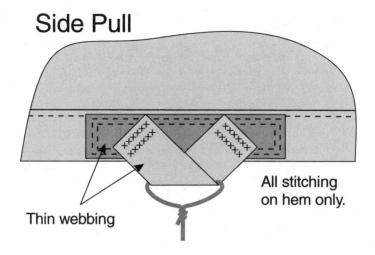

Thin webbing

All stitching
on hem only.

Lifter Patch

Material: 500 denier,
coated Cordura

2" diameter

2 lifter line attachment slits,
3/4" long, 1/2" apart

Sew Lifter Patch to tarp around
perimeter, two rows stitching

Tie lifter-line through loop
formed by the two slits

tarp body requires two pieces of material, each the length of your height-derived measurement (plus half-an-inch hem allowance for each end.) Each piece would be somewhere around 53 inches wide for a two-person tarp (plus seam allowances). Sew these two pieces together length-wise, using a flat-felled seam, creating one large piece. The center seam becomes the tarp's ridgeline. If adding beaks (see illustration) add them now. Then around all the edges sew the half-inch hem. Refer to the accompanying illustrations for the arrangement of the various reinforcements and attachment loops.

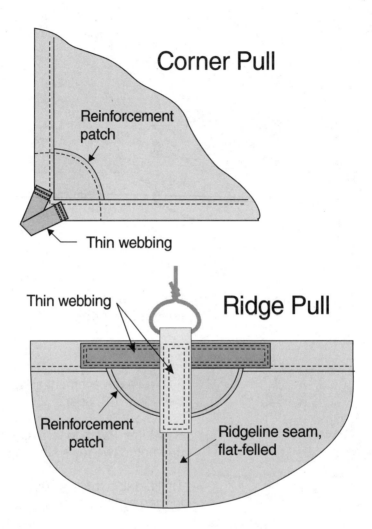

Corner Pull

Reinforcement patch

Thin webbing

Thin webbing

Ridge Pull

Reinforcement patch

Ridgeline seam, flat-felled

People have asked me about using Tyvek for tarps, ground sheets, and so forth. I think the interest in this material is based more on the name, which has sort of a fresh, exotic appeal to those unfamiliar with it. But Tyvek is a very common material that has been around a long time. Personally, I find it unsuitable for hiking and camping—mainly because it is not waterproof. People have tried various coatings, but I think the problems outweigh any advantages. For an inexpensive and far more workable alternative, I recommend ordinary 3 mil polyethylene. It is available at most hardware stores, perfectly waterproof, and surprisingly durable when properly used.

Flat-Felled Seam

Strong, and nice looking because it
hides the raw edges. Used for
waterproof stuff-sacks, tarp ridgelines, etc.

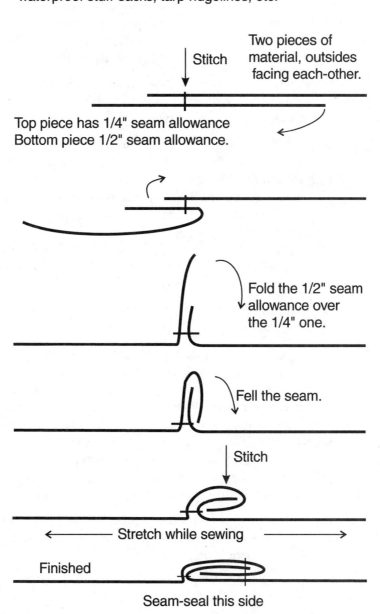

Stitch

Two pieces of
material, outsides
facing each-other.

Top piece has 1/4" seam allowance
Bottom piece 1/2" seam allowance.

Fold the 1/2" seam
allowance over
the 1/4" one.

Fell the seam.

Stitch

← Stretch while sewing →

Finished

Seam-seal this side

Quilt or sleeping bag

If you are thinking of trying a quilt, you can save a lot of money by making your own. Or you can make a sleeping bag by following the steps listed below. Manufacturers tend to complicate the designs of their sleeping bags in order to attract sales, but we hikers need only a simple quilt or bag. Making these at home is easy and straightforward, particularly with today's synthetic insulation, which does not require internal baffles built into the quilt or bag, as goose down does. You can purchase all the necessary materials from the mail-order outlets mentioned earlier.

The quilt simply drapes over us like a blanket. It consists of two sheets of thin, nylon fabric sandwiching the insulation. To make a sleeping bag out of it, simply fit both edges with a zipper, and fold it in half.

Inexpensive insulation will usually result in a much heavier product. For best results, use the newer brands of insulation; check with your mail-order outlet for availability. Currently, Jenny and I use Polarguard 3D or Primaloft. To achieve the desired thickness, simply double or triple the layers. (See the Quilt and Sleeping Bag chapter for temperature rating details.) The quilts we make for spring and summer hiking are made with two layers of 1" insulation. Our two-person quilt is 64" wide and 80" long. A one-person quilt would be 45" wide, and would exclude the insulated flap (see below).

Follow these steps, and you will have a quilt that is as effective as any sleeping bag on the market:

- Think of the quilt as a 2" thick blanket. Cut out two pieces of 1.1 ounce breathable nylon to the desired shape of this "blanket," as it would appear when laid flat on the floor. Remember that you start by sewing the pieces together inside-out, then later turn the finished product right-side out so that the seam allowances are inside. Sew the two pieces together around their edges, but leave the head end open like a giant pillow case. Consider a light-colored nylon for the upper layer, to minimize radiation heat loss, and dark-colored for the lower layer, which when exposed to the sun will dry the quilt much faster.

- While the "pillow case" is inside-out, lay it on top of your layers of insulation. Cut the insulation to the same size and shape as your "pillow case," then pin them in place.

- Following your line of stitching on the nylon as a guide, sew the

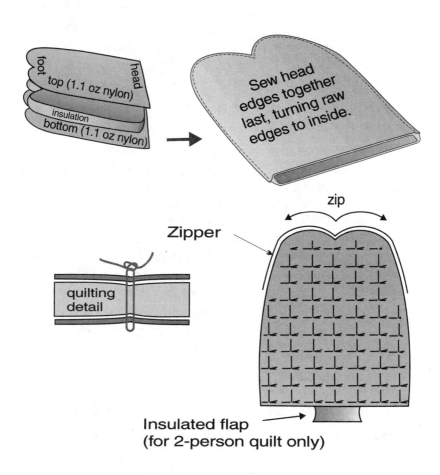

foot · head
top (1.1 oz nylon)
insulation
bottom (1.1 oz nylon)

Sew head edges together last, turning raw edges to inside.

zip

Zipper

quilting detail

Insulated flap
(for 2-person quilt only)

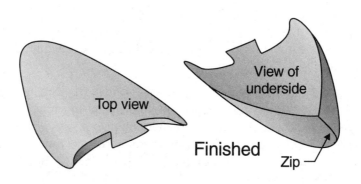

Top view

View of underside

Finished

Zip

insulation to the pillow case around its perimeter—except along the open edge at the head of the quilt. Use a long straight stitch.

- At the head end, separate the two layers of nylon, and sew the insulation only to the nylon layer next to it. This will allow you to turn the entire quilt right-side out without having the insulation shift out of position. It also makes the next step easier.

- Turn the quilt right-side out, and stitch the top edge closed, tucking in the raw edge of nylon.

- Quilting: stabilizes the insulation, keeping it from shifting and being pulled apart as you pull the quilt out of its stuffsack. Grid the bag off in 18" squares if using a continuous filament insulation such as Polarguard 3D, or 12" squares if using discontinuous filament such as Primaloft. Do this using a tape measure and a washable marking pen, simply marking each grid intersection. Insert a 12" length of synthetic yarn into the eye of a large hand-sewing needle (known as a tailor's or leathercraft needle). Poke the needle through the quilt at one of the gridpoints. An eighth of an inch from where the needle emerges, poke it back through the quilt the other way. The yarn now runs through the quilt rather like a staple, with its two ends sticking out one side. If the quilt is 2" thick, use a mandrel that is 2" wide—such as a yardstick or ruler. Lay the mandrel on the quilt, upright

between the two yarns. On top of the mandrel tie a square knot, and snug it up tight. When you pull out the mandrel you have a per-

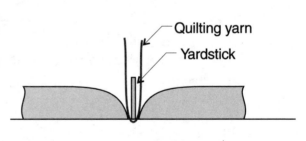

Quilting yarn

Yardstick

fect 2" loop in the yarn—matching the thickness of the quilt. Repeat the process at each grid mark.

- Sew on a full-length zipper if you want to make a sleeping bag, or sew only a 26" very lightweight robe zipper, starting at the foot and running up toward the head. This shorter zipper allows you to close only the bottom portion of the quilt, making a pocket for the feet. No matter the length of the zipper, it allows you to open the bag fully for faster drying.

When Jenny and I sleep together beneath the quilt, a gap forms between our neck and shoulders, permitting an undesirable draft. Our solution is to sew to the quilt an insulated flap of the same materials as the quilt itself, and about 12" wide by 8" tall. The flap hangs down between our necks and blocks the draft. Also, we sometimes sew a couple of Velcro patches along the sides of our quilts, and we glue the opposite patches to our foam pads. This helps secure the quilt over us.

The backpack

The accompanying illustration shows the construction details of my pack. To begin, you could take measurements from a commercial pack of the size you are interested in and transfer those measurements to paper, creating your own pattern. Or you could start with a commercial pattern. As mentioned in the Backpack chapter, my pack is 11½" wide, 9 1/3" deep, and 20½" tall, not taking into account its extension collar.

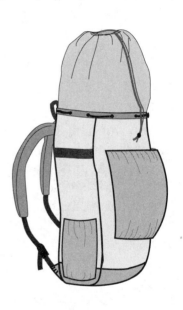

Whether using a commercial pattern or creating your own, you can customize the pack to suit your needs. You can omit most of the straps and fancy accessories.

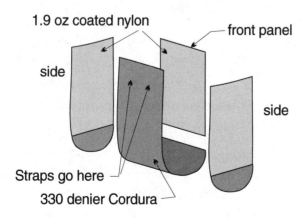

1.9 oz coated nylon

front panel

side

side

Straps go here

330 denier Cordura

You can add a water bottle pocket made of mesh on one side, a fuel bottle pocket on the other, and a large pocket on the back for stowing a wet tent fly or tarp. Along the top of the pockets make a small casing and run elastic through it to prevent the loss of the pocket contents. If your load will generally be below 20 pounds, you could dispense with the internal stays and the hip belt.

Reinforce all stress points with small patches of material in order to spread the load over a wider area and to reduce the chances of the stitching pulling out. The greatest stress occurs where the shoulder straps attach to the upper part of the pack. The reinforcement patches there need to be quite large. Another stress point is where the shoulder straps attach to the bottom of the pack. In this area do not attach the nylon webbing straps directly to the body of the pack. Rather, attach the webbing to a tripled layer of material, triangular in shape, and attach that to the pack.

1-1/2" webbing

rows of zig zag stitching

Stitch webbing to top layer of shoulder strap casing, not through entire strap. Do this before making the casing.

shoulder strap

3/4" webbing

For my home-made packs I use 330 denier coated Cordura® for both the bottom and the panel that rests against my back, and 1.9 ounce coated nylon for most of the remainder. Use the same kind of thread as with the previous projects. Triple-stitch everything, using a simple straight stitch.

Shoulder strap construction

The construction of the shoulder straps is not difficult. Use a heavy-duty size 100 needle, and ask your mail-order suppliers what they sell for pack strap foam.

To begin the shoulder strap, cut out four pieces of 330 denier Cordura, 13" by 3". These will become the casings into which you will insert the foam pieces. Before sewing the top and bottom halves of the casing together, stitch the nylon webbing to the top piece. Use 9 inches of 1 1/2" flat nylon webbing at the top, and 20 inches of 3/4" flat nylon webbing at the bottom. The top is wider because it secures directly to the pack. The bottom is narrower because it must feed into an adjusting buckle, and a 1½" buckle would be far too large. Leave 2½" of the wide webbing extending beyond the raw edge of the casing. Position the narrow webbing so that it overlaps the wide webbing by ¾". Sew the webbing to the top layer of the casing, as illustrated.

With the webbing now in place you can proceed with the rest of the shoulder strap. Use a straight stitch and sew the top casing to the bottom casing, along both edges, inside-out, with a 3/8" seam allowance. Leave the top and bottom open. Go back and double-stitch these edges for a stronger seam, then sear the raw edges of the casing all the way around. Now you can turn the casing right-side out, so that the webbing is on the outside and the side seams are hidden.

Cut the foam to the size of the casing, round off the corners slightly, and insert it into the casing. The foam should fit reasonably tightly, so you might find it a bit of a wrestling match to situate it correctly. Finish the top and bottom of the shoulder strap by tucking the raw edges of the Cordura inside, and sewing the ends closed.

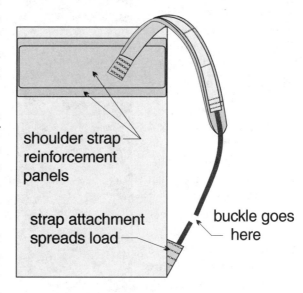

shoulder strap reinforcement panels

strap attachment spreads load

buckle goes here

Now you can stitch the free end of the 1½" webbing to the pack. Use large safety pins to position the strap to the pack temporarily. Try the pack on for fit, and adjust the placement of the straps to suit. Stitch the straps to the pack using four rows of zigzag stitches, half an inch apart. Be sure that you have at least two layers of reinforcing material underneath this high stress point.

Your basic pack should be ready to go. You can finish off the collar extension with a 1" wide casing, drawstring and toggle. You can even add a second casing and drawstring at the bottom of the extension collar so that you can cinch the pack closed when the collar is not loaded. There are many other additional features you can add: a narrow webbing strap across the sides to hang socks for drying, a haul loop at the top between the shoulder straps for lifting the pack. Be careful though, not to add too many extraneous features; keep it as simple and as light as possible.

Hiker's Friend Water Filter System

I designed the Hiker's Friend water filter system for our first thru-hike, and Jenny and I have used it during many thousands of miles of hiking, Arctic sea-kayaking, and canoeing. I first described the system in the first edition of this book; my feelings were that it is so simple in construction that just about anyone could make their own. So let's start with an overview of how this filter system works, then I will describe how to make one for yourself.

The Hiker's Friend system is gravity-fed, and therefore it requires no effort to operate, other than what is needed to hang it from a tree branch or other support. It works unattended, meaning that we are not slaves to the pump. As a package, it is considerably smaller and lighter than most filter units on the market.

It consists of only four parts: a circular sheet of waterproof nylon that forms a water bag, a filter cartridge, a suspension cord, and a 7½ foot length of clear tubing. The water bag is suspended at head height, and the tubing runs from the cartridge down to a water bottle at ground level.

Virtually any type of filter cartridge will work in the Hiker's Friend, as long as that cartridge has a tubing nipple at one end, for attaching a length of tubing. The tubing itself is available at most hardware stores.

The water bag is easy to make, even without access to a sewing machine. It looks like an upside-down parachute, but with a difference in the suspension. To make the bag, cut out a 30" diameter circle from a piece of lightweight, coated nylon fabric. Fold the circle of fabric in half three times to make a pie-shaped wedge, one-eighth of a pie. Mark each of the eight creases at the edge—these will be the equally-spaced suspension points around the circle's perimeter. As you did for the small ditty bag, you could melt a small hole at each suspension point, about an inch from the edge, and thread a 6-foot long cord through them. The stronger method is to sew a tab of webbing at each attachment point. Use 3/8" wide nylon grosgrain tape or twill, 3" long. Sear the ends to prevent fraying. You will need eight of these. Fold each piece of webbing in half to make doubled pieces 1½" long. Position one piece of ribbon at each of the eight suspension points. The folded-in-half ribbon should straddle the fabric, and extend beyond the fabric ¾" to accommodate the suspension cord. Note that I do not hem the edge of the bag. After sewing all eight tabs, feed the suspension cord through them.

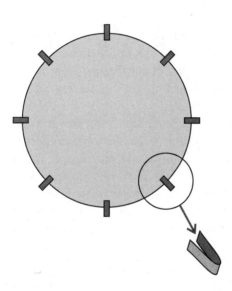

You now have a water bag that you can use with the Hiker's Friend filtration system, or by itself at camp for storing water. You can also use this bag as a shower by fitting it with a siphon tube and a small, plastic shower head.

To continue with the Hiker's Friend project, you need to attach the filter cartridge to the inside bottom of the bag, so that the cartridge does not float to the top and suck air. To keep the filter cartridge at the bottom of the bag, secure a 16" length of cord inside the bag, to its bottom. Tie an overhand knot in the middle of the cord, open the water bag and locate its center, lay the knot on the center, then reach under the bag to the outside and pinch the knot with the fabric. Use a piece of twine to wrap several times around this pinch, from the outside. Tie off the twine with a secure knot. Open the water bag and tie the filter cartridge in place, using the fixed cord. The tubing attaches to the cartridge inside the bag. The tubing then comes up and over the bag's rim, and descends to the water bottle at ground level.

Attach the tubing to the cartridge, then fill the bag by dragging it through the water like a parachute, or by holding it under running water, or by pouring water into it from a cookpot. Hang the bag from a tree branch, and start the siphoning flow by sucking on the free end of the tubing. Until the cartridge becomes saturated, it will expel air bubbles into the siphoning tube. These bubbles reduce the siphoning pressure and you need to get rid of them. To do this, simply raise the tube and permit the bubbles to float upward toward the tube's free end, and escape. When the tube contains only water, lower its free end into a water bottle. Note in the illustration that the tubing should J-bend upward before entering the collection receptacle. If the bag is dripping, unfiltered water might run down the outside of the tube. The J-bend prevents this water from contaminating the filtered water inside the water bottle. To stop the filtering, simply raise the tubing. To keep it raised when not in use, tuck the free end behind a suspension loop.

To change a clogged cartridge, simply untie it and replace it with a new one.

You can speed the filtering process by running the tubing directly through the bottom of the water bag. To do this, cut a hole in the bottom center of the water bag, the same diameter as the connection nipple of the cartridge you will be using. Wrap a thick rubber band (I use a "broccoli band" from the grocery store) around the bottom end of the cartridge to help seal the joint; the rubber band acts as a gasket. Then place the cartridge tip through the hole and lash the bag to the cartridge around the rubber band. Lash tightly using waxed artificial sinew, available at leather goods stores. To change the cartridge, carefully cut away the lashing, then use a new rubber band and a new length of sinew to lash a new cartridge in place.

Modifying a commercial umbrella

Most commercial umbrellas are constructed with various pieces that are not necessary to the umbrella's function. When I modify one of these umbrellas, these superfluous pieces are what I am after.

I begin by sawing off the J-shaped plastic handle, leaving a 3½" stub. This is just long enough to hold on to. Next, I pull off the plastic top-cap and discard it. And after hack-sawing the excess metal shaft above the canopy to within ¼" of the top of the fabric, I file the shaft's new top end smooth.

I then remove the springs and other nonessential components. Here is how: Each tine has a plastic end-cap, to which the fabric is tied. I pull three adjacent end-caps off their tines, then cut the thread holding the canopy to these tines. I do not cut off the end-caps. I am now able to slip the canopy over the top of the umbrella framework, just far enough to expose a small nail running through the top of the uppermost plastic assembly. This nail secures the assembly to the shaft. I carefully pry the nail out, and save it for later replacement. Then I lift the assembly off the shaft and set it temporarily aside.

At the bottom of the shaft, just above the plastic handle, is a slot containing the thumb release piece. Pressing this trigger will deploy the umbrella, but actually this trigger is unnecessary after my modification. A few inches above the slot is the trigger's anchor point, and if I use a small screwdriver to depress the anchor, I can remove the trigger piece and discard it.

The illustration shows what other components I remove for the umbrella modification. At the center of the canopy, on the outside, I sew a covering of coated fabric, 1½" in diameter. I then reassemble the unit, replace the nail, carefully pull the canopy back over, and pop the plastic end caps back over the ends of the tines.

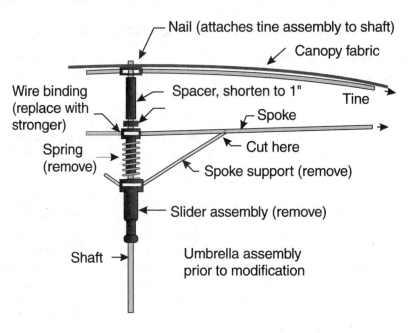

Nail (attaches tine assembly to shaft)

Canopy fabric

Wire binding (replace with stronger)

Spacer, shorten to 1"

Tine

Spoke

Cut here

Spring (remove)

Spoke support (remove)

Slider assembly (remove)

Shaft

Umbrella assembly prior to modification

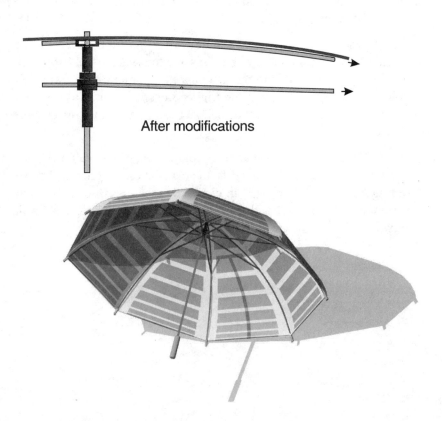

After modifications

Sewing projects for a winter's day

Sewing is an extremely effective way to save money on hiking gear, and it can be very rewarding. And once you gain more skill and experience, you may think of all sorts of other interesting projects. Here are a few more suggestions:

- Sew an eyeglasses loop inside your tarp or tent, to keep them handy yet out of harm's way at night. Sew on a second loop for your wristwatch.

- Pack cover—most commercial ones do not fit well, and they tend to leak profusely. Design one to fit your pack. Or, make a pack liner.

- Waterproof pack liner. This is a large waterproof stowbag, fitted inside your backpack.

- Eyeglasses bag—make it from soft fleece

- Watch band—make it with webbing and Velcro

- Tent peg stowbag

- Camera stowbag

- Cookpot stowbag—Use in conjunction with cook-fires, which blacken the pot

- Food bags

- Shower booties—These are easily made of lightweight coated nylon, with elastic around the top edges. The final product looks much like a pair of inverted shower caps.

- Stowbag for the Hiker's Friend water filter

Seam Sealing

Sealing the seams is usually the last step when making your own gear. And presently we must seal the seams of commercial gear made of silicone-impregnated nylon, because as of yet no way exists to machine-tape this type of material. Either way, seam sealing by hand is a job that is best done correctly the first time, and this means using the right compounds in the right ways.

―――――――――

Unfortunately, some widely distributed seam sealing compounds harden and begin flaking away within a few weeks of application, especially when exposed to strong sunlight. Even some of the more reputable tent manufacturers supply these inferior sealers with their products. Why? Probably because these particular compounds are easier to apply. However, seeing the results of your work exfoliating away is not a pretty sight. And speaking from experience, the act of removing the inglorious mess in order to repeat the job can be even more dispiriting. So before you start the process, test the compound in a few inconspicuous places on the item to be sealed. Expose these tests to sunlight for a few days, then try to scrape away the cured compound with your fingernail. If the compound hardens to the extent that it cracks when the material is crumpled, or if you can peel or flake the compound away, then do not use it.

My recommendations: On silicone-impregnated fabrics, use clear 100% silicone sealant, available at hardware stores. Diluting it, with a solvent such as alcohol, is unnecessary. On uncoated fabrics and urethane-coated fabrics, use Seam Grip or AquaSeal, both from the McNett Corporation. These two products work especially well when mixed with their accelerators (see manufacturer's instructions). The accelerator adds a bit of strength, and greatly shortens setting time.

Before seam sealing any item of gear, wipe away any dust or residues of manufacture using a damp cloth, or a cloth wetted with a mild degreasing solvent such as rubbing or denatured alcohol. These precautions will ensure that the sealant bonds to the fabric properly. After applying the sealant be sure to let it dry thoroughly. Also, avoid using the sealing compounds indoors; the vapors can make you sick. Even outside, work only in 10 or 15 minute intervals, allowing your respiratory system to recover and the compound's solvents to evaporate. The more "footage" you try to seal in a single session, the more likely the newly-sealed seams will land back on the material. This can smear the compound unattractively onto the main body of your project. So split the job into several short sessions, and allow several hours of drying time in between each one.

When it comes to sealing seams, two people are better than one. As one person stretches the seam apart, the other applies the sealing compound. This procedure exposes more of the stitching to the compound brush. If working alone, you can lay the piece down on a clean, hard surface and place a knee or a heavy weight on one side of it. Stretch the seam with one hand while applying compound with the other. Use a small bristle brush to apply the compound. If the bristles are insufficiently stiff, trim them shorter. And do not try to make a neat job. Neat jobs are far more prone to leaking, because they tend to lack sufficient coverage. Smear the compound on the seam half-an-inch wide to prevent water from wicking laterally through the fabric. Sealing the seams on one side of the item is usually sufficient.

When the job is complete, allow the sealant to cure undisturbed for a day or two. Before placing the finished product into its stuff sack, dust the sealing compound lightly with talcum powder. This will prevent the seams from sticking to themselves and later pulling bits of compound away. Finally, test the gear under a garden hose, or in the shower if you are working with clothing, and correct any leaks. On humid days, however, be aware that the cold water from a hose could cause condensation to form inside a tarp or tent fly, making it appear to be leaking. Look carefully for beads of water actually coming through the seams.

In camp, you can improvise sealing compound with lip balm, tree sap, or even peanut butter. For more lasting repairs, of course, use seam sealing compound. On longer outings you could place a small tube of compound in your drift box (as described in the Resupply chapter). Use it to repair small tears also. Tape the tears closed from one side, and apply compound to the other side.

Ray & Jenny's PCT 1994 Gearlist

In the interests of safety, please note that we are not recommending this list to anyone else. Always compile your own based on personal experience and needs.

Ray's packweight 8.44 lb
Jenny's packweight 7.12 lb
(Not including food, and clothing worn)

	Weight	Cost of materials	Hours to make
Ray's Gear			
Pack	13.5 oz	$10.40	12.0
Umbrella	9.0 oz	$12.99	1.0
Mylar umbrella covering, with rubber bands and tape for attaching mylar to umbrella	0.8 oz		
Sleeping quilt: PrimaLoft® synthetic fill, includes mosquito netting. 79" long, 58" chest, 44" foot	49.0 oz	$34.0	9.0
Sleeping bag stowbag, 2 ply W/B	2.5 oz	$6.00	3.0
Stove, fuel, windscreen, in coated nylon stowbag	24.8 oz		
Water bottle (empty soda bottle)	1.6 oz		
Ray's Clothing			
Hat: fleece	1.2 oz	$0.50	0.3
Shell jacket: breathable nylon	6.0 oz	$8.00	6.0
Mittens: fleece	1.0 oz	$1.00	1.0
Shell pants: breathable nylon	3.0 oz	$4.00	3.0
Socks: 2 pair thin nylon	1.2 oz		
Shower booties, coated nylon	0.8 oz	$0.50	1.0
Face towel: cotton, 12" square	1.8 oz		
Clothing stowbag (plastic garbage sack)	1.3 oz		
Ditty Bag #1, nylon mesh	0.2 oz	$0.50	0.5
Windex for cleaning eyeglasses and camera lens	0.8 oz		

Half a cotton bandana for cleaning eyeglasses and camera lens	0.1 oz		
Compass	0.8 oz		
Spoon: Lexan	0.2 oz		
Prescription dark glasses	1.2 oz		
Eyeglasses bag: fleece with velcro	0.2 oz	$0.25	0.5
Flashlight with single AAA battery and spare bulb	1.0 oz		
Pocket knife	0.8 oz		
Toothbrush	0.1 oz		
Dental floss	0.1 oz		
Hydrogen peroxide (antiseptic)	0.5 oz		
Cord	0.5 oz		
Ditty Bag #2, nylon	0.6 oz	$0.50	0.5
Medical kit: Betadine, Metronidazol, Diasorb, Amoxicillin, Campho-Phenique Antibiotic, zinc oxide, Mycelex (for athlete's foot), 1 T. salt in tiny resealable plastic bag	4.0 oz		
Sewing kit: heavy thread, 3 safety pins, 3 needles	0.1 oz		
Emergency fire starter kit in resealable plastic bag: small lighter, stick matches, birthday candles	0.9 oz		
Spare flashlight battery, size AAA	0.5 oz		
Valuables: traveler's checks, cash, credit card, driver's licenses, in resealable plastic bag	1.0 oz		
Toilet kit: toilet paper & Dr. Bronner's soap in plastic vial	2.0 oz		
Journal pad, maps & pen	2.0 oz		
Ray's Total Pack Weight	8.44 lb		

Jenny's Gear			
Pack	11.5 oz	$10.40	12.0
Umbrella	6.0 oz		1.0
Mylar umbrella covering, with rubber bands and tape for attaching mylar to umbrella	0.8 oz		
Tarp: 1.9 oz coated ripstop nylon, 8'8" square	28.0 oz	$15.0	5.0
Tent stakes: 8 aluminum, 7" long	2.5 oz		
Tent stakes stowbag: nylon	0.1 oz	$0.25	0.5
Ground sheet: 81.5" long. 48" wide at head, 34" at foot	6.5 oz	$13.99	0.1
Foam pads: two 3/8 inch thick closed cell polyethylene. 19.5" wide at shoulders; 17.5" at hips; 36.5" long	9.5 oz	$6.99	0.1
Camera with 1 roll film	6.0 oz		
Camera stowbag: coated nylon	0.5 oz	$1.50	0.5
Camera kit: 1 roll of film, spare battery, and bulb brush	1.4 oz		
Water bottle (empty soda bottle)	1.6 oz		
Water scoop: breakfast cereal cup, plastic	0.1 oz		
Water trough: cookie package, aluminum foil	0.2 oz		
Jenny's Clothing			
Hat: fleece	1.0 oz	$0.25	0.2
Shirt: Thermax, long sleeve	3.0 oz	$9.75	3.0
Shell jacket: breathable nylon	6.0 oz	$7.50	4.5
Mittens: fleece	1.5 oz	$0.75	0.3
Shell pants: breathable nylon	4.0 oz	$7.61	4.0
Socks: 3 pair, thin nylon	1.8 oz		
Shower booties: coated nylon	0.8 oz	$0.50	1.0
Half of a cotton bandana as towel	0.3 oz		

Clothing stowbag (plastic garbage sack)	1.3 oz		
Jenny's Ditty Bag, nylon	0.2 oz	$1.00	0.8
Flashlight with single AAA battery & spare bulb	1.0 oz		
Lighter	0.5 oz		
Comb	0.3 oz		
Toothbrush	0.3 oz		
Spoon: Lexan	0.2 oz		
Can opener: P-51	0.2 oz		
Repellent in pump spray bottle	1.8 oz		
Sunscreen	0.8 oz		
Note pad & pencil	0.3 oz		
Prescription dark glasses	1.2 oz		
Eyeglasses bag: fleece with velcro	0.2 oz	$0.25	0.1
Lip balm	0.5 oz		
Aspirin & vitamins together in small resealable bag	0.3 oz		
Foot Care in resealable bag: 13 adhesive strips, ½sheet Moleskin, full pack of 2nd Skin & dressing, white adhesive tape, clear first aid tape, 3 Q-Tips, 3 pieces Molefoam	3.5 oz		
Cookpot with lid: aluminum, 2 quart capacity	7.8 oz		
Cookpot stowbag: coated nylon	0.5 oz	$1.00	0.8
Jenny's Total Pack Weight	7.12 lb		

Ray's clothing worn			
Sun hat with wire rim	2.0 oz		
Shirt: polyester	4.0 oz		
Watch	1.5 oz		
Shorts: spandex	4.3 oz	$2.00	2.0
Socks: 2 pair, thin nylon	1.2 oz		
Shoes	22.0 oz		

Jenny's clothing worn			
Sun hat	2.0 oz		
Shirt: polyester	2.0 oz	$6.50	3.5
Underwear	0.5 oz		
Shorts: nylon/spandex	3.0 oz		
Socks: nylon	0.6 oz		
Shoes	21.0 oz		

Ray's Additional Gear			
Head net: no-see-um netting (used in central OR only)	1.2 oz	$1.00	0.5
Hat: fleece & 2-ply W/B covering (used in northern WA only)	2.5 oz	$1.75	2.5
Jacket: 2-ply W/B (used first few days only)	6.0 oz	$7.00	4.0
Sweater: lightweight fleece (carried through northern WA, rarely needed)	14.3 oz	$13.00	4.5
Wicking shirt: Thermax, long sleeve (used in WA only)	8.0 oz	$7.50	4.0
Shell mittens: breathable nylon (used in central OR only, for mosquitoes)	0.2 oz	$1.00	0.5
Wicking pants: Thermax (used in northern WA only)	7.5 oz	$7.00	3.0
Snow boots: Avia N'yati (used in WA only)	26.5 oz		
Socks: 2 pair, polyester & wool blend (used in WA only)	2.2 oz		
Shell booties: breathable nylon (used in central OR only, for mosquitoes)	0.2 oz	$1.00	0.5
No-Fog cloth in resealable plastic bag (used in northern WA only)	0.2 oz		
Water bag: 2.5 gal (used in southern CA only)	3.5 oz		
Ice axe, modified (used in northern WA only)	12.8 oz		3.0

Jenny's Additional Gear			
Hat: fleece (used in WA only)	3.0 oz	$3.50	1.5
Sweater: lightweight fleece (used in northern WA only)	14.0 oz	$13.00	4.5
Jacket: 2-ply W/B (used first few days only)	8.3 oz	$21.50	5.5
Shell mittens: breathable nylon (used in central OR for bugs and southern CA for sun)	0.2 oz	$1.00	0.5
Wicking pants: Thermax (used in WA only)	7.0 oz	$7.00	3.0
Snow boots: Avia N'yati (used in WA only)	25.0 oz		
Socks: 2 pair, polyester & wool blend (used in WA only)	4.0 oz		
Socks: 1 pair, Ragg wool (used in northern WA only)	3.8 oz		
Shell booties: breathable nylon (used in central OR for mosquitoes only)	0.2 oz	$1.00	0.5
Water bag: 2.5 gal (used in southern CA only)	3.5 oz		
Ice axe, modified (used in northern WA only)	12.5 oz		3.0

Going Solo

A common question that comes my way is: were I hiking solo, how much heavier would my pack be, considering that I would have to carry all the shared gear, including the tarp, quilt, stove, cookpot, and so forth.

Based on the preceding tables, the following list itemizes how my solo packweight might change:

Going solo - changes to Ray's 8.44 lb. baseline packweight	
Using a one-person quilt of Polarguard 3D rather than my Primaloft double would lighten my load by 16 ounces.	-16.0 oz.
Quilt stowbag, smaller by one third, lightens my load by 0.75 oz.	-0.75 oz.
The stove I would still need to carry, (in this example) but I need only half as much fuel, and a fuel bottle half as large. This lightens my load by 4 ounces.	-4.0 oz.
Windex, need only half as much.	-0.3 oz.
Smaller medical kit	-1.5 oz.
I would omit the prescription dark glasses and its case, because I now use a single pair of photo-grey eye-glasses.	-1.4 oz.
A one-person siicone tarp	12.0 oz.
Tent stakes and stowbag	2.6 oz.
Ground sheet for one person, space blanket material	1.25 oz.
Foam pad	4.8 oz.
Camera, film, kit	6.64 oz.
Water scoop & trough	0.3 oz.
Lighter	0.5 oz.
Can opener	0.2 oz.
Repellant	1.0 oz.
Sunscreen & lip balm, I don't use.	0.0 oz.
Aspirin & vitamins	0.17 oz.
Foot care bag	2.0 oz.
Cookpot for one person, and stowbag	5.0 oz.
Total added weight for Ray hiking solo	12.51 oz.

Poking at the Embers

If I must worship God,
then I will do so in the temple that He created.

— John Muir

To me there is nothing quite so welcome and satisfying as a little cook-fire, with its pot suspended over the heartening flames by a simple tripod of sticks. I feed small kindling into the fire every so often, while Jenny stirs the meal and digs around in a food bag. This is a relaxing, quiet time; a nice break from the hours of hiking.

The tripod standing over the cook-fire is sacred to me, in the sense that its three legs represent elements fundamental in us all; namely the physical, intellectual and spiritual. More specifically, each leg corresponds to our awareness in that particular realm, and our ability to function in it.

In order for the cook-fire tripod to serve its purpose, each leg must be strong and capable. If one leg is weak, then the whole tripod lacks strength. And so it is with us. When one of our "tripod legs" is underdeveloped, then we are limited, and this makes for a lopsided, weak and unbalanced journey through life. But when equally developed, the three legs work together and make us exceptionally capable in all our pursuits.

One of the benefits of hiking and camping is the escape they provide from the distractions of city life. Distraction is mainly what keeps us from walking our Paths, and from developing and strengthening all three legs equally.

In the same way that we develop our physical skills with exercise and resolve, and our intellectual skills with analysis and study, we strengthen the spiritual leg with meditation and prayer. But in nature our meditations and prayers can take on many forms. They can be as simple as walking quietly along a trail with senses wide open and with gratitude for the beauty all around. Pausing to admire the colors in a flower, we can turn that joy into a prayer. When the sky finally clears after several days of wet and clouds, we might rejoice in the sunshine, and send those feelings outwards. So we can easily use these gifts of nature as spiritual building blocks. And when meeting other people we can show them kindness by saying positive things, and whether intentionally or not we are passing along the Creator's love.

Drinking from a pure spring, I give thanks for the water of life. When I encounter wild animals, large and small, I think of them as kindred spirits with whom I am sharing the "wilderness cathedral." At other times I like to pray and meditate alone, sitting alongside a creek or upon a high rocky outcrop, giving thanks to Him who made it all and placed me here. Actually, my journeys are themselves a form of dynamic meditation, and during them I feel that I am honoring the Creator by appreciating his creation. And by giving thanks for all that he has created and cared for with such love.

When I learned of the Gospel some forty years ago, my life took on new meaning. The Bible spoke to me and changed my life's direction completely and much for the better. In a nutshell the tidings are these: By piling rocks we cannot reach the stars, and by practicing religion we cannot reach God's eminence. God loves the mountains, trees, and even our stealth campsites; otherwise why would he have created them? And he loves us too. And it is this love that prompted him, some two thousand years ago, to send Jesus to provide transit across the colossal gap between God and us. The wages of sin are death, not the physical death but the spiritual one. But Jesus paid the price of our sins. When we accept Jesus as Lord and Savior, we accept God's gift of spiritual life.

In terms of hiking, I think of nature as our compass, pointing the way to the Creator. The Holy Bible is our guide book, filling us with resolve, and providing directions at life's junctures. And Jesus provides us passage over the unwadable gap, to eventually triumph in our spiritual quests.

"For God so loved the world,
that he gave his only begotten Son,
that whosoever believeth in him should not perish,
but have everlasting life."
— John 3:16

The words 'born again Christian' mean different things to different people. I consider myself a simple follower of Christ. He lived simply, dressed modestly and spent quite a lot of time in the purity of wilderness. And I like to think that Jesus was a hiker. One of his last acts on earth was to sit with a few of his disciple friends before a fire. They roasted fresh-caught fish, ate bread, and perhaps sat long into the night talking heavenly subjects while poking at the embers.

Select Bibliography

Books are but stepping stones to show you
where other minds have been.

— John Muir

Hiking narratives and trail guides

Blind Courage, Bill Irwin. WRS Publishing: 1993. Autographed copies from Bill Irwin Ministries, Inc. P.O. Box 109, Sebec, ME 04481

The Longest Walk, George Meegan. Paragon House: 1989. An extraordinary seven year, continuous trek from the tip of South America to the top of North America.

The Long Walk, A Gamble for Life, Slavomir Rawicz. Harper & Brothers: 1956

Into a Desert Place; A 3000 mile walk around the coast of Baja California, Graham Mackintosh. W. W. Norton: 1995

The Walker's Journal, Robert Sweetgall. Creative Walkers, Inc.: 1986. Out of print, but a gem if you can find a copy. Describes his walk through all fifty states in 364 consecutive days. Sweetgall hiked across the country, not just once but twice. The objective of his long-distance walks, and they were remarkable endeavors, was to urge the public to exercise more. To that end he gave over 200 lectures to student bodies along the way. As our society grows ever more sedentary, Robert's purpose was to demonstrate to people that the human body is indeed designed for, and benefits from, rigorous exercise.

High Summer: Backpacking the Canadian Rockies, Chris Townsend. Oxford Illustrated Press (UK) and Cloudcap (USA): 1990. Details a pioneering trek along the Continental Divide, north from the American-Canadian border. Townsend has written a number of very fine adventure narratives and how-to handbooks.

Wilderness Walks, Twelve Great Walks in Scotland, Cameron McNeish and Richard Else. BBC Books: 1997. Along with a second volume, *More Wilderness Walks* by McNeish and Else, these two excellent books offer tremendous hiking possibilities for that part of the world.

First aid

Medicine for Mountaineering & Other Wilderness Activities; 4th Edition, James A. Wilkerson, M.D. The Mountaineers: 1992. Jim and I were members of the same climbing expedition to the Peruvian Andes in the late '60s. His book was the most thorough on the subject then, and it still is.

Wilderness Medicine 4th Edition; Beyond First Aid, William W. Forgey, M.D. ICS Books, Inc.: 1994. Contains a wealth of practical information, and is a great refresher on a subject that we all need to review on occasion.

Health and Nutrition

The Natural Farms Cookbook, Frank Ford. Harvest Press: 1978

Dry It-You'll Like It!, Gen MacManiman. Living Food Dehydrators: 1974. A book about dehydrating food, including recipes and plans for building your own food dehydrator.

Jane Brody's Good Food Book, Jane Brody. Bantam Books: 1987

Beating the Food Giants, Paul A. Stitt. Natural Press: 1993 (P.O. Box 730, Manitowoc, WI 54221)

Your Body's Many Cries for Water, F. Batmanghelidj, M.D. Global Health Solutions: 1995

Excitotoxins, The Taste that Kills, Russell L. Blaylock, M.D. Health Press: 1997

Traditional Foods are your Best Medicine, Ronald F. Schmid. Healing Arts Press: 1997

Mad Cowboy; Plain Truth from the Cattle Rancher Who Won't Eat Meat, Howard F. Lyman. Scribner: 1998

Richard Hittleman's Yoga: 28 Day Exercise Plan, Richard L. Hittleman. Bantam Books: 1969

Emerging Viruses: AIDS, Ebola & Vaccinations, Dr. Leonard Horowitz. Tetrahedron: 1997. Cogent arguments that these viral agents are man-made. Also excellent information on the dangers of vaccinations. Video and book available from Tetrahedron 1-888-508-4787 (tetrahedron.org)

Suppressed Medical Discovery Video, Dr. Robert C. Beck. "The Granada Forum: 1997"

> *Robert C. Beck, D. Sc. Lecture*, Audio Cassette Lecture, 1996

> *Robert C. Beck, D. Sc. Documentary and Protocol Video*, 1999

> Above Bob Beck video, audio cassettes, and "handout" available from: Sharing Health 1-800-224-0242

> Bob Beck-designed hardware available from:

>> Action Electronics 714-547-4425 (www.action-electronics.com/ps.htm)

>> Sota Instruments 1-800-224-0242 (www.sota-inc.com/products.htm)

Ice axe technique

Mountaineering: Freedom of the Hills, 6th Edition, The Mountaineers: 1999.

Natural History

Peterson Field Guides, edited by Roger Tory Peterson. An excellent series of field guides.

National Audubon Society Field Guide to North American Reptiles & Amphibians, J.L. Behler and F.W. King. Knopf: 1979

Bear Attacks: Their Causes and Avoidance, Stephen Herrero. Lyons & Burford: 1985. Information on bear ecology, behavior and attacks.

Rattlesnakes, Laurence M. Klauber. University of California Press: 1982

Preparedness

The Encyclopedia of Country Living, Carla Emery. Sasquatch Books: 1994

Making the Best of Basics—Family Preparedness Handbook, James Talmage Stevens. Gold Leaf Press: 1997

Personal growth

Flow, The Psychology of Optimal Experience, Mihaly Csikszentmihalyi. Harper and Row: 1990. Contains insights valuable to hiking and all human endeavor.

How I Found Freedom in an Unfree World, Harry Browne. Avon Books: 1973. When I first read this book in the mid 70's, it affected my thinking profoundly. It is not a hiking book, but it encourages a person to think for him or herself, and this is very applicable to hiking.

Sewing your own

Sewing Activewear, Cowles Creative Publishing, Inc. 1986. From the Singer Sewing Reference Library. Look for this excellent book at your local fabric stores.

Lightweight Camping Equipment And How To Make It, Gerry Cunningham and Margaret Hansson. Charles Scribner's Sons: 1976.

Wilderness philosophy and skills

Tom Brown's Field Guide to Wilderness Survival, Tom Brown, Jr. Berkeley Books: 1983. I heartily recommend all of Tom's books and classes.

Mutant Message Down Under, Marlo Morgan. HarperCollins: 1994. A compelling and instructive story of a walkabout with a small band of Australian Aborigines.

Blue Mountain Buckskin, Jim Riggs. 1995.

Craft Manual of North American Indian Footwear, George M. White. 1992.

Song of the Paddle, An Illustrated Guide to Wilderness Camping, Bill Mason. Firefly Books: 1988.

A Snow Walker's Companion; Winter Trail Skills from the Far North, Garrett and Alexandra Conover. Ragged Mountain Press: 1995.

One Life at a Time, Please, Edward Abbey. Henry Holt and Co.: 1988. A fun read, as are Edward Abbey's other books.

Index

Author's Profile

Ray Jardine holds a degree in Aeronautical and Astronautical Engineering from Northrop University, and worked in the aerospace industry as a specialist in computer-simulated space-flight mechanics. He retired at an early age to pursue his outdoor interests.

A mountaineer, he climbed most of Colorado's fourteeners, many in winter; and he climbed extensively across western North America. His highest peak was Peru's Huascarán, at 22,205 feet.

A wilderness instructor, he worked for the Colorado Alpine Winter Mountaineering School for two seasons, and Outward Bound for seven. In the process he backpacked several thousand miles. He also holds an EMT certificate from St. Anthony's Hospital in Denver, Colorado.

A rock climber for 25 years, Ray established some of the era's toughest climbs, including the world's first 5.12 graded climb: The Crimson Cringe, and the first 5.13: The Phoenix. He climbed extensively in Great Britain and across western America. His ascents in Colorado include seven Diamond routes. In Yosemite Valley he pioneered 50 first ascents, and was the first to free climb a grade VI, on El Capitan. He invented the protection and anchoring device known as the "Friend," which revolutionized the sport. And he originated the style of climbing used today that enables far more challenging routes to be climbed. According to Rock & Ice magazine, "The brilliance of his routes, the undeniable contributions of his designs, and his yet-unrealized visions of the future of the sport place Ray Jardine among the rarest of climbing revolutionaries."

In 1982, Ray and his wife Jenny put to sea aboard their ketch SUKA, (acronym for "Seeking UnKnown Adventures") and spent 3½ years sailing around the world.

Ray is also an avid hang glider pilot. He has logged some 400 hours aloft, flown to 16,000 feet, cross-country 50 miles, and thermal gained 9,100 feet (nearly two miles straight up). He has flown sailplanes and small powered craft, and he holds an Australian Restricted Private Pilot's License. He is also a PADI-certified scuba diver.

In 1987 he and Jenny thru-hiked from Mexico to Canada, generally along the **Pacific Crest Trail** in 4 months. Once wasn't enough, so in 1991 they thru-hiked the **PCT** again, in 3 months, 3 weeks. In 1992 they thru-hiked the **Continental Divide Trail** in 3 months, 3½ weeks. In 1993: the **Appalachian Trail** in 2 months, 28 days. And in 1994 they thru-hiked the **PCT** southbound in 3 months and 4 days, traveling at a comfortable pace while carrying very lightweight loads.

Ray coined the term "Triple Crown" in the March 1994 edition of his *Distance Hiker's Gazette*, and presented the first Triple Crown awards at the second annual ALDHA-West Gathering. He and Jenny founded the organization and ran it for three years.

Sea kayaking has also been a favorite pursuit. Ray and Jenny have paddled several thousand miles in areas such as offshore California, the Sea of Cortez, French Polynesia, Australia, Alaska and Canada. In 1988 they paddled from Anacortes, Washington 3,300 miles north to the Bering Sea. Continuing the trip in the summer of 1995, they paddled 600 miles along the rugged coast of Arctic Alaska in a kayak of their own design and aerospace composite construction. In the summer of 1996 they returned in yet another home-built kayak and paddled 1,400 miles to Monument 1 at the Alaska/Canada border. And in the summer of 1997 they paddled their third home-made kayak 975 miles down the Mackenzie River (Canada's longest), then across 200 miles of Arctic coastline until confronting pack ice. That same summer they paddled a canoe 575 miles down the remote Thelon River from Lynx Lake to the village of Baker Lake near Hudson Bay.

In 1998, Ray and Jenny were featured guests in the BBC television series *Wilderness Walks* with host Cameron McNeish, filmed during a six day hike through the Three Sisters Wilderness of Oregon.

The summer of 1999 they canoed across the Barrenlands of Arctic Canada, traveling down the Back River, up the Meadowbank River, over the Divide and down to the village of Baker Lake—736 miles in 40 days.

For stories and photos, see Ray's web site:
www.transport.com/~ray316
or search for "Ray Jardine's Adventure Page."

AdventureLore Press

P.O. Box 804, LaPine OR 97739

For information about out titles
see our web page at:
www.adventurelore.com

To order, telephone:
1-800-247-6553
or 419-281-1802